War Land on the Eastern Front is a study of a hidden legacy of World War I: the experience of German soldiers on the Eastern Front and the long-term effects of their encounter with Eastern Europe. It presents an "anatomy of an occupation," charting the ambitions and realities of the new German military state there. Using hitherto neglected sources from both occupiers and occupied, official documents, propaganda, memoirs, and novels, it reveals how German views of the East changed during total war. New categories for viewing the East took root along with the idea of a German cultural mission in these supposed wastelands. After Germany's defeat, the Eastern Front's "lessons" were taken up by the Nazis, radicalized, and enacted when German armies returned to the East in World War II. Vejas Gabriel Liulevicius' persuasive and compelling study fills a yawning gap in the literature of the Great War.

VEJAS GABRIEL LIULEVICIUS is Assistant Professor of History at the University of Tennessee.

Studies in the Social and Cultural History of Modern Warfare

General editor
Jay Winter, *Pembroke College, Cambridge*

Advisory editors
Paul Kennedy, *Yale University*
Antoine Prost, *Université de Paris-Sorbonne*
Emmanuel Sivan, *The Hebrew University of Jerusalem*

In recent years the field of modern history has been enriched by the exploration of two parallel histories. These are the social and cultural history of armed conflict, and the impact of military events on social and cultural history.

Studies in the Social and Cultural History of Modern Warfare presents the fruits of this growing area of research, reflecting both the colonization of military history by cultural historians and the reciprocal interest of military historians in social and cultural history, to the benefit of both. The series offers the latest scholarship in European and non-European events from the 1850s to the present day.

For a complete list of titles in the series see end of book

War Land on the Eastern Front

Culture, National Identity, and German Occupation in World War I

Vejas Gabriel Liulevicius

University of Tennessee

CAMBRIDGE
UNIVERSITY PRESS

PUBLISHED BY THE PRESS SYNDICATE OF THE UNIVERSITY OF CAMBRIDGE
The Pitt Building, Trumpington Street, Cambridge, United Kingdom

CAMBRIDGE UNIVERSITY PRESS
The Edinburgh Building, Cambridge, CB2 2RU, UK
http://www.cup.cam.ac.uk
40 West 20th Street, New York, NY 10011–4211, USA   http://www.cup.org
10 Stamford Road, Oakleigh, Melbourne 3166, Australia

First published 2000

Printed in the United Kingdom at the University Press, Cambridge

Typeset in Plantin 10/12pt [VN]

A catalogue record for this book is available from the British Library

ISBN 0 521 66157 9 hardback

Contents

List of maps	*page* vi
Acknowledgments	vii
List of abbreviations	viii
Introduction	1
1 Coming to war land	12
2 The military utopia	54
3 The movement policy	89
4 The *Kultur* program	113
5 The mindscape of the East	151
6 Crisis	176
7 Freikorps madness	227
8 The triumph of *Raum*	247
Conclusion	278
Select bibliography	282
Index	300

Maps

1 Eastern Europe before 1914   13
2 The German "Great Advance" of 1915 – Eastern Front   18
3 The Ober Ost state – main administrative divisions   60
4 The fullest extent of the German advance on the Eastern
   Front by 1918   207
5 Postwar Eastern Europe in the 1920s   250

Acknowledgments

My thanks for help and assistance in this venture are owed to many individuals and institutions. I am especially grateful to Thomas Childers of the University of Pennsylvania, the ideal advisor, Frank Trommler of the University of Pennsylvania, and Alfred Rieber of the Central European University, Budapest. Thanks for suggestions and comments are due to Michael Geyer, Thomas Burman, and Jay Winter, editor of the series in which this book appears. My grateful thanks also goes to Elizabeth Howard, editor at Cambridge University Press.

I gratefully acknowledge the support I was given in my studies and research by the Mellon Fellowships in the Humanities, the William Penn Fellowship of the University of Pennsylvania, the DAAD-German Academic Exchange Fellowship, and the Title VIII Postdoctoral Research Fellowship at the archives of the Hoover Institution at Stanford University. While researching, I was grateful for friendly receptions at the Bundesarchiv-Militärarchiv in Freiburg, the Bundesarchiv in Koblenz, the Geheimes Staatsarchiv Preussischer Kulturbesitz in Berlin, the German Foreign Ministry archive in Bonn, the Lithuanian State Historical Archive and the Lithuanian Academy of Sciences library manuscript section, both in Vilnius, the archives of the Hoover Institution in Stanford, and kind librarians at the University of Pennsylvania, the University of Freiburg, and the University of Tennessee.

For the production of maps for this book, I thank University of Tennessee's SARIF EPPE fund for its award, and Wendi Lee Arms for her skilled cartography.

Finally, my thanks go to my parents, to whom this book is dedicated, for their unfailing encouragement and support, and to my grandfather, who awakened my fascination for the past.

Abbreviations

Archival sources

BA   Bundesarchiv, Koblenz, Germany

BAMA   Bundesarchiv-Militärarchiv, Freiburg-in-Breisgau, Germany

GSTA PK   Geheimes Staatsarchiv Preussicher Kulturbesitz, Berlin, Germany

LCVIA   Lietuvos Centrinis Valstybinis Istorijos Archyvas, Vilnius, Lithuania

LMARS   Lietuvos Mokslų Akademijos Rankraščių Skyrius, Vilnius, Lithuania

Publications

BUV   *Befehls- und Verordnungsblatt des Oberbefehlshabers Ost.* BAMA PHD 8/20.

ZXA   *Zeitung der 10. Armee.* University of Pennsylvania Library; Special Collections.

KB   *Korrespondenz B.* BAMA PHD 8/23.

Introduction

During the First World War, the experiences of German soldiers on the Western and Eastern Fronts seemed worlds apart. These separate worlds shaped distinct "front-experiences" (even for soldiers who fought on both fronts) which proved to have important consequences both during and after the war, testimony to the impact of war on culture. While all was "quiet on the Western Front," a routine hell of mud, blood, and shell shock in the trenches, a different ordeal took shape for the millions of German troops in the East from 1914 to 1918. What they saw among largely unfamiliar lands and peoples, both at the front and in the vast occupied areas behind the lines, left durable impressions. These crucial first impressions in turn had profound consequences for how Germans viewed the lands and peoples of the East during the war itself and in the decades to come, until ultimately these ideas were harnessed and radicalized by the Nazis for their new order in Europe. In this sense, the eastern front-experience was a hidden legacy of the Great War. The failures of the First World War had vast consequences, for out of this real encounter over four years there grew a vision of the East which encouraged unreal and brutal ambitions. It is crucial to understand that when German soldiers invaded the lands of Eastern Europe under Nazi direction during the Second World War, it was not the first time that German armies had been there. Rather, the eastern front-experience of the First World War was an indispensable cultural and psychological background for what came later in the violent twentieth century, a preexisting mentality.

The aim of this study is to reveal the assumptions and ideas which derived from the eastern front-experience, shaped by the realities of German occupation. Above all, it seeks to understand the psychological outlines of this experience and the outlook on the East it produced. The very idea of a galvanizing, transformative front-experience was important in Germany during the war and in its aftermath, as millions searched for some compelling, redemptive meaning to the sacrifices of a global struggle ending in defeat. In the West, this front-experience was marked by industrial warfare, in a blasted landscape of mud, barbed wire, machine-gun nests, bunkers, and fortified emplacements facing no man's land, over which swept barrages, high explosives, and all the technological energies of terrible battles of attrition, the shattering and grinding trials of Verdun and the Somme. This western front-experience of the trenches, ran one important myth of the Great War, hammered a "new man" into being, a human war machine, the hardened "front fighter." After the war, the works of former shock-troop commander Ernst Jünger and the tidal wave of "soldierly literature" cresting in the late 1920s presented a new and brutal model of heroism in the person of the storm trooper, and a military model of society in the *Frontgemeinschaft*, the "community of the trenches," which had supposedly overcome the weaknesses of liberal individualism and class division in a true egalitarian moment. Technological modernity and materialism were also transcended, the passionate argument ran, by the *esprit* of an elite forged in battle and its transformations: these steeled "princes of the trenches" mattered more and more in modern battle, while ordinary individuals counted ever less. Even Remarque's pessimistic *All Quiet on the Western Front*, indicting authorities who had sent crowds of innocents into the "blood mill" of the West, still plaintively avowed that this generation had been changed by the experience, and while wounded and crippled, might represent revolutionary potential in its generational unity. While these ideas were clearly the trappings of myth rather than realistic social descriptions, myths have consequences. The mythologized western front-experience provided impetus and symbols for the militarization of politics and the acceptance of political violence in Germany between the wars.

As the mythical figure in the West gained in definition, growing clearer in outline, in the East limits were lost. There, with widened eyes, the German soldier faced vistas of strange lands, unknown peoples, and new horizons, and felt inside that this encounter with the East was transforming him because of the things he saw and did there. Armies in the East found themselves lost, far beyond their homeland's borders, in huge occupied territories of which most knew little. In general, before the war, ordinary Germans had little direct experience of the lands just to their east. Norbert Elias, later a famed sociologist, recalled that when the war broke out, even as a student he knew about Russia "nothing, absolutely nothing. The Tsar and the Cossacks, barbarous. The barbarous east – that was all beyond the pale."[1] During the course of the war, such hollow commonplaces were replaced by specific details and anecdotal generalizations about the East, drawing on the immediate, first-hand experience of soldiers, conditioned by occupation policies and practices.

The eastern front-experience thus illuminates modern German perceptions of the East, and about what sort of things could be done there.

While millions of soldiers were involved in the first-hand experience, many others at home were also touched by the propaganda of military authorities in the East and the enthusiasm for annexations in significant portions of the population. As will be shown, while the eastern front-experience of all the individual soldiers was not identical in every detail, they shared many broad assumptions and common features. The hallmarks of the eastern front-experience were significantly different from the typical features of the West, even for soldiers who experienced war on both fronts. Above all, the stay in the East was marked by the central fact of German occupation. Unlike in industrial Belgium and northern France, the occupiers seemed to face not modern developed lands, but what appeared as the East's primitive chaos. The second decisive difference came into focus as the war neared its end, a basic and essential point, though often forgotten. After the peace of Brest-Litovsk in March 1918, imposed on beleaguered Russia, it appeared to Germans that half of the war had been won. This central fact, that war in the East apparently had ended in German victory, made it all the more difficult to accept the failure that followed upon Germany's weakening in the West that same summer and the collapse into revolution at home. The perceived lessons and conclusions drawn from the eastern front-experience and its failures would constitute a hidden legacy of the first World War.

In scholarship on the First World War, the Eastern Front has remained to a great extent the "Unknown War," as Winston Churchill called it nearly seventy years ago in his book of the same name.[2] Since then, many standard works on the conflict have concentrated on western events, casting only occasional glances at developments on the other front.[3] Norman Stone's excellent *The Eastern Front, 1914–1917* finally gave a detailed account of the military history.[4] For an understanding of the role of the East in German war aims and internal politics, the appearance of Fritz Fischer's *Griff nach der Weltmacht* in 1961 and the explosive debates which followed were decisive.[5] Fischer documented annexationist demands in the East, indicating suggestive continuities between strivings of the *Kaiserreich* and the Nazi regime. Detailed monographs followed, investigating avenues Fischer had opened and seconding some of his conclusions.[6] Yet there never appeared in this scholarship, nor in general overviews of Germany's relationship with Eastern Europe, a comprehensive evaluation of the significance of the experience of the Eastern Front for the masses of ordinary German soldiers who lived it, and this encounter's cultural impact.[7] A clear view on the meaning of this episode in the East had yet to resolve itself.

In the last decades, historical research on the First World War took on a new impetus, as scholars focused on the cultural impact of the war that had ushered in modernity, breaking traditions, altering and recasting old certainties, and overthrowing empires. In these investigations, "culture" was not restricted to "high art," but was defined more broadly, in an anthropological sense, encompassing a society's values, assumptions, governing ideas, and outlooks. From the 1970s, new studies explored the first World War as a decisive experience shaping modern society. John Keegan's original work opened the way to a fresh understanding of war's cultural significance and its experiences in terms of ordinary lives, insisting that "what battles have in common is human."[8] The ascendancy of social history further strengthened emphasis on experience as a category of historical analysis, encouraging works looking beyond a chronology of military events to seek out the interpretations which participants in the First World War formed from their experiences. Paul Fussell's *The Great War and Modern Memory* sketched the myths of "the Great War as a historical experience with conspicuous imaginative and artistic meaning," as lived and reworked by British writers and poets.[9] Other studies provided social histories of trench warfare in the West.[10] Building on these efforts, cultural historians moved to assess the importance of the First World War in molding the distinctive contours of the modern. Robert Wohl's study of the mythologizing of the generation of 1914 demonstrated the war's impact across Western Europe, forming a powerful articulation of identity with profound political and cultural consequences for the turbulent interwar period.[11] Through close reading of symbols and memorials, George Mosse's *Fallen Soldiers* defined the conflict's role in shaping modern nationalism. Jay Winter's *Sites of Memory, Sites of Mourning* explored the cultural history of "mourning and its private and public expression," revising the earlier exclusive emphasis on radical discontinuity by showing how traditions played a crucial role in helping individuals and societies cope with the personal and collective loss of the war's more than nine million dead.[12] Most broadly, Stephen Kern's *The Culture of Time and Space, 1880–1918* and Modris Eksteins' *Rites of Spring: The Great War and the Birth of the Modern Age* claimed for the Great War the status of a watershed event, the defining moment for modernity, when basic human ways of apprehending reality were changed forever.[13]

Yet these illuminating examinations of the psychology of the front-experience and its ramifications focused almost exclusively on only one half of the war, the Western Front. Discussions of the First World War's cultural impact either completely neglected the eastern front-experience or allowed it only glancing, peripheral mention. It is striking to compare this omission with the volume of historiography on the Eastern Front in the Second World War. The contrast could not be greater, as the Second

World War in the East, marked by fierce ideological combat, harsh German occupation policies, and the events of the Holocaust in particular, has been studied in great depth. In particular, Omer Bartov's work on the front-experience of the East offered especially striking insights into the character and mechanics of the Nazi pursuit of war, while casting light on the soldiery's social context, the culture and beliefs which they brought into the ranks.[14] Yet this important body of work would likewise benefit from a clear view of the German encounter with the East which preceded the devastating Nazi invasion, when German troops returned to areas where their armies had been before.

The neglect of the Eastern Front in historiography of the First World War, then, is a striking gap. It might be explained in part by the remoteness of the events and area to western scholars. After the Second World War, it was believed that all but fragments of the German documentary material had been lost to bombings, especially at Potsdam, while archival holdings in the Soviet Union were inaccessible or unknown (in fact, though scattered and sometimes incomplete, significant documentary material survived).[15] Moreover, it seemed in those Cold War decades that Eastern Europe's complexity was no longer a vital issue, frozen in the apparent stasis of communist regimes. Even the crucial issue of ethnic identities in this region was treated most searchingly not by historians, but recorded as personal experience in the writings of Nobel laureate Czeslaw Milosz.[16]

The eastern front-experience still remains conspicuous by its absence in historiography. This is in itself a telling feature of the "Unknown War." The German eastern front-experience was so disorienting, conclusions drawn from it so unsettling, that it was not mythologized in the same ready way as the world of the western trenches in the decades after the war. Instead, it constituted a hidden legacy of great importance, formed out of a decisive episode in the history of Germany's relationship with the East, and holding crucial implications due to the "lessons" drawn from this encounter. Significant cultural assumptions about the East and a German civilizing mission there were shaped under the impact of war. And yet until now the eastern front-experience and its long-term legacy have remained *terra incognita* to historical scholarship.

This study explores the significance of that distinctive eastern front-experience. Its dramatic outlines emerge from a broad variety of sources, as the study ranges widely to capture the images, ideas, and characteristic assumptions recurring in German views of the East. These sources include official reports, administrative orders, propaganda bulletins, personal letters, memoirs, diaries, visual evidence by war artists and amateurs, army newspapers, poems and songs, and realistic novels by participants recording their confrontation with the East. Moreover, for a truly comprehensive, unretouched picture of German administration in the East, it is important to also draw on sources from parts of those native populations subject to German rule, as a crucial corrective and supplement to official German sources. This study uses the case of the largest ethnic group under military occupation in the northeast, Lithuanians, to provide native sources giving a "view from below" of the structures of the occupation (thus moving beyond narrow national history). This produces a more complete anatomy of an occupation, dissecting its impact on both occupiers and occupied and the clash of their cultures in the turmoil of war. Given the disorganized realities of post–1918 Eastern Europe, it is necessary to draw in not only official sources (for statistical evidence is sometimes impossible to adduce), but also popular native sources chronicling the occupation (sometimes in tendentious terms which need to be dissected critically, at other times offering recurrent motifs and charges which illuminate how natives experienced and understood the occupation). In addition, the use of Lithuanian sources indicates the impact of total war on a population in a corner of Europe less familiar in the West. This episode, while little known, is important to a full apprehension of the First World War's total European impact. It also forms a crucial chapter in Germany's longer relationship with neighboring peoples to its East, an interaction spanning centuries and marked as much by cultural exchange and influence as war and military domination. However, one should add that the very multiplicity of languages also presents a specific problem for any historical narrative on this area. In northeastern Europe's contested lands, each city and town bears many names in different languages (Lithuanian, Latvian, Estonian, Yiddish, Polish, Russian), each laying claim to the designated place. Since this study deals above all with German perceptions of the occupied East, which military authorities claimed as a "New Land" for German administration, this study uses German names given to the locations under occupation to reflect and trace those ambitions, providing current names as needed (while obviously in no way endorsing those ambitions).

For German soldiers, the eastern front-experience began with crucial first impressions and encounters, shaping how they regarded the East. Unexpected military triumphs in 1914 and 1915 brought German armies into possession of vast territories in northeastern Europe, along the Baltic coast. Mental pictures of a unitary and monolithic Russian empire, which most Germans held before the invasion, broke down before the varied and chaotic scene they now faced, a patchwork of distinct "lands and peoples." The occupiers confronted a strange landscape and foreign populations, with unfamiliar traditions, cultural identities, and histories.

Backdrop to all of this was the devastation of war, leaving the territories in desperate chaos, heightened by the frantic "scorched-earth policy" of retreating Russian armies. Seeing the East for the first time during war, in a whirlwind of human misery, dirt, disorder, disease, and confusion, produced visceral reactions in soldiers. These horrible sights seemed to be ordinary, abiding, and permanent attributes of the East they now surveyed, not just examples of universal human sufferings under the lash of war. Yet the very destruction and disarray held out an alluring possibility to officials. The army could bring order to these lands, making them over in its own image, to realize a military utopia and establish a new German identity charged with a mission of bringing *Kultur* to the East.

The result was the attempt to build a monolithic military state beyond Germany's borders, named "Ober Ost" (after the title of the Supreme Commander in the East, *Oberbefehlshaber Ost*). Poland, to the south, was put under a separate civil administration where different practices and political goals obtained, and thus for the most part lies outside of the scope of this study. Policies in Ober Ost, the largest compact area of German occupation, indeed had significant similarities to those pursued in other occupied territories, Belgium, northern France, and Poland: harsh economic regimes and requisitions, attempts at political manipulation, outbreaks of brutality against civilians, and the use of forced labor. In important respects, however, Ober Ost was different: in its purely military rule (excluding natives from administration), the relative unfamiliarity of lands and peoples of the region for Germans (compared to Belgium or Poland), and in the ideological terms on which this military state in the East was built. Belgium and Poland, as scholars have shown, were approached with prejudices and predispositions which shaped the occupation (fear of Belgian civilian snipers, long-standing anti-Polish sentiments), but the encounter with the East in Ober Ost created new terms for understanding the region.[17] The distinctive ideological understandings, occupation practices, and ambitions crafted in Ober Ost give this episode its importance.

In Ober Ost, General Erich Ludendorff, mastermind of the military state, and his officials built a huge machinery of administration in the occupied territories, jealously maintaining a complete monopoly of military control. Ober Ost was to be the embodiment of the army as a creative institution. This military utopia's ambitions went far beyond traditional conservatism or monarchism, instead showcasing a modern kind of rule, bureaucratic, technocratic, rationalized, and ideological. Under the slogan of "German Work," which claimed for Germans a unique capacity for a kind of disciplined and creative work that organized, molded, and directed, it would reshape the lands and peoples, making them over to pave the way for permanent possession. Out of this ambition there emerged two specific practices aiming to control and shape the occupied territories. In both cases, these practices were less unitary, step-by-step blueprints than assumptions and ambitions implicit in many different aspects and policies of the occupation regime. Precisely because they animated so many spheres of the regime's activity, it is instructive to examine these ideas and their ramifications.

A particular practice aiming to remake the area was called "movement policy," *Verkehrspolitik*, by which officials sought to place a severe grid of control over the territory and its native populations, directing all activity in the area and turning it to the uses of the military state, working towards a rational organization of the occupied spaces. It used modern techniques of surveillance, registration, and documentation to mobilize the resources, material and human, of the area.

The ambitious intellectual counterpart to this "movement policy" was a wide cultural program. Ober Ost's administration sought to form and manipulate the identities of different native populations, shaping them through the German Work of arbitration and cultural mentoring in special institutions designed for this purpose. In essence, the military state tried to dictate a culture for Ober Ost, where crude and untutored primitive peoples would be cultivated and ordered by German genius for organization. German soldiers, meanwhile, were also confirmed in their role as supervisors of German Work from above, separate from native populations below, in their own institutions of culture in the East: army newspapers, military homes, and theatre performances at the front.

At the same time, the eastern front-experience and practices of the military administration formed in German soldiers a specific view of the East and the sort of things that might be done there. Increasingly, the area was seen not as a complicated weaving of "lands and peoples" (*Land und Leute*), but as "spaces and races" (*Raum und Volk*) to be ordered by German mastery and organization. For many, a new German identity and mission directed against the East grew out of the eastern front-experience. The message of a mission in the East, already buttressed by concrete achievements, found ready reception back in Germany as well, where promises of future prosperity won by conquest attracted not only enthusiasts of the annexationist war aims movement, but ordinary Germans as well, enduring wartime privations. In the context of total war (demanding the complete participation and mobilization of entire societies, economies, and home fronts of nations) and the attendant militarization of education, the ground was further prepared in Germany for propaganda on the East's possibilities and promise.

Yet ultimately, fatal contradictions were built into Ober Ost's project for total control. Vaunting, overreaching ambition led to constant conflict between the utopian ends and brutal means of the state's policies, which sped towards immobilization. In 1917, as war in the East seemed to be won and Ober Ost's administration lunged at the chance to make its rule permanent, the state's political efforts seized up. Instead of successfully manipulating native peoples, yoking them to the program of German Work, the regime called forth desperate native resistance, as subject peoples articulated national identities in a struggle for survival. This study follows that catalytic process through Lithuanian sources, where outlines of a culture clash emerge, as natives championed their own values against the military's future plans. At the same time, the state was to have given soldiers an identity founded on the mission of *Kultur* in the East, but the results were disappointing. Collapse in November 1918, coming just after the euphoria of what seemed final victory in the East, was beyond comprehension for soldiers of Ober Ost and many Germans at home. Shame, fear, and disappointment created a furious rejection of the East and its dirty, chaotic "spaces and races."

Denial and hatred found expression in the rampage of *Freikorps* freebooters and German mercenaries in the Baltic lands after the war. This brutal coda to the eastern front-experience underlines that the First World War did not end neatly on November 11, 1918, but continued in reverberations and aftershocks into the postwar period. The experiences of the Eastern Front and Ober Ost were reworked in postwar Germany, forming an important backdrop to Nazi plans for realizing a racial utopia in the East. Categories of practice and perception which marked Ober Ost's rule were radicalized, forming an integral part of the Nazi ideology of biological war for "living space." Thus, the earlier military utopia's failure had enormous consequences, as the Nazi regime moved to cleanse and order the spaces of the East, emptied of those populations which Ober Ost's administration once tried to manipulate and form.

The significance of the eastern front-experience of the First World War is revealed in the disastrous ambitions built up in Ober Ost. Such ambitions, even after they ended in failure, enlarged the mental horizons of those who had seen the East, establishing radical new possibilities and practices, offering ideas and conclusions about the East's nature, its dangers and opportunities for Germany, forming a crucial cultural and psychological background and preexisting *mentalité* to be exploited and built upon by the Nazis. The lessons drawn from the failure of wartime plans in the East would have profound consequences, as they returned again in a more radical permutation in Nazi ideology.

NOTES

Translations are all my own, unless otherwise stated.

1 Norbert Elias, *Reflections on a Life*, trans. Edmund Jephcott (Cambridge, MA: Polity Press, 1994), 19–20.
2 Winston S. Churchill, *The Unknown War: The Eastern Front* (New York: Scribner's Sons, 1931).
3 Newer surveys offer more complete coverage: J. M. Winter, *The Experience of World War I* (Oxford and New York: Oxford University Press, 1989); Bernadotte E. Schmitt and Harold Vedeler, *The World in the Crucible, 1914–1919* (New York: Harper & Row, 1984); Holger H. Herwig, *The First World War: Germany and Austria-Hungary, 1914–1918* (London: Edward Arnold, 1997).
4 Norman Stone, *The Eastern Front, 1914–1917* (New York: Scribner's Sons, 1975).
5 Fritz Fischer, *Griff nach der Weltmacht. Die Kriegszielpolitik des kaiserlichen Deutschland, 1914/1918* (Düsseldorf: Droste, 1961); Wolfgang J. Mommsen, "The Debate on German War Aims," *Journal of Contemporary History* 1.3 (July 1966): 47–72.
6 Gerd Linde, *Die deutsche Politik in Litauen im ersten Weltkrieg* (Wiesbaden: Otto Harrassowitz, 1965); A. Strazhas, *Deutsche Ostpolitik im Ersten Weltkrieg. Der Fall Ober Ost, 1915–1917* (Wiesbaden: Harrassowitz Verlag, 1993); A. Strazhas, "The Land Oberost and its Place in Germany's Ostpolitik, 1915–1918," in *The Baltic States in Peace and War, 1917–1945*, ed. Stanley V. Vardys and Romualdas J. Misiunas (University Park: Pennsylvania State University Press, 1978), 43–62; Wiktor Sukiennicki, *East Central Europe During World War I*, 2 vols. (Boulder, CO: East European Monographs, 1984); Pranas Čepėnas, *Naujųjų laikų Lietuvos istorija*, 2 vols. (Chicago: M. Morkūno spaustuvė, 1976). Other studies: Georg von Rauch, *Geschichte der baltischen Staaten*, 3rd edn. (Munich: Deutscher Taschenbuch Verlag, 1990); Werner Basler, *Deutschlands Annexionspolitik in Polen und im Baltikum* (Berlin: Rütten & Loening, 1962); Börje Colliander, "Die Beziehungen zwischen Litauen und Deutschland während der Okkupation 1915–1918" (Ph.D. diss., University of Åbo, 1935); Stanley W. Page, *The Formation of the Baltic States: A Study of the Effects of Great Power Politics upon the Emergence of Lithuania, Latvia, and Estonia* (Cambridge, MA: Harvard University Press, 1959); Alfred Erich Senn, *The Emergence of Modern Lithuania* (New York: Columbia University Press, 1959); Marianne Bienhold, *Die Entstehung des Litauischen Staates in den Jahren 1918–1919 im Spiegel Deutscher Akten* (Bochum: Studienverlag Dr. N. Brockmeyer, 1976).
7 Walter Laqueur, *Russia and Germany: A Century of Conflict* (London: Weidenfeld & Nicolson, 1965); Günther Stökl, *Osteuropa und die Deutschen. Geschichte und Gegenwart einer spannungsreichen Nachbarschaft*, 3rd edn. (Stuttgart: S. Hirzel Verlag, 1982).
8 John Keegan, *The Face of Battle* (New York: Viking Press, 1976), 297.
9 Paul Fussell, *The Great War and Modern Memory* (Oxford: Oxford University Press, 1975), ix.

10 John Ellis, *Eye-Deep in Hell: Trench Warfare in World War I* (New York: Pantheon Books, 1977); Eric J. Leed, *No Man's Land: Combat and Identity in World War I* (Cambridge: Cambridge University Press, 1979).

11 Robert Wohl, *The Generation of 1914* (Cambridge, MA: Harvard University Press, 1979).

12 George L. Mosse, *Fallen Soldiers: Reshaping the Memory of the World Wars* (Oxford and New York: Oxford University Press, 1990); Jay Winter, *Sites of Memory, Sites of Mourning: The Great War in European Cultural History* (Cambridge: Cambridge University Press, 1995), 5.

13 Stephen Kern, *The Culture of Time and Space, 1880–1918* (Cambridge, MA: Harvard University Press, 1983); Modris Eksteins, *Rites of Spring: The Great War and the Birth of the Modern Age* (Boston: Houghton Mifflin, 1989).

14 Omer Bartov, *The Eastern Front, 1941–45: German Troops and the Barbarisation of Warfare* (New York: St. Martin's Press, 1986); Omer Bartov, *Hitler's Army: Soldiers, Nazis and War in the Third Reich* (Oxford: Oxford University Press, 1991).

15 Important documentary evidence is preserved at the Bundesarchiv/Militärarchiv in Freiburg (BAMA) and in Lithuanian archives in Vilnius (the Lithuanian State Historical Archives [Lietuvos Centrinis Valstybinis Istorijos Archyvas, LCVIA] and the manuscript section of the library of the Lithuanian Academy of Sciences [Lietuvos Mokslų Akademijos Mokslinės Bibliotekos Rankraščių Skyrius, LMARS].

16 Czeslaw Milosz, *Native Realm: A Search for Self-Definition*, trans. Catherine S. Leach (Garden City, NY: Doubleday, 1968).

17 See Werner Conze, *Polnische Nation und deutsche Politik im ersten Weltkrieg* (Cologne: Böhlau Verlag, 1958); Alan Kramer, "'Greueltaten': Zum Problem der deutschen Kriegsverbrechen in Belgien und Frankreich 1914," in *"Keiner fühlt sich hier als Mensch." Erlebnis und Wirkung des Ersten Weltkriegs*, ed. Gerhard Hirschfeld, *et al.* (Frankfurt: Fischer Taschenbuch Verlag, 1996), 104–39; E. H. Kossmann, *The Low Countries, 1780–1940* (Oxford: Oxford University Press, 1978), 517–44.

1   Coming to war land

When the First World War broke out in the summer of 1914, the nightmare which had haunted German leaders and military men for decades became real – they faced war on two fronts. Undaunted by the scale of this disastrous gamble, enthusiastic recruits were rushed to battle, hoping for quick, decisive, and dramatic victories. They little suspected the hells they hurried towards, or what transformations awaited them there. After the failure of the Schlieffen Plan, which aimed for decisive victory in a blow to France, the Western Front bogged down into a prolonged war of position and entrenchment, with great battles of attrition fought over small, bloodied salients, gas attacks and bombardments lasting days. These ordeals formed a western front-experience which affected a generation of young Germans and was mythologized into a potent political idea. Out of this experience came the lunge for a new model of heroism in the elite storm-troops, idealized by writers of the front generation like Ernst Jünger.[1] This myth claimed that a new man was born in storms of steel, hammered into being by the poundings of industrial warfare and the "battle of matériel." Shaped by "battle as an inner experience," the hardened front soldier of the West seemed an answer to the modernity of war.[2]

Away to the east, in fighting that carried German armies far from the borders of the *Kaiserreich*, a very different experience took shape. By contrast, the Eastern Front saw sporadic war of movement across vast spaces of inhuman scale, along a line of a thousand miles, twice the distance of the Western Front. Instead of being confined to the narrowed horizons of troglodyte bunkers and sapping trenches, soldiers in the East found their horizons widened to an extent that was nearly intolerable. In foreign lands and among unknown peoples, a new world opened before them. Its impressions and surprises left them reeling and directed disturbing questions back at them, robbed of previous certainties. Administering great occupied territories meant that they had to contend with the reality of the East each day, even as it held out to many fantastic hopes of possession and colonization. Their ambition to shape the future of these

Map 1 Eastern Europe before 1914

lands forced the conquerors to engage with the living past of the area. While the western front-experience appeared as a confrontation with modernity, the primitiveness of the East and its anachronisms sent the occupiers hurtling back through time. This sense of the primitive was heightened by the fact that in the East's open warfare, increasingly their own advanced equipment seemed insufficient, leading to a process of "demodernization" of the Eastern Front (repeated during the Second World War), as technology receded in importance.[3] From the start, a series of crucial surprises and disturbing first impressions marked the meeting with the East.

Over the four years of war, roughly two to three million men experienced the realities of the Eastern Front. Their precise number is difficult to pin down, given transfers, the moving of troops from east or west as the strategic situation demanded, casualties, and leave. In general, however, according to military statistics, troops fighting in the East numbered 683,722 in 1914–15, then 1,316,235 in 1915–16, building to 1,877,967 in 1916–17, and down to 1,341,736 in 1917–18. On average, 1,304,915 men served in the East in any given year (compared with an average of 2,783,872 in the West). Roughly twice as many troops (the ratio was 1:0.47) fought on the Western Front as in the East (though considerable numbers of these men may have fought on both fronts over the years).[4] In fact, since the above numbers count frontline troops rather than units serving behind the lines, one must assume that even more men saw the East than those statistics represent. One needs to note that among these millions of men, drawn from all parts of Germany and all levels of society, there were certainly some men for whom the East was not totally unknown: those living in eastern border areas were more familiar with this region, while others had traveled there on business. But for the bulk of these men, truly immediate, first-hand experiences of the East would present an unfamiliar scene.

War in the East began with a surprise, as assumptions of German war plans were reversed.[5] Schlieffen's doctrine envisioned a decisive blow to France, before turning on Russia's massive strength. Instead, the intended campaign of encirclement and annihilation in France bogged down, while the General Staff looked on with dismay at unexpectedly quick Russian mobilization. After Germany declared war against Russia on August 1, 1914, the commencement of hostilities brought disaster to East Prussia. Urged on by the French, Russian armies moved before they were entirely ready, to draw German forces away from the West. Two Russian armies rolled towards this tip of German territory, commanded by General Yakov Zhilinski: General Rennenkampf's northern First Army from Wilna (Vilnius) and Samsonov's southern Second Army from

Warsaw. Since Prussia's defenses were stripped to bring more manpower to the West for decisive victory there, the Russians at first enjoyed successes. Their advancing forces outnumbered von Prittwitz's defending Eighth Army by more than four to one. After the Battle of Gumbinnen on August 20, East Prussia was practically evacuated of German troops. Cossacks burned and plundered, taking hostages from the civilian population and deporting them east.

In this moment of disaster, General Prittwitz lost his nerve, insisting to general head quarters that the Eighth Army be withdrawn behind the Vistula. Imperial Chief of General Staff Helmuth von Moltke responded by relieving him of his command. On August 22, the aged General Paul von Hindenburg was called back from retirement and put in charge of the Eighth Army.[6] In fact, his appointment was nearly an afterthought, for the General Staff only needed someone of superior rank to lend authority to the tactical talent of newly promoted Major General Erich Ludendorff, famed for his dramatic role in taking the Belgian fortress of Liège, who was made Hindenburg's chief of staff.[7] A special train sped the duo to the front, where First General Staff Officer Lieutenant-Colonel Max Hoffmann already had matters in hand and had issued orders for the coming days, which the newly arrived leaders needed but to look over and approve.

By the end of the month, German armies rallied and defeated the Russians at Tannenberg, exploiting superior mobility and organization. A huge battle from August 26–31, 1914 led to the encirclement of Samsonov's army. Russian leadership under Zhilinski was spectacularly incompetent, with movement of the two armies in his command poorly coordinated and further impeded by long-standing personal animosity between Samsonov and Rennenkampf. Russian radio orders were sent uncoded and were intercepted by incredulous German listening posts. Over sixty miles and four days, in a landscape split up by strings of little lakes, the battle raged, until the agile mobility of German forces won out. Ninety-two thousand Russian prisoners were taken. General Samsonov, his army crushed, wandered off into the woods and shot himself. On the German side, naming the battle was a task of great symbolic significance. Afterwards, Ludendorff explained that rather than choosing one of the small locales with unmelodious names, "at my suggestion, the battle was named the Battle of Tannenberg, as a reminder of that clash in which the Order of Teutonic Knights had been defeated by united Lithuanian and Polish armies. Will the German now allow, as then, that the Lithuanian and especially the Pole take advantage of our helplessness and do violence to us? Will centuries-old German culture be lost?"[8] The symbolism conjured up by Tannenberg was muddled, but powerful: victory in 1914 redeeming an earlier defeat in 1410.

Victory here took on mythic proportions, coming at a time of dimly understood disappointments in the West. Overnight, Hindenburg became a god to Germans at home. On November 1, 1914, he was elevated to the position of Supreme Commander in the East, *Oberbefehlshaber Ost*, with extraordinary powers. In the partnership between the old field marshal and his chief of staff, Hindenburg provided the figurehead. This was announced by his very appearance: proliferating heroic paintings and photographs showed a square-edged figure seemingly petrified, frozen into impossibly upright bearing, topped by a blockish head with chiseled features and a bristle of severely cropped, grizzled hair. One coworker said he looked "like his own monument."[9] Behind this steady figurehead, Ludendorff provided dynamism and restless nervous energy. Hindenburg described the partnership as a "happy marriage."[10] The initials HL flowed together into one symbol of power. In the first year of the war, their spreading fame stood in sharp contrast to the stalemated failures in the West, all that Chief of General Staff Falkenhayn had to show after he replaced von Moltke.[11] Over the next months rivalry simmered between the popular champions of Tannenberg and the overall commander, soon reflected in a split in the officer corps and indeed also in Germany's political leadership, between two opposed camps, "Easterners" and "Westerners."[12] The "Easterners," led by Ludendorff, Hindenburg, and Hoffmann, insisted, true to Schlieffen's philosophy of battles of annihilation, that decisive victory could be gained against Russia, if they were but given sufficient reserves for larger encirclements. By contrast, Falkenhayn and the "Westerners" were skeptical of these claims and doubted the chances of an outright military victory, as they understood better the strategic strain of conflict on several fronts, the challenge of economic war as Germany was blockaded at sea, and the fundamental fact that the decisive result, if it came, would still have to be sought on the Western Front, not in the spaces of Russia. Over the next two years, this conflict escalated, with overall leadership of Germany's war effort as the prize.

From the Battle of the Masurian Lakes from early to mid September 1914, the Germans turned on Rennenkampf's army. After a battle over great areas of difficult terrain, the Russians were expelled from East Prussia. German armies moved on to take parts of the Suwalki area, but they were again lost to the Russians in their late fall campaign. To the south, Austria's attack into Russian Poland met with disaster. Austrian armies were turned back and pushed almost to Cracow by September. To staunch this development, Germany's eastern armies were reorganized to produce a new Ninth Army, which was set moving against Warsaw. But the Russians, now reaching full mobilization, heroically counterattacked at the end of September, threatening Silesia. Intensively using railway movement to offset Russian numerical superiority, Hindenburg and Ludendorff deflected the attack. Receiving new reinforcements from the West, they threw Russian armies back towards Warsaw, as winter closed the campaign.

With the start of the new year in 1915, German armies went over to the offensive in the East. They regained their foothold in the Russian empire after the winter Battle of Masuren in February 1915. By mid March, German front lines all ran on enemy territory. Falkenhayn temporarily moved his attention east to relieve the strained Austrian front, where Russian forces threatened the Carpathians and prepared to surge into Hungary. This shift eastwards was a mixed blessing for Hindenburg and Ludendorff, whose control there now was less absolute, yet they strained to realize their plans of annihilating battles of encirclement. The German "Great Advance" began on April 27, 1915, as part of the main offensive of the Central Powers all along the Eastern Front. In the north, German troops moved into the territories of what had been the medieval Grand Duchy of Lithuania. The immediate goal was to protect East Prussia from renewed attack and to distract from attacks to the south during early May. There, the southern armies achieved a breakthrough at Gorlice. In the north, in spite of the terrible condition of roads, progress was made. On May 1, 1915, the Germans took the larger city Schaulen (Šiauliai) in the Lithuanian lowlands, a center of railroad connections and industrial production. Not much was left of it: the city was burning, put to the torch by Russian troops retreating towards Riga, destroying 65 percent of the buildings.[13] In their withdrawal, Russian forces practiced a concerted "scorched earth" policy of destroying lost territory and emptying it of people. On May 7, 1915, the Baltic port of Libau (Liepāja) was taken by a combined German assault by land and sea, the first great fortress to fall in the string of Russian frontier fortifications. To the south, the Russians had been expelled from Galicia.

In May, the northern armies prepared their attack over the Njemen River, supporting the mid-July offensive on the Eastern Front, which aimed at the formidable fortress city of Brest-Litovsk. The Eighth Army, under General von Scholtz, attacked towards Lomza and Grodno. The Njemen Army, commanded by General von Below, crossed the Windau River on July 14, 1915. On August 1, 1915, Mitau (Jelgava) and Bauske were taken. The fortress of Kowno (Kaunas), another great strong point of Russian defenses, was besieged on August 6, 1915. It fell on August 18, 1915, to troops of Eichhorn's army, under the command of General Litzmann, who took the forts and mountains of supplies, 20,000 dispirited prisoners, and over 1,300 guns. The emptied city's population was reduced by more than 70 percent.[14] After Kowno's capture, German

Map 2 The German "Great Advance" of 1915 – Eastern Front

armies were in possession of most of Lithuania and Kurland. Now the way lay open to the area's largest city, Wilna, the most important rail artery of the Northwestern Territory. Fortress Grodno fell on September 3, 1915, the last stronghold on the Njemen River line of defense. To the south, Warsaw had been taken on August 5, 1915 and by later in the month most of Poland was in German hands. Ludendorff was allowed to make his move towards Wilna on September 9, 1915, still hoping for a dramatic encirclement. The Njemen Army struck east, in the direction of Dvinsk (Daugavpils). The Tenth Army under Hermann von Eichhorn attacked southeast toward Wilna.

After Kowno's fall, Wilna prepared for evacuation. Streets had long been crowded with carts of refugees fleeing east. Now the government departed, officials and agencies cramming the train station to bursting with packages and freight. With them, they took their monuments and statues, symbols of tsarist rule. Parishioners surrounded churches to prevent bells from being taken away. The city shut down, mail and telephone service severed. As the Germans neared, cannon were soon heard from three sides. Zeppelins floated over the city to drop bombs on darkened streets. The retreating Russians were determined to leave as little as possible to the advancing Germans. In the evenings, the city's fringes were lit by flames, as fire "evacuated" what railroads could not. The government sought to mobilize all local reservists, so that their manpower would not fall to the enemy. Soon planned measures turned to panic. Arson teams set fire to homesteads, farms, and manors, pillaging, looting, and driving people east by force. On September 9, 1915, the army chief ordered that all men from 18 to 45 were to retreat with the army. A crazy manhunt began, as natives and deserters hid or fled to the woods. Those caught by police were sent to collection centers to be moved out. Intensifying Zeppelin bombardments, shattering the train station and dropping explosives at random, announced the end. The last Russian regiments and Cossacks marched out of a city that seemed dead. In the dreamlike interval before the arrival of German soldiers, life slowly began to stir again, as locals organized civic committees, police militia, and newspapers. The last farewell of the Tsar's forces was the sound of explosions, as bridges were blown up.

Death's Head Hussars were the first Germans to reach the city center. For one native, it seemed a scene from the past, as if medieval Teutonic Knights were resurrected: "Almost as five hundred years ago, they were wrapped in gray mantles, only without the cross." When German troops marched into the city in parade formation, natives were impressed with their order and cleanliness, remarking on their unified bearing, "their sameness." Officers seemed much closer to their soldiers than in the

Russian army. Together, Germans seemed to present a unified front, as they ate together, talked together, joked together, and "looked upon the inhabitants of the conquered land with the same haughty mien."[15] Wilna and its fortifications were all in German hands on September 19, 1915. Despite the success, German northern armies lacked sufficient strength to effect the encirclement of which Ludendorff dreamed. The Russians succeeded in withdrawing in time, retreating towards Minsk. Brest-Litovsk fell on August 25, 1915 to Mackensen's army, while Prince Leopold of Bavaria's Ninth Army moved through the primeval forest of Bialowies. The vision of epic encirclement, replicating Tannenberg on a gigantic scale, was unrealized and Hindenburg and Ludendorff blamed Falkenhayn, who had not approved their plans. Thereafter, the duo's break with Falkenhayn was complete; their rivalry entered its most intense phase. As Falkenhayn turned his attention to Serbia and then back to the Western Front in 1916 (beginning his disastrous attempt to "bleed France white" at Verdun in the spring), the indispensable eastern commanders schemed to displace their superior.

By fall of 1915, the East's sweeping war of movement came to an end. Consistently, Russian armies in retreat managed to withdraw into the open spaces, establishing new fronts. With September's end, German offensive operations closed. In the north, the front stabilized on the banks of the Düna, short of the fabled Hansa city of Riga, which was too well protected for frontal assault. From Kurland's northern tip, the front of the Supreme Commander in the East ran all the way to the Austrian sphere of operations in the south.

On this new front line, German armies settled into a monumental work of building up fortified positions. Behind this wall, war and Russian scorched-earth policy ravaged rear areas. As it withdrew, the tsarist administration shipped entire factories east, destroying what it could not move. It evacuated or dragooned away masses of people. In particular, the defeated army scapegoated groups they considered "unreliable." Russians suspected Jews of sympathies for the invaders because they spoke Yiddish, a language related to German. Commander in Chief Grand Duke Nicholas Nicholaevich ordered the expulsion of tens of thousands of Jews from front areas at short notice.[16] Lutherans were considered suspect because of their religion, even if they were ethnic Lithuanians or thoroughly assimilated natives of German ancestry who spoke Lithuanian at home. Retreating Russian soldiers carried out summary shootings and hangings of Lutheran farmers as spies, burning homes and mills, and driving others away.[17] Even "reliable" populations were herded off. Kurland was left depopulated, losing three-fifths of its population. Crops were burned. German armies came into possession of lands in a state of desperate disorder. Refugees crowded the roads, streaming towards the cities where they huddled together in misery, while the prospect of famine and epidemics hung over the ruined territory.

The army's task was to establish "ordered conditions" in rear areas behind its front, securing lines of communication and supply. While Poland was placed under a civilian administration, Hindenburg's Tenth Army administered the areas of Russia's Northwest Territory. Under the Supreme Commander in the East, the territory was known as Ober Ost (also Ob. Ost). It encompassed the areas of Kurland, Lithuania, and Bialystok-Grodno, a space of 108,808 square kilometers (nearly twice the size of West and East Prussia combined, and at 42,503 square miles roughly 45 percent of the area of the United Kingdom today) with an ethnically diverse native population of close to 3 million.[18] Ober Ost was essentially the feudal fief of the Supreme Commander in the East, *Oberbefehlshaber Ost* von Hindenburg, invested with exceptional freedom of action. He personally, or more often through his energetic chief of staff, Ludendorff, directed not only military operations on the Eastern Front, but also day-to-day administration of the occupied territories. The supreme commander was the first cause of the Ober Ost state, to which he gave his name. His figure was the personification of that state, his will its law. Over the next year, while Hindenburg sat for portraits or hunted bison in ancient forests, his junior partner Ludendorff built up a huge machinery of military administration, driven by an obsession to "create something whole" and lasting here, even while scheming to supplant Falkenhayn. The area over which the supreme commander held sway also expanded over time, as Hindenburg was charged with the command of the front with the Austrians as far south as Brody, east of Lemberg, after threatening Russian successes of the Brusilov offensive in Galicia in June 1916.[19] By the time their intrigues brought Hindenburg and Ludendorff to Germany's High Command on August 29, 1916, Ober Ost had grown into a formidable and independent military state in the East, a military utopia.

The experiences of the fronts in East and West took shape in markedly different ways for German armies. The East remained, at least potentially, a war of movement, after the West bogged down into a war of positions, trenches, and bunkers. Offensives here still held the promise of breakthroughs. And yet this was an elusive promise, for as one officer observed of this fighting, "it burns at all points and nowhere is there a uniform and straight front line, at which a decisive result could be won."[20] Even the process of fortification and digging-in marking war in the West assumed another character here, as German forces secured large areas and then sank into the vast landscape.

To begin with, combat on the Eastern Front was even costlier than in the West, proportionately, in terms of deaths and other casualties during the first two years: especially in the first year, when losses per unit exceeded those in the West by more than a quarter. The great advance of 1915 came at great expense; one division reported daily losses of more than 200 men. Afterwards, western losses predominated, but memories of tremendous initial casualties were another crucial first impression of the East. During the course of the entire war, losses on the Eastern Front (due to death, wounds, and disease) were one-quarter lower than in the West. In relation to the overall numbers of men, there were two-fifths less dead, only half as many missing, and one-third fewer wounded than in the West. However, another defining feature was the role disease played in losses in the East. During the entire war, in the West there were 2.8 sick cases for every one wounded man, in the East there were 3.7 sick cases for each wounded. Medical officers struggled to combat the East's epidemiological "gigantic danger": typhoid, malaria, cholera, and that "most uncanny enemy", typhoid spotted fever, a disease unknown in Germany, carried by lice. Yet this urgent task was impeded by primitive conditions and apathetic natives who, it was claimed, were less affected than Germans by the diseases they carried, given their habitual state of "high-grade lice-infestation."[21] The twin horrors of violent death and disease hovered over the Eastern Front, characteristic hallmarks for German soldiers.

Arriving in the East, German soldiers often found themselves lost, even though just over the border from Germany. The very proximity of such strangeness heightened the force of new impressions. According to Ludendorff, he and his soldiers knew "little of the conditions of the land and people [Land und Leuten] and looked out on a new world."[22] Many had to learn on the spot everything they needed to know about these lands.[23] First impressions were crucial, for once formed they determined how soldiers and officers viewed and treated the lands and peoples under their control. The army had made no plans in advance for administration of the newly occupied territories. Moreover, the reality they saw overthrew their earlier vague views of the East. From a distance, it had seemed to them a monolithic, frozen Russian empire, but now it dissolved into a chaotic, ragged patchwork of nationalities and cultures.

When the Kaiserreich looked to the East in the decades before World War I, it saw an absolutist monarchical state, apparently unified. For the broader German public, Imperial Russia conjured up images of repression, backwardness, and despotism. The "Russian threat," looming ever larger before 1914, evoked visions of Cossacks and inexhaustible peasant armies, unending human waves, and the sheer potential power of the

"Russian steamroller," poised to overwhelm central Europe. Germany's left hated tsarism for its role as "Gendarme of Europe" for the Holy Alliance. Ordinary Germans viewing the East before the war worked on traditional assumptions that it needed to be understood in dynastic terms. Above all, people to the east were understood as subjects of another imperial sovereign, all vaguely Russian in character, whatever else they might be.

The traditional background of German perceptions of the Russian empire was a tangle of dynastic sympathies and relationships, influencing foreign policy from the Holy Alliance of 1815 to Bismarck's 1887 treaty of conservative solidarity. Bismarck insisted there were no fundamental conflicts between Imperial Russia and Imperial Germany. Yet after Bismarck's dismissal in 1890, "mutual terror" grew up between Germany and Russia. Fears grew of Russian surprise attack and nightmares of the Slavic advance of peasant giants gained currency in the popular imagination. Increasingly isolated by its diplomatic blunderings, Germany's foreign policy turned to the preservation of Austro-Hungary, threatened by Pan-Slavism and even more by its own ossified incompetence. By 1910, a conviction that continental war was inevitable was established in the minds of leading personalities, feeding a "politics of cultural despair." The new chancellor, Theobald von Bethmann Hollweg, revealed his deep fatalism when he sighed at the futility of planting trees on his estate at the Oder River, convinced that Russians would soon take over the area. Adding fuel to this fire, the 1890s saw the hoisting of the banner of a new politics to win for Germany the international position it believed it merited by its economic muscle. The cry for *Weltpolitik* went out across large segments of imperial society, as an outlet for the political energies of the confined population. Industrial and agricultural interest groups encouraged these demands, seeking new economic possibilities. Some ultranationalist propagandists looked east. Ernst Hasse, the theoretician of Pan-Germanism, called for a return from the colonial scramble to a European policy in his *Deutsche Politik* (1908). The views of the activist right wing on Russia were represented by Constantin Frantz, author of *Weltpolitik* (1882–83) and one of Bismarck's sharpest critics, who urged war on the East, Paul de Lagarde, whose *Deutsche Schriften* (1905) urged expansion to take territory for the race, and Friedrich Lange, whose *Reines Deutschtum* (1904) preached racial war.[24] These extremist ideas drew increasing support from nationalist and expansionist pressure groups, foremost among them the Pan-German League.[25] Another group, the League of the Eastern Marches, also nicknamed Hakatisten after the founders' initials, agitated for German settlement in the eastern provinces to weaken the Polish minority there. Its influential membership of industrialists, agrarian notables, and academics were a voice to be reckoned with in domestic politics.

Repatriated Baltic Germans, in particular, carved out a special position in forming public opinion on Russia and the East. The emergence of Pan-Slavism in the 1860s and policies of Russification in the Baltic provinces put increasing strain on their position as a "peculiar institution" within Imperial Russian society. Articulate Baltic Germans resettling in Germany energetically presented their grievances and often partisan understanding of Russian realities to the public.[26] Increasingly influential after 1905, they did not create fear of Russia in Germany on their own, but gave more distinct, anecdotal form to common apprehensions from the experience of their own minority ethnic group. During the war, they were in the forefront of the most ardent annexationists.

Set against the tradition of autocratic sympathies was German revolutionary sentiment. At the start of the nineteenth century, German student radicals planned attempts on the life of Tsar Alexander I and the Polish risings stirred liberal sympathies among the middle class. Russia's role in suppressing the 1848 revolutions was not forgotten. Indeed, it was on the left that the most durable antipathy toward the Russia of the Tsars (and the conservatism of the Russian peasantry) was found. Engels declared that "hatred of Russia is the first German revolutionary sentiment." In 1848, as Russia intervened in Hungary, Marx and Engels called for revolutionary war against the gendarme of the Concert of Europe. Bebel and Liebknecht again took up the cry in the 1890s. This revolutionary myth of Russia would have important effects in 1914, as the socialist party's ready voting of war credits in August and the war aims of the German left reflected the special position Russia occupied in its world of thought. The Russian issue, thus, was to be a decisive component in German socialist enthusiasm for the war effort.

Another revolutionary "myth" of Russia was dreamed by succeeding generations of German artists and thinkers. The originator of modern nationalism, Johann Gottfried Herder, praised the naturalness of eastern and northern peoples, while condemning German imperialism. His philosophy had revolutionary impact on the consciousness of Slavic and Baltic intellectuals. *Sturm und Drang* movement members Klinger and Lenz discerned in Russia and its people a spiritual breadth not to be found in their own civilized Europe. Later, the same quality was appreciated by Wagner and Nietzsche, Spengler and Thomas Mann. Rilke even considered Russia his spiritual homeland. For many, the East was not only an exotic setting for the imagination, but seemed a *tabula rasa*, where man was still young, a noble savage for all that he was in chains. Generally, the picture of Russia in the public imagination of the early twentieth century was based mostly on the reading of Russian novelists, as well as popularizing critics interpreting Russian culture for German readers, reducing it to distilled images and generalizations of each artist's "message."[27]

By no means, however, was German academic scholarship ignorant of the East and the Russian empire. While teaching in Slavonic studies was established in 1842 at Breslau, it took on new momentum with the 1902 founding of the Seminar for Eastern European History and Geography in Berlin, directed by Baltic German historian and publicist Theodor Schiemann.[28]

In spite of scholarly work, however, even educated Germans did not know much in detail of lands to the east. Famed sociologist Norbert Elias recalled that, as a student (in spite of growing up in Breslau, in eastern Germany) in 1914 he knew nothing about Russia except that it was "barbarous" and far away.[29] Popular perceptions of the East, as well as much academic work, rested upon a set of common assumptions shared by many Germans about Eastern Europe, views influenced by German rule over parts of Poland since the eighteenth century. These stereotypes about Prussian-Polish territories and Poles were "potentially and actually transferable to the Slavs in general" and in practice functioned as justifications for rule over minority populations in Prussia.[30] The most important disdainful assumption posited a "cultural gradient" (*Kulturgefälle*) sloping away from Germany to the Slavic East, plunging down into barbarism the further one ventured. Dirt, underdevelopment, and anarchy were assumed to be characteristic conditions of these lands, summed up in the imprecation "*Polnische Wirtschaft!*" (Polish economy), synonymous with mismanagement. By contrast, some popular authors and historians argued, Germans had carried culture and development to the East, in a supposedly timeless and elemental "Drive to the East," *Drang nach Osten*, over past centuries, a notion well established by the 1860s.[31] These general, vague, but commonly held assumptions conditioned the way Germans viewed the East in 1914, and found expression in a ditty chalked on the side of a rail wagon carrying troops in the war's first heady days: "Tsar, it's an almighty shame / That we have to first disinfect you and your gang / And then thoroughly cultivate you!"[32]

In sum, there had been a sense of Russian uniformity in the *Kaiserreich*'s vague impressions of the East, whether seen as military threat, despotism, dirty backwater, or romantic tableau. But these popular visions were radically upset when German armies arrived in the East in the summer months of 1915. They now saw a reality on the ground quite different from their preconceptions. What seemed in peace a unitary empire now broke down completely before their eyes. With overarching

Russian administration gone, the lands were revealed as distinct, various, and more complex in their present and past than Germans had suspected. Non-Russian peoples there had their own languages, traditions, and historical memories forming cultural and nascent national identities. Where before Germans spoke of the area as a part of an empire, an undifferentiated "Russia," they now understood the occupied territories in terms of a collection of "lands and peoples" – "*Land und Leute.*"[33] From now on, newly arrived Germans had to contend with all the onslaught of impressions thrust at them by the territories to be administered, struggling to understand the foreign lands, peoples, and living histories of this place.

Most immediately, the landscape and scale of the spaces of the East left newly arrived occupiers shaken. Ober Ost's areas were separated from East Prussia by shallow, flat lowland, with marshy woods and crossed by many rivers. Rippled lines of hills marked the coast of the Baltic waters and yielded to a slowly rising east of hilly lands scoured by river valleys, filled with marshes and a multitude of little lakes. Further to the east, the land opened out on to the vastness of Russian plains, a premonition of gigantic steppes beyond.[34] The area seemed a place of transition between the different worlds of Germany and the Russian empire.

The area's geographical situation had been of decisive importance in shaping it into the place the occupiers now saw, giving the territory its distinctive mix of peoples and densely woven texture of history and myth. Through the ages, it had been in the historically fateful position of being a crossroads of Europe, a "war land" situated along the great European plain extending from Russia's frozen north to the Baltic coast and on to northern Germany.[35] This great plain was a natural corridor for the movement of peoples, channeled between the Baltic's waves and the watery Pripet marshes to the south. Thus, from time immemorial this place was a point of meeting and conflict between East and West. Distinct families of peoples pressed in from all sides: here Germanic peoples, there Slavic. Great campaigns moved through this corridor, most memorably Napoleon's disastrous invasion of Russia's depths in 1812. Topography read like destiny.

Geography had determined the region's texture of history and ethnicity, and now confronted the Germans, leaving them shaken. Again and again, the occupying soldier felt that he was losing himself in the open, empty spaces of the East. The breadth of sky, the earth's flatness and expanse grew oppressive. The further east armies moved in 1915 and in the later great advances of 1918, the more this landscape revealed itself in its openness, the plains in their endlessness. All this left the occupier as a tiny figure struggling to explain his presence. One soldier recorded the experience of the steppe taking him "into its spell" as he walked further into its emptiness, until "In the distance, at the horizon, a brighter line now bordered the blackness. There lay the East, the Russian endlessness. He stared into this land, which in its distant expanses makes the eyes wide and yet directs the gaze inwards, which leads people into infinity, and yet leads them back to themselves."[36] Another recalled being "constantly amazed at the wide stretches of land without settlement."[37] Such sights called up a powerful inward reaction in the newly arrived soldier. His gaze was drawn eastwards, towards this mysterious, powerful expanse. It was apparent even in towns, as one official sensed in Kowno. Everywhere, he wrote, one felt "free horizon. The main roads as well are laid out so broadly, that one sees constantly the proverbial Russian sky spanned above. It seems indeed so mystically wide, as if it curved constantly away and only struck the earth somewhere behind the horizon."[38] The endlessness and emptiness seemed to grow more intense the further east one went.[39]

The occupiers met another disturbing impression in the huge, primeval forests, so different from the managed woods they knew in Germany. Imaginations reeled at their sheer scale, their endless areas, and what might be hidden in the wild, brooding darkness. Forests hid howling wolves, bears, elk, deer. Even bison roamed in the primeval forest of Bialowies, long since vanished elsewhere in Europe.[40] On seeing one, an official marveled that "it seemed like a picture from the grayest prehistoric times."[41] Natives told soldiers disjointed stories of supernatural beings living there. What astonished Germans even more was that the woods here were not cultivated at all, untouched by the organized, planned, scientific forestry practiced in Germany. Trees were not thinned, forest floors not cleared, remaining thick, impenetrable tangles of growth: oaks, pines, ghostly pale birches, brambles, briars, fallen trunks and branches. A soldier's diary recalled such "mighty root work and grotesque tree figures," woods where "many branches have been toppled, broken by snow or wind, and lie like a mighty pile of ruins, like a desolate garden of tangled marble columns." An official marveled at mounds on the forest floor, into which one sank.[42] The trees were also immensely old; cut down, some pines showed up to 250 rings of growth.[43] These great woods lived their own life and death, oblivious to human presence in "eternal, unbreakable, holy and closed peace," a "thousand-fold family which has grown together."[44] The chaotic tangle of massive unities made it seem that no human had walked through them since time began. Germans recognized these as fabled *Urwälder* – ancient, "original" forests which covered Europe in prehistoric times and retreated here to make their last stand. Awe at this spectacle was touched by apprehension for soldiers, because the impressions which the ancient forests made refuted a part of their own understanding of themselves as Germans: people at home in wooded nature, romantic inheritors of a tradition of tribal independence born under German oaks, described by Tacitus.[45] Nature was not acting upon them as it was supposed to, for they were decidedly not at home here, and this called into question earlier complacent assumptions about themselves. Arnold Zweig's novel of Ober Ost, *The Case of Sergeant Grischa* (the great war novel of the Eastern Front), recalled forests as dangerous places which sent people hurtling back through time by their primeval quality, back into more primitive states.[46]

Baltic weather gave the land its physical character. Rain fell constantly through spring, summer, and autumn. It could not drain off into the poor soil and gathered into extensive rivers and lakes, marshes and bogs. One soldier's diary complained: "A gentle spring rain comes down during the entire day, and one comes to believe that the earth will simply be flooded away."[47] When rains cleared, the land was bathed in strange, pellucid light – the sky a striking, immediate blue, arched vast over the plains. Then mists and fog crept in, through the forests and down valleys, a twilight of uncertain shapes and living forms. Finally, rain would begin again. Winters were harsh, as Siberian winds brought infinities of snow to cover the land. One awed official felt "deep impressions of the unmeasurable extent, loneliness, and winter majesty of the Russian forests."[48] A captain recalled marching forward in snow three feet deep, needing to relieve exhausted men leading the column every thirty minutes.[49] Drifts erased roads and covered villages, while wolves ranged at night, emboldened by hunger.[50] Soldiers could freeze to death at their posts. Winter was slow to loosen its grip on the land, even with the thaw. With spring, the snow-covered land became sodden.

This affected the ground underfoot, leaving it marshy. Advancing troops moved with difficulty through the swamps, along uncertain trails that only locals really knew. Ground was spongy, perennially wet, and footing uncertain. Travel here seemed a nearly superhuman undertaking. Roads were wretched, impossibly rutted and dusty when dry, most often seas of mud and mire, swallowing carts, trucks, and horses. As vehicles drove alongside roads to avoid the growing swamp at the center, the width of some roads expanded to fifty meters.[51] The infamous roads left perhaps the most powerful impression on newcomers.

All of this brought soldiers' attention to the soil. The first cause of the land's peculiar features lay in the nature of the ground, the character of its earth. The occupiers experienced and remarked on it.[52] Ground was permanently wet, permeated with standing water. It was completely undrained and seemed totally uncultivated. New arrivals saw the territory as a badlands. One official characterized this as "*Unland*," to express the intensity of its desolation.[53] Yet there was also something more, a spirit of the place that worked in on them. A "profound stillness" lay over the landscape.[54] Other soldiers mused on the "melancholy" and "trace of sorrow, which never entirely disappears from this land."[55] It possessed a unique character, which they felt they had to grasp to gain a firm position.

Many documents from the occupation attest to the strength of these first impressions and attempts to come to terms with them. By some means, the place's "unique character," "*Eigenart*," had to be apprehended. Soldiers recounted the scenes in army newspapers, official publications, and in letters, diaries, memoirs, and novels. Albums of sketches and photographs recorded images arresting the attention of the occupiers. Army publications such as *The Lithuania Book* and *Pictures from Lithuania* presented landscape scenes and ethnographic sketches, to catalog, order, and fix the unfamiliar.[56]

As soldiers sought to account for the strangeness of these lands, many seized on the idea of "*Kultur*." Chief among the ecstatic "Ideas of 1914" mobilizing German society was the claim that the Great War represented a conflict of opposing national life philosophies. Supposedly, on the Western Front, organic German *Kultur* clashed with the mere "civilization" of Western democracies.[57] German intellectuals asserted that French and British achievements were only hollow technical attainments, based on a shabby materialism. German *Kultur*, meanwhile, was real, rooted, organic, spirit-infused, and given wings by idealistic philosophy. The Eastern Front, however, was different: here a juxtaposition of *Kultur* and civilization could not work out. And yet *Kultur* emerged as one of the great issues of the Eastern Front, where it took on a different sense, made crassly literal. Here *Kultur* did not merely mean high art; it meant civilization as such. *Kultur* was even taken back to its original sense of agricultural cultivation, of working the land, even drainage. Germans rendered war in the East as a clash between *Kultur* and its negation – sheer "*Unkultur*."[58] In this view, German cultivation and transformative energies faced here only empty badlands, wastes. The new arrivals saw a place that seemed to them little worked, or "cultivated," compared to Germany. With every step into the wilderness, they weighed in their imaginations how this piece of nature would have been tamed, controlled, divided, subdivided, cultivated and shaped, back home.[59] Crossing into the East, one official noted,

I have never seen a border like this, which divides not just two states, but two worlds. As far as the eye could see, nothing but a scene of poverty and *Unkultur*, impossible roads, poor villages and neglected huts and a dirty, ragged population with primitive field agriculture, a total opposite of the blooming German landscape in neighboring Upper Silesia.[60]

Perhaps Germans could cultivate and overcome this strangeness. Looking out over the landscape, they saw not only what was there, but what it might become.

At the same time, the wild, "uncultivated" lands were also inhabited. At first, this land of war seemed nearly emptied of people. Great numbers fled as the war approached, or were dragooned away by retreating Cossacks. Natives who hid in the forests to wait for the front to pass now slowly struggled back. The distribution of people had been sparse before the war, and was even more so now. Ober Ost's population density was below that of Germany's emptiest areas. With twenty-seven people per square kilometer, it stood at about half that of East Prussia, a quarter of that of Germany as a whole.[61] In all of Ober Ost, 1,300,000 were estimated to have fled their homes (of an original population of 4,200,000), with Kurland losing 54.4% of its peacetime population, Lithuania 26.6%, Wilna-Suwalki 46%, and Bialystok-Grodno 37.35%. Generally, roughly a third of the prewar population had fled or fallen victim to the war.[62]

German armies also faced populations striking in their helplessness, now disproportionately made up of women, children, and the old. Refugees flooded Wilna and other cities, in numbers overwhelming the limited resources of native relief committees, and soon disease and famine gripped the urban centers. For the occupiers, seeing the lands for the first time, these initial impressions were crucial, shaping the way they responded to the territory and its peoples.[63] It was decisive that they first saw the lands under fire and the sword, for they took the abnormal conditions and effects of war to be characteristic of the place, part of its essential character.

Facing something new and unknown in the diverse native populations, the first imperative for the occupiers was to understand the categories and varieties making up this confusing mix of peoples. Somehow, the complexity had to be distilled, reduced to essences, but the task of defining these peoples was no easy matter. Definitions of identity were notoriously fluid here and even now still in the process of historical development. In their new Ober Ost, Germans faced a bewildering array of unfamiliar peoples with alien customs, histories, and views of the world.

In villages and lone steadings, along the roads, advancing German armies met the territory's largest group, the peasant people of the Lithuanians. They spoke an archaic language, the oldest living Indo-

European tongue, a linguistic coelacanth fascinating to scholars. Along with other Baltic tribes, they had inhabited these shores since 3000 BC. In the Grand Duchy of Lithuania, they had been Europe's last pagans, practicing animistic religion, worshiping trees, snakes, and bees. A 200-year Baltic crusade by the Teutonic Knights failed to baptize them by force (though managing to wipe out the related Old Prussians, and taking their name). On meeting the Lithuanians, one German official character-ized their history as the fight of a "nature-people against western *Kul-tur*."[64] For all practical purposes, the countryside only truly accepted Roman Catholic Christianity in the eighteenth century. Even then, what evolved was a complex synthesis of older beliefs with new religion.[65] This slow assimilation reflected the peasant people's supposedly characteristic stubbornness and conservative nature.[66] Over the last decades, as pros-pering independent farmers pressed their children to become educated, a class of intelligentsia came into existence, taking up the project of forming a national consciousness, clashing with the different political conceptions of local Poles and Russians.

The third Baltic tribe, besides the Lithuanians and extinct Prussians, were the Latvians in Kurland to the north, until recently likewise largely a peasant people, though advancing industrialization centered in Riga and larger towns produced strong urbanization, an industrial working class, and middle class.[67] Historical circumstances formed them into a people distinct from their cousins to the south, falling under German rule in the thirteenth century, yoked into serfdom by colonial masters. Lutheran faith came to them through their German lords, while southern areas under the Polish–Lithuanian Commonwealth retained Catholicism. With Lutheranism, Latvians also gained their own literary language and thus a basis for growing national consciousness. Strengthened by sharp social and class conflict, this evolved into a frightening intensity of mutual hatred and violence between Latvians and German Baltic Barons, erupt-ing during the 1905 Revolution.[68] A third of the Latvian population was displaced by the war.[69]

Another peasant people came into focus only gradually, known as Belarusians, "White Russians," or "White Ruthenians."[70] Even their proper name was uncertain. They were a Slavic tribe concentrated mostly to the south and east. After a first encounter, one official called them "very good-willed and submissive, but standing culturally at an extraordi-narily low level."[71] Historically, their identity was formed by being cut off from the Eastern Slavs by the Grand Duchy of Lithuania's rule. Lacking even the beginnings of an educated class (at least in the occupied terri-tories), their passivity and voicelessness shocked the Germans.[72] Such shadowy indistinctness was disconcerting. Was this the wreckage of a people, doomed to extinction, or one in the process of being born? Belarusians were further split into different confessions, Roman Catholic and Orthodox. Because Catholic clergy were Polish, the religious affiliation, as with Lithuanians, conditioned overwhelming cultural and linguistic tendencies to assimilate, further confusing ethnic identity.

In the cities and towns, soldiers were often surprised to find a group speaking a German dialect, the Eastern Jews. Alone among local peoples, *Ostjuden* were able to communicate with Germans, either through their cognate Yiddish or polyglot learning. One official called them "indispensable," "born translators."[73] *Ostjuden* played a unique role in these diverse lands, a history dating back to happier days of the Grand Duchy's religious toleration, invited as settlers in the fourteenth century, fleeing persecution in the West. Lithuanian Jews developed a distinct historical character, giving rise to the name "Litvak."[74] Wilna was called the "Jerusalem of Lithuania," where the "Vilna Gaon" Elijah Ben Salomon taught, a center of learning and focal point for the Jewish enlightenment. Jews lived for the most part in towns and cities, making up a larger percentage of their inhabitants, working at small trades and living in difficult conditions. Before the war, some traveled the countryside as horse traders and peddlers, valued by peasants for the news they brought.[75] Generally, relations with local peasants seemed good.[76] Before the war, Jews and Lithuanians cooperated to present candidates for Duma elections.[77]

Poles or Polonized local noble families made up the politically dominant land-owning classes and nobility, especially in southern areas, Wilna and Suwalki, and towns. Their cherished historical memories recalled the Polish–Lithuanian Commonwealth, and their language, culture, and romantic, messianic nationalism were Polish. Yet some jealously asserted a distinct Lithuanian political identity, defined in the formulation *"gente Lituanus, natione Polonus"* – "Of the Lithuanian tribe, Polish nation." This produced escalating conflict with Lithuanian intellectuals, whom they labeled *Litwomany* (Litho-maniacs), as opposed to merely regional identity, *Litwiny*. Catholicism's identification with Polish identity and language made church politics a battleground of ethnic friction.

Most Russians in the territory, brought in under tsarist attempts at Russification, were now gone. In 1915, administrators, police, schoolteachers, and Orthodox priests, the entire administrative apparatus, fled with the Tsar's troops. Only some simple Russian farmers remained. More dangerous were other Russians who went to ground here: deserters, retreating soldiers trapped behind the lines, ever more escaped POWs, small sabotage units left behind, and spies. Armed and dangerous, they skulked in forests and swamps, forming bandit groups which terrorized the countryside.

The largest ethnic German communities were in the old German Baltic provinces of Kurland, Livland, and Estland (the last two conquered later, by February 1918). Here the occupiers met the legendary "Baltic Barons." Baltic Germans flaunted their tribal character: fierce tempers, aristocratic appearance, and curiously flat accents. Though insisting on their Germanness, Baltic Germans were also deeply embedded in local history. Their identity was above all aristocratic, for they had been loyal servitors of the Romanovs, occupying leading positions in the provinces (in spite of their small absolute numbers) and Russia. After emancipation of the serfs, social and economic developments produced growing class and national antagonism with Latvians and Estonians, exploding in the 1905 Revolution and ensuing reprisals.[78] Afterwards, Baltic Germans organized clandestine settlement programs to bring Germans to Kurland.[79] Their towns, officials rhapsodized, appeared to have been transplanted from Germany, so homelike did they seem.[80] Kurland's chief announced that the "order, cleanliness, and civilization" created by the Baltic Germans was characteristically German, and when compared to Lithuania, "no other example makes clearer the cultural superiority of the German race."[81] Yet under the surface, unsuspected complexities were ready to emerge.

Last to be brought under German control were the Estonians, in 1918. An aboriginal Finno-Ugric people speaking a language unrelated to Baltic tongues, their history paralleled that of Latvians.[82]

Other peoples showcased the strange syntheses characteristic of the region. Numbering 2,000 in Kurland's northern corner, Livonians were by origin a Finnic people assimilated to Latvian culture across the racial divide.[83] There were traces of other peoples, descendants of settlers, Mennonites and Calvinists seeking religious toleration, or isolated Frenchmen lost in Napoleon's 1812 retreat from Russia and assimilated into the local population. There were also small Tatar and Muslim communities. Tatars were brought here in the fifteenth century as prisoners, then bodyguards for the Grand Dukes. Compounding confusions of identity, some Tatars belonged to the Karaite sect, professing non-Talmudic Judaism.[84] Different groups had been stranded here by the tides of history.

This entire scene was unsettling for Germans. Terms of ethnic identity here were confusing and explosive. To one official the area seemed, "viewed from above . . . a cauldron, in which all kinds of peoples and currents simmered together wildly."[85] Fundamental rules they knew from home did not seem to apply, for ethnicity here seemed at once

crucial and yet unstable, in flux. Everywhere were people whose surnames were messes of ethnicity (or living testimony to the accretion of
history and identity, depending on one's view). Even so, surnames were
not reliable indicators of what a person's hotly professed identity would
turn out to be. Rather, ethnicity seemed very much determined by choice.
"Elective ethnicity" ruled. Families splintered along many planes of
fracture, different branches ending with different permutations of names
and allegiances.[86] Newly arrived Germans, trying to discern order in the
land, found this disconcerting. Asked their nationality, natives would
answer, "I am from here."[87] Many understood themselves as *Tutejszy*,
"locals." Other peasants might answer "Catholic" or "Christian." Officials complained that "with the low level of education of the population,
nationality conditions cannot be at all exactly ascertained." An early
analysis reported,

Objectively determining conditions of nationality comes up against the greatest
difficulties. It happens, that one party defines a community as "pure Polish,"
while the other party defines the same community as "pure Lithuanian." Yet even
where statements are in such stark contradiction, one may not always assume
their falsification by one side or the other. It is indeed often difficult to decide,
whether someone is a "Lithuanian" or "Pole" or "White Russian" or "Great
Russian." There are "Lithuanians" who speak no word of Lithuanian, and vice
versa there are committed "Poles," in a religious or other tradition, who speak
only Lithuanian. Often members of one family count themselves to different
nationalities. The low level of education of the population worsens the chaos even
further and opens the door to national agitation of every kind.[88]

Other surprises underlined this ethnic complexity, especially the amazing
case of the "three Smiths" in the Lithuanian town of Mariampol. Besides
a family by the German name of Schmidt, there were also in this multilingual area families named Kowalski and Kusnjetzow, which likewise mean
"smith" in Polish and Russian. But German observers noted that

We discover, with a sense of distress, that all three have distanced themselves far
from their national identity. Because . . . Mr. Schmidt, who on top of everything
else carries the [German] given name Heinrich, professes himself an incarnate
nationalist Pole, Mr. Kowalski as a thorough Russian and the apparently Muscovite Mr. Kusnjetzow as a genuine German. And the situation is no better with the
confessional identity of the three: the Pole Schmidt is Roman Catholic, the
Russian with the Polish name of Kowalski is Orthodox, while Mr. Kusnjetzow, in
spite of his Russian name, belongs to the Evangelical community.[89]

Even as ordinary people lived these contradictions, the flip-side of such
effortless syntheses could be growing ethnic conflict, fired by social and
economic tensions, encompassing ecclesiastical politics, education, and
coloring class conflict.[90] As war promised to redraw borders, strife began

in earnest. Germans found themselves buffeted by competing ethnic claims from all sides.

This confusion bothered soldiers because their own national identity was a recent construct, and often in question. The German Reich, cobbled together only forty years before, was fragmented, despite loud and unconfident assertions of chauvinists to the contrary. German regionalism and tribalism were persistent realities. Eastern Germany had unassimilated Poles and Slavic minorities. Alsace-Lorraine presented complications in the West, with its German-speaking French patriots. Bavaria and other principalities resisted Prussian predominance and asserted separate regional characters. For some this Great War (sometimes referred to as the "War of Peoples") promised to finally cement the German identity of an empire born from the Franco-Prussian war in 1871. Kaiser Wilhelm II declared all divisions transcended: "I know no parties any more, only Germans." Reality was much more vexatious, as events in the East made clear. On marching into Wilna, troops projected a unified German front, yet local Polish girls with flowers sought out Prussian Poles, singling them out for kisses as liberators of the city, "pearl of the Polish crown."[91] At the very moment of arrival, then, cracks appeared in the wall of one German identity. From now on, soldiers with Slavic names occupied an awkward position. As the guardsman Kazmierzak in Zweig's novel meditated, "experiences since the beginning of the war have made the Prussian soldiers with Polish names suspect – well, because of the uncertainty. They are observed even more keenly than the others, with the exception of the Alsatians."[92] Ober Ost's ethnic riot directed unsettling questions back at the occupiers. The sheer variety of peoples could seem astonishing and objectionable to new arrivals used to different certainties. It was disconcerting for them to see how much ethnicity depended on historical circumstance and (to them this seemed most obscene) on personal choice and commitment.

Whatever feelings came to them at the sight of this variety, one thing was clear to Germans. They could not view the lands as they had before, as merely "West Russia," in dynastic terms, provinces of a monolithic empire, and its people's identity that of subjects of the autocratic Tsar. The view of "empire and subjects" dissolved, as the newcomers now saw them as distinct and variegated. Now they were understood as "*Land und Leute*," "lands and peoples," discrete unities of territory and ethnicity with characters all their own. A complicated and war-wrought history had made this place, giving the region its unique character as a land of syntheses, anachronistic survivals, and local adaptations.

German soldiers sensed a living history in the peoples and their ways, from which they were excluded, standing apart. It seemed that once a thing happened, it stayed on forever, absorbed and retained, present in visible traces and echoed memories. To begin with, these same Baltic peoples described by Tacitus had been here since the Christian era's beginning. Once reaching across northern Russia to Moscow, their territories contracted with the press of other peoples to this last stand, hemmed in on all sides. Yet, in one of the paradoxical historical movements which seemed to play themselves out so often, the Baltic Crusades beginning in the thirteenth century backfired, actually forging anarchic Lithuanian tribes into a state. In their new territories, crusaders built *Zwingburge*, "castles of subjugation," as strong points to hold down natives. German settlers were introduced and native Prussians slowly extinguished. The Teutonic Knights intensified their biannual raids against Europe's last pagan outpost, Lithuania. In a brutal version of the "Grand Tour," crusaders from the West came to fight, including Chaucer's Knight. The Order of the Teutonic Knights' "Lithuanian Way Reports," essentially Baedeker guides for pillage and rapine, allowed crusaders to raid with accuracy from south and north. But this pressure from both sides led to the consolidation of independent Lithuanian tribes under Grand Duke Mindaugas in 1236 and resurgent paganism in a warlike state, holding off the Teutonic Knights to the west and raiding Russian lands to its east, expanding at a terrific rate. By the early fifteenth century, under Grand Duke Vytautas the Great, Lithuania extended from the Baltic coast to the Black Sea – Europe's largest state. In 1410, allied Polish and Lithuanian armies defeated the order at Tannenberg, a blow from which it never recovered. The Grand Duchy's resistance proved decisive for the region, stopping wholesale colonization of the northerly Baltic provinces, by cutting off overland routes for concentrated settlement by German Eastland trekkers and farmers. Yet the Grand Duchy eventually waned before the growing power of Muscovy and Sweden. Out of necessity and dynastic politics, Lithuania drew closer to the Kingdom of Poland, culminating in constitutional fusion and the creation of a joint commonwealth. Decline and then partitions by surrounding powers followed. This area fell to Russia, which abolished the very name "Lithuania," renamed as "Northwestern Territories." At the same time, other forces were at work, as the gospel of language and *Volk* spread by Johann Gottfried Herder had a catalytic effect on the national renaissances of the area's peoples.[93] Inspired by his high estimation of their idioms, local intellectuals strove to develop literary languages. This was accompanied by a series of chain reactions set off by failed Russification policies, as the autocracy's attempt to play ethnic groups off against one another only produced resentful, heightened consciousness on all sides.[94] Most strikingly, after suppressing the 1863 revolt, Russia banned printing of Lithuanian in Latin letters, seeking thus to remove Lithuanians from Polish influence, bringing them closer to Orthodoxy by way of Cyrillic print. Instead, this precipitated another paradoxical reversal, as common people, who had little interest in such matters before, became radicalized. A broad secret movement grew up to resist the policies, personified by "book-bearers," simple people slipping across the border from German Prussia with sacks of books printed in Tilsit. Ordinary smugglers turned into popular activists, while secret schools spread across the countryside, producing the tradition of the "School of Trouble," a system of clandestine education.[95] Russian policy inadvertently galvanized and radicalized a population. Henceforth, national identity was inextricably bound up with the idea of education, a hallmark of the Lithuanian movement.[96] The rise of independent farmers after emancipation from serfdom provided a social basis for the growth of a local intelligentsia. The 1905 Revolution gave further evidence of natives' insurgent mood, producing demands for political and cultural autonomy.[97] An enormous diaspora across the Atlantic supported these demands.[98] Not least among the surprises in the East for Germans was finding that those they had understood above all as subjects of the Tsar were often embittered opponents of his regime.

The history which unfolded before the newcomers recorded a string of failed outside attempts to rule and reshape the place. Neither landscape nor people offered German soldiers anything to which they could attach their own past. Moreover, the past was here everywhere present, visible and felt, an overlay of legend, tradition, and memory. History seemed not strictly chronological, but present and the land itself adrift in time, so retentive that once a thing happened, it was no longer to be dislodged, but endured in an infinity of echoes. Past traces coexisted out of all context, in archaic, original survivals, uncultivated, absolutely primitive.

The sense of history pressing in on the new arrivals came also from the ground underfoot. Among its many disconcerting qualities was how much history it seemed to hold.[99] Army engineers' spades, building fortifications, found burial sites and weapons from a dim past of Baltic–Indo-European tribalism. Dynamiting outside Mitau in 1916 to loosen sand could produce a shower of human bones, iron and bronze artifacts.[100] Army newspapers reported prehistoric finds in the trenches.[101] The most startling element was that here the prehistoric level was so close to the surface. A thin recent layer instantly gave way to dense past. An army scholar marveled that "at a depth that by our standards is improbably shallow (1/2–2 meters), there lie here the remnants of past millennia." Intact finds of antiquities were made only centimeters from the surface, "so that immediately under the layer of top-soil, the old world is exposed."[102] Military scholars again adverted to the concept of *Kultur* to explain this phenomenon, speaking of "culture layers," "culture ground," and "culture earth." The ground's specific nature demonstrated for them a shallowness of modern history. Clamorous prehistory was visible above ground as well: hill forts by the hundreds reminded that this had long been a war land. Roadside crosses and chapel poles were everywhere, an insistent pre-Christian tradition, sometimes massed on holy hills.[103] These were all uncanny sights.

A key feature was disconcerting simultaneity. Scholars marveled that an ancient hoard dug up near the front contained coins centuries apart, a numismatic museum unto itself. In the countryside, newcomers saw natives farming with nearly prehistoric tools.[104] Towns were riots of architectural simultaneity, styles densely topping one another, adaptations of western forms used quite differently here. Buildings of improbable age and condition were not pulled down, but still used. Yet the whole jumble seemed to cohere. In the same way, the territory held different peoples, in what Germans took to be different stages of historical development, existing side by side.

Facing this unfamiliar mess of history, soldiers stationed in Ober Ost looked for their own historical models. Somehow, they had to fit themselves into this eclectic yet cohering foreign jumble, to give meaning to their presence here. To the present mind, this need may seem strange. Yet in a time when historical memory was denser than in our own age, this was a crucial fundament of identity. In that "pre-post-modern" age, the historical search was frequently not accurate, but nonetheless intensely driven. Too often, historians treat another period's consciousness as *tabula rasa*, when in fact every human consciousness is affected by traces of the past, even if only in roughly caricatured form. Ludendorff himself, upon his arrival, stood on a rise above Kowno's old town and felt himself battered by the past, in billowing winds of time. Always a man with an eye to his own repute, public opinion, and posterity, here he felt history call on him to justify his presence.

In army newspapers, official publications, and personal documents, Germans recorded their avid search for hints of their own fit in this area, looking back to parts of their own imagined pasts. The most ancient was that of the great movements of peoples in the Dark Ages, a tribal model hovering before readers of the *Song of the Nibelungs*. The newcomers tried squinting at the hill fortresses looming before them. Could they discern "German" lineaments in these prehistoric shapes?[105] This past proved after all too shadowy to yield an identity for a modern, eastwards-moving German. On a different tack, army newspapers took up medievalizing poses, trying to link the region to Germany in a common culture of the

Middle Ages.[106] Invaders compared themselves to Teutonic Knights moving eastward and building a state in Prussia, carrying the *Drang nach Osten*, a sensed continuity asserted in the naming of the Battle of Tannenberg.[107] This was the place of genesis for the Prussians, at once the least German and most German of all German tribes, cobbled together from a fraternity of adventurers. Their identity was born at the borders, where the word *Deutsch* first took on its ethnic meaning. Back in central Europe, it had earlier simply meant "of the common people." But in the Eastern Marches, crusaders were known as "*Teutsche Herren*," "German Lords." Meanwhile, native pagans were defined, in a chilling formulation, as "*Undeutschen*." Yet comparisons with that age were troubling, since the Baltic Crusades were ultimately unsuccessful and the Order's castles only hulking, weathered ruins.

At last, when other possible models failed them, the occupiers seized on a most potent historical "memory" from their own arsenal of historical imagination. It was not even bound to the area, and thus could not be a perfect match. But in viewing the ravages of global total war, the image that often presented itself to soldiers was the Thirty Years' War, which rolled over Germany again and again from 1618 to 1648. Most prominently, they saw themselves as the war people of Schiller's drama *Wallenstein's Camp*, the *Landsknechte* freebooters of popular memory. This model gave expression and some meaning to their rootlessness and brutalization.[108]

The reason for this was the unique place which the Thirty Years' War occupied in the German popular historical imagination, with the status of national myth. If myth may indeed be said to be "history that everyone knows" (Michel Tournier), then the Thirty Years' War stands on the threshold of myth in German historical consciousness. From 1618 to 1648, Germany became the stage for an apocalyptic European war. The prolonged experience of helpless suffering left an enduring cultural legacy; having been Europe's battleground was the common experience of German peoples. Memory of the ordeal acquired a special function in modern German thought, art, literature, and drama, as Germany's first experience of total war, indeed afterwards known as "*der große Krieg*." Not merely religious, the war mobilized all the resources on the scene, drawing combatants from all over Europe: French, Spanish, Swedes, English, Scots, Irish, Greeks, Cossacks, Poles, and Finns in quick succession. These foreign forces poured in to "protect" "German Liberties," so that in the name of their own freedom, Germans were forced into complete prostration, Germany made over into a new landscape. Rough historical estimates find that a quarter of the population was lost, while areas stalked by plague saw more than half swept away. The countryside lay abandoned, unpeopled. Helpless, the individual endured, accepted his fate, or went under, in an unending ordeal of suffering and loss. And the war moved on and on.

In spite of its similarities to modern total wars, the Thirty Years' War represented in popular memory not a "World War" so much as a "World of War."[109] In the German historical imagination, the Thirty Years' War appears not as a time, but almost a place. It was difficult to conceive of a "historical event" lasting thirty years. Moreover, the war seemed even less historical as no one could point to significant outcomes, since the war, lasting a lifetime, ended not with successes, but with the exhaustion of contending powers, called off without decisive resolutions. Most significantly, the panorama of desolate landscapes made the war a place in popular historical memory.

In this war landscape, one German figure looms up, one figure alone, embodying possibilities of freedom of will and action, less a character than a towering, unyielding shell of black armor, the carapace of an austere moral attitude. This figure is a being named Wallenstein. By the "accident" of his name, the evoked figure seems hardly human, more like a mountain or cliff, a topographical feature: literally, "Rearing Stone." This "new man," opportunist and renegade, seems a juggernaut in dark armor moving across the landscape, a huge warlord in a world of war. This popular vision of Wallenstein is actually not unlike the historical Albrecht von Wallenstein, a larger-than-life Bohemian noble, who placed a private army at the disposition of the Kaiser. Made Duke of Friedland ("Peace Land"), after more victories the Kaiser declared him "Generalissimo of the Baltic and the Ocean Seas," then supreme commander *in absolutissima forma*, "with special powers." When Wallenstein moved to set up as an independent potentate in Bohemia, he was assassinated by his own officers. Encased in such titles, radiating extraordinary powers and dangerous freedom of action, it is easy to see why Wallenstein became a mythological figure, sole embodiment of moral possibilities against a background of general helplessness.

Below Wallenstein's towering figure, at his base, the landscape was in motion with armies. Most at home there was the freebooting mercenary *Landsknecht*, compounded of severe discipline and rapacious freedom. *Landsknechte* were the war's chosen people, their multiethnic armies called *Kriegsvolk*, war people or a race of war, whose only homeland was war – "La guerre est ma patrie," as a military saying went. As the war moved, so moved their homeland: the *Lager* (camp), the march, and the slaughter of pitched battle. Over time, religion no longer united armies, but only common loyalty to war. They created their own language, a mix of international military jargon and Yiddish, Polish, Gypsy, and romance languages. The armies were a nation of war on the move. The Thirty Years' War they inhabited was a landscape unto itself, surging with figures and moralities.[110]

The powerful model of the Thirty Years' War housed in German popular historical memory broke to the surface and seemed revived, then surpassed, in the First World War. This new Great War supplanted the earlier "*grosse Krieg*," taking on many of its images in the process. Such an invocation of precedent was not unconscious, cultivated by artists and propagandists. Noted war writer Walter Flex published a story collection set in the Thirty Years' War, entitled *Wallenstein's Visage*. Alfred Döblin wrote his epic novel, *Wallenstein*, during the global conflict. Rilke's *Five Hymns*, composed in the war's first drunken days, invoked a consuming war-god reminiscent of Grimmelshausen's frightening colossus in *Simplizissimus*, the "German Hero" bestriding the world. These literary tropes took on political significance, as Field Marshal Paul von Hindenburg was turned into that towering hero, in place of Wallenstein. A cult of personality was constructed around the field marshal. In Berlin, Hindenburg was literally set up as a titanic figure. There, and in towns throughout Germany, huge wooden statues of Hindenburg were erected in public squares (Berlin's statue was three stories tall).[111] People drove nails of gold, silver, and iron into the wooden titan signifying donations to war charities. By this common effort, the huge figure became metal-clad, armored, a visible projection of collective will.

Even as some soldiers of Ober Ost hunted for a historical sense for their presence, some clue of continuity or mission, and army newspapers carried articles and sketches searching for historical parallels, the search for traces of themselves in the region's history was consuming, yet ultimately without satisfying results. The past in the present was too irreducibly visible and unfamiliar here, creating much of the area's insistent picturesqueness. For soldiers, the land was a collection of unfamiliar scenes and traces of the past, in which the new arrival could not find any reflection of himself.

There was an added special difficulty for German Jews in the administration. Moving east and meeting *Ostjuden*, they were suddenly even more sensitive to their own difference as "Germans of the Mosaic confession." They confronted what they agreed was their own unassimilated past and this encounter produced reactions in many, sometimes creating personal crises and changing lives. Arnold Zweig, a writer in the cultural administration, came away with a commitment to Zionism.[112] A character in his novel, military judge Posnanski, found himself drawn to Hassidic piety, while yet identifying with German culture and the West. His week was spent in German military courts, his Sabbath at Hassidic prayer houses in the Jewish quarter.[113] Not all reacted thus; another German Jewish soldier recalled that this encounter at first left him somewhat shaken, but then the cultural "gap" between himself and *Ostjuden* confirmed for him his Germanness: "I could not be anything but a German."[114]

These encounters opened up a set of disturbing questions. German attempts to find historical models for their presence could not overcome this strangeness. They would need to "write themselves in" in some other way. Unexpectedly, German identity was thrown into this crucible of war in the East. The sum of powerful first impressions was that the new conquerors were in control, yet in many other respects disoriented. This fact conditioned policies and the ambitions which grew out of them in Ober Ost, against a backdrop of the constant struggle of German soldiers to find a place for themselves, without losing themselves in the process.

German understanding of the place's unique character was founded on the fact that they were lost in the filth and wreckage of war in the East. The devastation produced only months before seemed to reflect the region's essential character, its deeper nature. The East appeared diseased, lice-ridden, uncannily empty and depopulated.[115] One group of soldiers advancing into Kurland met with the terrifying news that the village they were to be quartered in had been decimated by plague. As one recalled,

It was a horrifying sight, these villages, deserted, half burned out and haunted by hungry crows, in which only on occasion, out of a stark, barricaded house with blind, covered windows, from a disgusting door crack would lean out a sad figure, wasted down to bones, which in terrible greeting would vomit on the doorstep and then immediately crawl back into the darkness of these unhealthy, forbidden houses.

Extensive measures for disinfection needed to be taken, but could not quell anxiety, for "there remained the uncanny feeling of being delivered up to such an invisible and treacherous enemy, against which there is no effective weapon, even with the greatest caution."[116] What soldiers saw of the remaining people was also disturbing: ethnicities in flux, languages running together, and communities overlapping. Boundaries of all kinds were obscure and the variety was overwhelming.

Most important of all was the revelation of natives' prostration and weakness before the army. It came to seem that they were not so much people to whom terrible things had happened as the sort of people to whom disasters always happened, somehow due to their own nature. According to a popular native source, this was confirmed at the outset of the occupation in a disastrous way, when frightened villagers (of a population now made up mostly of women and the old) tried to kiss the hands of surprised German officers, begging for leniency. That moment was an eye-opening revelation of the invaders' power and native helplessness. After their first surprise, a popular native account claimed, officers eventually held out their hands as a matter of course.[117]

Towns and cities yielded potent visions, concentrating the region's foreign impressions for soldiers stationed there.[118] The largest city, Wilna, seemed caught in a dreamlike brooding, affecting those who came there. Wilna was founded by Grand Duke Gediminas, legend said, at the urging of a prophetic dream of a howling iron wolf. It was used as a cult center for the burning of bodies of the pagan Grand Dukes. The ancient Lithuanian capital of Vilnius, rendered as "Wilna" by Germans, was both the administrative center and centerpiece of the region's foreignness. A good part of its strangeness lay in its eclectic character. Scores of different cultures from all cardinal directions ran together. The city was "more than a geographical expression." There was, and always had been, a multiplicity of cities in that one place, all meeting on the one spot, yet distinct: Lithuanian Vilnius, pagan heart of the Grand Duchy, focus of attention for intellectuals' nationalist stirrings, Polish Wilno of palaces and churches, official Russian Vilna, the Wilna of German traders, "Jerusalem of the North" of the Litvaks. Some Germans found this mixture exotic, others distasteful, as one commented: "Upon closer examination, the city view was in many respects alien and disharmonious. Over half a thousand years the most different influences from Occident and Orient had brought forth a queer cultural mixture which matched the presently still existing mess of nationalities."[119] There was little for a transplanted German mind to cling to in this setting.

Official guidebooks published by the administration presented the city's strange sights, interpreting them for soldiers on leave, steering them away from perilous surroundings and instructing them on how to behave. The guidebooks were less comprehensive guides to the place than guides to correct bearing and etiquette for soldiers. They warned of spies, usually forward women. Soldiers were instructed that their behavior was watched everywhere: "German discipline and order are our marching companions. The population of the occupied territory judges the entire German people by *your* behavior. To pay attention to appearance, salutes, and a worthy bearing is the duty of a German warrior." The booklets tried to set the terms for soldiers' encounters with the cities. A 1916 guidebook for soldiers new to Wilna started the visitor's itinerary with a visit to the delousing station. Afterwards, it directed him to those spots that would seem familiar: old or new German houses. At the confluence of the two rivers rose the castle hill, from whose tower fluttered the austere and familiar colors, black–white–red, of the Prussian flag. The city's German evangelical church was a "piece of the homeland." The soldier might be drawn to the "German Street," once the merchant quarter, with solid German houses. But once he stepped down it, it became clear what a different world he had entered. This was the *Judengasse*, the Jewish quarter. Soldiers were instructed on how to react to sights and sounds of life redolent of foreignness, Oriental mystery. "The scenes of the street, foreign to your eye, strike you as strange," the guidebook ordered.[120]

Booklets could only mediate or frame the strangeness; they could not make it go away. Towns heightened the impression soldiers had of being ungrounded. Footing was uncertain, on streets overlaid with perilous, rickety boardwalks of narrow, slick planks. The city center was a confusing welter with "no sign of a planned layout, with terrible pavements and open gutters in which sewage flowed."[121] Chaotic pedestrian traffic was a constant source of complaint, as soldiers jostled against ragged natives in narrow alleys and archways. Underfoot, multilayered history again announced itself. To officials' disgusted amazement, cleaning of one particularly filthy urban thoroughfare struck proper cobbled pavement underneath, buried for decades under trash and dirt.[122] Natives were as surprised as the soldiers. In another case, cleaning exposed a human skeleton – it was unclear how or when it had ended up there.[123] Germans were impressed by Wilna legends of an entire city underneath the visible one on the surface, excited by the discovery of underground passages.[124] Here, the streets (those above ground) were of quaking earth, with no proper pavement. One stood on a swaying, uncertain base of mud, stamped earth, or rickety boardwalks. The physical reality and the spiritual combined to produce metaphors for the unfamiliarity of the place.

When occupiers considered how they themselves were regarded by subject populations of the rear areas, they worried over their own standing in native eyes. When so outnumbered, a formidable and assertive self-presentation, an imposing "bearing" summed up as "*Haltung*," was crucial. By projecting a resolute image, the occupiers could compensate for their small numbers. Prestige demanded that they keep their distance from native populations. Army publications instructed soldiers in proper bearing: how to feel at home while keeping their distance, resisting going native.[125] But this imperative of an authoritative German bearing opened the door to all the difficulties of defining who or what was German, a carryover from the fragmented *Kaiserreich*. Yet this trouble simultaneously held promise, as a special, urgent case of a larger project, as thinkers at home looked to war as a transformative experience, finally offering a redemptive chance to transcend the flawed realities of fractured imperial German society, achieving some new, triumphant ideal.[126]

The answer seemed to lie in the concept and slogan of "German Work" – "*Deutsche Arbeit.*" A characteristically *German* kind of work would give German lines and features to the land, putting their stamp on the place, changing it so that the occupiers would at last recognize themselves in the transformed territories. "German Work" shaped and ordered: drew borders, rationalized, defined, oversaw, channeled energies. Thus, the army would change the place, giving German form to foreign, alien content. The source of the slogan was Wilhelm Heinrich Riehl's *Die deutsche Arbeit* (1861), proposing the idea of a systematic style of work typical of Germans.[127] Riehl's thought was an influential contribution to a nineteenth-century national debate on work, an effort to contend intellectually with the Industrial Revolution's wrenching dislocations, especially distressing in Germany's late, accelerated development.[128] Riehl was an important figure in German culture, though quickly shrouded in anonymity. He is significant as a case of German liberalism's crisis after 1848 and the creation of alternative models of society in reaction.[129] Though soon written off as a popularizing, unsystematic thinker, his ideas, cut adrift, gained tremendous currency up to the present, detached from their obscure creator's name (Riehl is, for instance, regarded as the father of *Volkskunde*, ethnography). In *German Work*, Riehl proposed that German craftsmanship offered a model of unalienated, spiritually meaningful labor. Riehl argued that "every people works according to its own nature." Work methods were keys to national identity, since "the soul of the nation springs from its idea of work, as out of its practice of work." Work was in its highest form "a deed springing from *moral motives*, striving after *moral goals*, which combines with *utility for ourselves* also *benefit for other people.*" In its highest moral sense, then, work had little to do with the materialistic money-grubbing of liberal capitalism. The truest work was realized by the German people, in their guilds and estates, as "the German spirit, in fact, seizes and realizes work in its purest moral greatness and in its richest and best differentiated fullness of variegation."[130] The real significance of Riehl's contribution lay not in its bombastic argumentation, but in the formulation itself. The title alone was of greatest consequence, burrowing into popular imagination. The term "German Work" was taken up in political writing at least a decade before the war in reference to colonial activities. It truly came into its own in the war, as a way of expressing hopes that this conflict was not merely destructive, but a chance for Germans to build a new world.

In the East, the term was further charged in the formulation of "*Kulturarbeit,*" "culture work," taken up by the administration's spokesmen, coupled with the powerful complex of *Kultur*. In the East, notions of "German Work" and "culture work" were fused, for they were self-evidently one and the same. Germans of the *Kaiserreich* defined themselves (not without pathos, given the imperfect result) as a state-building people. The German, then, was someone who administered and gave order. Through German Work, Germans would find for themselves an identity, justifying their own presence in the East. All this would be achieved by their nation's quintessential institution, the army. One official was quoted as announcing, "Here, without question, we are the bringers of *Kultur!*"[131] The occupiers repeated the term over and over as an explanation of their presence. It rang through the administration's official and propagandistic documents, permeating the military state's self-presentation. The first issue of its public relations periodical, *Korrespondenz B*, carried a manifesto which solemnly concluded, "Ober Ost is a young land for the art of German administration. Success must justify its actions."[132] Ultimately, this meant that the means of German Work justified any ends, in this *tabula rasa* of the East.

German Work was neither a bloodless ideological construct nor mere motivational slogan, but rather implied a new way of looking at the eastern territories. Specific claims about the land followed from it. Officials asserted that, in spite of all outward appearances, the new land around them was in fact *not* unlike Germany, merely unworked. It resembled Germany, only "of course more frequently interrupted by swamps and wasteland, than we are used to seeing in the homeland." In fact, the sights

constantly summon up before the eye of the imagination familiar pictures of the *Heimat*. Only that here the scale is larger, lines drawn out further, and borders between nature and the work of man seem erased. But that is probably due more to lack of exploitation of the land than to its unique character [*Eigenart*] and does not apply to the areas where human activity could develop itself more briskly.[133]

This argument also ultimately derived from Riehl. In his influential book, *Land and People* (*Land und Leute*), he posited a mutual relation between a people's character and their territory. Any land received its face and features from those who worked it, making it over.[134] Foreign land could thus physically "become" "German," with intensive cultivation. German Work thus dictated a specific prescription for the work to be accomplished, and Ober Ost derived its program and mission from this conception. Ludendorff, newly arrived in the East, resolved "to take up in the occupied territory the *Kulturarbeit* which Germans over many centuries had done in those lands."[135]

Under Ludendorff's direction, the army's "culture work" and German Work set out to transform the occupied territories. In the process, Germans' sense of their own identity would be transformed. German identity in Ober Ost was defined as a specific way of doing things, a working and

organizing spirit. Means were defined as ends. Not content, but *method*
and *form* were important. This semantic slant fitted to perfection the
Administration's comprehensiveness and the scope of its ambitions. It
was the ideal chance for the army, which had presented over centuries the
image of an unpolitical tool of the state. Now it would reveal itself as a
creative power. Ober Ost would be the outward expression of the army's
animating spirit: in Schiller's words, "Spirit, which builds itself a body."
Ultimately, it was a chance for Ludendorff, who exulted as he saw his will
permeating the administration. Only later would it become clear that
turning *Kultur* into a mere means emptied of content, and defining
German identity as rule over others, would be a disastrous development
for both occupiers and occupied. Seizing on the ideology of German
Work, the army prepared to build a military utopia which would change
the place. The most durable product of the venture, however, would be
the transformation which took place within individual soldiers, creating a
specific way of viewing and treating the lands and peoples of the East.

NOTES

1 Ernst Jünger, *In Stahlgewittern. Aus dem Tagebuch eines Stosstruppführers* (Leipzig: R. Meier, 1920), and *Der Kampf als inneres Erlebnis* (Berlin: E. S. Mittler &
   Sohn, 1922).
2 Bernd Hüppauf, "Langemarck, Verdun, and the Myth of the *New Man* in
   Germany after the First World War," *War and Society* 6.2 (September 1988):
   70–103; Fussell, *Great War and Modern Memory*, 36–74.
3 Adolf von Schell, *Battle Leadership* (Columbus, GA: Benning Herald, 1933;
   rpt., Quantico, VA: Marine Corps Association, 1988), 66. On the Second
   World War: Bartov, *Hitler's Army*, 12–28.
4 *Sanitätsbericht über das Deutsche Heer (Deutsches Feld- und Besatzungsheer) im
   Weltkriege 1914/1918*, vol. III, *Die Krankenbewegung bei dem Deutschen Feld-
   und Besatzungsheer* (Berlin: E. S. Mittler & Sohn, 1934), 34–35, 138–39*.
5 Strategic overview details from: "Die Eroberung des Gebietes," in *Das Land
   Ober Ost. Deutsche Arbeit in den Verwaltungsbezirken Kurland, Litauen und
   Bialystok-Grodno. Herausgegeben im Auftrage des Oberbefehlshabers Ost. Bear-
   beitet von der Presseabteilung Ober Ost* (Stuttgart: Verlag der Presseabteilung
   Ober Ost, 1917), 3–8; Erich Ludendorff, *Meine Kriegserinnerungen, 1914–
   1918* (Berlin: E. S. Mittler & Sohn, 1919); Paul von Hindenburg, *Aus meinem
   Leben* (Leipzig: S. Hirzel, 1920); Stone, *Eastern Front*; W. Bruce Lincoln,
   Passage Through Armageddon: The Russians in War and Revolution, 1914–1918
   (New York: Simon & Schuster, 1986).
6 John W. Wheeler-Bennett, *Wooden Titan: Hindenburg in Twenty Years of
   German History, 1914–1934* (New York: William Morrow, 1936).
7 Roger Parkinson, *Tormented Warrior: Ludendorff and the Supreme Command*
   (New York: Stein and Day, 1979); D. J. Goodspeed, *Ludendorff: Genius of
   World War I* (Boston: Houghton Mifflin, 1966).

8 Ludendorff, *Kriegserinnerungen*, 44–45.
9 BA N 1031/2, Gayl, 79.
10 Hindenburg, *Leben*, 78.
11 Holger Afflerbach, *Falkenhayn. Politisches Denken und Handeln im Kaiserreich* (Munich: R. Oldenbourg Verlag, 1994).
12 Robert B. Asprey, *The German High Command at War: Hindenburg and Ludendorff Conduct World War I* (New York: William Morrow, 1991), 112–13.
13 Jonas Puzinas, *Rinktiniai raštai*, vol. II (Chicago: Lituanistikos Instituto Leidykla, 1983), 272.
14 BA N 1031/2, Gayl, 47.
15 Petras Klimas, *Iš mano atsiminimų* (Vilnius: Lietuvos enciklopedijų redakcija, 1990), 42.
16 Israel Cohen, *Vilna* (Philadelphia: Jewish Publication Society of America, 1943), 359.
17 Antanas Gintneris, *Lietuva caro ir kaizerio naguose. Atsiminimai iš I Pasaulinio karo laikų, 1914–1918 m.* (Chicago: ViVi Printing, 1970), 246–57.
18 *Das Land*, 431.
19 Wheeler-Bennett, *Wooden Titan*, 68.
20 Bernhard von der Marwitz, *Stirb und Werde. Aus Briefen und Kriegstagebuchblättern des Leutnants Bernhard von der Marwitz* (Breslau: Wilh. Gottl. Korn Verlag, 1931), 32.
21 *Sanitätsbericht über das Deutsche Heer*, vol. II, *Der Sanitätsdienst im Gefechts- und Schlachtenverlauf im Weltkriege 1914–1918 und Stichwortverzeichnis für I., II. und III. Band* (Berlin: E. G. Mittler & Sohn, 1938), table 5, and vol. III, *Die Krankenbewegung*, 34–35; Hermann Koetzle, *Das Sanitätswesen im Weltkrieg, 1914–18* (Stuttgart: Bergers Literarisches Büro & Verlagsanstalt, 1924), 80–90; M. Schwarte, ed., *Der grosse Krieg*, vol. IX (Part 2) (Leipzig: Barth, 1923), 529–38.
22 Ludendorff, *Kriegserinnerungen*, 146.
23 Erich Zechlin, "Litauen und seine Probleme," *Internationale Monatsschrift für Wissenschaft, Kunst und Technik* 10.3 (December 1, 1915): 257–86.
24 Laqueur's *Russia and Germany* presents the best overview of these trends.
25 Hans-Ulrich Wehler, *Das Deutsche Kaiserreich, 1871–1918* (Göttingen: Vandenhoeck & Ruprecht, 1973), 92–94; Roger Chickering, *We Men Who Feel Most German: A Cultural Study of the Pan-German League, 1886–1914* (London: Allen & Unwin, 1984).
26 Hans Rothfels, "The Baltic Provinces: Some Historic Aspects and Perspectives," *Journal of Central European Affairs* 4.2 (July 1944): 117–46.
27 Robert C. Williams, "Russians in Germany, 1900–1914," *Journal of Contemporary History* 1. 4 (October 1966): 121–49.
28 Michael Burleigh, *Germany Turns Eastwards: A Study of "Ostforschung" in the Third Reich* (Cambridge: Cambridge University Press, 1988), 13–15; Friedrich Kuebart, "Zur Entwicklung der Osteuropaforschung in Deutschland bis 1945," *Osteuropa* 30 (1980): 657–72.
29 Elias, *Reflections*, 19–20.
30 Burleigh, *Germany*, 3–6.
31 Ibid.; Wolfgang Wippermann, *Der "Deutsche Drang nach Osten." Ideologie und*

Wirklichkeit eines politischen Schlagwortes (Darmstadt: Wissenschaftliche Buchgesellschaft, 1981).

32 Ernst Johann, ed., *Innenansicht eines Krieges. Bilder, Briefe, Dokumente, 1914–1918* (Frankfurt-on-Main: Verlag Heinrich Scheffler, 1968), 21.

33 "Land und Leute," in *Das Land*, 9–22; BAMA N 196/1, Heppe, vol. V, 128.

34 R. Schlichting, *Bilder aus Litauen. Im Auftrage des Chefs und unter Mitarbeit zahlreicher Herren der Deutschen Verwaltung Litauen* (Kowno: Kownoer Zeitung, 1916), 9–11.

35 Norman J. G. Pounds, *Eastern Europe* (Chicago: Aldine Publishing, 1969), 11–13.

36 BAMA PHD 8/23, Alfred Schirokauer, "Der deutsche Soldat in der russischen Steppe," *KB* 6 (November 15, 1916). *Korrespondenz B* (*KB*) was Ober Ost's public-relations periodical.

37 Victor Klemperer, *Curriculum Vitae. Erinnerungen, 1881–1918*, vol. II (Berlin: Aufbau Taschenbuch Verlag, 1996), 462.

38 Richard Dehmel, *Zwischen Volk* und Menschheit. Kriegstagebuch (Berlin: S. Fischer Verlag, 1919), 449.

39 BAMA N 196/1, Heppe, vol. V, 48.

40 BAMA PHD 8/23, "Urwald von Bialowies," *KB* 1 (October 11, 1916).

41 BAMA N 196/1, Heppe, vol. V, 64.

42 Marwitz, *Stirb*, 99, 97–98, 103–4; BA N 1031/2, Gayl, 263.

43 BAMA N 196/1, Heppe, vol. V, 61.

44 Marwitz, *Stirb*, 134.

45 Simon Schama, *Landscape and Memory* (New York: Alfred A. Knopf, 1995), 23–134; Elias Canetti, *Crowds and Power*, trans. Carol Stewart (London: Victor Gollancz, 1962), 173–74.

46 Arnold Zweig, *Der Streit um den Sergeanten Grischa* (Potsdam: Gustav Kiepenheuer Verlag, 1927), 42–43.

47 Marwitz, *Stirb*, 76.

48 BAMA N 196/1, Heppe, vol. V, 57.

49 Schell, *Leadership*, 42.

50 BAMA N 196/1, Heppe, vol. V, 116.

51 Ibid., 69.

52 Marwitz, *Stirb*, 17, 79.

53 BAMA N 196/1, Heppe, vol. V, 48.

54 Schlichting, *Bilder*, 28.

55 BAMA N 196/1, Heppe, vol. V, 54; Marwitz, *Stirb*, 95.

56 *Das Litauen-Buch. Eine Auslese aus der Zeitung der 10. Armee* (Wilna: Druck und Verlag Zeitung der 10. Armee, 1918); Schlichting, *Bilder*.

57 George L. Mosse, *The Crisis of German Ideology: Intellectual Origins of the Third Reich* (New York: Schocken Books, 1981), 6; Fritz Stern, *The Politics of Cultural Despair: A Study in the Rise of the Germanic Ideology* (Berkeley: University of California Press, 1961), 196–97, 207; Peter Gay, *Weimar Culture: The Outsider as Insider* (New York: Harper & Row, 1968), 72–74, 91; Roland Stromberg, *Redemption by War: The Intellectuals and 1914* (Lawrence: Regents Press of Kansas, 1982), 147–49; Günther Mai, *Das Ende des Kaiserreichs. Politik und Kriegführung im Ersten Weltkrieg* (Munich: Deutscher Taschen-

buch Verlag, 1987). Norbert Elias recalled that in prejudices about eastern countries, "culture was always the main principle" (*Reflections*, 20).

58 BAMA N 196/1, Heppe, vol. V, 133.
59 *Das Land*, 11.
60 BAMA N 196/1, Heppe, vol. V, 16.
61 Schlichting, *Bilder*, 11; *Das Land*, 431.
62 BA N 1031/2, Gayl, 124; *Das Land*, 89.
63 BAMA N 98/1, von Gossler, 65.
64 BAMA N 196/1, Heppe, vol. V, 123.
65 Ibid., 123–24.
66 Manfred Hellmann, *Grundzüge der Geschichte Litauens und des litauischen Volkes*, 4th edn (Darmstadt: Wissenschaftliche Buchgesellschaft, 1990), 107.
67 Alfred Bilmanis, *A History of Latvia* (Princeton: Princeton University Press, 1951); Andrejs Plakans, *The Latvians: A Short History* (Stanford: Hoover Institution Press, 1995).
68 Rauch, *Geschichte*, 26–27.
69 Ibid., 36.
70 Nicholas P. Vakar, *Belorussia: The Making of a Nation* (Cambridge, MA: Harvard University Press, 1956), 1–4; Jan Zaprudnik, *Belarus: At a Crossroads in History* (Boulder, CO: Westview Press, 1993).
71 BAMA N 196/1, Heppe, vol. V, 54.
72 *Das Land*, 17–18; BAMA PHD 8/23, "Die Weißrussen," *KB* 6 (November 15, 1916); "Die Weißruthenen," *KB* 35 (June 6, 1917).
73 BAMA N 196/1, Heppe, vol. V, 17. Steven E. Aschheim, *Brothers and Strangers: The East European Jew in German and German Jewish Consciousness, 1800–1923* (Madison: University of Wisconsin Press, 1982), 139–214, and "Eastern Jews, German Jews and Germany's Ostpolitik in the First World War," *Leo Baeck Institute Year Book* 28 (1983): 351–65.
74 Solomonas Atamukas, *Žydai Lietuvoje. XIV–XX amžiai* (Vilnius: Akcinė bendrovė Lituanus, 1990).
75 LCVIA F. 641, ap. 1, b. 53, "Verwaltungsberichte Rossienie," *Verwaltungsbericht für die Zeit vom 1. Oktober 1917 bis 31. März 1918. Georgenburg*, 25.
76 Egmont Zechlin, *Die deutsche Politik und die Juden im Ersten Weltkrieg* (Göttingen: Vandenhoeck & Ruprecht, 1969), 224–25.
77 Hellmann, *Grundzüge*, 130; Senn, *Emergence*, 10.
78 Rauch, *Geschichte*, 26–28.
79 Werner Conze, "Nationalstaat oder Mitteleuropa? Die Deutschen des Reichs und die Nationalitätenfragen Ostmitteleuropas im ersten Weltkrieg," in *Deutschland und Europa. Historische Studien zur Völker- und Staatenordnung des Abendlandes* (Düsseldorf: Droste Verlag, 1951), 207.
80 GSTA PK, I. HA. Rep. 84a, nr. 6211b, *VII. Verwaltungsbericht der Militärverwaltung Kurland. Oktober 1917*, 47.
81 BAMA N 98/3, Gossler, 25–26.
82 Toivo U. Raun, *Estonia and the Estonians*, 2nd edn (Stanford: Hoover Institution Press, 1991).
83 *Das Land*, 20–21.
84 Cohen, *Vilna*, 451–68; BAMA PHD 8/23, "Tataren," *KB* 41 (July 18, 1917).
85 BA N 1031/2, Gayl, 134.

86 Zechlin, "Litauen," 282; The most famous case is that of two brothers, Narutavičius (Lithuanian form) and Narutowicz (Polish), whose ethnic choices led them in different directions. The former became a member of the Lithuanian nationalist movement and signatory of Lithuania's independence declaration, while the latter became Poland's first president: Senn, *Emergence*, 8.

87 BA N 1031/2, Gayl, 135.

88 Zechlin, "Litauen," 258, 282–83.

89 BAMA PHD 8/23, "Die drei Schmidts von Mariampol," *KB* 68 (November 19, 1917).

90 Hellmann, *Grundzüge*, 127–28.

91 Klimas, *Atsiminimų*, 42.

92 Zweig, *Grischa*, 23.

93 Stöckl, *Osteuropa*, 24–28; Ulf Lehmann, "Herder und die Slawen. Probleme des Geschichtsbildes und Geschichtsverständnisses aus historischer Perspektive," *Jahrbuch für Geschichte der sozialistischen Länder Europas* 22.1 (1978): 39–50.

94 Theodore R. Weeks, *Nation and State in Late Imperial Russia: Nationalism and Russification on the Western Frontier, 1863–1914* (DeKalb: Northern Illinois University Press, 1996).

95 Algirdas Greimas and Saulius Žukas, *Lietuva Pabaltijy. Istorijos ir Kulturos bruozai* (Vilnius: Baltos lankos, 1993), 134–35.

96 Zechlin, "Litauen," 283.

97 Egidijus Aleksandravičius, "Political Goals of Lithuanians, 1863–1918," *Journal of Baltic Studies* 23.3 (fall 1992): 227–38.

98 Roughly one-third of Lithuanians lived abroad before the war, especially in the United States and Canada: Romuald Misiunas and Rein Taagepera, *The Baltic States: Years of Dependence, 1940–1990*, rev. edn (Berkeley: University of California Press, 1993), 7.

99 Franz Frech, "Vorgeschichtliches aus Kurland," and K. Bohneberg, "Die Vorzeit im Schützengraben," in *Das Land*, 400–9.

100 Frech, "Vorgeschichtliches," in *Das Land*, 401.

101 BAMA PHD 8/23, "Prähistorischer Fund an der Ostfront," *KB* 15 (January 17, 1917); "Im Schützengraben-Museum," *KB* 19 (February 14, 1917); K. Bohneberg, "Prähistorisches aus dem Schützengraben," *KB* 22 (March 7, 1917); (Special Collections, Van Pelt Library, University of Pennsylvania, Philadelphia) Berns, "Vorgeschichtliche Gräberfunde im Osten," *Der Beobachter. Beilage zur Zeitung der 10. Armee* 140 (July 18, 1918). All subsequent citations of *Der Beobachter* refer to the Special Collections of the Van Pelt Library at the University of Pennsylvania.

102 Bohneberg, "Vorzeit," in *Das Land*, 404.

103 Greimas and Žukas, *Lietuva*, 23.

104 Schlichting, *Bilder*, 18.

105 Rudolf Häpke, "Die geschichtliche und landeskundliche Forschung in Litauen und Baltenland 1915–1918," *Hansische Geschichtsblätter* 45 (1919): 19–20; BAMA PHD 8/23, "Ein germanischer Ringwall in Litauen," *KB* 98 (March 8, 1918).

106 (Special Collections, Van Pelt Library, University of Pennsylvania, Philadel-

phia) "Hans Sachsens Pfingstbesuch in Wilna," *Zeitung der 10. Armee* 87 (June 10, 1916); "Lustige Hans-Sachs-Spiele im Soldatenheim Allenstein," *Zeitung der 10. Armee* 89 (June 14, 1916). All subsequent citations of *Zeitung der 10. Armee* refer to the Special Collections of the Van Pelt Library at the University of Pennsylvania.

107 Sven Ekdahl, "Tannenberg/Grunwald – Ein politisches Symbol in Deutschland und Polen," *Journal of Baltic Studies* 12.4 (winter 1991): 271–324.

108 Marwitz, *Stirb*, 46; BAMA N 196/1, Heppe, vol. V, 21, 67. After Ober Ost's collapse, attractions of the Thirty Years' War model were full-blown in the Freikorps rampage. Later, they recurred on the Eastern Front in the Second World War. Bartov, *Eastern Front*, 93, 155–56.

109 Michael Howard, *War in European History* (Oxford: Oxford University Press, 1976), 37.

110 Herbert Langer, *Kulturgeschichte des 30 jährigen Krieges* (Stuttgart: W. Kohlhammer, 1978).

111 Wheeler-Bennett, *Wooden Titan*, 77–78; Winter, *Sites*, 82–83.

112 Jost Hermand, *Arnold Zweig* (Reinbek bei Hamburg: Rohwohlt Taschenbuch Verlag, 1990).

113 Zweig, *Grischa*, 122.

114 Klemperer, *Curriculum*, 484.

115 BAMA PHD 8/23, "Gesundheitspflege in Bialystok. Schmutziges aus einer Großstadt," *KB* 34 (May 30, 1917).

116 Marwitz, *Stirb*, 126–27.

117 J. Šilietis, *Vokiečių okupacija Lietuvoje, 1915–1919 m. paveikslėliuose ir trumpuose jų aprašymuose* (Kaunas: "Varpo" B-vės spaustuvė, 1922), 116.

118 BAMA PHD 8/23, Herbert Eulenberg, "Wilnaer Strassenbild," *KB* 26 (April 4, 1917); Paul Monty, *Wanderstunden in Wilna* (Wilna: Verlag der Wilnaer Zeitung, 1916); Oskar Wöhrle, "Wilna – Ein Kultur – und Städtebild," in *Das Land*, 42–59.

119 BAMA N 196/1, Heppe, vol. V, 130; Klemperer, *Curriculum*, 683.

120 *Ich Weiß Bescheid. Kleiner Soldatenführer durch Wilna* (Wilna: Verlag Armeezeitung AOK 10, 1916), 9, 18.

121 BAMA PHD 8/23, Paul Monty, "Wilnaer Bürgersteig," *KB* 8 (November 29, 1916); BAMA N 196/1, Heppe, vol. V, 133.

122 BAMA PHD 8/23, "Das wiedergefundene Straßenpflaster," *KB* 7 (November 22, 1916); 95 (February 26, 1918).

123 BAMA PHD 23/65, "Der Knochenmann in der Murawieffstraße," *Grodnoer Zeitung*, 269 (November 15, 1917).

124 (Special Collections, Van Pelt Library, University of Pennsylvania, Philadelphia) "Unterirdischer Gang in Wilna," *Scheinwerfer* 24 (July 27, 1916); Weber, "Nochmals der 'Unterirdische Gang in Wilna,'" *Beobachter* 158 (September 15, 1918). All subsequent citations of *Scheinwerfer* refer to the Special Collections of the Van Pelt Library at the University of Pennsylvania.

125 Friedrich Bertkau, "Das amtliche Zeitungswesen im Verwaltungsgebiet Ober-Ost. Beitrag zur Geschichte der Presse im Weltkrieg" (Ph.D. diss., University of Leipzig, 1928), 18–19. Bertkau led Ober Ost's press section; his thesis discussed his work there.

126 Roger Chickering, *Imperial Germany and the Great War, 1914–1918* (Cambridge: Cambridge University Press, 1998), 9.
127 Wilhelm Heinrich Riehl, *Die deutsche Arbeit* (Stuttgart: J. G. Cotta'scher Verlag, 1861).
128 Joan Campbell, *Joy in Work, German Work: The National Debate, 1800–1945* (Princeton: Princeton University Press, 1989).
129 Woodruff D. Smith, *Politics and the Sciences of Culture in Germany, 1840–1920* (Oxford: Oxford University Press, 1991), 40–44.
130 Riehl, *Die deutsche Arbeit*, 3, 3, 5, 12.
131 Klemperer, *Curriculum*, 467.
132 BAMA PHD 8/23, "Ob. Ost," *KB* 1 (October 11, 1916).
133 *Das Land*, 10–11.
134 Wilhelm Heinrich Riehl, *Land und Leute* (Stuttgart: Cotta, 1854).
135 Ludendorff, *Kriegserinnerungen*, 138.

2 The military utopia

After unexpected conquests and the first impact of disorientation, the German army rushed to make over the land and peoples in the territories taken by the end of the great advances in fall 1915, seeking to establish facts on the ground which would justify keeping the area forever. General Ludendorff eagerly devoted himself to the task of ruling Ober Ost's territories, with the "firm resolution, to create something whole."[1] After Poland was wrested from the control of the Supreme Commander in the East in August 1915 with the creation of a separate civil Government General of Warsaw, Ludendorff resolved that this would not happen with his lands to the northeast.[2] Instead, he announced, "since they have taken Poland from me, I must find another kingdom for myself" in Lithuania and Kurland.[3] These lands were to remain a preserve for the military, where the army would build up a state, an expression of the military as a creative institution, in fact the quintessential German institution, with a mission in the East: civilizing, modernizing, carrying *Kultur*. These ambitions were fused into a utopian vision, which was the moving spirit behind the building of the Ober Ost state and yet also produced within it fatal contradictions.

While the future of these territories was unclear, the army sought to create a durable order before peace came, setting the terms for later disposition of the lands. To create "something whole," occupation authorities pursued a threefold policy: they aimed to impose their own form and order on the lands, then to use the lands to the fullest extent, towards the final, long-range goal of progressively making over the territory. First there was the obvious necessity of securing areas behind the front, establishing lines of communication and supply, order and quiet among the subject peoples. Next, officials would move to a total mobilization and comprehensive economic exploitation of land and people. Successes of rational management by the army were to convince Germans at home and natives here that the regime should be permanent. Finally, in a utopian climax, came the progressive remaking of the lands and peoples, through intensification of control and administration. Total control, of a sort not possible in the West, opened the possibility of creating something truly unprecedented, new, and "whole." The problem, as would quickly become evident, was that these goals were frequently in conflict.

Ludendorff himself was the war god who called this military utopia into being. From his office, scanning maps of the area, he envisioned the state as an extension of his own personality and was awed by his own creation: "My will permeated the administration and in it gained creative joy."[4] So strong was the animating spirit Ludendorff built into the administration that it continued to unfold even after he and Hindenburg left in August 1916 to direct Germany's Supreme Command, replacing their disgraced superior Falkenhayn. At the same time, Ludendorff took away from Ober Ost a wealth of experience which would influence his organizing of Germany's effort to wage "total war" from 1916, as he mobilized economic resources in the Hindenburg Program, demanded compulsory labor and the militarization of working conditions in the country's factories through the "Auxiliary Service Law," and marshaled propaganda to fire a tiring population with annexationist fantasies through a program of "Patriotic Instruction," as all of these measures pushed civil authorities ever more to the margins in the face of a "silent dictatorship."[5] Policies practiced in the East could be imported back to Germany's embattled home front.

In fall 1915, Ludendorff began to organize the administration in a way that would keep the lands under military control. When the areas had first been conquered, they were administered directly by the armies ranged across them. Behind a twenty-mile strip of operation area at the front lay the rear area (*Etappe*) commands of each of the armies. Special rear area troops and military police took up positions to fight espionage and "to maintain peace in the land."[6] By March 1916, the land was divided into special rear area administrations: Lithuania (Etappe 8), Suwalki-Wilna (Etappe 10), Bialystok (Etappe 9), and Grodno (Etappe 12), all run by administration chiefs. The administration was frequently reorganized, especially in the southern areas, producing constant confusion. Ludendorff set about centralizing control, yet he faced the problem of doing this while retaining exclusively military control in the area. To this end, he established a central administration in the staff of the Supreme Commander in the East, officially consecrated in the administration's "constitution," the "Order of Rule" of June 7, 1916.[7] The territories were divided into administrations, with administration chiefs responsible to both rear area inspectorates and directly to the central administration.[8] Both of these, in turn, were under the Supreme Commander in the East, who stood at the summit where all the confused chains of command met.

Thus Ludendorff built a justification for continued military rule: the Supreme Commander in the East had to be the highest post, mediating between all the armies and officials, coordinating their efforts. Civilian control was fended off, giving Ober Ost a "special character" as a military state, while other occupied areas, Belgium and Poland, received civil administrations.[9]

Ludendorff built up a central bureaucracy, a body whose size and character reflected at once both the ambitions of his military utopia and the administrative chaos typical of Ober Ost. Ludendorff collected a large staff, necessary because of "the size of the task and expanse of the area to be administered."[10] Ludendorff aimed to give his administration a distinctive "special character." Out in the East, "German," "military," and "expert" were to become synonyms. The size of the staff grew and grew, by a process that seemed unstoppable.[11] All of the staff was to be purely military, while civilians drawn into the work of the administration were made subject to military law.[12] For competent administration, Ludendorff collected experts from the ranks, but also recruited civilian personnel, intending to make them over into military men. For simple matters of administration, he believed in taking on energetic people without specific training: "here, clear will, general knowledge, and sound common sense could replace much that was lacking." In developing agriculture, forestry, courts, finances, church, and schools, however, there was no room for amateurs. At first it was difficult to get men out in the East, but later, as the administration "gained a certain reputation, it became easier."[13] This was a land of unlimited possibilities, luring personalities who strained for expansive freedom of action. A high official noted that his section attracted young officials wanting independence of action and upward mobility in their careers. To secure the best, Ludendorff extracted information about those applying for duty in Germany: in one case, writings on Lithuania by a young archivist, Dr. Zechlin, came to his attention, so he was transferred from his unit to Ober Ost, as an expert on the region's history (later, Zechlin would be ambassador to Lithuania in the interwar period).[14]

The number of officials working in Ober Ost's growing state can be roughly estimated. One official reported that at its high point the central administration numbered 601 upper-level positions, including military details and economic officers. Of that number, 190 officials worked in forestry and agriculture, 110 in medicine and veterinary duties, and the remaining 301 at internal administration and justice.[15] Below the central administration were regional divisions. One of these, Lithuania, had 2,084 men in September 1916: 201 officers and higher officials, 362 middle-level officials, 878 lower officials and policemen. At this time, Ober Ost had five such areas, so an estimate would suggest more than

10,000 men involved in the administration as a whole.[16] However, the administration's size fluctuated. The chief of Military Administration Lithuania noted that in early 1918 he had over 9,000 subordinates.[17] Since Kurland remained alongside as a parallel unit, one might estimate a total of roughly 18,000 officials and workers. Throughout the occupation, then, the administration as a whole probably numbered between 10,000 and 18,000 men. Besides men in the administration itself, millions of German soldiers served on the Eastern Front and in the rear areas and many came to know Ober Ost.

The administration drew in a broad range of men from different walks of life in civilian existence. In principle, these officials were either no longer usable at the front or specialists with important skills, or both. Among higher officials, the largest group was involved in government at home. Officials included archivists, professors of theology and philosophy, advisors to the Prussian culture ministry, doctors, liberal parliamentary deputies, art historians, lawyers (one, military mayor of Schaulen, later headed the German Academic Exchange Service between the wars), Prussian regional governors, estate owners, merchants, foresters, writers, artists, teachers, and a Lübeck city senator (administering captured Riga). All parts of Germany were represented in the administration, one official reported, though the Prussian element at the top was marked. Another postwar German report cited 485 officers and higher military officials in Ober Ost, not including those in the economic sector. Of these upper officials, 74.84% were Prussians (while Prussians represented just over 60% of all Germans). The report noted their religious confession: 83.71% were Protestant; 14.85% were Catholic; and 1.44% Jewish (by contrast, in Germany's entire population, Protestants were about 62%, Catholics about 37%, and Jews about 1% of the total). Thus, especially Protestants, and to a lesser extent Jews, were overrepresented. Education was also emphasized among these upper officials: 335 of the 485 had university or technical higher education. Most of the officials were middle-aged. Agricultural officials were mostly from Pomerania, East Prussia, and Silesia and were thus able to adapt their skills to similar climatic conditions. In Kurland, Baltic Germans were also included in the administration. A handful of men had served in the colonies, perhaps carrying over some of their administrative experience to this new territory. In the administration's upper levels, officials were also bound together by common memberships in university dueling fraternities, earlier friendships, or family ties. An official announced that this elite "felt like a big family."[18]

Another important visible quality of the military state was that it consisted entirely of men. Visits by family were "strictly prohibited," one official reported. This was also enforced at the administration's upper levels, for "Ludendorff had strictly insisted from the start that no wives would follow their husbands into the occupied territory," and this rule endured.[19] After 1916, German women were brought in as secretarial staff, but the state remained conspicuously male.

Not only experts crowded in to the administration, since officials provided places for friends and relatives, and important individuals pressed their wards on the state in the East. Prince August Wilhelm of Prussia's inclusion was a mixed blessing for officials in Bialystok-Grodno, as his ceremonial status and dynastic duties interfered with mundane bureaucratic duty.[20] The administration became a curious mix of ambitious competence and even more ambitious incompetence. Besides being exclusively military, it was also to be exclusively German. Authorities assiduously denied any local initiative, claiming natives were incapacitated by their "great cultural backwardness."[21] Moreover, there was to be a clear division of labor in the ideology of "German Work," since obviously *Deutsche Arbeit* could only be done by Germans. To make this absolutely clear, the "Order of Rule" decreed that official titles of all offices bore the prefix "German."[22] Separation between ethnic groups, rulers and ruled, was strictly drawn and vigorously maintained. A general precept written into the "Order of Rule" stated that no native could command or be set above any German. Natives could only be drawn in to work as helpers, and then received no pay for their services, could not refuse service or resign from assigned responsibilities.[23]

Yet the collection of Germans assembled to rule Ober Ost was problematic. The men heading the administration were, to a great extent, Prussians. Their Prussian character and experience colored their perceptions, assumptions, and methods in the East.[24] Especially among technical experts, jurists, and staff of the cultural administration, German Jews were strongly represented. Arnold Zweig, himself a German Jewish official, suggested in his novel that other officials resented them, questioning their Germanness.[25] Victor Klemperer, also of German Jewish origins, worked in the press section. In peacetime he was a journalist and scholar of literature (today he is famed for his later studies of the Nazis' manipulation of language in propaganda, and his diaries depicting life in the Third Reich). Klemperer observed that it was easiest for the administration to find translators for Hebrew and Yiddish, among German Jews, and their presence gave a pretext for anti-Semites' slanderous claims of the "Jewification' [*Verjudung*] of the Eastern rear areas."[26]

It was also important to have soldiers who spoke other local languages. This brought in two groups with an uneasy German identity. Soldiers who spoke Polish were mostly Prussian Poles. Their allegiance could prove problematic, when their sympathies and cooperation with local Poles, tacit or overt, created resentment among other natives.[27] A handful of soldiers from that part of East Prussia known as Lithuania Minor were Prussian Lithuanians able to communicate with Lithuanian natives.[28] However, their German nationalism could be exaggeratedly chauvinistic, to compensate for their origins and non-German last names. Differences in religious confession also came into play, creating tension between Protestant Prussian Lithuanians and Catholic natives. A secret report on the ethnic situation in Ober Ost from May 1916 asserted that natives distrusted Prussian Lithuanians so much that they preferred to deal with a "genuine German."[29] These groups were only the most dubious cases in a generally muddled scene. Zweig's novel pointedly emphasized the many Slavic names and differences of regional identities in the ranks: Bavarians, Frisians, Rhinelanders, all in tension with Prussian officers.

Such as they were, these German military experts approached their tasks with vigor, as energetic and confident bearing would have to overcome general lack of knowledge about the place. Trusting to will and organization, their confidence created a characteristic trait of the state, as immediate needs became springboards to gigantic, monstrous, and impossible ambitions. Ludendorff explained the problem and what he saw as its solution:

We worked in conditions that had been for us until then completely unknown, in addition in a land wrecked by war, in which all the bonds of state and economy had been broken. We confronted a population foreign to us, which was made up of different, often mutually feuding tribes, which did not understand our language and for the most part rejected us internally. The spirit of true and selfless discharge of duty, the inheritance of a hundred-year-old Prussian discipline and German tradition, animated all.[30]

With time, officials came to know the place, but at first Ober Ost was like "a colonial land, which lies unexplored before its owner."[31] Yet rule could not wait for a comprehensive understanding of lands and peoples. Instead, in this improvisational work, Ludendorff insisted that the essential keynote was daring experimentation and unsparing administrative absolutism, "to act quickly and energetically in unknown circumstances." Vigorous decision and bold experimentation were essential, "to work not bureaucratically, but according to the requirements of the situation. Thank God there was no 'precedent,' that grave-digger of free power of decision."[32] This scheme, where action was unhampered by "procedure" or "precedent," was a blank check. Any sort of action or program, if carried through with the rational organization of German Work, was justified in these new lands.

Map 3 The Ober Ost State – Main Administrative Divisions

To steer the entire state, Ludendorff organized an extensive central administration during the fall of 1915. It was ensconced in Kowno. At the top of the structure was the Supreme Commander in the East and his staff. On the tier below, special administrative sections were established under the quartermaster general, General von Eisenhart-Rothe, on No-

vember 4, 1915.[33] Together, these offices, part of the supreme commander's staff, formed what was essentially Ober Ost's interior ministry.
Section V (Politics) was most important, handling the military utopia's
relations with civil and military authorities in Germany. Internally, the
section steered the entire administrative system, regulations growing out
of all the departments, and political problems, especially nationality
questions. First headed by Hindenburg's son-in-law, von Brockhusen, it
passed to Captain von Gayl on November 11, 1916. Coming from a
Prussian military family, before the war von Gayl followed a bureaucratic
career, leaving to head the private East Prussian Settlement Society in
1910. His activism in encouraging German "inner colonization" in the
Eastern Marches, which first brought him to Ludendorff's attention, was
matched by Pan-German ideas, antipathy towards Poles, and anti-Semitic sentiments. After the war, von Gayl was a member of the Prussian
state council and Prussian plenipotentiary; in 1932, he briefly served as
interior minister in von Papen's cabinet.[34] Working together with von
Gayl's section were other special sections: the Gendarme Inspectorate,
Press Section, and *Verkehrspolitik* (movement policy) Section. Section VI
(Finances), run by Financial Councilor Tiesler, guided economic policy,
collected taxes and revenues, and managed state monopolies. Section
VIIa. (Agriculture) exploited the land and directed feeding of the armies
and native population, under Count Yorck von Wartenburg. Its sister
section VII b. (Forestry) controlled the territory's principal natural resource, its great wealth of forest. Section VIII (Churches and Schools),
led by Prussian Culture Ministry Councilor Altmann, was essentially
Ober Ost's culture ministry, regulating relations with clergy, educational
policy, and projects of "art and scholarship." Courts were the responsibility of Section IX (Justice) under Senate President Kratzenberg. Postal
and communications systems were managed by Section X (Post). In a
duplication of responsibility, Section XI (Trade) under Major Eilsberger
steered economics in industry and monetary policy. Likewise, in agriculture, Section XII (Land Cultivation) competed with other economic
sections. Such overlap led to constant infighting, perversely expressed in
steady competitive expansion of sections and their staffs. In the field, rear
area commanders came into conflict with adminstration officials. Ludendorff was the indispensable arbiter in administrative chaos, wielding the
final word: "I had to function in a balancing capacity."[35]

Below the central administration were administration chiefs ruling the
territory, at first divided into six military administrations: Kurland,
Lithuania, Suwalki, Wilna, Bialystok, and Grodno. Administration chiefs
were responsible to both the rear area inspectorates of individual armies
and to the central administration. This confusing subordination meant

that only the supreme commander and his deputy had a clear overview and freedom of action. Progressive centralization of territorial units followed. In May 1916, Wilna and Suwalki merged into Administration Wilna, later united to Lithuania in March 1917, forming Military Administration Lithuania. In November 1916, Bialystok and Grodno were united. Then this larger unit, too, was subsumed by Military Administration Lithuania in February 1918, with only Military Administration Kurland left alongside.[36]

During most of the occupation, the most important units were Military Administrations Kurland, Lithuania, and Bialystok-Grodno. Kurland was led from Mitau by Major Alfred von Gossler, a former Prussian regional governor, conservative Prussian parliamentary deputy, and Reichstag member. He later called this the high point of his life.[37] Inhabited by Latvians and Lithuanians, Kurland made up about one-fifth of Ober Ost's area. It was severely depopulated by the war, with entire areas lying empty and half its inhabitants gone. Only about fourteen people remained to a square kilometer. To the south lay Military Administration Lithuania, ruled from Wilna. Taking in the entire Lithuanian-speaking ethnographic area, it covered Russia's former provinces of Kowno, Suwalki, and western parts of Wilna *gubernia*. Lithuania formed Ober Ost's core, with more than half of its area and two-thirds of the total population. The land was inhabited by Lithuanians, with concentrations of Poles to the south, along with Belarusians. Its towns were a mix of peoples, with Jews often in the majority and heavy Polish representation. Wilna, with a population of 139,000, was Ober Ost's only sizeable city. Military Administration Lithuania was headed by the controversial Prince Franz Joseph zu Isenburg-Birstein. Even Ludendorff's indulgent estimation of his favorite acknowledged Isenburg's impulsive nature.[38] Isenburg's autocratic rule produced repeated crises, mounting to scandals in the Reichstag, finally resulting in his sudden removal in early 1918. Furthest south was Military Administration Bialystok-Grodno, ruled from Bialystok by von Heppe, a Prussian bureaucrat.[39] The area was inhabited for the most part by Poles and mainly by Belarusians in the southeast. Jews made up more than a fifth of the population. When Bialystok-Grodno fused with Lithuania in February 1918, von Heppe took over in Wilna as chief of Military Administration Lithuania.

Each military administration Chief had under him a staff mirroring the central administration. This symmetry meant that with every expansion of a central staff section, corresponding exponential growth took place below.[40] Military administrations were rigorously divided to ensure systematic, rational, and intensive control and exploitation. Each broke down into regions, subdivided into districts, on the Prussian model, though here districts were nearly three times larger. An officer was appointed district captain to lead each of these most basic units. District captains wielded unlimited power over local natives, appointing mayors and official heads for communities. They had economic staffs like the supreme commander, with economic officers to direct economic exploitation. Each district was divided into six or seven office districts led by office heads, whose areas were broken down into estate districts and communities with headmen. Infinite subdivisions placed a grid of control over the wide land.

While the administration sought to present the picture of effective centralization, local officials in fact exercised great independence. Remote from central control, many reveled in their power over subject populations. The "Order of Rule" gave them considerable personal autonomy, with control over their own finances once they satisfied the central administration's demands. Isolated in the countryside, lonely officials found themselves lost, sinking into the mire of the foreign land. One official recalled a young soldier wounded in the West and installed as administrator of an abandoned estate, who "suddenly, probably because of the weight of his responsibilities, was seized by delusions, wandered through the forests during the nights and caused wild shoot-outs."[41] Some reacted with aggression, flaunting total control over natives. Abuses were rife, as area captains filled their own larders and storehouses with requisitioned goods, popular native sources charged.[42] Central authorities could not control the behavior of subordinates in remoter areas. If the army took from the land what it needed, claiming everything as its property, the same lordly treatment was applied to natives. In the streets, natives were required to make way for German officials, saluting and bowing. Violence became increasingly routine, with reported public beatings. There were numerous complaints of German soldiers raping and mistreating native girls and women, while men trying to defend them were beaten and threatened with death.[43] Brutality toward natives went unchecked from above, due to the imperative of presenting a unified front. This contradiction, however, drove an ever deeper wedge between the image of the state and reality on the ground, what was happening "out there," as the popular mood grew ugly.

Despite its monolithic image, Ober Ost was wracked by administrative chaos within. Overlapping competencies, confused chains of command, sections' ambitions to expand produced a constant hum of conflict.[44] Other bodies also worked in the territory with an independence which clashed with the administration's plans. The important military Railroad Directorate became a state within a state.[45] The central office of military police in the East also made its demands. Because of differing political aims, according to von Gayl, Ober Ost and the civil administration of Poland in Warsaw clashed and were in a "state of war . . . until the bitter end."[46] Finally, and most intolerable to officials, the distant Reichstag could be heard, periodically demanding civil administration (in both senses of the term) for these occupied territories. Frustrated officials tried to overcome these problems of organization with more organization, which one later confessed they viewed as a "magical force," in spite of mounting disappointments.[47] All through the occupation, they waged a constant struggle for centralization, yet these efforts ran up against their own striving to expand the power of their offices and collided in turn with the jealous self-importance of lower officials in their private domains. Kurland's chief von Gossler reported that at one point his disagreements with the central administration led to his telephone line being severed.[48] Hand in hand with efforts to expand went shirking of responsibility. Based on personal observation, Zweig's novel painted scenes of constant departmental infighting. At the base of the administration were "countless police officers, area commanders – small, anxious people, who could lose their comfortable position in the occupied territory for a dereliction of duty." They "often rescued themselves through the panacea of not being officially responsible. Whatever was outside the small, narrowly circumscribed area of responsibility of Watch-Master A. or of Area Command B. was out of the solar system."[49] As units bickered with one another, an official observed: "I had the same impression I have had before and since, that as soon as officers in the rear areas are not busy enough, there are veritable orgies of pettiness, selfishness, and quarrelsomeness."[50] Staff often disregarded the order they administered, and allowed the higher ranks special treatment and exemptions. Class conflict in the ranks was heightened by different views of the war. While most ordinary soldiers hoped for a quick peace and return home, officers and officials had more to expect from continued war: careers and estates in the occupied territories. Deep divisions and internal conflict wracked Ober Ost, even as it presented itself as a monolithic, total state. What united the feuding offices and ambitious staff was a common vision of rule.

Ober Ost's plans called for intensive exploitation of the lands and its financial arrangement was geared toward the goal of autarchy. The occupied territory would be run from its own resources, while providing for armies in the East, placing no demands on the Fatherland. In Germany itself, autarchy had been a long-standing dream of nationalist politicians, but took on greatest urgency during the war, as Britain's naval blockade choked the economy, dependent on imports for a third of its food and many vital raw materials, and income from exports.[51] That economic self-sufficiency which eluded the *Kaiserreich* was achieved in

Ober Ost, the military boasted. Even better, it actually sent back resources to Germany. The first complete economic plan was drafted for
fall 1916.[52] Ober Ost's hunt for revenue was comprehensive and ruthless.
Import duties, taxes, state monopolies, and state enterprises yielded
considerable sums. Of necessity, collection systems had to be as simple as
possible, even if they placed great burdens on the poor. More complicated and equitable revenue collection was not possible, officials argued,
because of the lack of trained German personnel, absence of any previous
documentation on the territory, and the natives' primitive level of understanding.[53] As a result, the administration concentrated on tolls, indirect
taxes, and monopolies. Its cigarette monopoly was a stunning success. At
Ludendorff's urging, the same model was applied to other products:
liquor, beer, sugar and saccharin, salt, and matches.[54] As a direct tax, the
administration used the most basic and primitive head tax. Taxes were
also levied on all sorts of regulated activities and property. Most notorious
was the famous "dog tax," treated as a grand joke by occupiers, but
bitterly resented by natives.[55] At first, state enterprises built and run by
Ober Ost brought little profit, because of high start-up costs, yet their first
goal within the war economy was not profit, but maximum productivity in
supplying army needs. Financially, the end result was considered a great
success, as Ober Ost operated without subsidies from Germany, thus
fending off control from the Reich.[56] Further reinforcing its self-sufficiency, Ober Ost created its own currency, "East money," which natives
distrusted and were reluctant to accept.[57] While German banks were
invited to invest in the area, Ludendorff managed to completely exclude
from Ober Ost the war corporations mobilizing the economy in Germany
and other occupied territories, a high official noted.[58]

In pursuing autarchy, economic policies envisioned intensive exploitation of all the land's resources. Ober Ost based its economic programs on
the 1907 Hague land-war conventions, which made occupiers responsible for maintaining ordered circumstances, but in fact used them as
cover for a severe regime. The land echoed with the sharp explanation –
"*Krieg ist Krieg*," "War is war" – as soldiers requisitioned native property.[59] The regime weighed heavily on the land and the "inquisitions," as
natives called them with bitter humor, were brutal.[60] The working assumption was that everything in the land belonged to the army. In the
cities, people were turned out of their homes, businesses, shops, and
apartments.[61] In return for confiscated property, owners were given "receipts." The word *Schein* soon entered the small working vocabulary of
shouted German words which all natives understood. From small confiscations, the state as a whole moved to the very largest. Each harvest was
confiscated entire and had to be sold to the army at prices which it fixed

itself. All trade was a state monopoly and it was forbidden to sell land. The "Order of Rule" laid down the principle guiding this strange new form of state: "The interests of the army and the German Reich always supersede the interests of the occupied territory."[62]

The principal productive resource of these lands was agriculture. The agricultural section's task was difficult, as contradictory aims jostled each other. A relentless regime of requisitions formed its foundation. In the occupation's first months, requisitions were brutal and unsystematic. Troops took livestock and food from farmers at gun point, with no pretense of eventual repayment, as no receipts were handed out.[63] There were reports of brutalities which outraged the population. A nobleman's diary recorded news that the pastor of Panemunė parish, Staugaitis, had been clubbed to death by a drunken soldier, in the presence of an officer, for resisting confiscation of clover feed.[64] Natives expected that with regular military administration and the passing of the front, requisitions would be reduced. To their horror, demands increased, and the system became increasingly brutal and systematic. Economic officers strove to rationalize the regime, collecting statistics on the unknown land or ordering local clergy to do so. What followed seemed to natives a statistical psychosis, as soldiers appeared intent on counting all trees in the forests and fish in the lakes.[65] Orders to collect statistics on their own parishioners put pastors in a very difficult position, fearing (as they put it) that people would finally have to give a receipt for every bite they ate. Farmers agonized that counting of cattle would soon be followed by confiscation.[66] Drawing on collected information, much of it impressionistic, district captains and economic officers drew up quotas determining how much grain, milk, eggs, and animals farmers had to deliver. Once lists were drawn up, their authority was final, trumping material reality. A native source claimed dead chickens had to be brought in as proof before being struck from the sheets.[67] Milk was required in strictly defined quantities, even from old and sick cows. Such schematic requirements disregarded the real conditions of households and countryside society. Norms did not take into account numbers of people dependent on each farmer, kin and hired hands. Estates whose owners had fled and holdings judged insufficiently productive were seized and managed by German officers. In Lithuania alone, a thousand estates lay abandoned.[68] Farmers around seized estates were drafted to work there, in addition to needing to tend to their own farms. Deadlines for delivery of the harvest were so abrupt that farmers often did not have time to take in their own share. The orders of one little town's commander stated simply, "Attention! . . . Whoever does not complete field work in the given time or does it badly, will have his land taken away."[69] Finally, officials confiscated hand mills and took over larger mills and thresheries, to ensure that no grain eluded them.[70] The crazed rigor of the statistical work and severe confiscations masked chaos and improvisation: in three years of occupation, no general norm for requisitions was ever established.

Even with the more systematic regime, abuses continued and popular resistance grew. Troops gave farmers requisition receipts to be turned in later for remuneration (when was not clear, perhaps after the war; soldiers joked that the English and French would pay). Yet natives reported slips often simply said in German, "The bearer of this note is to be hung immediately" or "This note is worth nothing."[71] Lest the system break down, the administration began to accept requisition slips issued by the armies, to quiet the population. Yet cash awards for requisitioned goods were paid out in "East money," distrusted by locals. Moreover, administration prices for goods it bought up were below those of Poland's government general. Naturally, brisk smuggling shot up, enraging Ober Ost officials, whose own price-fixing had created this situation.

Extraordinary transport difficulties hampered the economy. Farmers were forced to work as wagoners, with their own carts of prehistoric structure. But rutted roads and miserable travel conditions disrupted military planning. Transport might take days, while requisitioned food rotted. Some forced service pitted ethnic groups against each other, while also offending religious convictions, as holidays were not respected. In the first days of Easter, natives claimed officials forced Christian farmers to transport brandy for the Jews of Alunta (Owanta).[72] Birsche's officer reported shutting down a market day, because its festive atmosphere distracted people from work.[73]

In ordering requisitions of livestock, data had first to be collected, cattle counted. Peasants hid their animals in cellars or drove them to secret forest clearings. Yet economic soldiers eventually managed to build up the necessary lists for an "ordered utilization."[74] Horses were mustered at "compulsory markets" where peasants were required to bring their animals and accept whatever price officials offered, then sign documents certifying the sale as voluntary, natives claimed.[75] Failure to meet norms for grain requisitions meant that all livestock was confiscated. Families had their last cow taken away, even if children needed milk. In such desperate cases, natives often resisted, and met crushing violence, shot down or savagely beaten.

Horse requisitions were carried through with exceptionally urgent severity, since the German army for the most part did not manage to mechanize its transport, but relied on horses. The small, tough animals, of the *Žemaitukai* breed, were valued highly and had been exported to Germany before the war. Yet these confiscations were crippling to farmers, who lost not only a crucial part of their economy, but also what they considered a member of the household. Peasants were ordered to present themselves and their horses for "horse reviews." Native sources record such a review, commanded for September 18, 1917 in Kroniai, Koschedary District. Farmers appeared on time, but when officials were several hours late, they allowed their horses to graze nearby. When the officials arrived and found the horses absent from the precise spot, punishments began. Thirty horses were picked out and their owners given one fifth of the normal price (the rest withheld as a fine for disobedience). The same commission then confiscated a further fourteen horses, because farmers misunderstood orders prescribing a specific kind of halter. The confiscated horses were sold on the spot to unknown private persons, not to the farmers, who tearfully begged to be allowed to buy them back.[76] The horses were so valuable that any pretext would do for seizing them. Farmers soon refused to transport goods, since their horses might be confiscated on the way.[77] As a result, urban centers starved. Ober Ost's policies abounded with such contradictions. With horses confiscated, agricultural productivity sank even further, as requisition quotas increased.[78] As a veterinary report noted, the confiscations produced strange economic distortions; tired, bad horses commanded higher prices than good ones, as they were less likely to be requisitioned.[79]

Economic officers collected raw materials with military uses. Anything that could conceivably be used was gathered and sent to Germany's war industries: furs, rags, and scrap metal. Local Jews were recruited to help in collections. Ludendorff averred, "The Jew was indispensable in this, as a middle-man."[80] Yet "raw material" was strangely defined. Troops came to requisition organ pipes from churches as scrap metal. There were reported incidents of economic troops bursting into churches during mass to seize altar candles.[81] In a Kowno suburb, tables set with food for Easter celebrations were requisitioned. From Jewish households, soldiers reportedly carried off sabbath candlesticks and Hanukkah menorahs.[82]

Over time, little confiscations grew into larger ambitions for ownership and expropriation. Increasingly, hard reality was obscured by alluring economic and agricultural fantasies. In its utopian intensity, the administration looked beyond immediate needs, to grandiose and unrealistic future plans. In the first planting year, 1916, officials set out to plant every acre of arable land, envisioning a "complete exploitation" or "complete tilling."[83] Ober Ost urged German agricultural associations to assist in development. On confiscated estates, agriculture could be practiced on a fantastic scale unknown to these lands. Ober Ost imported agricultural machinery of all kinds, introducing gigantic motor plows which amazed natives.[84] The result of this ambition was a disastrous first harvest, with tremendous waste of seed, for real conditions were not taken into account. Ludendorff acknowledged, "we expected too much of the area to be planted."[85] As a result, the situation in the cities, especially Bialystok, was "practically desperate," an official reported, provoking hunger riots and strikes.[86]

From this disappointment, officials concluded they needed to aim for longer-term goals: the utopian outlook remained. The agricultural sections conducted systematic experimentation with seeds, to see which took best to the soil.[87] Harvests could be doubled, they announced. These plans were celebrated in Germany, to create enthusiasm for keeping this gigantic farming reserve. In November 1916, the administration sponsored an Ober Ost fruit exhibition in Berlin.[88] Fourteen thousand people came to view tangible products of German Work: fresh fruits, marmalade from Ober Ost's jam factories, canned preserves, dried fruits and vegetables. Throughout the occupation, officials looked at the land with a view to changing it. Confiscated estates under military management were a crucial part of this ambition. Officers installed as overseers and managers came to feel ever more at home there, treating the property and people as their own.[89]

That utopian outlook, intent on permanent possession, was an important part of the eastern front-experience, distinguishing it from that of the West. Here, Kurland's chief explained that anyone with an "eye to the future glimpses in the not too distant future a through-and-through German, blossoming land."[90] Reflections on the present state of the land were not flattering. They claimed it seemed a hundred years behind Germany. Even elementary soil drainage was unknown here. Natives accepted the land as it was: "dire situations of wetness are regarded, it seems, as an inevitable fate, just as the incredible growth of weeds in most of the fields, which is an unavoidable consequence of the backwardness of the entire state of *Kultur* of the land." Native farming seemed hopelessly archaic and indolent. One scene in particular astounded soldiers: "Our soldiers love to relate how farmers plow around large and small stones in their fields, rather than making the effort, once and for all, to smash up the larger stones and to remove the pebbles." Yet even here there was, in fact, more going on than the occupiers recognized. Such behavior reflected not merely some essential laziness in native character, but their animistic sense that the stones, which had risen to the surface over years, had spirits and a right to be where they were. The entire country was full of holy stones and boulders, revered since pagan times, here not so very distant. Germans marveled at the prehistoric stick plows used by natives and their primitive "three-field system" of cultivation. Even local breeds of swine were closer to wild boars, it seemed, than to German varieties.

People lived together with their animals, a constant source of amused comment. In all, this was a "primitive natural economy." Natives' undemanding ways of life indicted them, revealing primitive "peoples of nature" rather than "peoples of *Kultur*" imposing their will on the environment. The verdict was clear: "the battle of *Kultur* against nature is here still in its infancy." For soldiers, coming to Ober Ost seemed to be a trip back into the past: "Exactly as in the days of our medieval colonization, even today the superiority of the German plow is evident over the un-German [*undeutschen*] 'Hake.' The Lithuanian 'Zocha,' only a hook covered with iron, must make way for the swing plow introduced from Germany." In this return to the past, Germans were bringing the future to these lands.[91]

From the first, the contrast of these lands with Germany was constantly before soldiers and officials, promising that the land could be changed and could become "German." Every trip by railroad seemed to demonstrate this: "For the untrained observer, the view of the condition of the fields on either side of the East Prussian border serves as proof. A single look out of the window of the rail-car determines, whether one is on the Russian or German side, even though on both sides it is the same soil and the same climate." Later, all through the occupation they worked through the experience:

The way in which agriculture is managed here is an inexhaustible topic of conversation among our soldiers. The differences between Germany and this occupied territory press in on even the most stupid eye. In Germany, regular furrows reach the furthest corner of the usable land, every tree in the forest is trimmed and looked after, planned order rules everywhere. In Ober Ost, except where the German has already created change, the field and meadow, tree and bush are left to themselves, and man is not their lord, but their guest, who is satisfied with that which the fields and gardens generously allow, instead of thinking about improvements with the pencil in hand for calculations.

What they imagined they faced here was sheer "prehistoric un-*Kultur*."[92]

Of the devastating conclusions drawn from this view of the land, one in particular was a decisive turn, as Germans thought about native peoples and themselves. Officials speculated that Eastern peoples only lived off earlier German accomplishments and work, letting them run down. Incapable of producing *Kultur* or work themselves, the peoples of the East and Russia envied the "productive work of Germans in Germany." They coveted German land, completely

overlooking the fact that the higher productivity of the lands in German hands is not a gift of nature, but the result of a heightened investment of capital and work – something which they, as yet, have shown themselves to be in no way capable of. Every piece of land which falls into the hands of the Muscovites, no matter how high its *Kultur*, must sink, with a merciless inevitability, to its natural level of productivity in a short span of time, after the reserves of the earlier, higher *Kultur* are used up and exhausted.

Peoples of the East were parasitic, incapable of real work, unlike "other, more joyously creative and productive races." Eastern "culture" was in fact "nothing but the night of apathy and the emptiness of the void."[93] From their utopian vision of the land, the occupiers drew conclusions about the characters of races, their own and those of subject peoples.

As officials planned agricultural fantasies, they considered measures over the next decade to continue the wartime "pioneer work of *Kultur*." Radical improvements and investment would begin as soon as peace came. German management would cultivate and change natives, implanting "cleanliness, order and accuracy." Lands and peoples would be possessed together: "If one could breed the people to order, cleanliness, honesty, punctuality, and duty (which is not the least of the problems faced here, which would have to be taken up and will not be easy and simple to solve) this area could become a bread basket of wheat and cattle, wood and wool, of the very highest value."[94] Projections for the future culminated in the plans for this "*Neuland*," organized by the administration by fall 1917, which explored in detail possibilities for development over coming decades.[95] According to Kurland's chief, this was the last chance in world history to "create truly *German* land." Kurland "was ideal settlement land," which "we now only need to hold and populate in order to possess a new, complete, and valuable piece of Germany!"[96]

Ober Ost officials insisted that they had here a *real* utopia, compared to the fantasies of armchair annexationists in Germany, who lusted after Mesopotamia and exotic overseas possessions. This was already real, they soberly insisted, and offered solid prospects for a glorious future and coming wars:

Our East-land is neither a utopia-land nor a paradise-land – it will always train a person to hard work, if it is to be richly productive. But if German Work succeeds in opening the land, if the *Heimat* can count on East-land cattle and meat, wheat and flax, butter and eggs, in future wars, then the German will know why he kept watch in this . . . wilderness over the course of years and days, winters and summers. Perhaps then he will consider the war economy of the army administration which, in the midst of a world in flames, cultivated the land.

In this "real" utopia in Ober Ost, land and war were tied together in a vision of the East taken by plow and sword. As soldiers and officers looked out of train windows and asked, "What does this land mean for us?," finding agricultural fantasies a constant topic for conversation, the compelling vision of the East, land, and war, gained purchase.[97]

One of the most visible development projects already taking place was industrial production. When German armies arrived, there was very little industry. Only some larger towns had factories and modest manufacturing centers. The administration took over what had not been destroyed and built its own factories in Libau, Kowno, and Bialystok, where requisitioned goods were processed for the army or to be sent back to Germany. All sorts of installations grew up. It was the army's boast that it took pressure off Germany's increasingly strained industry, as the economy was mobilized to offset Britain's naval blockade, which produced the hunger of the 1916–17 Turnip Winter. Ober Ost alone supplied a third of the meat eaten by armies in the East. The administration established potato drying centers, stations for processing straw and wood, sawmills, factories for mass production of marmalade, preserves, and drying of mushrooms in huge quantities. By the summer of 1917, 610 military dairies were at work.[98] These enterprises were visible testimony to the army's organizational skills.

Above all, the army turned to Ober Ost's real prize, the enormous forests. Troops required gigantic quantities of lumber at the front for fortifications, while railroad structures likewise made great demands.[99] Bridges needed to be built and sinkholes in the roads had to be firmed up with boards to be passable. Firewood was essential to survival in the harsh weather. Beginning already in 1915, the army undertook a program of forestry of huge dimensions. The work was so important that it was made independent of other administrations, creating more bureaucratic conflict. The largest and most important area was the primeval forest of Bialowies, led by Bavarian Forestry Councilor Major Escherich, as administrative chief. In postwar Germany, Escherich later led the right-wing terrorist group, Org-Esch (Organisation Escherich).[100] Many visitors from Germany came on tours to this "monstrous enterprise," claimed as the biggest in Europe. A network of roads and railroads was built through the forest, while "a small army of POWs" and press-ganged natives provided labor: one official mentioned 5,000 workers in early 1916.[101] Trees were tapped for sap and resin, yielding valuable chemicals, while burning produced charcoal. Army sawmills supplied their own needs, as well as more wood for the Western Front. Exploitation went beyond purely military needs, as lumber was also sold to private German firms. The best wood was sent to the Reich, where cellulose timber supplied production of gunpowder and explosives, such as nitroglycerine, and paper manufacture. Quantities being cut were so large that eventually military reports went over to merely noting the value of shipments in marks. Lauded "scientific forestry" was less in evidence, as one official confessed, in the face of ravenous orders, though Ludendorff later denied strip-cutting.[102] For kilometers to either side of rivers and roads, forests were cut down. Areas lay waste, a stubble of stumps or dead trees killed by being tapped to drain away their valuable sap. Natives looked with dismay at clear-cut wastes.[103]

These economic policies seemed to yield substantial rewards. According to statistics gathered after the war, during the entire occupation in Lithuania, 90,000 horses, 140,000 cattle, and 767,000 pigs were requisitioned. Studies estimate that during this period, the administration removed various resources valued at 338,606,000 marks, while importing goods and materials worth 77,308,000 marks.[104]

These ambitious plans created huge demand for labor to man industries, military farms, the formidable railroad and engineering works. Everywhere, manpower shortages appeared. The administration found it needed to arrange the "drafting and transfer of local surplus workforce."[105] POWs and even refugees displaced from the front were organized into work gangs, while army estates used neighboring peasants for unpaid labor, as their own steadings were left untended.[106] As a result, they could not meet their requisition norms and were punished for this, caught in the vicious circle of Ober Ost's war economy. Soon, however, the workers' numbers did not suffice. In mid 1916, the administration ordered that all adult men and women in the territory could be put to work.[107] According to the "Order of Rule," natives had no right to refuse assigned duties.[108] Resistance was punished with up to five years of prison. Forced labor battalions were set up and marched to work at harvests and road building.[109] In September 1916, Schaulen's mayor, Lieutenant Morsbach reported efforts at a "complete calling-up" of people for labor, which led to ordering between 610 and 650 men and women to all kinds of work, organized into six "columns." Morsbach noted that he made use of the right to draft people for work without pay.[110] A report from Kurland noted in October 1916 that "the lately undertaken recruitment of men capable of work has understandably caused some disquiet, all the more because the recruitment, due to the speed with which it was enacted, was not executed without mistakes."[111] In the winter of 1916/17, mobilization increased.[112] One official noted that ordering of workers' conditions "forms the center of gravity of the entire administration."[113] In the Lithuanian area, numbers in the gangs reached 60,000, shuttled around the country, from one work project to another. Conditions and exertions were terrible, yet each worker was allowed only 250 grams of bread and a liter of soup each day. As a result of poor nourishment, many reportedly died of exhaustion. For a day's hard labor, workers received 30 to 60 pfennigs. The wage later rose to one and a half marks. Though additional provision was promised for those with families, it was not paid out. Even the old and sick were not exempt from labor. Natives were forced to work in the cold without suitable clothing, under armed guard. When their workday ended at 4 p.m., natives were driven back to unheated barracks and locked in for the night, without warmth or light. In Schirwintai District, a work battalion supposedly was unable to escape and burned to death when their barracks caught fire (the official bulletin denied this, yet the incident continued to be mentioned after the war in Lithuanian sources. The official denial, blaming foreign distortion of news, stated that the barn was not locked, no one died in the fire, and that in fact it was caused by workers' negligence.)[114] Work gangs were ravaged by disease: typhus, dysentery, tuberculosis, cholera, and lung inflammation. Of 237 workers of Work Battalion A.-K. 806 in Baisegola in Kiedany District, at one point (apparently in fall or winter 1916) only 89 workers were capable of work, all the rest were sick.[115] POWs were treated even worse. In December 1917, a popular native source claimed, about a hundred burned to death in their barracks on Stripelkiai estate in Meshkuchai.[116] As it became more difficult to fill work battalions, military press-gangs roamed towns and scoured the country-side by night. Localities were forced to present the ordered numbers of workers (it was understood that some of these workers were also to be shipped to Germany).[117] Troops reportedly surrounded churches during mass to seize worshippers as they came out. Once he was pressed into labor, a native's family often lost its only wage earner and knew nothing of what had become of him. An official in Birsche District commented:

Here, assignment to a Civil Worker Battalion is considered a great disaster by the inhabitants. People are thinking above all about the extraordinarily high mortality number, as well as about those who return, often miserable and sick. One can sympathize with this thought process; on the other hand one must also keep in mind that the Lithuanian is by nature given to whining. Probably almost every family tries to get its members out of the Civil Worker Battalions.[118]

Some workers were enlisted to work in Germany, where manpower shortages in factories and agriculture were also dire.[119] Studies after the war put the number of workers, in forced labor or enlisted, at 130,000 in Lithuania alone.[120] A German postwar report put the number of forced laborers in the civil worker batallions at 5,033 in June 1917 (along with 1,007 voluntary workers), after disease and escape had reduced their numbers.[121] Increasingly, men escaped to the woods to avoid forced labor, swelling the growing bandit groups. After escalating native pro-tests, the army formally dissolved forced labor battalions on September 20, 1917. In fact, some continued to operate, as workers were designated "volunteers" and slaved on as before.

Ober Ost's economic policy was highly contradictory. While the regime managed to extract significant quantities of agricultural products and resources from the damaged land, the voraciousness of its immediate demands undercut long-term goals for developing the area. One result, however, was unambiguous. The condition of natives became unbearable. Famine gripped the cities, with thousands dying in Wilna during the winter of 1916/17.[122] The following spring brought hunger to the countryside as well. There, the poor were hardest hit, since they had earlier relied on independent farmers for work and aid in times of trouble. The farmers were now themselves reduced to penury by requisitions. In the crisis, many turned to banditry. The popular mood turned against the Germans, where before it had been tentative, expecting normalization and the return of order. This was a decisive development, for German authorities themselves argued from the first that natives' political sentiments were above all a function of their economic well-being. As the regime produced economic terror, local native relief organizations won credibility among the populations. Ordinary peasants who had cared nothing for politics now were forced into political understanding in ethnic terms. Paradoxically, the administration produced the objective conditions for a growing national consciousness, commitment, and stiffening opposition to its own rule. Intoxicated to blindness by the omnipotence of his own will, Ludendorff brushed the matter aside: "Sparing the area of the Supreme Commander in the East at the cost of the homeland out of false feelings of humanity would have been an absurdity."[123] Because of their belief in the transcendent power of organization, officials were unable to see the contradictions in their own policies and unrealistic expectations, finding it easier to blame the lands and peoples for the failures.

Exploitation of the land was buttressed by an enormous body of orders and commands. The "Order of Rule" declared that the Supreme Commander in the East "exercises the complete legislative, judicial, and executive state power."[124] A particular instance of German Work was the administration of law. Every district received a district court for natives. While the Hague conventions demanded that inhabitants be judged by laws of the occupied country, the administration twisted this principle to its own purposes in a remarkable way. First of all, officials questioned how much law existed here before the war, "considering the confused Russian circumstances."[125] Officials chose a Russian legal code published in 1903, but never put into effect. Russian laws had to be translated into German so that German judges could rule according to their dictates. This was yet another testimony to German Work, as Ludendorff noted after the war with bitter pride: "I believe that no other people besides the

Germans would go to such trouble for areas taken in war." Yet for all that, "the German judge here in the poor, lice-infested Lithuanian towns delivered legal judgments according to foreign laws with the same objectivity and the same seriousness as in Berlin according to his own laws. Who will equal us in this?"[126] In fact, the judicial apparatus operated with increasing arbitrariness, avoiding constraints of "precedent" and "procedure" which Ludendorff despised. Courts were independent of German legal norms at home. Russian law was administered "in German fashion," in German language which natives could not understand. The end result was that rulings could be made with great severity and no chance of appeal. The Supreme Commander in the East expressly released judges from personal liability in making decisions in the East.[127] This reinforced the division of labor envisioned in German Work, as Ober Ost law was applicable only to natives, while Germans were to be judged by German law. Law became a tool of policy, as the legal system was not separated from the administration.[128] Punishments were brutal, with crippling fines for slight infractions and death sentences for a native's possession of a weapon. One official serving on courts martial which handed down death sentences said that "the distress and wailing of the poor war victims cut into my heart very much, but I could not do anything to help, in view of the inexorable nature of military law."[129] Death sentences were also given in cases of "espionage" and "war treason," most often alleged sabotage.[130] While records concerning the number of executions are not clear, according to estimates after the war, in Lithuania at least a thousand executions took place.[131] With so little separation of powers, the judiciary had no real independence, but simply enforced orders. Reflecting policy imperatives, a fiscal motivation increasingly crept in to the courts, as a report conceded, with the inclination to impose ever greater financial penalties for meaningless offenses, since these brought profit, while incarceration cost money.[132]

How law was subordinated to the military state's interests is vividly portrayed in Zweig's great realistic novel, *The Case of Sergeant Grischa*. This development forms the central story, culminating in an indictment of the entire system of military rule. Zweig's story (published in 1927) is based on a real incident which he learned of while working in the press section. Grischa, a Russian prisoner of war, escapes from a labor camp. When caught by military police, he claims to be someone else, a deserter who crossed over Russian lines to return home to Wilna. According to orders, any deserter who does not turn himself in to a police station within three days is considered a spy and is to be shot. Even after it becomes clear that the prisoner is innocent of espionage, is in fact another man altogether, the system grinds on and has him executed: "The

Divisional Court Martial works like a machine: once it has caught a man, it draws him through its gearwork and releases him as a corpse." It cannot afford to admit its fallibility. Moreover, officials were afraid that this deserter's example would infect troops and break their discipline. A handful of officials, gripped by crises of conscience, try to save him (in the process, Zweig illuminates the chaotic inner workings of the state's conflicting offices), but they are overruled by Schieffenzahn (Ludendorff), who delivers the ultimate maxim: "the state creates justice, the individual is a louse."[133] In Ober Ost, policy is the primary concern, not justice. In the novel, this moment brings on a crisis of identity for more sensitive and just officials, because Schieffenzahn's revolutionary modern creed of the state runs counter to two older traditions: Prussian and Jewish conceptions. For old General von Lychow, representative of the Prussian *Junker* tradition, the state deserves respect because it upholds a justice greater than itself: embodying it, not creating it. For Jewish military judicial counselor Posnanski, law itself derives its value only by reference to transcendent principles. Seeing it made a mere instrument of the state revealed the courts as a sham and facade for an edifice of naked power.

Floods of orders issued from the military utopia. With its goals of total control, it passed regulations on every aspect of life and activity. Regulations prescribed traffic, restrictions on movement, curfews, trade monopolies, agriculture, animal husbandry, cleanliness, even down to orders on the baking of cakes (on March 3, 1916, the administration fixed Wednesdays and Saturdays as days when baking was allowed). In 1916, Schaulen's mayor ordered that loaves of bread be stamped, so their provenance could be determined.[134] A huge body of regulations grew up, yet language problems created great difficulties, as natives were expected to conform to orders though not fully informed of them. Often natives did not know what they were being punished for. Summaries of orders in native languages were eventually posted on special "order boards" set up in the towns. Translations were often so bad that they were nearly incomprehensible (because of an orthographic mistake, one legendary announcement read in Lithuanian, instead of "The German court judged," "The German excrement shitted").[135] Native languages, moreover, often lacked technical terms equivalent to idioms of German "officialese." A translation post annexed to the press section grappled with the problems, but could not keep pace with the massive volume of new regulations. The problem was finally "solved" by fiat: when laws appeared in German, they went into effect regardless of whether they were understood. Thus, the problem was "happily resolved. It was specifically determined, that for all orders and regulations, the German language sufficed."[136] The result was the worst sort of legalism, on its face systematic and orderly, but in fact stunningly arbitrary in application. Since orders and laws were unknown or not understood, the peasantry characteristically withdrew into itself, hunkering down. As they withdrew, their passivity paralyzed the territory's workings: "people were eaten up inside with worry over this infinity of orders, but the more they worried, the less they obeyed."[137] Impoverishment and transgressions, known or unknown, forced many to the move of last resort: fleeing to the woods to hide or to join bandit groups. While Ober Ost's guiding vision was a regime where German Work from above channeled native energies and initiative, its policies instead produced paralysis and rejection among the natives.

Troops of German police called *gendarmes* were deployed throughout the territory to keep order and enforce the state's will. Their commander was General Rochus Schmidt, an "old East African," who had served in the colonial forces, perhaps transferring his colonial perspective to Ober Ost.[138] For the most part older soldiers withdrawn from front duty, since Germany could not spare trained police, Schmidt's untrained gendarmes notoriously abused their power over native populations. Ludendorff blithely excused the matter: "Perhaps individual gendarmes regrettably contributed to the later bad feeling. How were they to step before an unfriendly population in a foreign land without enough knowledge of the language, and accomplish anything? . . . I only want to present all the difficulties, which the German men had to deal with in a foreign land."[139] Gendarmes' responsibilities included enforcing requisition norms, hunting down secret schools, controlling native movement, and suppressing smuggling. Eventually, they would also have to move to crush native armed resistance. Spread thinly across the territory, stationed in remote locations, their small numbers meant that their actual control was limited. Often localities only saw gendarmes race through, stop to give orders in incoherent translations of local languages, then disappear. Where they settled in, however, their control could be arbitrary and absolute. The brutality of some of these untrained policemen could not be effectively checked, as they raged in private kingdoms far from central control. Official brutality from above converged with private brutality from the lower ranks below. Police interrogations were accompanied by beatings and torture in the jails, native sources claimed. Natives could be arrested on suspicion and held for two to three months without charge.[140]

Growing banditry not only threatened Ober Ost's control, but was also a symptom of its ambitions and abuses. Bands grew steadily, reaching crisis proportions in 1917.[141] Originally, small bands of Russian soldiers cut off during retreat led furtive lives in the forests, only coming to villages to beg for bread.[142] Over the next two years, however, their numbers swelled, augmented by escaped POWs and natives driven into this outlaw existence by requisitions and manhunts for forced-labor battalions.[143] Bandits became more aggressive and soon district captains reported that in addition to terrorizing natives, they killed soldiers.[144] As native farmers were ordered, under pain of punishment, to inform on bandits, their relations with the bandits changed. Growing more desperate and confident, bandits attacked whole villages. Farmers were robbed and threatened with death if they informed the authorities. Some bands numbered a hundred men, becoming strange conglomerations of nationalities, including German deserters. Bands began to tax villages, hold courts, and demand requisitions, in a peculiar imitation of Ober Ost. In some forests, they built up regular fortresses and camps. In this fight, natives were caught in the middle. Since Ober Ost punished possession of firearms with the death penalty, natives were helpless, unable to defend themselves. German efforts "made the inhabitants a tool in this fight," native relief organizations complained. One report hoped for good results from a "sharpened approach against the population and the Russian bandits."[145] An official regretted this tactic, but explained that "towards the population, which I was fundamentally sorry for, I couldn't do otherwise than go at it with the greatest energy and sharpness," including taking hostages, and levying fines.[146] The regime directed most measures against the natives, punishing those who gave shelter or food to escapees, even when threatened. Police had to be informed of any chance meeting or contact. Even suspicion or rumors of support brought fines of hundreds or thousands of marks levied on localities, while greater collective punishments were imposed on areas where Germans were shot at, holding the entire area responsible. Soldiers sometimes faced an unsettling phenomenon, finding their own deserters among captured bandits. They had to be "re-Germanized."[147] Military police tried provocations against locals, using stool pigeons pretending to be escaped prisoners, who then betrayed anyone charitable enough to offer bread.[148] In the end, however, police simply gave up fighting against bands in many parts. Authorities traveled in rural areas with trepidation. Woods were cut away from paths in more dangerous areas to avoid ambush.[149] Night was given over to bandits and smugglers. Unofficially, police at last concerned themselves only with attacks or threats to Germans and the military; natives were not protected. Gendarmes did not respond to natives' complaints or simply told them to pay the tributes demanded by bandits. Natives lost the last reason to trust gendarmes when they could not expect protection from the army. Ober Ost's claim of establishing "ordered circumstances" was equivocal, and its police measures only produced a final alienation of the natives.

As another subcategory of order, Ober Ost concerned itself with public health, in characteristically authoritarian fashion. The area seemed a sinkhole and breeding ground for disease, its hygienic conditions shocking, cities now inhumanly crowded, jammed with refugees. All this was taken to reflect the character of the land "in which various epidemics are native." An official account reflected blandly, "Human life does not count for much in Russia."[150] The task was clear: "thus, the sanitary and medical establishment had to be built from the ground up in Ober Ost, so that serious dangers would not be constantly lurking behind the army's back and at the *Heimat*'s borders."[151] Measures would have to be coercive, as the army "gave special attention to the hygienic circumstances of the population."[152] Among natives, "hygienic conditions were completely primitive and understanding of these problems and inclination to cooperate were in general absent."[153] "Sanitary police measures" evolved into a large program. Eventually, a head section "S," standing for *Santitätswesen*, or "medical affairs" was established in the administration's main department, charged with "general and special hygiene of the land," with a hygenic institute.[154] Delousing stations were established in rural and urban areas.[155] Attention focused on the cities, which special plague-troops combed for sick people. The ill were taken to quarantine centers; houses boarded up, plastered with red warning signs, entire neighborhoods closed off.[156] Inoculations were forced on the population and people were driven in crowds for delousing at military bathhouses. "Sanitary police" searched homes to see that they were kept clean. Authorities regulated prostitution, with medical examination of prostitutes, 70 percent of whom they initially estimated to be infected with venereal disease. It appears that the army ran its own military brothels. Posters in Kowno gave directions on condom use, disinfection after intercourse, obligatory registration of prostitutes' permits, and measures in the event of infection.[157] A wide array of prohibitions and orders sought to check the area's dangers. It was forbidden to sell food in the streets. Deaths had to be reported and registered at command posts within one hour. It was forbidden to wash corpses and funeral processions were banned; the dead could be accompanied to the graveyard only by one person carrying a cross and two with candles. Dogs and cats were destroyed in the cities, as Germans feared that they carried disease.[158] Orders instructed natives on the correct way to make outhouses and inspections followed up on these improvements.[159] The countryside presented identical problems, as Birsche's District Captain Löslein reported: "the lack of cleanliness among the population is unbelievably great." He noted the "evil state" of toilets, unsanitary tearooms and bakeries, and reported that he had established daily inspections and levied fines to compel cleanliness.[160] Overall, the administration aimed to change native behavior, habits, consciousness. Such "education" would take a long time: "full successes could only ripen over decades, if native populations themselves could be educated to an understanding of the importance of health problems and brought to a committed cooperation in their resolution."[161] Natives, in fact, reacted very differently.

When the natives noticed that "the Germans feared diseases no end," there followed a disastrous development on both sides.[162] After they learned of this fear and saw its effect on soldiers, they used it as one of their only means to avoid requisitions and physical abuse. One of the words in the German vocabulary they quickly learned was "*Krank*." By shouting "Sick, sick!," they could defend themselves, one popular native source claimed.[163] Officials used disease-prevention as an excuse for keeping the territory shut off.[164] It was a disastrous dialectic, conditioning German views of a "dirty East." Memories of cleansing Ober Ost and hygiene programs endured even after the war. Ludendorff congratulated himself: "the conditions of the land stabilized and life there returned to ordered courses. The German's sense of order and his understanding of hygiene won through."[165] The lands and peoples had been reformed by the spirit of German Work.

Ultimately, more important than administrative details was the spirit of the army administration. It animated Ober Ost's offices and unfolded with remarkable continuity even after Hindenburg and Ludendorff left to assume the supreme command in August 1916. Instead of being an apolitical institution, the army would create a state after its own spirit. The motivating ideology of German Work made the methodical use of power an end in itself. Great, overreaching ambitions in Ober Ost's utopian vision sanctioned a brutal, arbitrary, and violent rule which undercut its own goals. Paradoxically, the imperatives of creating a state that appeared monolithic and total in its claims ultimately frustrated the rationalizing spirit. From within, Ober Ost was wracked by constant reorganization, unstaunchable floods of orders and regulations, confusing rungs of subordination, duplicated responsibilities, institutional rivalries, abuses, and violence both random and calculated. Over time, the image the military state projected diverged ever more from the reality of its rule. Rather than recognize this, its utopian vision insisted on two great programs which would seek to possess the lands and peoples of Ober Ost, by controlling native movement and native culture. The army hoped to claim for its own what it had made over.

NOTES

1 Ludendorff, *Kriegserinnerungen*, 145.
2 Hans Zemke, *Der Oberbefehlshaber Ost und das Schulwesen im Verwaltungsbereich Litauen während des Weltkrieges* (Berlin: Junker & Dünnhaupt Verlag, 1936), 6.
3 Quoted in Martin Kitchen, *A Military History of Germany from the Eighteenth Century to the Present Day* (Bloomington: Indiana University Press, 1975), 220.
4 Ludendorff, *Kriegserinnerungen*, 160–61; BA N 1031/2, Gayl, 50.
5 Gerald D. Feldman, *Army, Industry and Labor in Germany, 1914–1918* (Princeton: Princeton University Press, 1966); Jürgen Kocka, *Klassengesellschaft im Krieg. Deutsche Sozialgeschichte, 1914–1918* (Göttingen: Vandenhock & Ruprecht, 1973).
6 Ludendorff, *Kriegserinnerungen*, 146.
7 BAMA PHD 8/20, "Ziffer 259. Verwaltungsordnung für das Etappengebiet im Befehlsbereich des Oberbefehlshabers Ost (Ob. Ost)," *Befehls- und Verordnungsblatt des Oberbefehlshabers Ost* 34 (June 26, 1916), 269–89. Henceforth, these orders are cited as *BUV*.
8 BAMA N 196/1, Heppe, vol. V, 95.
9 Kurt G. A. Jeserich, *et al.*, eds., *Deutsche Verwaltungsgeschichte*, vol. III, *Das Deutsche Reich bis zum Ende der Monarchie* (Stuttgart: Deutsche Verlagsanstalt, 1984), 899–907.
10 Ludendorff, *Kriegserinnerungen*, 147; Hans-Joachim von Brockhusen-Justin, *Der Weltkrieg und ein schlichtes Menschenleben* (Greifswald: Verlag Ratsbuchhandlung L. Bamberg, 1928).
11 BAMA N 196/1, Heppe, vol. V, 90.
12 BAMA PHD 8/20, "Ziffer 259. Verwaltungsordnung für das Etappengebiet im Befehlsbereich des Oberbefehlshabers Ost (Ob. Ost)," *BUV*, 34 (June 26, 1916): §2, p. 269.
13 Ludendorff, *Kriegserinnerungen*, 148.
14 BA N 1031/2, Gayl, 74; 224.
15 Ibid., 160.
16 *Skizzenmappe der 'Kownoer Zeitung'*, nr. 27 (September 3, 1916).
17 BAMA N 196/1, Heppe, vol. V, 127.
18 Rudolf Häpke, *Die deutsche Verwaltung in Litauen 1915 bis 1918. Der Verwaltungschef Litauen. Abwickelungsbehörde Berlin.* (Berlin: Reichsdruckerei, 1921), 32–33. This is the occupation regime's official closing report; BA N 1031/2, Gayl, 161.
19 Ibid., 49, 254.
20 BAMA N 196/1, Heppe, vol. V, 91.
21 *Das Land*, 93.
22 BAMA PHD 8/20, "Ziffer 259. Verwaltungsordnung für das Etappengebiet im Befehlsbereich des Oberbefehlshabers Ost (Ob. Ost)," *BUV*, 34 (June 26, 1916): §4.1, p. 270.
23 Ibid., §§8.2 and 8.4, p. 270.
24 Häpke, *Verwaltung*, 32.
25 Zweig, *Grischa*, 333.

26 Klemperer, *Curriculum*, 466.
27 "Denkschrift zur gegenwärtigen Lage Litauens," in *Der Werdegang des Litauischen Staates von 1915 bis zur Bildung der provisorischen Regierung im November 1918. Dargestellt auf Grund amtlicher Dokumente*, ed. Petras Klimas (Berlin: Paß & Garleb GmbH, 1919), 38. Lithuanian natives complained that gendarmes ordered them to speak Polish: LMARS, F. 23–47, "Vokiečiai Lietuvoje," list of complaints, 2.
28 Klimas, *Atsiminimų*, 61.
29 (Hoover Institution Archives) Germany. Oberste Heeresleitung. Box 2, folder 5, untitled memorandum from Ober Ost (Wilna, May 5, 1916), 110.
30 Ludendorff, *Kriegserinnerungen*, 148.
31 *Das Land*, 93.
32 Ludendorff, *Kriegserinnerungen*, 148, 152.
33 BAMA N 196/1, Heppe, vol. V, 82; Zemke, *Schulwesen*, 7–8.
34 BA N 1031/2, Gayl.
35 Ludendorff, *Kriegserinnerungen*, 155, 146, 156.
36 Ibid., 149; BAMA N 196/1, Heppe, vol. V, 120.
37 BAMA N 98/1, Gossler, 59.
38 Ludendorff, *Kriegserinnerungen*, 149.
39 BAMA N 196/1, Heppe, vol. V, 88.
40 Brockhusen, *Menschenleben*, 131.
41 BAMA N 196/1, Heppe, vol. V, 80.
42 Šilietis, *Okupacija*, 56.
43 "Denkschrift," in *Werdegang*, ed. Klimas, 36; Šilietis, *Okupacija*, 34–38; Gintneris, *Lietuva*, 313. On harassment, Tadas Daugirdas, *Kaunas vokiečių okupacijoje* (Kaunas: Spindulio B-vės spaustuvė, 1937), 42, 55.
44 BAMA N 196/1, Heppe, vol. V, 95.
45 Häpke, *Verwaltung*, 83. On conflicts with railroad units: LCVIA F. 641, ap. 1, no. 53, "Verwaltungsberichte Rossienie," *Verwaltungsbericht 30. Jan. 1916*; LCVIA F. 641, ap. 1, no. 53, "Verwaltungsberichte Rossienie," *Verwaltungsbericht 29. März. 1916*, 5.
46 BA N 1031/2, Gayl, 188.
47 *Das Land*, 243.
48 BAMA N 98/1, Gossler, 68.
49 Zweig, *Grischa*, 97.
50 BAMA N 196/1, Heppe, vol. V, 59.
51 Henry Cord Meyer, *Mitteleuropa in German Thought and Action, 1815–1945* (The Hague: Martinus Nijhoff, 1955), 116–36; Gordon A. Craig, *Germany, 1866–1945* (Oxford and New York: Oxford University Press, 1978), 357.
52 BAMA N 196/1, Heppe, vol. V, 104; *Das Land*, 95–96.
53 *Das Land*, 98; Ludendorff, *Kriegserinnerungen*, 157.
54 Ludendorff, *Kriegserinnerungen*, 157; *Das Land*, 100–1.
55 BAMA PHD 8/20, "Ziffer 29. Hundesteuerordnung für die dem Oberbefehlshaber Ost unterstellten Gebiete," *BUV* 4 (December 27, 1915): 64–65; Ludendorff, *Kriegserinnerungen*, 157.
56 Ludendorff, *Kriegserinnerungen*, 157–58; *Das Land*, 95.
57 LCVIA F. 641, ap. 1, b. 52, *Verwaltungsbericht für IV Vierteljahr 1916. Birsche*,

29. *Dezember 1916.*, 12.

58 BA N 1031/2, Gayl, 145.

59 Klimas, *Atsiminimų*, 45; Gintneris, *Lietuva*, 364; Daugirdas, *Kaunas*, 64; Mitau. *Bilder aus deutschen Soldatenheimen. Ausschuß für Soldaten- und Eisenbahnerheime an der Ost- und Südfront* (Berlin: Furche Verlag, 1917), 45.

60 Klimas, *Atsiminimų*, 50, 69, 156, 158.

61 Ibid., 43.

62 BAMA PHD 8/20, "Ziffer 259. Verwaltungsordnung für das Etappengebiet," *BUV* 34 (June 26, 1916): §6.2, p. 270.

63 "Denkschrift," in *Werdegang*, ed. Klimas, 36.

64 Daugirdas, *Kaunas*, 48.

65 Klimas, *Atsiminimų*, 66.

66 LCVIA F. 641, ap.1, b. 52, *Verwaltungsbericht für März 1916. Kreisamt Birsche*, 28.

67 Šilietis, *Okupacija*, 74.

68 Klimas, *Atsiminimų*, 45; *Das Land*, 238.

69 LMARS, F. 23–47, 6.

70 Gabrielė Petkevičaitė-Bite, *Karo meto dienoraštis* (Vilnius: Vaga, 1966), 667.

71 Šilietis, *Okupacija*, 76; Gintneris, *Lietuva*, 305, 315–16; Daugirdas, *Kaunas*, 51.

72 "Denkschrift," in *Werdegang*, ed. Klimas, 35.

73 LCVIA F. 641, ap.1, b. 52, *Verwaltungsbericht für Februar 1916. Kreisamt Birsche*, 13.

74 Ludendorff, *Kriegserinnerungen*, 153.

75 Klimas, *Atsiminimų*, 53.

76 "Denkschrift, die wichtigsten Mißstände," in *Werdegang*, ed. Klimas, 72–73.

77 Klimas, *Atsiminimų*, 53.

78 Ibid., 106.

79 LCVIA F. 641, ap. 1, b. 52, *Verwaltungsbericht des Militärkreisamts Birsche für das I. Vierteljahr 1917.*

80 Ludendorff, *Kriegserinnerungen*, 155.

81 Klimas, *Atsiminimų*, 46, 59.

82 Cohen, *Vilna*, 364.

83 *Das Land*, 243; Marwitz, *Stirb*, 137; BA N 1031/2, Gayl, 146.

84 Klimas, *Atsiminimų*, 53; LCVIA F. 641, ap. 1, b. 53, "Verwaltungsberichte Rossienie," *Verwaltungsbericht. 29. April 1916*, 10.

85 Ludendorff, *Kriegserinnerungen*, 152.

86 BAMA N 196/1, Heppe, vol. V, 97.

87 *Das Land*, 195–96.

88 BAMA PHD 8/23, "Die Ob. Ost-Obsterzeugnisse in Berlin," *KB* 4 (November 1, 1916).

89 Klemperer, *Curriculum*, 466.

90 BAMA N 98/3, Gossler.

91 *Das Land*, 189; 190; 228; 247, 201; 190; 228.

92 Ibid., 190; 228; 232.

93 Ibid., 210.

94 Ibid., 211, 219; 223.

95 Strazhas, *Ostpolitik*, 246–53.

96 BAMA N 98/3, Gossler, 28.

97 *Das Land*, 251, 224.

98 Werner Butz, "Die kriegswirtschaftliche Nutzung des besetzten Ostraums im Weltkrieg, 1914–1918," *Wissen und Wehr* 23 (1942): 227.

99 Ludendorff, *Kriegserinnerungen*, 155.

100 *Bialowies in deutscher Verwaltung. Herausgegeben von der Militärforstverwaltung Bialowies* (Berlin: Verlagsbuchhandlung Paul Parey, 1919); Ludendorff, *Kriegserinnerungen*, 152, 156.

101 BA N 1031/2, Gayl, 264; BAMA N 196/1, Heppe, 59–63. Zweig's novel depicts such a POW labor camp, Forest Camp Nawarischky.

102 BA N 1031/2, Gayl, 147; Ludendorff, *Kriegserinnerungen*, 155.

103 Valentinas Gustainis, "Nepriklausoma Lietuva: kaimiečių ir jaunimo valstybė," *Proskyna* 3. 6 (1990): 172.

104 Čepėnas, *Naujųjų*, II, 91–92; M. Urbšiene, *Vokiečių okupacijos ūkis Lietuvoje* (Kaunas: Spindulio B-vės spaustuvė, 1939).

105 BA N 1031/2, Gayl, 239.

106 LCVIA F. 641, ap. 1, b. 52, *Verwaltungsbericht für III. Vierteljahr 1916. Kreisamt Birsche*, 5; Klimas, *Atsiminimų*, 106.

107 BAMA PHD 8/20, "Ziffer 259. Verwaltungsordnung für das Etappengebiet," *BUV* 34 (June 26, 1916): §88, pp. 288–89.

108 Ibid., §8.4, p. 270; Linde, *Deutsche Politik*, 62–65; Strazhas, *Ostpolitik*, 38–42; Čepėnas, *Naujųjų*, II, 95–99.

109 Gintneris, *Lietuva*, 233–41; BAMA N 196/1, Heppe, vol. V, 61. One report noted the problem of resistance to being drafted for labor in building roads: LCVIA F. 641, ap. 1, b. 52, *Verwaltungsbericht für Februar 1916. Kreisamt Birsche*, 34; another indicated that "idle people" were drafted into two worker units, and mentioned a unit of "unemployed" sent from Kowno (who were quite useless at work, unsuited to labor), while army farms were worked by people from surrounding villages: LCVIA F. 641, ap. 1, b. 52, *Verwaltungsbericht für III. Vierteljahr 1916. Kreisamt Birsche*, 5; on *Arbeiterkolonnen*, including those moved in from Kowno: LCVIA F. 641, ap. 1, b. 52, *Verwaltungsbericht für IV. Vierteljahr 1916. Birsche, 29. Dezember 1916*, 166. Escaped *Zivilarbeiter* were also arrested by police when encountered: LCVIA F. 641, ap. 1, b. 52, *Verwaltungsbericht des Militärkreisamts Birsche für das II. Vierteljahr 1917*; LCVIA F. 641, ap. 1, b. 53, "Verwaltungsberichte Rossienie," *Verwaltungsbericht für die Zeit vom 1ten Oktober bis 31ten Dezember 1916*. German accounts during the Second World War also mentioned "forced drafting" for labor, especially work on roads, in the occupied territories: Butz, "Die kriegswirtschaftliche," 228.

110 BA 238/8, Morsbach. Bürgermeister von Schaulen. Zu Abteilung IV. Schaulen, September 27, 1916.

111 GSTA PK, I. HA. Rep. 84a, nr. 6210, *V. Verwaltungsbericht der Deutschen Verwaltung Kurland. Oktober 1916*, 36. Similar effects on morale: GSTA PK, I. HA. Rep. 84a, nr. 6210, *Verwaltungsbericht der Deutschen Verwaltung Wilna-Suwalki, 3 Vierteljahr 1916*, 53; GSTA PK, I. HA. Rep. 84a, nr. 6210, *Vierter Verwaltungsbericht der Deutschen Verwaltung Bialystok Juli–September 1916*, 20.

112 "Denkschrift . . . Mißstände," in *Werdegang*, ed. Klimas, 74.
113 LCVIA F. 641, ap. 1, b. 53, "Verwaltungsberichte Rossienie," *Verwaltungsbericht für die Zeit vom 1. April bis 30. Sept. 1917*, 28.
114 "Der Scheunenbrand von Schirwinty – eine Tartarennachricht," *KB* 57 (October 11, 1917).
115 "Denkschrift . . . Mißstände," in *Werdegang*, ed. Klimas, 75.
116 Šilietis, *Okupacija*, 125.
117 LMARS, F. 23–47, "Vokiečiai Lietuvoje," list of complaints, 4.
118 LCVIA F. 641, ap. 1, b. 52, *Verwaltungsbericht des Militärkreisamts Birsche für das II. Vierteljahr 1917*, 9. The same report also noted that prostitutes, whose healing cost the circuit much, were sent to female worker columns.
119 Häpke, *Verwaltung*, 86–87; Linde, *Politik*, 64; Ulrich Herbert, *A History of Foreign Labor in Germany, 1880–1980: Seasonal Workers / Forced Workers / Guest Workers*, trans. William Templer (Ann Arbor: University of Michigan Press, 1990), 87–119; Lothar Elsner, "Ausländerbeschäftigung und Zwangsarbeitspolitik in Deutschland während des Ersten Weltkrieges," in *Auswanderer – Wanderarbeiter – Gastarbeiter. Bevölkerung, Arbeitsmarkt und Wanderung in Deutschland seit der Mitte des 19. Jahrhunderts*, ed. Klaus J. Bade (Ostfildern: Scripta Mercaturae Verlag, 1984), 527–57; Friedrich Zunkel, "Die ausländischen Arbeiter in der deutschen Kriegswirtschaftspolitik des 1. Weltkrieges," in *Entstehung und Wandel der modernen Gesellschaft*, ed. Gerhard Ritter (Berlin: n.p., 1970), 280–311.
120 Urbšiene, *Ūkis*, 125.
121 Häpke, *Verwaltung*, 81.
122 Ibid., 106–107, 109; BAMA N 196/1, Heppe, vol. V, 79.
123 Ludendorff, *Kriegserinnerungen*, 154.
124 BAMA PHD 8/20, "Ziffer 259. Verwaltungsordnung für das Etappengebiet," *BUV* 34 (June 26, 1916): §1, p. 269.
125 Ludendorff, *Kriegserinnerungen*, 158.
126 Ibid.
127 Häpke, *Verwaltung*, 67–68.
128 BAMA N 196/1, Heppe, vol. V, 104.
129 Ibid., 59.
130 LMARS, F. 9, BF-3117, "Ob. Ost ir jo štabo įvairūs įsakymai," "Zentralpolizeistelle des Oberbefehlshabers Ost," 34.
131 Čepėnas, *Naujųjų*, 114.
132 Häpke, *Verwaltung*, 67.
133 Zweig, *Grischa*, 128, 357.
134 BAMA PHD 8/20, "Ziffer 102. Verordnung betreffend Kuchenbackverbot," *BUV* 14 (March 11, 1916): 144–45; (Hoover Archive) World War I Subject Collection, box no. 19, folder "Germany. Proclamations. Lithuania," "Bekanntmachung," Kowno, dated February 24, 1916; BA 238/8, Morsbach. *Tätigkeitsbericht des Bürgermeisteramtes Schaulen von Mitte August bis 30. Sept. 1916.*
135 Klimas, *Atsiminimų*, 68.
136 *Das Land*, 130.
137 Klimas, *Atsiminimų*, 66.

138 BA N 1031/2, Gayl, 160.
139 Ludendorff, *Kriegserinnerungen*, 151.
140 Klimas, *Atsiminimų*, 73, 91, 109.
141 LCVIA F. 641, ap. 1, b. 52, *Verwaltungsbericht des Militärkreisamts Birsche für das I. Vierteljahr 1917.*; Klimas, *Atsiminimų*, 107; Gintneris, *Lietuva*, 344–52; Strazhas, *Ostpolitik*, 208–11.
142 BAMA N 196/1, Heppe, vol. V, 62–63.
143 LCVIA F. 641, ap. 1, b. 53, "Verwaltungsberichte Rossienie," *Verwaltungsbericht 29. August 1916*; GSTA PK, I. HA. Rep. 84a, nr. 6210, *V. Verwaltungsbericht der Deutschen Verwaltung Kurland. Oktober 1916*, 36; Klimas, *Atsiminimų*, 156; Gintneris, *Lietuva*, 349.
144 LCVIA F. 641, ap. 1, no. 52, *Verwaltungsbericht für April 1916. Kreisamt Birsche*, 21; LCVIA F. 641, ap. 1, b. 52, *Verwaltungsbericht für III. Vierteljahr 1916. Kreisamt Birsche*; LCVIA F. 641, ap. 1, b. 52, *Verwaltungsbericht für IV. Vierteljahr 1916. Kreisamt Birsche*; LCVIA F. 641, ap. 1, no. 53, "Verwaltungsberichte Rossienie," *Verwaltungsbericht 29. August 1916*, 3–4.
145 "Denkschrift ... Mißstände," in *Werdegang*, ed. Klimas, 79; LCVIA F. 641, ap. 1, b. 52, *Verwaltungsbericht für III. Vierteljahr 1916. Kreisamt Birsche*, 7.
146 BAMA N 196/1, Heppe, vol. V, 76. On arrests of civilians: LCVIA F. 641, ap. 1, b. 53, "Verwaltungsberichte Rossienie," *Bericht über die militärischen Massnahmen in den Kreisen Rossienie und Georgenburg vom 19/XI – 19.XII.16.*
147 Klimas, *Atsiminimų*, 65.
148 Gintneris, *Lietuva*, 346.
149 Klimas, *Atsiminimų*, 90; Gintneris, *Lietuva*, 365.
150 *Das Land*, 119.
151 Ibid.
152 Ludendorff, *Kriegserinnerungen*, 152. Regarding impact on Jewish communities, see Pam Maclean, "Control and Cleanliness: German-Jewish Relations in Occupied Eastern Europe During the First World War," *War & Society* 6. 2 (September 1988): 47–69.
153 *Das Land*, 119–20.
154 LMARS, F. 9, BF–3117, "Ob. Ost ir jo štabo įvairūs įsakymai": "Neueinteilung" order (dated April 1, 1918), signed by Freiherr von Gayl. The first subsection was charged, among other things, with "Treatment of prostitutes and their welfare."
155 In Rossienie, a Jewish ritual bath was to be commandeered for this purpose: LCVIA F. 641, ap. 1, b. 53, "Verwaltungsberichte Rossienie," *Verwaltungsbericht für die Zeit vom 1ten Oktober bis 31ten Dezember 1916*; LCVIA F. 641, ap. 1, b. 53, "Verwaltungsberichte Rossienie," *Verwaltungsbericht für die Zeit vom 1 Januar bis 31ten März 1917.*
156 LMARS, F. 23–15.
157 Documentary evidence surviving from the administration itself does not mention this, but other sources do: Magnus Hirschfeld, *Sittengeschichte des Ersten Weltkrieges*, rev. 2nd edn (Hanau: Schustek, 1966), 231–54; (Hoover Archives) World War I Subject Collection, box no. 19, "Germany. Proclamations. Lithuania." On German military brothels in general: Asprey, *German High Command*, 181.

158 Klimas, *Atsiminimų*, 45, 54.
159 Ibid., 72; LCVIA F. 641, ap. 1, b. 52, *Verwaltungsbericht für Februar 1916*. *Kreisamt Birsche*, 10–11; LCVIA F. 641, ap. 1, b. 53, "Verwaltungsberichte Rossienie," *Verwaltungsbefehl* [sic] *28. Feb. 1916*, 2, 7; LCVIA F. 641, ap. 1, b. 53, "Verwaltungsberichte Rossienie," *Verwaltungsbericht 29. März. 1916*, 3.
160 LCVIA F. 641, ap. 1, b. 52, *Verwaltungsbericht für Februar 1916*. *Kreisamt Birsche*, 10–11.
161 *Das Land*, 126.
162 Klimas, *Atsiminimų*, 45.
163 Šilietis, *Okupacija*, 121.
164 Klimas, *Atsiminimų*, 137.
165 Ludendorff, *Kriegserinnerungen*, 160.

3   The movement policy

The first, most daunting challenge confronting German rule in the East was a matter of sheer scale: the extent of the captured spaces. When the great advances of 1915 ended by fall, the Eastern Front stabilized, and Germans found themselves in possession of 160,000 square kilometers (62,500 square miles) of new lands, which seemed to be "in wild disorder."[1] The army would have to impose its own control. From this strategic imperative, the administration leapt to a vastly more comprehensive vision and ambition, summed up under the name of "*Verkehrspolitik*" – the "movement policy," which would pave the way for permanent possession of these new lands. *Verkehrspolitik* was a startling, modern vision of controlling the land totally, by commanding all movement in it and through it. Ober Ost, just to the east of Germany, was closed off, reserved for the military and its purposes. Its land was then divided up, creating a grid of control in which military authorities could direct every movement: of troops, requisitioned products, raw materials, all resources including manpower. Eventually, authorities sought to mobilize not only native manpower, but also the native ethnicities as collective units, aiming to define their place in the larger cultural plan for these territories, through a program of cultural work. What *Verkehrspolitik* accomplished on the ground, a parallel cultural program tried to duplicate within people's heads, changing their identities. As the military set out to control all the space and movement under its administration, military authorities were possessed by a vision of a total control and channeling of energies, direction and supervision. With these energies harnessed, the new lords would make over the land in their own image, moving towards final possession through colonization.

The very term *Verkehrspolitik* is itself of great significance. "*Verkehr*" is difficult to pin down in English, because it carries an entire evocative complex of meanings: some broad, others specific. It means traffic, movement, communications and relations, or (most broadly) any kind of interaction. The term's very expansiveness is crucial, because ambitions attached to *Verkehrspolitik* would move from the narrow, necessary, and specific, to the all-encompassing, impractical, and impossible. The German term *"-politik"* works in contradictory ways. Translated as either "policy" or "politics of," it suggests that the object in question is within the realm of political negotiation, but then signifies that the matter is under state supervision, after all. The expression itself was not absolutely new, dating at least to the 1880s (i.e. *Realpolitik*, *Aussenpolitik*, *Weltpolitik*). Yet with the First World War, the term underwent a slight change in meaning, for earlier formulations had denoted *kinds* of policies, while the new usage defined concrete *objects* of policy. An explosion of terms coupled with *"-politik"* began, a linguistic trend enduring today in coinages such as "settlement politics," "East politics," "population politics," "school politics," "environmental politics." Above all, the new term suggested state control, planning, and arbitration. Thus it is no accident that the term surfaced in Ober Ost, as possibilities for control were greatest over subject populations in occupied territories, but new practices could then be imported back home, to be used there. *Verkehrspolitik* marks an expanding psychological horizon of political possibilities, possibilities for control. It is also telling to note that the term was first used most commonly as an adjective (*verkehrspolitische*), underlining the way in which practices, once established, then grew into articulated programs.[2]

To begin with, the military vision of *Verkehrspolitik* grew out of the concrete necessity of ordering the area. Lines of communication and supply to the front had to be secured. Next, the army turned to economic exploitation of the territory, for the harvest stood in the fields ready to be taken in, with no time to waste. Because transport was so crucial to military operation, here Germans noted the most vivid devastation of Russian "scorched-earth policy." Burned-out hulks of railroad stations and store sheds, dynamited water towers and bridges, toppled railroad cars and locomotives were "the outward signs that are well known by each participant in the fighting on the Eastern Front." A huge effort lay ahead for construction troops, and especially for railroad troops, so that "trade and movement [*Verkehr*] could eventually be steered into normal courses."[3] Soon, officials declared that reconstruction alone would not suffice. By their standards, the transportation net had been shockingly primitive even before its willful devastation. Compared to German railroad maps, Russia's rail net looked absurdly small for such expanses. The wretched roads on which columns of troops and supply moved forward left profound first impressions. With rain, roads turned into dangerous seas of mud, "a wild broth, in which falling horses would drown."[4] They would have to be brought up to German standards. All through the transport system, "it was a matter not only of rebuilding that which was destroyed, but also of creating that which was new."[5] After securing lines of communication and movement, the army faced other pressing concerns. The next imperative was to control potential espionage and banditry. In this mess of foreign peoples, authorities suspected everyone, and precautionary measures were extensive and extreme. "Ordered circumstances," as the mantra went, had to be maintained. Then authorities moved toward a "positive" goal of intensifying the territory's economic exploitation. Requisitioned goods and crops had to flow back to Germany and to supply troops on the Eastern Front. Manpower resources likewise had to be directed. These were the practical goals of the movement policy, but *Verkehrspolitik* then grew into a comprehensive ambition, with a new ordering of the territory as its aim. It would be an order very different from the one before the war and "rested on completely different points of view than the anti-movement [*verkehrsfeindliche*] fundamentals of Russian legal and administrative practice."[6] The ultimate implicit goal of *Verkehrspolitik* was permanent possession of the land. Although the future was still unclear, some sort of colonization was hoped for. Even as the administration kept the precise forms of its final goals flexible, it went about laying down the groundwork for keeping the area.

The Supreme Commander in the East entrusted the program to a special section of his staff, the *Verkehrspolitik* Section.[7] Until the fall of 1917, it worked alongside other administrative sections. As work progressed, the new Supreme Commander in the East, Prince Leopold of Bavaria (replacing Hindenburg here upon his promotion), united the *Verkehrspolitik* section with his staff's political section in October 1917, as an integral head inspectorate.[8] *Verkehrspolitik* section officers retained the same competencies as before, but now their task had been moved to a central position in the Supreme Commander in the East's staff. The *Verkehrspolitik* section's area of operations also expanded, as ordered on August 25, 1917.[9]

The section's duty was the comprehensive ordering of the area and its populations. Officially, it was to bring into accord "the total movement in the area behind the front and the area of operations, both with the changing military situation and requirements following from it with regard to counterespionage, unburdening of the rail system, etc., as well as, on the other hand, with the necessary economic development of the land." Many competing interests, economic, political, and financial, were to be taken into consideration in forming policies, but the overriding interest in any instance was always the army's demand for security and "ordered circumstances":

A consequence of this was the necessity of a stricter control of the increasing movement, where, while sparing the economic interests of the occupied land as much as possible, the military essentials were given their proper weight. The activity of the *Verkehrspolitik* Section, therefore, had to be made independent and had to be brought into the closest association with the difficult political and economic questions of the territory, as large as it was diverse.[10]

The vast project of totally reordering the land was too comprehensive an ambition to be limited to the workings of the *Verkehrspolitik* section alone. In fact, the program's principle carried over into all areas of administration. Measures for *Verkehrspolitik* were built into many orders, edicts, directives, and proclamations, promulgated by officials of all administrative realms and enforced by the different varieties of police. The *Verkehrspolitik* section itself worked closely with the administration's intelligence officer and the Central Police Office in the East, which was concerned most with counterespionage, but cooperated with "political policing" and participated in "the control of *Verkehr*."[11] Help from the administration as a whole was needed to realize the ambition and thus the motivating ideas of *Verkehrspolitik* permeated Ober Ost's administrative practices.

The first step in a new ordering of the land would be to control the area by demarcating it and assessing its resources and possibilities. The land had to be divided, mapped, and surveyed in depth. The administration's first measure was to close off the territory. To the East the front served as a barrier, while in the West, the newly occupied territory was severed from Germany, as an area of military operations. The administration emphasized the importance of closing off the East for the benefit of the homeland. The East was presented as dirty, disease-ridden, chaotic, swarming with spies, bandits, revolutionaries, and other shady characters. Isolating it would ensure that none of these influences crept into Germany. Authorities maintained strict control at the East Prussian border. To repel infectious diseases, on October 17, 1915 the field medical chief ordered that all railroad crossings on the eastern borders were to be sealed off so no soldiers crossed over without delousing. Larger delousing stations were established for troop trains, while rail lines also had movable delousing stations fitted into train cars. Border guards examined freight and requisitioned goods, especially livestock, for traces of sickness or pestilence. All trains coming from the east or southeast "had to be thoroughly disinfected, if possible with materials which at the same time deloused."[12] Human travelers had to show "delousing-certificates" before being allowed to cross over to the West. The imperative was the closing-off of the East. At the same time as it was being exploited, the East was also feared.

After the territory was closed off, it was cut up, divided and subdivided again, to create a grid of intensive control. It took quite some time to achieve the uniformity of administrative divisions which Ludendorff and his staff envisioned. The supreme commander finally passed an order defining the structure on June 7, 1916.[13] All through the war, borders were shifted, units divided up or united, while administrative chaos reigned. Moreover, Ober Ost was a growing war state, expanding east in fits and starts with new conquests.

Officials divided the territory according to the ordered pattern, carving it up into administrations, these into administrative regions, and finally subdividing these into smaller districts. Units were separated from each other administratively and physically, the better to control each smaller division, their internal borders guarded by police and stationed troops. Natives were not allowed to move over the official boundaries. As local captains observed in their reports, the object was a constantly "intensifying administration" and exploitation to meet the needs of military authorities, who would control the movements of natives, direct the flow of goods, requisition material, all in a rational organization and division of labor.[14] The military's imposition of a grid of control created enormous hardship for native populations, for borders were often drawn arbitrarily, ignoring actual givens of the land, patterns of settlement, social organization, and centuries-old trading ties. Natives sometimes could not cross boundaries to visit neighbors, relatives, even parish churches. Traveling Jewish merchants lost their livelihood entirely.[15] Huge fines, crippling penalties, and confiscations were imposed by military courts or district captains for infractions of these borders.[16] Resentful native intuition of what was happening was keen; according to popular sources, ordinary people imagined *Verkehrspolitik* as a spider's web, directing their movements and requisitioned property inexorably to central points of control and collection.[17] In a typical peasant response, natives drew back into themselves and their households, frustrating German expectations of revitalized economic activity.

As the area was divided, military authorities undertook intense mapping. This cartography was the basis for rational, planned exploitation of Ober Ost's territory and eventual German settlement. Considerable mapping had been done before the war, under the aegis of military geography, since a special emphasis on this field had been a tradition of the German general staff.[18] Now more precise cartography ensued, as the extensive spaces were subjected to an astonishing series of wartime geographic, geological, and agricultural surveys.[19] The authorities brought in Professor Kaunhowen from the Regional Geological Institution in Berlin to conduct thorough investigations. Economic officers working alongside district authorities submitted reports on the conditions they found in the locales. Most of all, they were interested in the state of the soil. District Janischki's exemplary economic officer sent in report after report on the nature of the ground and the possibilities it held.[20] Since military administrators intended to become "masters of all that they surveyed," they planned, quite logically, to survey everything. Economic officers built up card indexes of land ownership, which would be useful for intensifying economic exploitation, as well as for eventual confiscation and redistribution of land.

Native populations also became objects for statistical consideration. Military Administration Lithuania carried out a "people and livestock count" (*Volks- und Viehzählung*) – the description speaks volumes about the occupiers' perspective.[21] Set at first for January 15, 1916, in the confused conditions it had to be postponed until June 1, 1916. Aggregate results were presented on July 8, 1916, but it was soon clear that they were impressionistic, with suspect numbers.[22] A new census would have to be carried out, confirming officials' disgust with these lands, where the simplest tasks could not be done right. Results of earlier ethnic surveys, however, were published in a much-publicized public relations product of Ober Ost, the "Map of the Division of Peoples."[23] It showed a wild patchwork of shadings – a *"Raum,"* or space, belonging neither to Poland nor Russia proper, which was a jumble of ethnicities and "uncommonly tangled questions" of identity. The map was worth a thousand words, its burden clear to anyone who saw it: such an ethnic mess, with no majority in a concentrated area of settlement, could not be trusted to rule itself. And who better to rule the area than a *Volk* from outside, it argued, a disinterested *Volk* with a sufficiently high level of *Kultur* to produce such a map in the first place. The preface concluded, "Political problems arise of themselves from the ethnographic situation. It is left to readers to draw conclusions. Here, too, the decision stands at the tip of the sword."[24] The "Map of the Division of Peoples" was a quintessential product of German Work.

Verkehrspolitik's ultimate end was permanent possession of these lands through some form of settlement. The army set about preparing for all happy eventualities. Von Gayl, later head of the political section, had first attracted Ludendorff's attention with a memorandum about ethnic German settlement in the East. Once in the East, von Gayl was ordered to give lectures, and was dispatched to look for fabled lost ethnic German settlements in the occupied territories (with a view to resettling them in East Prussia), with disappointing results.[25] His overview of the new lands, however, revealed other possibilities. For his part, Ludendorff spent his first half year in the territories dreaming up plans and then moved to take action. On April 27, 1916, he ordered administration chiefs to prepare information on prospects for settlement in their areas by the fall. Specifically, reports had to summarize population statistics and religious affiliations of natives, exact assessments of land quality and who owned it, and estimates of land available for settlement.[26]

Ludendorff then looked back in the Reich for support for these plans, applauded by annexationists in the war aims debate who sought eastern agricultural lands to "balance" gains of industrial areas in Belgium and northern France. Among them, one of the most active and clamorous was Government President of Frankfurt on the Oder, Friedrich von Schwerin, active in formulating policies to weaken Polish land ownership in Prussia before the war and head of the "Society for the Encouragement of Internal Colonization." Von Gayl, who had done similar work, admiringly called him "the father of modern settlement." Schwerin pestered the chancellor's office with memoranda demanding new eastern colonial lands, resuming an imperial mission, adding that these lands should be emptied of people through expulsions, as Pan-Germans also recommended.[27] In November 1916, Schwerin traveled in the area, aided by Ober Ost, gathering information on settlement conditions.[28] Shortly thereafter, Schwerin founded, with the approval of the High Command, the "New Land" company in Berlin, which aimed to support German settlement in the East and Alsace-Lorraine (later in the war, this company founded a sister-branch, the Kurland settlement society). Noted land reformer Adolf Damaschke also agitated for German eastern settlement. In principle, plans for settlement found support in the Reich government. Ober Ost's position was presented in a memorandum prepared by Ludendorff's political assistant, von Gayl, and approved by the High Command. Its essential point was that depopulated areas of the territory would be filled in with a "human wall" of new German settlers, securing it for all time.[29] The Foreign Ministry welcomed the idea. A first meeting took place on February 13, 1917. It was followed by a March 31, 1917 meeting in Berlin hosted by the Foreign Ministry, with representatives of the Interior Ministry, War Ministry, and General Staff. Now discussion already concerned only the specific details of arrangements to be made. Von Gayl drew out a map for his report. This was a fateful move, opening the question of shifting the ethnic color patches of peoples represented on the map. Later in 1917, as the war entered a new stage with revolutionary upheavals in Russia, negotiations for a victorious peace in the East at Brest-Litovsk, and Germany girding for its last gamble on the Western Front, plans for settlement had to be adjusted to fit new realities, but a decisive mental threshold had been crossed and moving of ethnic populations became a thinkable option. Finally, by fall 1917 officials gathered information into a larger plan for exploitation of these territories as German colonial land.[30] The plan projected profits expected over the coming decades. Plans for settlement were begun; actual settlement would have to wait.[31] This was the result of another conflict of aims in the military administration, since ambitions for total control of the area would not allow, in the short term, for the arrival of German settlers. A land rush would open the area to increasing control from the Reich, exactly what military authorities were determined to avoid. Authorities deferred requests for information on estates for sale made by military men in Germany, yet waiting lists were begun.[32] Ober Ost's planners' ambitions for total control paralyzed them when they sought to move toward realizing their mutually contradictory aims. Meanwhile, however, within the closed territory all kinds of experiments in social organization and rationalization of labor could take place in this "New Land," with forced labor and experimental subjects readily to hand. Military agronomist Kurt von Rümker performed agricultural experiments in breeding plant hybrids.[33] Ludendorff envisioned a "human wall" of pure Germans in the East, bracketing other unreliable, weaker, and less cultured ethnicities. Settlers could not be bourgeois Germans, but rather soldiers turned into farmers on the model of medieval "fighting farmers" (*Wehrbauer*), holding the land with "sword and plow." The area would be a military preserve, launching ground for the next decisive war expected by Hindenburg, a vast parade ground, a land consecrated to war.[34]

After dividing the territory and defining a grid of control in late 1915, officials needed to define ways in which movement *could* take place, stipulating legitimate channels of ordered transportation and communication. They created corridors of movement: rail lines, roads, waterways, post and telegraph connections. Military authorities presented this as an archetypal example of organizing German Work and were quick to point out (no matter that it was an overstatement) that they created these networks almost from nothing, considering how primitive conditions had been upon their invasion, establishing the victors' claim to this land.

The rail system's condition presented serious problems for the front and for building of fortified positions, bunkers, and shelters. Retreating Russians destroyed much of the network, blowing up bridges over the Njemen and other larger rivers, burning down stations and watering systems. The telegraph system was removed wholesale. Rails were torn up on some lines, ties removed. The Military Railroad Authority, engineering and construction troops, and telegraph-troops (Norbert Elias, later a famed sociologist, was among these communication units) began reconstruction.[35] Converting the railroad from Russian gauge to German standards was an effort of gigantic proportions, and rich in symbolic significance for the new owners, seeming to put a seal of possession on their new realm. Because of its crucial role, the railroad directorate under Field Railroad Chief in the East Colonel Kersten, became a virtual state within a state in Ober Ost.[36] Later, its exalted position created problems as it competed for manpower with the administration. Yet progress against enormous odds was swift. Kowno's crucial railroad bridge was usable by late September 1915 a month after the fortified city was taken, while after Christmas 1915, regular service was restored.

Next the military set about expanding the present system of movement. The railroad directorate built a great railroad works in Libau on the coast. Merely maintaining the constructed system demanded effort: "provisional water containers froze up in winter, and all sorts of surmountable and insurmountable barriers had to be overcome."[37] In the first winter of 1915, crisis struck the rebuilt bridges, as ice floes came over the Windau and Njemen rivers. The situation was tense at the Njemen bridge in Kowno, at the time the only connection to Germany by rail, but the new work held up against nature's battering, a satisfying omen for uniformed onlookers. Considering further innovations, German technical experts were crushingly dismissive of the earlier system. Russia had not used the ports of Windau and Libau at all, declared Ludendorff. The land deserved to be taken from them by someone who would really use it. Other Njemen bridges were finished, while great new railroad lines between Tauroggen-Radwilischki and Schaulen-Mitau were completed in May and August 1916. Ludendorff announced that these "rail lines opened the land in a cultural sense. The land is indebted to us for this."[38] This net of railroad lines connected to smaller lines at the front, supplying troops. Built for military utility, these stretches could also play a role in the land's future development. Improvements were already yielding benefits, while promising greater things for the future.

Good roads were essential for troop movement. In fall and spring, the situation was hopeless, as constant rain and melting snow flooded every road, turning it into "an impassable morass": "Some army horses, having survived enemy fire unscathed, fell victim to the treacheries of the Eastern theater of war and drowned in the quagmire or collapsed through exhaustion."[39] In summer, deep sand created difficulties. Wagon wheels had to grind their way through, making achingly slow progress. The invaders found that the best time for travel was in winter, when skis moved over the land lightly, freely, and made of themselves a track, which would, however, eventually disappear. All too easily, it seemed to them, the land reverted to its original untamed nature. If road quality was bad, the sparseness of layout made Germans shake their heads. Damning verdicts on the territory's abysmal level of *Kultur* and its former masters followed:

"No other example characterizes better the Russian road system in the occupied territories, or, more precisely, the system of roadlessness than this fact, which is simply incomprehensible to Western concepts of *Kultur.*" Such contrasts were all the more striking because of outrageous disparities of scale. Finally, just to seal the case, there were aesthetic quibbles:

What there is of highways is, even by our standards, almost uniformly good, except that here they lack tree growth as a frame, which in Germany somewhat beautifies even the most desolate highway. The straight line of many highways is characteristic, taking no account of arable land and slopes, nor of the proximity of larger localities. What there is otherwise of land roads, does not give joy to either man or animal.[40]

Everywhere, road systems demanded radical improvement, even where spared "scorched earth" treatment. Russians managed to blow up most important bridges, but surviving ones were poorly constructed. Officials outlined a program: "Thus the first task was the rebuilding of the work of destruction completed by the Russians, the second the improvement of roads everywhere, where a constant movement of troops and convoys took place." It seemed that construction troops sank entire forests of logs in the "bottomless roads of the East," to firm up the ground.[41] When military authorities surveyed their own work, the sheer numbers were staggering. In Military Administration Bialystok-Grodno alone, from the offensive's close in fall 1915 to the end of the year, they had built 434 bridges, some with icebreakers, including a great bridge over the Bug River. Great highways from Grodno to Lida, Kowno to Dünaburg, and Tauroggen to Mitau were improved into first-rate condition.[42] Troops, gangs of native forced laborers, and POWs worked at improving everywhere else.[43] But there were limits to the new building of highways, and maintenance alone required great efforts. Construction troops built snow fences, protecting the most important roads in winter. They laid out wide roads for safety through rougher parts, cutting away forests in great swathes to either side to prevent ambushes. But in spite of all the problems, the occupiers saw vivid successes, which they believed were "readily acknowledged by the population." Of course, it did natives little good, as their movements were severely restricted.[44]

Authorities wanted to expand river traffic as well, taking pressure off heavily used railroads. Here, too, they were loud in their amazement at the state of things in these backward territories, a "picture of complete neglect by the Russian government . . . swamped canals and unregulated rivers."[45] Waterways would be even harder to transform than the rail system. Authorities focused on the greatest rivers, the Memel (Njemen) and Bug. Plans were drawn up for improvements on the Aa and Windau, then connections were made for travel between these areas and Germany proper. The army had larger plans to turn the Memel into a great concourse all along Germany's far new eastern frontier. Such plans found enthusiastic echoes in Germany. Lübeck's chamber of commerce harassed Ober Ost with unsolicited suggestions (and handed out awards of the Hansa cross to curry favor).[46] But even on the plane of future plans, the military's own conceptions won out.

The military administration reestablished telegraph and telephone connections, crucial for army operations. Earlier installations were thoroughly destroyed, stations burnt down or standing empty, stripped of equipment, and no post officials remained.[47] German field services, however, were so efficient that their advance was little hampered. As the administration settled in, it constructed a telegraph, telephone, and post network under Field Postmaster Domizlaff.[48] In November 1915, it established the ponderously named German Post and Telegraph Administration for the Postal Territory of the Supreme Commander in the East, based in Kowno, working with the Reich's postal service.[49] Private communication, though restricted, was again up and working by January 15, 1916.

Soon telegraph wires stretching over huge spaces covered the territory, an image which seemed emblematic of German occupation. In Zweig's novel it was laden with significance, a recurring symbol of the military state. Army newspaper mastheads showed landscapes overdrawn with communications wires, visible testimony to *Verkehrspolitik*.[50]

The field post was important for troop morale, sustaining connections to Germany, as Ludendorff emphasized. By 1917, thirty-eight offices operated in the area designated "Postal Area Ober Ost," with its own stamps and network of offices dotting the country. Native use of the postal service was severely restricted, though allowing them limited use seemed necessary to keep control of traffic, for otherwise clandestine systems of communication were sure to develop. Post offices, then, became posts of control. An official account stated, "The comparatively small number of postal stations form points of collection for *Verkehr*, in which all inhabitants of the postal area may take part." Military district offices and office directors controlled traffic between post areas and the land at large. Monopolizing collection and distribution, they functioned as *Verkehrsvermittler*, "mediators of movement." The central concerns to be met were again military demands, "which above all required surveillance of *Verkehr*." Thus, orders limited length and content of letters, which could only be written in German to make censorship easier, even though few natives understood the language. German functioned, as authorities put it, as exclusive *Verkehrssprache*, "language of traffic."[51] To bring funds into the territory, military authorities allowed natives to send requests for money to relatives in America, principally Lithuanians and Jews.[52] They were only permitted to send preprinted cards, with messages to be checked off or circled, precautions against espionage. Thus, "use of the telephone could not until now be allowed to the population, for reasons that are obvious."[53] All communication was to be kept within channels defined by *Verkehrspolitik*. Any correspondence outside official mail was forbidden and harshly punished. The administration asserted its monopoly on *Verkehr* with jealous vigor.

After creating channels for movement, the administration regulated and policed what limited movement was allowed. The aim of limiting individuals' movement was often at odds with other aims of the military state, especially economic imperatives. Ludendorff admitted, "restrictions on personal movement, which we had to lay on the land with a view to military security, prevented freer development" of trade.[54] But administrators would not relinquish the ambition of *Verkehrspolitik*, and overrode such considerations. Perhaps even stricter *Verkehrspolitik* would be the answer.

The *Verkehrspolitik* section built a substantial body of orders and regulations to enforce its program. Ober Ost's official handbook stated its operative principles in nearly metaphysical terms:

First of all there had to be found a way suited to actual practice which would realize the principle of the new *Verkehrspolitik* beginning with the occupation of Ober Ost – adaptability to the special conditions and needs. For the management of the operation of the business, two possibilities presented themselves: centralization and decentralization. The *Verkehrspolitik* Section chose neither of the two as the sole principle, but rather sought the solution of problems of *Verkehr* in an interrelation of centralization and decentralization, which has vindicated itself.

Where military interests were involved, centralization was required. Ober Ost was also a rear area and staging area of operations, not merely a civil administrative region like Warsaw and Belgium. A degree of decentralization, however, had to be allowed for economic reasons. The administration defined types of movement: transit travel, near-border travel, longer stays, and inner travel. The first three types of movement were under centralized control. Only travel within internal borders was nominally decentralized. Transit travel was ordered by "a decree, which gives to the *Verkehrspolitik* section alone the right to approve any travel into or out of the area." Its monopoly was complete: "No person, at any point, no matter in which direction, may therefore cross the border without the permission of the *Verkehrspolitik* Section of the Supreme Commander in the East." Permission took the form of a certificate for transit travel (*Durchreiseschein*). The importance of such an arrangement was manifold:

there arises the possibility of uniformly controlling the tasks of *Verkehr* throughout the area. Only this measure guarantees that superfluous trips do not take place, that *Verkehr* with foreign lands can be prevented and minimized in the interest of counterespionage, that the *Verkehr* of trade in regard to goods and food, to which the border is closed, can be supervised and that the companies with purchasing power can be directed to the trading offices in Germany or to the official offices for trade. Also, the solution of the worker question could only be achieved in the desired way by such a strict centralization. For only in this way is there the possibility to seize all the available manpower and to shift it about, so that the surplus of workers arrives in the area where it can find fitting implementation because of the shortage of manpower for agriculture or industry.

The policy also served in other aspects of the manpower question. Authorities could shuttle civil and criminal prisoners, used for heavy labor. The *Verkehrspolitik* section would determine which travel was valid, weighing "the necessity of all travel and the trustworthiness of all persons in question." Travel in border areas was also centralized. Some workers and tradesmen had to be allowed to commute across on a regular basis, so relevant regulations were brought together in the "Order for the Regulation of Near-Border Movement." A border pass (*Grenzschein*) could be issued for a longer period, allowing crossing of borders. Likewise, the section made arrangements for regulating longer stays. A special pass (*Aufenthaltsschein*) was needed for stays of any length in Ober Ost, also bestowing benefits on the holder, marking him off from natives: it "has as its aim . . . also the improved condition of the holder of the certificate (German from the Reich or ally) relative to the native population." The importance of documentation was elevated to a cornerstone of administration, as authorities sped towards the "execution of the principle followed by the Supreme Commander in the East, that every person, in whatever place and for whatever purpose they might find themselves in the occupied territory, must be in possession of some identifying certification – [which] further occasioned the introduction of the pass requirement for the native population of the occupied territory." Every native over the age of ten was issued personal identification to be carried at all times. The Supreme Commander in the East set up the Foreign Office Ober Ost (Auslandstelle Ob. Ost) to handle any relations with the outside world, serving as the military state's foreign ministry. The region itself was totally cut off: "As to the East the front, so in the West the border of the Reich presented a barrier, difficult to cross, established in the interest of the military."[55]

Finally, control of "internal movement" (*Innenverkehr*) was nominally "decentralized." All this meant, in fact, was that the *Verkehrspolitik* section delegated its supervisory function at lower levels to local military authorities, so that district captains took over where the *Verkehrspolitik* section left off.[56] There, movement was also ordered schematically on the daily, ordinary plane. The native was allowed to move outside of his or her home in the district only by day and on foot, but as soon as he or she intended to use a horse, wagon, skis, rail, or waterway, he or she had to apply to the district captain for a permission pass. If the native needed to cross area borders, he or she needed to procure a travel pass. Travel after curfew, by night, required a night pass. One quickly reached the limits of this severely circumscribed "decentralization." The *Verkehrspolitik* section reserved the right to direct longer trips, changing of residences, and any traffic involving bicycles, cars, or motorcycles.[57] It wished to document and approve every movement. Passes were required for walking at night, taking in guests, for the use of one's own cart or vehicle, for prostitution. Passes proliferated, as even dogs were issued passes (certifying that their "dog tax" had been paid). After authorities established that movement required documentation, they extended the "principle of documentation" to all units of movement in the territory: each inhabitant.

Immediately upon the occupation, after closing off the territory, the administration wanted to register everyone under its control. Ober Ost would issue documentation to all inhabitants, announcing that "in this case, military interests above all were decisive, on the other hand, however, also interests of national economy."[58] Everyone over ten was to be documented, to facilitate rationalized control. This was an immense task, demanding documentation for 3 million people in a war-torn, devastated land. Special units were set up to process the entire country. In December 1915, thirteen pass commando units (*Paßkommando*) were formed, charged with "identifying the population and issuing passes."[59] Eventually these units spread out over the entire territory, behind the front. The staff consisted of fourteen officers and some 600 men: photographers, translators, and writing staff.[60] Every commando was divided into three to four groups, of ten to twelve men each, led by an older NCO or sergeant. Each received a district for processing – "*Bearbeitung.*"

Official sources describe a typical session of this work, which is worth examining in detail, since one may discern the categories of practice built into *Verkehrspolitik*.[61] The work was systematized, so the routine was almost always the same. A larger native farmhouse was chosen in the countryside. The local gendarme orders all natives to come at specific times for processing. The natives have arrived, all sitting on benches in their best clothes, "all the nationalities thrown together." Jocularly, the official account notes, "being photographed is for them something new, hitherto unknown and means for most of them a celebration." In fact, popular native sources later claimed they were locked into barns with animals for whole days awaiting processing.[62] Natives awaiting treatment sit with numbers pinned to their chests. Earlier, soldiers had given them numbers to hold, but these too often were mixed up, a frustrating impediment to smooth operation. The officer in charge again checks the numbers of the "victims, radiant with joy." Before being photographed, each native pays a mark for the procedure. Then they are herded forward in groups: "Generally, the people, to use a drastic comparison, have to be led like a flock of sheep. Otherwise there would be a wild confusion and quick and conscientious work would be impossible." Natives are divided into groups of five, and led "out to the yard, where the photographer and his assistants are already waiting for the victims." The five are installed on a bench with seats marked off, to keep them stationary. They are photographed all together and moved on. "But the next are already standing ready for the same procedure." The group whose photograph had just been taken is marched out to the next room, where writers wait. On a white card, for the index, is entered information yielded by "a great quantity of questions." After language difficulties, soldiers determine the name, religion, birth, residence, and number of children. The native is then led to a measuring rod at the wall to ascertain his height. His inked index fingerprint is pressed on to the card and in the blue Ober Ost pass. The subject moves to another writer, who copies the card's information into the pass. The locality's headman or scribe identifies the person and signs the pass. Afterwards, the account records, the native's ink-stained "offending finger is carefully wiped off on the hair or on the lining of the skirt." Finally, "the seriousness of the procedure is past and each trolls out of the house on to the street, satisfied and cheerful." In this way, 150 or more persons are processed (*"behandelt"*) in a single day. The pass is stamped across the picture pasted into it, official stamps pounded on, and checked again before being distributed. Pass Commandos kept their own central archives, passing card indexes to district offices. Passes, meanwhile, "end up in the more or less clean pockets of their owners" to be shown on demand to military authorities. By the time of the official account in 1917, 1,800,000 natives had been registered. Authorities astonished themselves with a survey of their surveys. More than 12,000 pens and 177 liters of ink had been used. The importance of the passes, essential for comprehensive and rational *Verkehrspolitik*, was hammered home again and again to the subject populations. If a native lost a pass, the required new one cost ten marks. The official account stated, "this high fine has shown itself to be absolutely necessary, because only so was it possible to make clear to the numerous people who lost their passes, that the pass is an important document, which one must store carefully in one's possession." Natives without passes were arrested and fined. Through *Verkehrspolitik* measures, the administration aimed to form a modern, subservient ethos among subject populations. Relentless orders were to produce a new consciousness, in which natives learned to see themselves in a new way: as objects of statistics, holders of identifying papers, pieces moved about over a map. The outcome, however, was only terror on the part of natives, to whom the reasoning behind actions was not explained. This pass-issuing episode is crucial because it gives a view in on the categories of practice put into operation here: through the prism of *Verkehrspolitik* people became "populations" and statistical objects to be "processed." The army carried through its program of reshaping people by the means it knew best: compulsion and force.

Ordinances reached down to regulate even the most ordinary movement. Authorities directed and rationalized the flow of traffic in towns, instructing natives precisely how to walk on the sidewalks. In Schaulen on August 16, 1916, military mayor Morsbach established the duty to yield right of way. Native sources later reported the order's tortured Lithuanian wording as: "All men and women and children in the city must politely greet the German officers of the German army. Further, all inhabitants must give right of way in the street to German soldiers and if need be should step down from the boardwalk. Resistance will be sharply punished." Morsbach's own report spoke vaguely of orders "concerning polite demeanor of the civilian population towards officers and men of the German army" and mentioned punishing three persons for violating this rule.[63] The army sought to habituate natives to this treatment and inspection. Soldiers surrounded churches and detained people without passes as they came out of mass until their children fetched the documents from home, apparently for the sole purpose of demonstrating the papers' importance, popular sources claimed.[64] Duty instructions for eastern railroad police emphasized how important it was that surveillance be normalized, people habituated to it, and civilians drawn in to assist: "If in this way the *public is educated to collaborate*, then as a rule every suspicious action or conversation must come to the attention of the traveling rail inspector and give him pointers for further observation."[65] It was a continuing process:

Such inspections of entire compartments are to be undertaken frequently – merely *for the purpose of habituating the travelers to the carrying of sufficient forms of identification.*

In general one is to proceed on the assumption that the observation of the inspection of travelers at the present time will (when correctly understood) have a calming effect on people with ordered circumstances, while creating unease among people with bad consciences – which is exactly what is aimed at.[66]

Habituated to control, inspection, and following orders, natives needed above all to understand their proper position in the system's division of labor. The military's German Work, distinguished by organizing genius, would direct and move native populations, which needed only to allow their raw, undirected energies to be harnessed.

As authorities intensified *Verkehrspolitik*, they stressed cleanliness. An obsession for "cleanliness" as understood by Germans was central to the envisioned order of classification and control. If *Verkehrspolitik* was claimed as German Work and a "deed of *Kultur*," *Kultur* itself was also understood as a German level of cleanliness and social discipline. For *Verkehrspolitik* to function smoothly, natives had to internalize the discipline of cleanliness as an integral part of their role in the new division of labor. Those prized possessions, the roads, had to be kept clean. In extensive orders, authorities in the towns charged natives with maintenance of roads and thoroughfares. Individual houses were responsible for cleaning sections of sidewalk. Out in the countryside, villages were assigned roads to clean and keep clear of snow in winter and spring.[67]

The same discipline would be extended to populations. As the task shifted from the lands to the peoples, a crucial aspect of the policy of cleaning the dirty East was the need to enforce a social hygiene on natives.[68] The very idea of epidemics spreading back to Germany transfixed Hindenburg and Ludendorff with disgusted horror. Venereal diseases in the pestilent towns loomed up for them as a special nightmare: an official source claimed that at first 70 percent of Wilna's prostitutes were infected.[69] The entire East appeared not only dirty and disordered, but diseased and contagious. Lice seemed omnipresent in the East, at the front and behind the lines. Cities were full of filth and rubble, crammed with ragged, exhausted, and grimy refugees. Moreover, the new conquerors made few allowances for the fact that many of these conditions had everything to do with the war – this was simply the way things were in the East. Yet it was something which the new ordering could not tolerate. Besides the destruction of cats and dogs, authorities moved to clean populations. Land and space became objects of treatment, and likewise the populations, as human matériel. Intensive, brisk education of native populations was required. At present, one official in the countryside noted, one could not use natives as food inspectors, since "in my experience the land population lacks the necessary sense of responsibility, conscientiousness, and a sense for order."[70] The army would teach natives cleanliness, by force if necessary. Native populations were policed;

with the classification of natives went compulsory cleaning. Special "plague troops" moved about the towns, quarantining neighborhoods and hospitalizing people with contagious diseases.[71] Compulsory cleaning of local populations took place at the administration's military baths and disinfecting stations. An official account spoke of "regulary repeated . . . compulsory delousing" of 1,800 people daily in Bialystok.[72] Troops drove groups of natives to the baths by force, according to native sources. Afterwards, those who had been "processed" were presented with certificates. On occasion, vaccines were administered there, with little explanation to those being treated. Natives viewed these measures with fear, their dismay due not to misguided satisfaction with poor personal hygiene, but the abrupt way in which these benefits were conferred. Vaccinations were sometimes noted in natives' passes.[73] Later, native sources claimed this "processing" was accompanied by incidents not mentioned in official German accounts. In towns, native women who still had gold hidden away reportedly used it to bribe their way out of compulsory visits to the baths, fearing mistreatment by soldiers when thus exposed.[74] Years later, natives sometimes recalled the vaccinations and health measures as one of the few positive legacies of German occupation, for all that the measures were resisted at the time. It is a cruel irony that in a later era, perverted echoes of this useful work in the East were heard in another kind of "processing," when "showers" provided the cover for mass murder in Nazi death camps.

What was characteristic here was the coercive, arbitrary, and often violent way in which people were treated, processed, and worked over, as an extension of a wider program of cleaning roads and towns. People came to be seen by the occupiers as objects of policy. This was another decisive turn in outlook, as peoples were turned into populations, to be ordered, numbered, documented, cleaned. They were regarded in aggregate, as dirty populations of dirty people, units of administration, manipulation, and hygiene. In this "biological warfare," native people could come to be regarded together with vermin, the ever-present lice of the East, which were being exterminated. In Ober Ost, often cleanliness was next to violence.

In the program of "cleaning" the East, a crucial concept was deployed, that of "*Raum*." *Raum* can be very roughly translated into English as "space," but in fact the term has in German a complex of allied meanings which carry decisive implications. They suggest concepts of "clearing" and "cleaning': "*aufräumen*," "*räumen*." The whole program of *Verkehrspolitik* involved these concepts in the control of spaces. "Spaces" had to be ordered, cleared, and cleaned. While *Raum* was presented as a neutral, descriptive term, it in fact prescribed an entire program in one word.

Moreover, the concept was at once delimiting and yet also expansive, just like Ober Ost itself. *Raum* defined a given area, but since the concept homogenized space, the area which was "treated" could keep expanding, endlessly. This was a significant turn in thought, for what the new occupiers had begun to see as distinct "lands and peoples" (*Land und Leute*) now came to be viewed as "spaces and races" (*Raum und Volk*), objects of control. In particular, a new concept increasingly came to the fore, that of "*Ostraum*," the East Space, designating the occupied areas whose political future still hung in the air.

Violence was built into efforts at enforcing the cleanliness necessary for a functioning of *Verkehrspolitik*. It was used both to keep "order" and to keep distance, as the division of labor demanded. The least infraction of an order by a native, or even misunderstanding or hesitation in its execution, could meet with storms of furious blows. This practice grew into episodic public brutality against civilians, according to native sources (grudgingly confirmed in some cases by German officials).[75] Increasingly, the occupiers were brutalized themselves, collectively, when their acts of violence met with little official reproach. It was important that the army show an undivided front, the reasoning went, while forceful correction of one of their own might lead native populations, with their low cunning, to believe that they could play Germans off against one another.[76] Thus, the epidemic of public beatings by officers continued. There was casual violence in the streets. In the spring of 1917, an officer in Rosieny district reportedly made this a specialty of his, beating men and women, including old people, in several villages.[77] This spontaneous, ordinary violence was possible because the larger program of control was itself built on systematized, rationalized coercion and violence. Symbolic of the regime's systematized brutality in these prisons was a contraption which native sources claimed was essentially a beating machine, a wooden scaffolding for stretching out victims and conducting rationalized violence with scientific precision.[78] It was another grid of control in miniature. Violence also maintained distance between occupiers and subject populations, as public beatings in the streets were usually occasioned by a perceived infraction of the duty to yield way, failure to salute, or some other imagined sign of disrespect. Violence, then, reasserted the ordering. A terrible self-reinforcing dialectic evolved. Natives reportedly noticed German fear of epidemics and tried to play on this reaction, simulating sickness.[79] While this was a way of avoiding being struck or touched, it in turn reinforced the revulsion felt by the occupier, who then moved to more drastic measures.

Verkehrspolitik represented a radical ideal of total control of Ober Ost's occupied territory, the better to exploit, mobilize, and possess the land.

The administration worked on the assumptions of this vision, which grew out of necessities the invaders first confronted: maintenance of order and effective economic exploitation. From those first necessary tasks, the vision swelled into a grandiose, total ambition. The program of *Verkehrspolitik* involved not merely volumes of orders issued to meet its imperatives of control, but also prescribed a new ethos to be imposed on subject native populations. *Verkehrspolitik* was both a means and an end in Ober Ost. The program placed the land in a brace, clamped in the jaws of a vise, in brackets holding it ready for the new forms it would be shaped into. The ambitions of *Verkehrspolitik*, however, were so total and unlimited that failure was preprogrammed, as the administration, in its military utopianism, pursued mutually contradictory goals (total military security and control of native movement, clashing with economic revitalization), with the result that none of them were achieved. But most decisive was the simple fact that the very monstrous ambition had been thrown up, erected as a vision of the future for military administrators. Now reality was measured not against reasonable expectations, but against this vision of *Verkehrspolitik*. No reality could meet such utopian requirements. This failure had momentous consequences, for soldiers came to look out over the East through the prism of *Verkehrspolitik*, its categories becoming points of reference to those who put it into action on a daily basis. They took aboard administrative categories by which the *Verkehrspolitik* section tried to get a firm grip on the territory: homogenized, uniform, "neutral" categories of "spaces" and "populations" to be controlled and ordered, cleansed and reshaped. These categories came to determine how German soldiers saw the East.

NOTES

1 Häpke, *Verwaltung*, 22. The total area taken in the East was larger than that of Ober Ost alone, as it included rear areas and front line zones under the control of armies. *Das Land*, 79.
2 Thus, earlier sources most often mention the *Verkehrspolitische Abteilung*, using the word as an adjective, before reference to *Verkehrspolitik* itself becomes common.
3 *Das Land*, 155.
4 Ludendorff, *Kriegserinnerungen*, 142.
5 *Das Land*, 155.
6 "Verkehrsregelung," in *Das Land*, 165.
7 Verkehrspolitische Abteilung.
8 BAMA PHD 8/20, "Ziffer 652. Bekanntmachung," *BUV* 91 (October 8, 1917): 693–94.
9 BAMA PHD 8/20, "Ziffer 636. Verordnung über die Ausdehnung der Verkehrspolitischen Abteilung Ob. Ost," *BUV* 88 (September 1, 1917): 679.

10 *Das Land,* 165.

11 Thus, the Central Police Office for the East's mission statement notes that it participates in "the control of *Verkehr*": LMARS, F. 9, BF–3117, "Ob. Ost ir jo štabo įvairūs įsakymai," "Zentralpolizeistelle des Oberbefehlshabers Ost," 34.

12 *Sanitätsbericht über das Deutsche Heer (Deutsches Feld- und Besatzungsheer) im Weltkriege 1914/1918 (Deutscher Kriegssanitätsbericht, 1914/18),* vol. I, *Gliederung des Heeressanitätswesens* (Berlin: E. S. Mittler & Sohn, 1935), 285.

13 Ludendorff, *Kriegserinnerungen,* 151.

14 LCVIA, F. 641, ap. 1, b. 52, *Verwaltungsbericht für Monat April 1916. Kreisamt Birsche* (May 1, 1916), 4; LCVIA F. 641, ap. 1, b. 52, *Verwaltungsbericht für März 1916. Kreisamt Birsche,* 6. The formulation of intensifying administration is also repeated elsewhere: BAMA N 196/1, Heppe, vol. V, 85, 110.

15 LCVIA F. 641, ap. 1, b. 53, "Verwaltungsberichte Rossienie," *Verwaltungsbericht 29. April 1916,* 14.

16 Yet reports complained of difficulty in policing these borders: LCVIA F. 641, ap. 1, no. 52, *Verwaltungsbericht für April 1916. Kreisamt Birsche*; LCVIA F. 641, ap. 1, b. 52, *Verwaltungsbericht für III. Vierteljahr 1916. Kreisamt Birsche,* 6.

17 Šilietis, *Okupacija,* 53.

18 Derwent Whittlesey, *German Strategy of World Conquest* (New York: Farrar & Rinehart, 1942), 29–30.

19 Ernst Tiessen, *Die Geographie des östlichen Kriegsschauplatzes* (Berlin: Concordia, 1914); Wilhelm Leitner, *In den Rokitno-Sümpfen. Kriegserfahrungen eines Geographen.* (n.p.: Stellv. Generalkommando I. Armeekorps, Abt. K., [1917]); J. Dreyer, *Die Moore Kurlands nach ihrer geographischen Bedingtheit, ihrer Beschaffenheit, ihrem Umfange und ihrer Ausnutzungsmöglichkeit. Herausgegeben mit Unterstützung der Verwaltung des Oberbefehlshabers Ost* (Hamburg: L. Friedrichsen, 1919); Karl Gäbert and Hans Scupin, *Bodenschätze im Ostbaltikum* (Berlin: Gebr. Borntraeger, 1928); Bruno Skalweit, *Die Landwirtschaft in den litauischen Gouvernements, ihre Grundlagen und Leistungen* (Königsberg: G. Fischer, 1918); Ernst Ferdinand Mueller, *Statistisches Handbuch für Kurland und Litauen nebst Übersichten über Livland und Estland. Mit einem bibliographischen Anhang zur Wirtschaftskunde Rußlands* (Königsberg: G. Fischer, 1918); Max Friederichsen, *Landschaften und Städte Polens und Litauens. Beiträge zu einer regionalen Geographie. Auf Grund von Reisebeobachtungen im Dienste der "Landeskundlichen Kommission beim Generalgouvernement Warschau"* (Berlin: Gea Verlag GmbH, 1918); Albert Thielecke, "Deutsche landeskundliche Arbeit im Weltkriege. An der europäichen Ost- und Südost-Front und in den anschliessenden Etappengebieten" (Ph.D. diss., Friedrich-Schiller University, Jena, 1936).

20 Robert Stupperich, "Siedlungspläne im Gebiet des Oberbefehlshabers Ost (Militärverwaltung Litauen und Kurland) während des Weltkrieges," *Jomsburg* 5 (1941): 348–67.

21 BA N 1238/8, Morsbach, *Tätigkeitsbericht des Bürgermeisteramtes Schaulen von Mitte August bis 30. September 1916.*

22 One official prefaced reference to it, "insofar as one wanted to follow the results of the census": BAMA N 196/1, Heppe, vol. V, 88. Sukiennicki,

however, argues for their relative reliability: *Europe*, I, 159–63; Senn, *Emergence*, 21.

23 *Völkerverteilungskarte*. This might also be translated as "Map of the Distribution of Peoples," since both senses apply. *Völker-Verteilung in West-Rußland* (Kowno: Verlag der Kownoer Zeitung, 1916). A second edition was published in 1917.

24 *Völkerverteilung in West-Rußland*, 2nd edn (n.p.: Druckerei des Oberbefehlshabers Ost, 1917), preface.

25 BA N 1031/2, Gayl, 39.

26 Work on prospects for settlement of German farmers reported in LCVIA F. 641, ap. 1, b. 53, "Verwaltungsberichte Rossienie," *Verwaltungsbericht 13 Juli 1916*, 7. A later report indicated good prospects, while settlement would also "accelerate the Germanization" of the area: LCVIA F. 641, ap. 1, b. 53, "Verwaltungsberichte Rossienie," *Verwaltungsbericht 29. August 1916*, 10.

27 Martin Broszat, *Zweihundert Jahre deutsche Polenpolitik*, rev. edn (Frankfurt-on-Main: Suhrkamp, 1972), 183.

28 Stupperich, "Siedlungspläne," 357.

29 Ibid., 362; On memorandum, BA N 1031/2, Gayl, 201.

30 LCVIA, F. 641, ap. 1, b. 971. For detailed analysis: Strazhas, *Ostpolitik*, 246–53; A. Strazas, "Die deutsche Militär-Verwaltung 'Oberost' – Prototyp der geplanten Kolonialadministration 'Neuland' (1915–1918)," *Wissenschaftliche Zeitschrift der Pädagogischen Hochschule "Dr. Theodor Neubauer," Erfürt-Mühlhausen, Gesellschafts- und sprachwissenschaftliche Reihe* 8 (1971): 39–44.

31 Kurt von Rümker, *Bevölkerungs- und Siedelungsfragen im Land Ob. Ost* (Berlin: Paul Parey, 1918); Stupperich, "Siedlungspläne," 348–67.

32 LCVIA, F. 641, ap. 1, b. 54.

33 Kurt von Rümker and R. Leidner, *42 Sortenanbauversuche im Verwaltungsgebiete des Oberbefehlshabers Ost* (Berlin: Paul Parey, 1918).

34 Wheeler-Bennett, *Wooden Titan*, 126.

35 Elias, *Reflections*, 23; Josef Wenzler, *Mit Draht und Kabel im Osten. Aus dem Tagebuch eines Telegraphisten* (Karlsruhe: Badenia, 1918).

36 Häpke, *Verwaltung*, 83.

37 Ludendorff, *Kriegserinnerungen*, 141, 155.

38 Ibid., 142.

39 *Das Land*, 158.

40 Ibid., 157–58.

41 Ibid., 158–59.

42 Ludendorff, *Kriegserinnerungen*, 142.

43 A report notes resistance to drafting for road building: LCVIA F. 641, ap. 1, b. 52, *Verwaltungsbericht für Februar 1916. Kreisamt Birsche*, 34. "Jews of the city Rossiene and other unemployed people" were forced into road work: LCVIA F. 641, ap. 1, b. 53, "Verwaltungsberichte Rossienie," *Verwaltungsbericht 29. Sept. 1916*, 12–13.

44 *Das Land*, 159.

45 Ibid., 156.

46 Stupperich, "Siedlungspläne," 361; BAMA N 98/1, Gossler, 88.

47 *Das Land*, 160–64.

48 Ludendorff, *Kriegserinnerungen*, 144.
49 *Das Land*, 160.
50 PHD 23/87 *Nowogrodeker Kriegszeitung* showed castle ruins with telegraph lines leading off to the horizon, a suggestive image uniting past and future. PHD 23/63 *Ostwacht. Lukowver Feldzeitung.*
51 *Das Land*, 161–62.
52 Ludendorff, *Kriegserinnerungen*, 160.
53 *Das Land*, 163.
54 Ludendorff, *Kriegserinnerungen*, 155.
55 *Das Land*, 166–79.
56 Ibid., 171.
57 Ibid., 172.
58 Ibid., 173.
59 LMARS, F. 9, BF-3117, 32.
60 *Das Land*, 173.
61 This section's information from "Ober-Ost Paß," in *Das Land*, 173–77.
62 Šilietis, *Okupacija*, 63.
63 Puzinas, *Rinktiniai*, 272; Gintneris, *Lietuva*, 374; Šilietis, *Okupacija*, 118; BA N 1238/8, Morsbach, *Tätigkeitsbericht des Bürgermeisteramtes Schaulen von Mitte August bis 30. September 1916.*
64 Gintneris, *Lietuva*, 373.
65 BAMA PHD 8/95, *Dienstanweisung für die Eisenbahnüberwachungsreisen in den Bezirken des I., II., V., VI., XVII. und XX. A.-K.. Zentralpolizeistelle Osten beim Oberbefehlshaber Ost* (December 24, 1915), §7, p. 5.
66 Ibid., §8, p. 6.
67 LCVIA F. 641, ap. 1, b. 52, *Verwaltungsbericht für April 1916. Kreisamt Birsche*, 19. Communities were also charged, on pain of fines, with guarding telegraph lines against sabotage: ibid., 12; LCVIA F. 641, ap. 1, b. 52, *Verwaltungsbericht für IV. Vierteljahr 1916. Birsche*, 29. *Dezember 1916*; LCVIA F. 641, ap. 1, b. 52, *Verwaltungsbericht des Militärkreisamts Birsche für das II. Vierteljahr 1917*, 5; LCVIA F. 641, ap. 1, b. 53, "Verwaltungsberichte Rossienie," *Verwaltungsbericht 27. Nov. 1915*, 6; LCVIA F. 641, ap. 1, b. 53, "Verwaltungsberichte Rossienie," *Verwaltungsbericht 29. August 1916*, 19.
68 *Das Land*, 119–26.
69 Ibid., 124.
70 LCVIA F. 641, ap. 1, b. 52, *Verwaltungsbericht des Militärkreisamts Birsche für das I. Vierteljahr 1917*, 6.
71 *Sanitätsbericht über das Deutsche Heer (Deutsches Feld- und Besatzungsheer) im Weltkriege 1914/1918* vol. I, *Gliederung des Heeressanitätswesens*, 274.
72 Ibid.; *Das Land*, 123.
73 LCVIA F. 641, ap. 1, b. 53, "Verwaltungsberichte Rossienie," *Verwaltungsbericht für die Zeit vom 1 April bis 30 Sept. 1917.*
74 Šilietis, *Okupacija*, 122; BAMA PHD 23/42, "Chef der Militärverwaltung Litauen. Wilna, 23. April 1917. Verwaltungsbefehl XXXV" orders delousing civilians, "if necessary with exercise of a stronger pressure": 4.
75 Šilietis, *Okupacija*, 117–19.

76 One report concerning invalid requisition orders worried that revealing conflict between offices would lower German status in native eyes: LCVIA F.
641, ap. 1, b. 52, *Verwaltungsbericht für Mai – Juni 1916. Kreisamt Birsche*, 23.
On effect of orders on local population: LCVIA F. 641, ap. 1, b. 53, "Verwaltungsberichte Rossienie," *Verwaltungsbericht für die Zeit vom 1. Oktober bis 31.
Dezember 1917. Georgenburg*, 23–24.
77 LMARS, F. 23–47, "Vokiečiai Lietuvoje," list of complaints, 8.
78 Petras Ruseckas, ed., *Lietuva didžiajame kare* (Vilnius: Vilniaus žodis, 1939),
167.
79 Šilietis, *Okupacija*, 121.

4   The *Kultur* program

Amidst war, the German army devoted a surprising amount of energy to ambitious cultural policies in the occupied territories, forming an integral part of the project of the Ober Ost state, as Ludendorff had conceived it, in his ambition to "build something whole" in the East. While *Verkehrspolitik* controlled the land, borders, and movement, a program of *Kultur* would accomplish the same on the spiritual plane, controlling entire peoples, their national identities, and future development.

Ludendorff, newly arrived in Kowno headquarters, conceived his *Kultur* program on a late autumn day in 1915, while walking out to survey his new land. From Kowno's surrounding heights, he looked out over the quiet, ancient, low-roofed settlement at the confluence of the Njemen and Neris rivers and was overpowered by historical memories surging around him. He recalled, "On the other side of the Njemen lies the tower of an old castle of the Teutonic Order as a sign of German *Kultur* work in the East, and not far from that is a landmark of French plans for world domination, that height from which Napoleon observed the fording of the river by the great army in 1812." Overlooking the ominous fact that these earlier projects ended in failure, Ludendorff was caught up in the glory of this moment and exclaimed: "Powerful historical impressions stormed in on me. I determined to take up in the occupied territory the *Kultur* work which Germans had done in those lands over many centuries." Considering the area's ethnic diversity, this was an ambition of huge dimensions, for a program of German *Kulturarbeit* would actually involve forming the native peoples and creating culture for them, since, Ludendorff believed, "left to itself, the motley population cannot create any *Kultur*."[1] Ethnic conflict raged in the area, but such friction, Ludendorff contended, simply made German mediation all the more necessary.

The program of *Kultur* offered much to Germans as well, as their chance to finally "write themselves into" the region's history. With a mission of German Work, their presence gained meaning. Most importantly, the program ensured that German custodianship would be permanent, Ober Ost more than a temporary expedient. As with the movement policy, the occupiers sought to control and direct all cultural activity. First, they would introduce order, *Ordnung*, then proceed to cultivation, *Bildung*, forming the *Kultur* and indeed the national identities of ethnicities. To impose order, cultural policies first asserted state control, a monopoly of military administration. To preserve "ordered circumstances," the supreme commander banned all political activity. By default, culture became politics. The administration would control and direct all cultural activity, underscoring this area's fragmentation and need for control from above. In such ethnic confusion, a people from outside, people with a genius for organization, were needed to provide the framework and arbitration for cultural flourishing, the reasoning went. To bolster this claim, the administration worked to project a monolithic image of Ober Ost, announcing its claims to Germany, to natives, and to German soldiers. Next, the administration could begin to shape a culture for Ober Ost. The administration's *Kultur* policies "bracketed" native cultures, giving German form to native content. The result might be described as "German in form, ethnic in content." German Work would brace the inchoate, primitive energies of the ethnicities, surrounding their cultures with German institutions. Ober Ost's cultural policies had three aims. First, they sought to project a compelling image of the state and its civilizing German Work in the East. Second, native culture was to be bracketed by German institutions which would define native identity and direct their development. Finally, cultural policies also aimed to provide German soldiers with a sense of their mission. These last two projects of constructing identities for the occupied and the occupier defined their specific roles in the division of labor of German Work.

By these standards, the program of *Kultur* which Ludendorff built into Ober Ost was a great success, as in the short space of two years, from 1915 to late 1917, it created a durable image of the military state and its mission of German culture-work. Yet the program's very success would prove damning, for when a political change of course was demanded in 1917, the administration found it could not jettison the built-in assumptions of the program. Called upon to let native peoples express themselves politically (at least enough to "voluntarily request" German annexation), the state had invested too heavily in the ideology of German Work to do so effectively, finding that the categories it had created with its *Kultur* program proved durable and unyielding. The ambitious cultural policies obscured the complex, often negative interaction with subject ethnicities. Even the effort of defining them and their place in the structure of German Work was done from a distance and from on high. The program's "constructive" aims often hardly impinged on native consciousness, except in the regime's coercive measures. This was the program's fatal flaw, for Ober Ost's claims diverged ever more from reality on the ground, a fact which became fully clear only in 1917.

From its beginning in the fall of 1915, the *Kultur* program involved many different sections of the administration. The task was too large for any one section alone, so the press section, political section, school and church section all collaborated. Among these, the press section held pride of place, charged with creating a compelling image of Ober Ost's work. It was created as an independent section on December 5, 1915. The same order also made all press a monopoly of the Supreme Commander in the East, under his censorship. Captain Friedrich Bertkau, Ludendorff's press advisor, headed the press section (with a staff of about seventy).[2] Before the war, he worked in the famous Ullstein publishing house. After being severely wounded in action, Bertkau led the press section from November 1915 to February 1918. To give the cultural administration a level of intellectual seriousness, Ludendorff collected an "academy" of intellectuals. Eventually, it included authors already famous before the war, Arnold Zweig, Herbert Eulenberg, and Richard Dehmel, artists such as Hermann Struck, and scholar Erich Zechlin, and the philologist and journalist Victor Klemperer.[3]

The press section worked to create a media network in the occupied territories, institutions serving as German outposts of culture, their very existence vividly demonstrating how German administration could be at home here. Ober Ost took credit for any signs of cultural revival: "As a fire over the steppe, so the war carried over the grass of the West Russian press and with its flames devoured the pitiful growth. However, as after the forest fire the ground becomes better, so in this case also the field was prepared for a new sowing. The sower came when the Administration of the Supreme Commander in the East drew into the land."[4] The press section established local German newspapers throughout the territory (*Kownoer Zeitung, Wilnaer Zeitung, Grodnoer Zeitung*). In choosing titles, editors deliberately picked names of towns to underline their local nature. Though printed in German, they were intended to provide natives with information on the war from the army's perspective, promulgate orders, and generally, in incidental articles, to juxtapose the disorganization and cruelty of Russian rule with the new regime of German Work. Politics were to be excluded, to keep peace between different ethnicities. The newspapers' central goal was outlined: "It was self-evident that these newspapers see their principal task as the diffusion and strengthening of German prestige and therefore had, in the first place, also to appear in German language."[5] As so often happened in Ober Ost, the very means chosen undermined the official goal. For the most part, newspapers appeared in German (Grodno and Bialystok's were multilingual, with Polish and Yiddish sections), which the natives they were to address could not understand. The only concession made to this reality was to print German text in Latin type rather than Gothic, "in order to meet at least half way the understanding of the population which one wanted to address."[6] In its opening issue, Wilna's newspaper stated its mission: to be

a pioneer of German peace-work – . . . to deepen understanding for German spirit and German manner, for German discipline and order. Above all, however, it wants the trust of the population. Deeply rooting itself in the ground of the land, it will share with it joy and suffering – it will become at once a representative of the German Fatherland in the East and a representative of the East in the German Fatherland.[7]

Newspapers were to be outposts of German culture planted in the East, at home in a foreign land. With countless articles on the area's character, unique sights, and impressions, the papers strove to show that they had found their place.

Thus, the press section's principal aim was to present a picture of the occupied territory and Ober Ost state to the outside world, emphasizing the area's unique character, complex diversity, and how German administration was successfully managing it, as no one else could. To influence opinion at home, the section published the periodical *Korrespondenz B* from October 1916. Carrying information about the area's character, history, and achievements of German Work, it was sent out to newspapers in Germany and provided official wire service information.[8] Its sketches, translations, poems, and scholarly articles were intended for reprinting. Ober Ost's military artists published many visual representations of the area. Etcher Hermann Struck produced a sketchbook, while military presses published postcards and collections of photographs, among them *Pictures from Lithuania*.[9] The administration published its own propaganda book, *The Land Ober Ost*. Essentially a handbook or "owner's manual" to the territory, it presented Ober Ost as it wanted to be seen. After introducing the "lands and peoples" in all their varied disorder, it offered extensive accounts of German achievements, ending with arrays of statistical overviews. The book's subtitle carried its true message: "German Work in the Administrative Areas of Kurland, Lithuania and Bialystok-Grodno."[10]

As a sophisticated manager of public relations, the press section coordinated contacts with Germany's press, as its officials held press conferences, a striking wartime innovation, and encouraged numerous propagandistic, wildly enthusiastic travel accounts in Germany's press.[11] Journalists came for carefully choreographed tours, which soon became routine, led by officers jokingly called "bear keepers," and accommodated in special guest houses. One conscientious official understood that these visits from the "Superpower of the Press" were necessary, but complained that their frequency was distracting. Kurland's chief noted that hardly a week went by without important visitors. Among the many notables were the Kaiser, the mayor of Lübeck, twelve other German mayors, imperial ministers, Hugenberg, the director of the Krupp works, and Swedish explorer Sven Hedin visited Ober Ost and related his experiences in his war book, *To the East!*.[12] To introduce the occupied territory to Germans at home, the administration sent war exhibits to Dresden, Leipzig, Cologne, and Danzig, featuring selected products of the Ober Ost press.[13]

The most striking achievement was Ober Ost's 1916 *Atlas of the Division of Peoples in West Russia*.[14] This folio was an eloquent *apologia* for the military regime's existence. The title said it all – but the map, a motley explosion of flecks of ethnicity, was worth a thousand words of annexationist propaganda. It announced to Germany the area's diversity, showing that it was no unitary empire, as earlier imagined. The map aimed "to spread the awareness that that state-structure, which before the war was considered a uniform Great Russian empire, is to a large extent formed out of territories of independent ethnicities, who do not stand nearer to Muscovite nature than to us."[15] All sorts of future possibilities opened up with the map of peoples.

The press section also acted as an interface with native populations, though one worker called the lack of familiarity with native languages "probably the sorest point of the entire administration."[16] The translation post coped with floods of military orders issuing from the state. Serious problems arose, especially involving "translation of concepts that were completely foreign to the shallow culture of this land."[17] As a remedy, the translation post instituted a card catalog of official language. Its systematic catalog of "officialese" rendered German concepts in native languages: Polish, Russian, Belarusian, Lithuanian, Latvian, and Yiddish. Just as card catalogs were to get a grasp on the population at large, this index captured or fixed languages. By 1917, official accounts boasted, it held almost 8,000 words. This measure was to ensure a unified image of the occupation regime to natives, "and above all to help avoid inconsistencies in publicly published announcements, as these detract from the Administration's prestige." The occupiers introduced concepts which native peoples had not possessed before, albeit a vocabulary of coercive measures, bureaucratic arbitrariness, and state power. In the spring of 1918, the press section turned this into a *Seven-Language Dictionary*.[18] The way in which the dictionary was presented is also revealing. In this land of anachronisms, its preface stated, "the development of the language of each individual nation kept step with its cultural development." This meant that "many of the languages in question lacked a whole set of expressions. For many words firmly embedded in the German language of administration, there were in those foreign languages no words whose meaning corresponded exactly to those of the German word – one had to decide on more or less daring new creations." Creating new languages for subject peoples, their "lexical work had in this case not only confirmative significance, but rather very often constitutive meaning." All the languages

had in common, understandably, the lack of expressions for all those concepts which had only come into being in the most recent times, especially during the world war, and above all there was a lack of words precisely for the expressions constantly recurring in the daily work of the administration, in the area of German administrative, judicial, and military activity. Here as well, there had to take place a work of creation by the Translation Post. It was necessary to create once and for all given expressions, so that these concepts in their full meaning would be firmly and indelibly imprinted on the spirit of the population.

While defining later lexical development, it promised for now "to avoid fragmentation and squandering of intellectual energy and to become the first basis for the uniform development of language in given limits." In creating these new languages of administration, *"Amtssprachen,"* experts insisted that their work was really merely a neutral one of systematizing, for "editors have tried to seize the spirit of the languages – they have listened to the unaffected attempts of the people, when they tried to create words for the new, unfamiliar concepts out of their original instincts." German organization thus gave form to native "original instincts" and incoherent drives, making the administration the arbiter for each native culture's linguistic development. The political section's official Lithuanian newspaper, *The Present Time (Dabartis)*, tried to create a new, official dialect in its pages, which "had already evolved into a kind of official language in the course of the years of occupation." In both Lithuanian and Latvian, "a huge number of new expressions had to be created." With White Ruthenian, the oldest Slavic language with strong foreign admixture, the translation post had to define the language, "a matter of linguistic virgin land." Identical difficulties arose with Yiddish, incorporating words from many languages, making it unclear which of several possible variants to choose. Notwithstanding these difficulties, editors emphasized that their work was not theoretical, but grew out of real and necessary practice: "The words are taken out of the people and are intended for the people." The editors hoped that the dictionary's "next edition will perhaps appear already in peacetime, or at any rate in a time of the livelier mutual approach of the German people and those neighbor-peoples." At the same time, the dictionary defined the unequal terms of that coming "mutual approach." The single most telling fact about the dictionary was that even though it was multilingual, translation ran all in one direction: from official German language into the other languages. One could not, for instance, look up a Yiddish word to find its German equivalent. The process was a one-way street, with German the language of command. It is a paradigmatic image for Ober Ost's project, where native "content" was ranked and fixed in a German grid. Order flowed in one direction only.

The press section managed every aspect of the way in which the military state was presented. All press underwent double censorship, before and after being typeset, in a regime given to ridiculous excesses of caution.[19] To regulate all cultural material entering Ober Ost, a book-checking office was created on July 15, 1916, as a special press section office (later that year, a branch opened in Leipzig).[20] Its very nature brought on a crisis of conscience for writer Richard Dehmel, who worked there and came to see this as a "sin against the German spirit."[21] Academic and journalist Victor Klemperer, on the contrary, was disconcerted at how quickly he grew into his censorship duties, reflecting, "How an office can turn one's head! . . . I forbid or prepare for forbidding!" Eventually, he too came to doubt the whole system.[22]

The press section's efforts ranged far afield. In a letter to the War Press Office's central censorship post in Berlin dated September 10, 1916, it requested that all notices on Ober Ost in Germany's press first be approved by its office, since frequently there "appeared in the German press articles and news items about the Ober Ost territory, containing incorrect or unwelcome information."[23] Ober Ost's active press programs demonstrated how settled the administration was, projecting a convincing picture of permanence.

Authorities now sought to understand the "national characters" of different ethnic groups. In Ludendorff's first estimate, "The population confronting us, except for the German parts, was foreign to us." He and his soldiers knew "little of the conditions of the land and people [*Land und Leuten*] and looked out on a new world."[24] All through the area were scattered other minority groups.

Most of all, advancing armies were surprised to encounter the Jewish population – pleasantly surprised, since for all their unfamiliar appearance, Yiddish, or "*Jiddisch-Deutsch*," as it was sometimes called, offered a connection.[25] As Ludendorff put it, "The Jew did not yet know which face he should show, but he made no difficulties for us. We could also make ourselves mutually understood . . . while with Poles, Lithuanians, and Latvians this was almost nowhere the case."[26] Compared to the discrimination and hardships visited on Jewish communities under Russian rule, Ober Ost's professed maxim of absolute neutrality towards ethnic groups seemed to represent considerable improvement in their condition, at least nominally and relatively. Officials noted the initial, hopeful friendliness of the Jews.[27] Victor Klemperer observed, "The Jews are well disposed towards us and speak German, or at least half-German." He noted that the administration valued "a good relationship with the Jewish population, where it found German language skills, ties to German *Kultur*, and which it was inclined to make its ally."[28] Some officials, however, imbued with anti-Semitic views, were suspicious.[29] The officer at District Office Birsche remarked that in his area "Jews are living here everywhere in considerable numbers: a cancerous wound of this land."[30] Other authorities sought to cultivate this relationship, thinking to form an element friendly to the Germans.[31] At the same time, however, there were dissenting voices; one secret report on ethnic politics from May 1916 warned that "it is a widely held misconception to consider the Jews of Russia as special friends of Germany," arguing that in fact they followed no national politics, but only economic interest.[32] Von Gayl insisted that "in the mix of peoples . . . they were a disturbing, often unfathomable factor in every political calculation."[33]

The question of how anti-Semitic ordinary German soldiers and officials were upon first meeting the *Ostjuden* has no unequivocal answer. The documentary sources yield an ambivalent record, showing both expressions of sympathy and interest as well as a range of anti-Semitic responses, including casual prejudices, slurs, and active hatred. Years later, the anti-Semitic von Gayl insisted that the Jews were set against the Germans, in spite of their outward friendliness. He noted that soldiers mocked and poked fun at Jews: "our soldiers saw in everyday life mostly the comical side of the Jews' demeanor, whom they liked to play tricks on. They loathed them also because of ineradicable filth which they spread about themselves, but only a few saw further and sensed the danger which there began to appear for our people."[34] By von Gayl's lights, there was not enough committed anti-Semitism for his taste. In 1916 in Schaulen, a report noted, the military mayor forced Jewish women to clean a square. Some soldiers and officers look on, commenting and apparently mocking the women, but other officers denounced the mayor "in the harshest terms," leading to an inflamed mood.[35] One must conclude that there was a range of responses in this ambivalent scene.

In the fall of 1915, Ludendorff sought a more precise understanding of the ethnic landscape, but attempts at censuses were unsatisfactory. Religious confession further complicated matters. Belarusians, for instance, were divided into Russian Orthodox and Roman Catholic segments. In spite of their common Catholic confession, Lithuanian and Polish groups often clashed in local ecclesiastical politics. Scarcely to be fathomed was a further fact: language (so important a determinant to German concepts of national identity) did not completely define ethnicity, either. Natives might fiercely identify themselves as Lithuanians, without being able to speak the language. Conversely, others were proud of their Polish identity, while speaking Lithuanian at home. Most scandalously, sometimes it could not even be ascertained what language was spoken at home. Mixing of Lithuanian, Polish, and Belarusian had produced a hybrid called "common" or "plain" language, and in any event, life was of necessity multilingual. One official criticized soldiers in Kurland for assuming that anyone who spoke German there was in fact German.[36] Terms of national identity seemed unfamiliar and dangerously unstable to the newcomers.

Shocked, Ludendorff found that his administration "discovered" a nationality invisible before: Belarusians. This left a profound impression: "At first they were literally not to be found. Only later was it revealed, that they were an extremely diffused, but superficially Polonized tribe, which stands on such a low level of *Kultur*, that it can only be helped by long influence."[37] This revelation was a great jolt. Here were people who seemed to have lost their ethnicity – "Poles had taken his nationality from him, without giving him anything in exchange."[38] One officer observing Belarusian peasants noted that they were good natured "but culturally very backward and indolent. Their shelters, clothes, and economic modes were of a primitiveness, which I would not have considered possible in twentieth-century Europe."[39] It was even unclear what this newly discovered group should be called. The name "Belarusian" or "White Russian" implied too close a relationship to Great Russians. Finally, the administration labeled them "White Ruthenians." Their lack of national consciousness seemed to offer possibilities for manipulation. A secret report on ethnic politics in Ober Ost from May 1916 strongly suggested that "the German future in this land depends on White Russians experiencing a renaissance and confronting the Poles." It warned against trying to germanize them, since that would only drive them further into Polish influence. By contrast, "if one succeeds in causing a rebirth" of the White Ruthenians, the Polish cause would be weakened (and pressure removed from nearby East Prussia's ethnically mixed marches). The writer argued that a small group of Poles had parasitically lived off this disoriented group, drawing upon it for recruits to its own nationality.[40] How a cultural rebirth could be engineered remained an open question, however, though the possibilities seemed tantilizing. From late fall 1916, Ludendorff ordered support for Belarusians through cultural policies.[41]

Before launching a nationalities policy, the army collided with fundamental questions. Most basically, it was unclear (and remained so) how to even define these nationalities. Was each a "tribe" – *Stamm*? "Nation-tribe" – *Volksstamm*? "Nation-let" – *Völkerschaft*? It seemed clear, at any rate, that none of these groups, as yet, was a *Volk* – a fully fledged "nation," like the Germans. Thus, the administration used many terms for "nations in embryo." The most bizarre formulation was that of "*Fremdvölker*," "*Fremdvölkischen*," "*Fremdstämmigen*" – "foreign peoples," "foreign nationals," or "foreign tribes," applied to peoples living in their own ancestral lands. Such tortured rhetoric invited welcome conclusions. Groups only in the process of becoming true "nations of culture" (*Kulturvölker*) could be objects for German tutelage in their developmental process. Once again, out of necessity came vaunting ambition. From trying to understand the foreign peoples encountered in the newly conquered East, German authorities moved to define who they were, what their identity was to be. The term most often used for native peoples was "*Völkerschaft*" – "ethnicity," "tribe," "mini-nation," or "nation in process" (this study uses "ethnicity," a translation capturing the ambivalent incompleteness suggested in German) accented what ethnicities were becoming, under German military tutelage.

The administration declared strict neutrality towards different ethnic groups. This "Chief Principle" was written in to the "Order of Rule," the Ober Ost's constitution of June 1916: "The different people-tribes of the area under command are to be treated by all German officials on equal terms."[42] The administration was to be strictly apolitical, a neutral broker from outside, its activities disinterested mentoring and arbitration. Officials repeated their insincere protestations of no politics.[43] Yet in the absence of politics, *Kultur* was the key to control and legitimation for that control. In a beatific state of supposedly apolitical administration, "the population was led with quiet confidence."[44] The maxim of neutrality toward all ethnic groups justified the German position of overlordship.

Through culture, authorities sought to define the characters of peoples, distilling their ethnic "essence" to position them in an appropriate place in a larger structure of German cultural tutelage. Cultural policy was in fact the military state's nationalities policy, bracketing native cultures in German institutions imposed from above: press, schools, and work rooms. Next, the military would proceed to form the peoples held in the brace. The German concept for "education," *Bildung*, was taken to its literal meaning, of "forming." As a political section official announced, "We are the ones who bring *Bildung* and no one else."[45] In fact, while great attention was paid to publicizing attainments of German Work, a clear problem lay in how much never reached native masses. This was a drama, enacted with a native "cast of millions," that said ever more about the occupiers and their crises of confidence and purpose.

The press section supervised such native press as military authorities allowed to operate. Yet only some ethnicities were allowed to publish newspapers; others had newspapers published for them by the army. The administration refused repeated requests from Lithuanians, the largest ethnic group, for a newspaper of their own. There was no need, authorities explained, because they themselves published one, *The Present Time* (*Dabartis*). It began publication in September 1915, in Tilsit in East Prussia, where the seat of Military Administration Lithuania remained in the first months of occupation and later was moved to Kowno together with the administration, placed under the political section. Steputat-Steputaitis (a Prussian–Lithuanian member of the Prussian diet, and a reserve officer) headed the paper, staffed by germanized Lithuanians from East Prussia. Aiming to create a mood receptive to incorporation into Germany, the newspaper had no credibility among Lithuanians because of its tendentiousness.[46] The administration's Belarusian newspaper, *The Voice* (*Homan*) had similar effect.[47] Nationalities allowed to publish newspapers were still hampered by strict censorship to head off anything resembling political activity.[48] Eventually, Lithuanian complaining finally wore down military authorities. With changing political requirements in the fall of 1917, they allowed an independent newspaper, *Lithuania's Echo* (*Lietuvos Aidas*), which began to appear in Wilna in September 1917 and soon created considerable problems. Official reports after the war judged the press project to have been largely a failure.[49] Internal security concerns and severe censorship meant that it never had enough independence to achieve credibility among the populations it was meant to influence.[50] Ober Ost's ambition of gaining a foothold in native consciousness through an influential press failed.

Even larger hopes centered on the administration's school policies, and because of this, failure in this area was especially significant.[51] Educational policy spun out of control from the very beginning. When Germans occupied the territories, they found the system in ruins and there for the taking, a paltry 602 schools. Before the war, illiteracy was high, and instruction in native languages had not been allowed (with some slight liberalization after 1905). After 1914, Russian teachers fled and many larger schools evacuated to Russia's interior, students and all. Ober Ost's school and church section took over the remaining educational system.

What happened next was a startling example of native intransigence and "troublemaking." Throughout their tenure, Ober Ost authorities were engaged in a running fight with locals, who had their own program and agenda. The opening act took place with the spontaneous founding of native schools all through the territory by natives, a thousand new private schools springing into existence.[52] They operated under wretched conditions. Buildings were lacking, destroyed or taken over for military purposes, and few trained teachers remained, since a substantial part of the native intelligentsia had fled with the Russians. Finally, as instruction in native languages had been proscribed, there were virtually no textbooks. Naturally, then, the keynote of these schools was improvisation. Absent trained teachers meant intrepid village high school girls shouldering the work of the land schools, supported by local farmers and drawing on traditions of secret schools in the territory during periods of Russification.

Sensing a threat in this spontaneous activity, in the first months authorities' efforts concentrated on banning the schools or bringing them to heel. They complained of unqualified teachers, unsystematic teaching programs, and unhygenic class settings. Most importantly, school foundings were seen as political actions, by which natives asserted their own agendas, eluding state control. In ethnically contested areas, especially Wilna-Suwalki and Bialystok-Grodno, competition between ethnicities could potentially disrupt Ober Ost's main objective, maintenance of order. Officials repeatedly banned founding schools, especially in Suwalki, occupied earliest. On July 16, 1915, area captains were ordered to list Polish schools and to keep them to German purposes. On October 28, 1915, Administration Lithuania's chief forbade new private schools. Yet natives generally disregarded the rules and continued to establish schools. Birsche's embarrassed district captain reported that "newer evidence has demonstrated the existence of a larger number of schools than noted in the earlier report. In my next report, I will be able to name the individual schools."[53]

Unable to put into effect a positive program, officials concentrated on trying to keep native energies within limits. On December 22, 1915, a military order made all education a monopoly of the Supreme Commander in the East. Even though Ober Ost claimed to be bringing *Kultur* and education to the primitives of the East, its educational policy at first consisted of the stricture – "*Verboten*," forbidden. Frequent directives attempted to head off the mushrooming educational institutions in the towns and countryside.

The spontaneous schools and other national agitation in the region apparently were a catalytic moment for Ludendorff, transforming his sense of the horizon of possibilities before him. His encounter with the spirit of Polish schools, in particular, radicalized Ludendorff's already intemperate outlook, revealing the tremendous mobilizing potential of such directed education. Ludendorff later recalled, "I was shown by various Polish readers how a national consciousness can be cultivated through teaching materials. There, Danzig, Gnesen, Posen, Wilna were Polish cities."[54] Directed education could actually call a nation into being. These impressions were later echoed in Ludendorff's "Patriotic Instruction" program, unleashed in the summer of 1917, once he was in the high command, seeking to mobilize all of Germany's material and spiritual resources to wage "total war."[55]

Once Ober Ost asserted its education monopoly, regular policies were needed. On December 22, 1915, Hindenburg issued a body of exhaustive public orders (with a secret supplement) concerning educational policy, "Guidelines for the Revival of the Educational System,"[56] prepared by Major Altmann, advisor to Prussia's Culture Ministry. These orders sought to impose administration control on all educational activity. The final decision on any educational question lay with the Supreme Commander in the East. Even private lessons required permission from the military authorities. The ultimate goal of Ober Ost's educational system was to "accustom youth to obedience towards the laws, respect for the German authority and its armed might, as well as discipline and order."[57] The most important innovation was the "national school" principle, as schools were founded on the basis of children's "mother tongue," overturning tsarist precedent when native languages of instruction were generally forbidden. While this new principle led to tremendous political problems in areas of mixed ethnicity, that very friction made Ober Ost an indispensable arbiter. The Supreme Commander in the East had the final say in determining which was the dominant mother tongue in cases of doubt. Until 1917, the administration was constantly involved in proxy conflicts between nationalities over schools. From the outset, authorities clashed with Great Polish agitation by landlords and priests in Wilna region, who envisioned a large independent Polish state within the former borders of the Polish–Lithuanian Commonwealth. With time and official adjudication, the number of schools in the region changed: Polish ones declining, Lithuanian increasing. Belarusians pulled their children out of the Polish schools. After 1917, control of schools was relaxed, due to new political circumstances.[58] In 1918 there were 1,350 public primary schools: 750 Lithuanian, 299 Polish, 164 Jewish, 89 White Ruthenian, 81 German, and 7 Latvian.

The guidelines also prescribed the method of teaching German: a required subject from the first grade and given as much time as possible in all following grades. Teaching was not to rely on translation, but rather on an inductive "natural" method of learning from "within" the German language.[59] Yet this ambition was tremendously difficult to put into effect, for few native teachers could speak German, much less teach it "from within." The administration intended to provide German "military teachers" from the ranks, but with pressing manpower shortages throughout the entire war effort, the task was impossible. Those teachers assigned to native schools found it very hard going. As Ludendorff noted, "Later, one held against us the fact that they spoke only German to the children who voluntarily presented themselves. The teachers, unfortunately, knew no other language."[60] In fact, bad feeling was created when military teachers replaced native instructors, who were reportedly fired without explanation.[61] Natives complained about brutal treatment of their children at the hands of Prussian pedagogues. The administration tried another tack, founding German schools for children of other nationalities, yet natives resisted these schools. In Varena, for instance, of eighty children registered at the local school, only ten remained when the school was made German. A remarkable exception was noted in attendance of German schools by Jews. In 1916, there were 65 German schools; in 1917, 169. Of these, Jews alone reportedly attended 26 in 1916 and 164 in 1917. After 1917, as the administration began to unravel, they decisively turned away to their own Jewish schools.[62] In Kurland, educational policy stressed energetic germanization. Chief von Gossler's memoir recalled, "from the start, I considered the school problem from the perspective of how the aim of the future germanization of the Latvian population could be most quickly and securely reached." In a 1915 speech he outlined three central maxims: "(1) every Latvian must learn German, (2) no German will be forced to learn Latvian, (3) all unreliable and bad elements . . . among the teachers – will be eradicated."[63]

In general, school policies constituted another case where ambitions outran resources. Unable to impose their program, officials fell back on proscription. The curriculum was dictated, often to absurd extremes. It was unclear how history could be taught, when it was a punishable offense to engage children in "discussion of military and political questions of the past, present, or future."[64] The administration registered schools, only grudgingly handing out permission to institute new ones, hunted down unauthorized schools, and punished organizers with crippling fines and imprisonment. Inspectors monitored schools, teaching plans, textbooks. Before being certified, native teachers were ordered to take special courses organized by military authorities, which stressed German language and German method. It is unclear how much they achieved, since in terms of mutual understanding, it appears that ground was lost, rather than gained. Teachers frequently complained that they were subjected to abuse and their cultures ridiculed, and seminars became hot-beds of secret resistance by young teachers.[65] The army also limited higher education. In Wilna, university courses were organized at the "People's University," until these were forbidden. Ludendorff forbade the establishment of a Polish university in Wilna.[66] Lithuanian requests to establish an agricultural school in Dotnuva were refused by von Rümker, Ober Ost's agricultural authority, on the grounds that they had not yet as a people progressed to the point where that was practical.

These programs' ultimate aim was to produce client nationalities within a German framework. They were blocs to be manipulated, under the guise of "mediation" between them by a "neutral" military administration. Hindenburg's secret orders on school policy forbade "any germanization." Instead, authorities aimed at gaining a foothold in each pupil's consciousness through language lessons and inculcating German manner, a German way of doing things, and German method. As Hindenburg's secret orders instructed, "if German nature should win influence in the inner working of the school (the teaching plan, style of teaching, teaching materials, and so on), this would be of lasting benefit for Germany, regardless of the political future of the land."[67] Children's minds could be colonized from within through teaching "German from the inside," winning the next generation of natives. This educational process would finally produce distinct blocs of ethnic groups, accustomed to German manner and method, but requiring German supervision. The refusal to allow institutions of higher learning revealed central assumptions of the *Kultur* program, as a hierarchy was established within a division of (cultural) labor. Natives had no need for an intelligentsia, for German tutors and custodians could fill that role. Von Gayl later summed up the basic conception: "with a firm but gentle guiding by the reins, the Lithuanian countrypeople could certainly be led to a higher level of culture and a satisfactory life of their own, pulled away from the influence of the Polish landlords as well as that of their own intellectuals, in the framework of the German cultural sphere, without giving up their own national properties."[68] In particular, Ludendorff and his officials envisioned using nationalities here to offset the Poles, dividing and conquering. Von Gayl recalled that Ludendorff "saw in Poland a danger for the German East, especially an East Prussia surrounded by Poland . . . In the Lithuanians he saw a counterweight against Poland which was worth preserving . . . Ludendorff saw all questions of the occupied territory only from the perspective of what benefited Germany and never from sentimental inclinations toward any border people."[69]

Ultimately, schools policies were another failure, for natives fell back on a tradition of clandestine schooling, and education became a focal point for sullen resistance. For all sides, it was decisive that a state founded on the claim of bringing *Kultur* to eastern wastelands pursued a policy consisting mostly of shutting down schools and stamping out grassroots educational efforts.

The same implict cultural division of labor was built into the exhibition of artists' and craftsmen's studios, the Wilna *Arbeitsstuben*, "work rooms," a preeminent institution for a bracketing of native culture, as folk artists and artisans worked under German supervision.[70] Work Rooms already existed before, as private schools or charities, but German authorities centralized these efforts. Sponsored by Ober Ost, "work rooms" supported native artists: local Germans, Jews, Lithuanians, Poles, Belarusians. The Wilna "work rooms" exhibition was opened in June 1916 by the German city administration.[71] This achievement seemed to testify to the reconstructive, creative powers of German Work, which produced an exhibition less than a year after taking the city.

The exhibit's guidebook offers a view of the institution's organization and real goals.[72] It opened with thanks to German experts for help in organizing the exhibition. In the showrooms, "products of old and new Lithuanian, White Ruthenian, Polish and Jewish arts and crafts from Lithuania were united."[73] Displays featured not high art, but ordinary artisan crafts, house wares, pottery, carvings, weavings. Such profane objects demonstrated how little craft forms changed over the ages, with old and new sometimes hard to tell apart. Yet such continuity and fidelity to traditional forms were presented as mere absence of historical sense and order, as if some crudely expressed, unchanging ethnic essence underlay this art. This ahistorical perspective suggested a permanent essence at the core of ethnic identities. Even if artifacts, new and old, were mixed historically, the show still asserted a principle of division, segregating exhibits by ethnicity with separate rooms devoted to artifacts from different "tribes": Poles, Lithuanians, Jews, and Belarusians. There was, however, no German section, for the message here was precisely that these separate ethnic worlds were only to be brought together by the Germans. In the Lithuanian section, a large display held 300 woven bands, Lithuanian *juostos*, a trademark of native culture. Their ornamental patterns were significant. Those brought together were of many different ages, and yet the earliest, from 1725, were in continuity with contemporary ones. Underlining this timelessness and archaism, the exhibition promised live demonstrations of handicrafts and older trades. Native work itself would be performed, under the occupiers' supervision.[74] The permanent exhibit would be an instant museum of archaic cultures; the living work and ways of these peoples turned into instant ethnography. Art objects and crafts were offered for sale to German soldiers as truly authentic souvenirs to take home. This was a further purpose of the exhibitions, to define, direct, and control traffic between Germans and locals, through this interface. Most of all, their attention was directed to the overarching organization of German Work, bringing together native efforts. Many thousands of soldiers passed through the exhibition, sat in the café taking refreshments and reading "all the German newspapers of the occupied territories of Russia," bought authentic native souvenirs, and took in the greater message. The "work room" institution expressed a specific ideology, centering on work: that of local peoples and of higher *Deutsche Arbeit*, in a division of labor. By its nature, German Work was an overarching effort, supervising the work of others. In the larger campaign of German Work, "work rooms" were the starting point for more comprehensive ambitions.

German occupiers faced in these conquered territories a past into which they could not effectively insinuate themselves, while the region's dense tangle of living historical associations denied the conquerors a place. If the reproach to their presence could not be met by the historical roles tried on, it might be overcome by annexing the past, assimilating it to their own project. German officials would function as custodians of history for native populations, using German Work to interpret and define the area's past. Ostensibly, this selfless effort was all for the benefit of locals, themselves incapable of such achievements. German management would reveal their own histories and identities, and thus possess their futures.

From the occupation's beginning, authorities set about assessing damage to local art-historical treasures, as part of their larger cataloging and information gathering. Many motivations were involved, not least among them genuine scholarly interest and a sense of responsibility. Accounts enumerated in great detail Russian destruction or wholesale hauling away of cultural objects: statues, church bells, archives. Reports emphasized Russian depradations, minimizing damage done by German guns. This asymmetrical reporting reflected sensitivity to reports from the Western Front, where Germans were smarting from Allied propaganda. German destruction of Belgium's Louvain's library in 1914 was used to damning effect in the battle for international opinion, presented as definitive evidence that Germans were "Huns" making war on civilization itself. By way of amends, Germany sought to compensate with the civilizing mission in the East.

Administrators emphasized the physical neglect of great art-historical treasures under Russian rule (exaggerations of its extent only underlined how indispensable their own efforts were). Important buildings had been allowed to fall into disrepair. Museums and archives languished in poor, obscure lodgings. Everywhere there was the same frozen disorder. Germans were shocked to find that no systematic records of the area's art-historical features existed.[75] The cultural administration devoted itself to the task, mobilizing German scholars and writers. German rule would be very different, it promised. It was as if the region's history had only been discovered by the new arrivals. Reports noted, "with the very shallow *Kultur* spread over the Lithuanian land, the number of museums and libraries is correspondingly small."[76]

First, the administration needed to list and inventory the treasures now in its keeping. It is striking how quickly attention was given to questions of preservation, even while war raged. In fall 1914, Paul Clemen, noted preservationist and professor of art history at Bonn, was charged with preservation efforts on the Western Front, then from fall 1915 also the Eastern Front.[77] The War Conference for Monument Preservation in Brussels on August 29, 1915, urged protective measures for the eastern occupied territories. Clemen traveled in Poland and Ober Ost to observe and direct efforts. At the front, concerned officers did what they could, salvaging altarpieces of churches. With occupation of the towns, the supreme commander appointed experts to secure archives and libraries. In the countryside, military district offices were ordered to collect all pictures, books, and movable icons. With the establishment of "ordered conditions" and methodical administration, preservation efforts intensified, aiming at more systematic, comprehensive overviews "of which valuable architectural monuments in the land had been damaged by military operations and needed urgent care, which libraries and collections in public or private hands were existent and which cultural evidences of Germanness from old or new times were to be found in Lithuanian territory."[78] From the first, great attention was given to discerning older traces of German culture, even when evidence was fragmentary or dubious. Brickwork that seemed Prussian in technique suggested that a certain structure might represent "one of the furthest monuments of the penetration of this art into the East."[79] It seemed that any meaningful achievement in these wastelands must indicate earlier German presence, even when speaking of relics as "German" was a feat of anachronism.

Enthusiasm continued unabated. As the occupation settled in, the administration encouraged conservation. In April 1917, Jena art history professor Paul Weber was appointed conservator for architectural and art-historical monuments and advisor on questions concerning art to Military Administration Lithuania. He traveled about, personally taking note of newly discovered treasures, and presented his results in a book, *Wilna: A Forgotten Site of Art*, published by the Tenth Army newspaper's Wilna press.[80]

Curators rejoiced at their finds, announcing, for instance, that Wilna was "to some extent for the first time discovered for European art history through the war."[81] Officials cataloged with gusto, taking special care to underline German traces. The administration cataloged everything exhaustively: museums, private libraries, libraries of societies, art collections, churches, castles ruined and intact, palaces, manor-houses, cloisters, statues, memorial columns, the huge wooden synagogues of the Litvaks. They established a central archive of architectural monuments, gathering photographs and information. Other projects behind the Eastern Front, like the Polish Government General's surveys, also extended to Ober Ost. Concern for preservation was imposed on lower administrative levels, whose regular reports included mention of monuments.

The work before cultural officials was extraordinary, with so much here that was strange and new to their senses. Even when artistic forms seemed familiar, there was a shock hidden within the whole, as peculiar things happened to styles they knew from European tradition. Scholars as well as casual onlookers were struck by the riot of simultaneity in the cities, where architectural styles and forms from many different epochs and traditions coexisted, intertwining, achieving improbable syntheses.[82] Styles obsolete in the West arrived here a generation late, mutated. Wilna in particular showed anachronistic survival and disorder. Its thirty-six great churches represented beautiful culminations out of joint with time. Spires and houses abutted each other in a clutter of ages, and yet there was in the whole a kind of vital coexistence, coherence uniting such variety. German custodianship extended to prehistoric ages, which here seemed so disconcertingly close to the present, in more haunting simultaneities.[83]

Demands on the appreciation of scholars could become overpowering, but in that case there was the proven antidote of devoting oneself to searching for the familiar: finding German traces in this chaos. One expert blandly averred that certain local works "are immediately conspicuous through their artistic quality and thus announce themselves as imports."[84] If Lithuanian nobility evidenced past strength of character, another official explained, it was also true that they possessed German background.[85] Reports announced discovery of a supposed Germanic ring fort, and scholars discussed the possibility of ancestral Goths having passed through the area.[86] In this way, the sheer variety could be dismissed. But German traces were limited and searchers all too often reduced to mourning what had been lost, while in other cases, the designation "German" was anachronistic. Cataloging went forward with immense condescension and didactic ponderousness, often overcoming a sense of appreciation. Great wooden synagogues from the seventeenth and eighteenth centuries represented striking achievements in native

Jewish architecture, creating startling new forms. Even here, custodians took it upon themselves to instruct religious communities in the care of their own sacred objects, urging "special protection, which they have until now evidently mostly been denied."[87]

Ober Ost's publicity machine celebrated these efforts: order and system imposed on earlier confusion and neglect. The classifying and ordering work itself was on display, demonstrating genius for organization and system. Publications intended for Germany featured these accomplishments of *"Kulturarbeit."* The *Tenth Army Newspaper* featured a series on monuments. At home, scholarly articles announced the new wonders discovered in the East.

Even at the war's end, as Germany braced for Ludendorff's final gamble, the 1918 spring Western offensive, Ober Ost exhibits continued to stress German Work. The Tenth Army's Wilna-Minsk exhibition was a great act of classification.[88] Visitors passed from room to room, each devoted to one of the different subject nationalities under German custodianship. The official guide is extremely illuminating. It speaks of needing to come to terms with the strangeness of the surroundings, to visualize previous ages here and in new lands taken in the East. With great application, organizers set about "discovering" German traces and influence. Descriptions of artifacts quizzed – "German Work?" The guide pointed out, "Those with little acquaintance with eastern art are especially amazed by strong German influence."[89] Guild masterpieces represented the labor of Wilna masters, "after all, mostly Germans," while "the dependence of the local works on German art is already explained by the fact that the masters, for the most part, had come from German cities."[90] The supposed lowering of standards was due to foreigners: "With increasing contamination of the guild system by foreign influence, especially Jewish, the quality of work sinks quite considerably."[91] Yet some of the strangeness was irreducible, not to be explained away. The seeming antiquity of new native art was striking, showing that "the connection with older art has been strongly retained with old technique."[92] A Belarusian manuscript in Arabic script seemed emblematic of the peculiar fusions of cultural worlds characteristic of the area. Even when these features could not be assimilated, the very fact that they were cataloged and displayed by German scholarship was presented as the crucial achievement.

While scholars cataloged and mentored native cultures, a cultural program was needed for the Germans themselves. To rule and make over these lands successfully, they needed a strong sense of purpose, reinforced by institutions for Germans alone, giving soldiers posted here a feeling for their mission. While Ober Ost set about defining and proctoring native cultures, it was necessary to "watch the watchers." A set of institutions of *Kultur* for soldiers instructed them in their proper position and role in the frame of German Work.

Even as soldiers carried German culture, they risked an erosion of their own identity in what were now lands without limits, lacking what occupiers were prepared to recognize as "culture." Increasingly, occupiers' actions showed the perils of this setting. Officials hinted darkly at problems endemic to rear areas. One was disgusted, as the "demoralizing effect on men and even officers was expressed in all manner of unhappy phenomena."[93] In the practice of the administration, they were losing their own sense of limits, civilization. One popular native source claimed soldiers, drunk or elated at the loss of bounds, had on occasion ridden naked through town streets.[94] The populations that looked on were considered too primitive to mind. Strictures that obtained in the West fell away, limits vanishing especially in the treatment of natives. Public violence against locals occurred. Natives complained of being used as hunting dogs by the Germans.[95] A popular source claimed natives were on occasion harnessed in teams to plows and photographed while German officers watched: an especially revealing scene, in view of claims being made of German "cultivation" of these lands and peoples.[96] It was a literal rendering of the administration's goals, harnessing native energies under the direction of German Work. But beyond increasing brutality, there were also more langorous dangers of simply going under in the great mass of peoples and expanses.

The administration worried over "fraternization" with natives, obsessed with disease, an anxiety expressed in scores of orders and directives. A principal reason was fear of epidemics of venereal disease incapacitating vast numbers of troops, as Hindenburg and Ludendorff both commented in their memoirs on the danger of these unclean lands. Ober Ost's administration gave orders on prostitution, determined to control it, and mobilized its health section.[97] Ober Ost's censors also aimed to eliminate "dirty literature" which might further inflame soldiers.[98] The military administration apparently ran its own supervised brothels.[99] By contrast, "tea parlors" in the towns, frequented by soldiers and officers, were an unregulated danger. This pointed to another peril, for feeling at home, soldiers might begin to see the world through the categories of these lands, rather than those they had brought with them. The administration wanted its men to come to feel at home, but not by slowly sinking into place and going native. Rather, soldiers had to be educated to their loftier position as supervisors, overseers, and orderers. How to reconcile goals of consolidating and assimilating with the simultaneous push for expansion and annexation?

The answer was to be found at the farthest edge of the aggressive moving border of German military power: up at the front. After late 1915, positions hardened into trench warfare, as in the West. It was a point of pride for Germans that their civilization and *Kultur* were carried right up to the outermost limits of their control, the most advanced trenches. Military officials and front newspapers lauded the care that went into creating ordered circumstances, even in these blasted ditches, dugouts, and foxholes, where German conditions were always complacently contrasted with the bestial state of life in opposing Russian earthworks. German trenches were marked by elaborate work, dug in deep, and carefully furnished inside. Photographs and sketches showed their celebrated domesticity, mimicking the *Gemütlichkeit* of German family parlors. A semblance of cultured life took place here: reading, cultivation, "front art." These achievements were actively encouraged by the command. Regulations celebrated trench domesticity, discerning its psychological importance.[100] Orderly comfort maintained in these most extreme surroundings were testimony to the building spirit of German Work. A distinctive attitude was embodied: the idea of *"Einbauen"* and *"Einrichten,"* terms that crop up frequently in the newspapers and memoirs. "Building-in," or fortifying, and "furnishing" or "equipping" were key concepts. As soon as a new position or territory was taken, German presence was thus established, founded, grounded. *Einbauen* and *Einrichten* promised security, and perhaps even a measure of "coziness" amid devastation.[101] These values were repeated in a variety of new military institutions in the occupied territory: "soldiers' homes," front newspapers, and military theatre. These institutions existed on the Western Front as well, in fact originated there, yet were significantly changed in the East, where they had a tone of desperate urgency. In the mental geography of soldiers, they were intended to spread over the land, making it over as German and recognizable, as strong points. Settling in was both means and goal, a sort of vindication, for the German Work of remaking the landscape promised to give meaning to their presence. Each of these cultural institutions took up the task.

"Soldiers' homes" were established in the towns to keep soldiers on leave above and apart from native populations, enclaves of German domestic order in foreign surroundings, where a "German soldier, as a man of higher *Kultur*" could never get used to being quartered in the filthy hovels of natives, with their large families.[102] Homes multiplied, cropping up at the front and behind the lines.[103] Staffed by "sisters," volunteers from Germany, homes offered inexpensive bed and board, and many amenities besides: coffee, reading rooms, piano rooms, evening entertainments, lectures, slide shows, musical evenings, readings of German poets, and theatrical pieces. One report exclaimed that "the soldiers' home is the purest institution of *Bildung*," and proudly concluded that so-called "German barbarians, one could say, take the university with them to the front!"[104]

The very phenomenon of "soldiers' homes" indicates the outlines of a distinct eastern "front experience." The *Fronterlebnis* celebrated in the books of Jünger and others was that of the West: men and machines battling in devastated trench landscapes. By contrast, the experience on the Eastern Front was quite different, its hallmarks the fight against invisible enemies of boredom and alienation, losing oneself in the landscape, going native. Being in the East meant a struggle for community and identity in vast expanses. Ludendorff's evaluation of the homes was telling: "From my perspective, one could never overdo it in this regard. The Soldiers' Homes corresponded to a deep need in the East."[105] Soldiers were exhorted to: "Stay German! If you want to restore yourself or rest, go into the Soldiers' Homes," advised Wilna's guidebook.[106] Suggested "places of entertainment" were only two: the German city theatre and "soldiers' homes." In army newspapers, reports multiplied of the founding of "soldiers' homes." Readers soon had the sense of there being so many of them that they must cover the landscape. In this mental geography, after all the publicity, the view must have seemed to a little less foreign to them.[107] Each home, a report announced, was "a new monument of truly German nature planted in the occupied territory."[108] But German custodians would still stay above and apart from natives in these institutions devoted to this apartness of the rulers. There soldiers were safe from the contaminating influences of mingling with locals, frequenting "tea parlors" and brothels. A married soldier's poem agonized over urban erotic temptations: "I go through the alleys, / And what I see displeases me. / And that which I am thinking, it's also not modest / Yet I cannot stop."[109] In the words of a pastor visiting "soldiers' homes," this was a "fight behind the front," and German institutions strengthened weakening men.[110] It was crucial for soldiers to maintain their distance as the ruling people. At the same time, the picture of "soldiers' homes" and their importance was propagated at home in Germany, in the periodical press and in booklets, assuring civilians at home that even at this remove, German soldiers were unchanged, intact.[111]

In the program of *Kultur* to keep soldiers German, the administration gave an important position to the soldiers' newspaper, the *Soldatenzeitung*, also known as *Frontzeitungen*, *Kriegszeitungen*, or *Armeezeitungen*. Many kinds appeared on the Eastern Front, keeping soldiers connected to the homeland and giving meaning to their presence in the East. While front newspapers were also published in the West and sprang up there first (made possible by more stationary forms of warfare), distinctive, urgent needs obtained in the East. Individual units founded newspapers, but were encouraged from above as well. Ludendorff provided army newspapers with wire service. The first eastern newspaper was "*The Watch in the East*," begun in 1915. By 1917 there were already eight on the Eastern Front, growing enormously, the largest reaching press runs of twenty to thirty thousand and more.

These newspapers were decisive in combating "the manifold desolation of the war of position: 'The long Russian winter . . . with the specter of boredom and numbness.'"[112] To improve morale, editorial staffs sought to involve troops, including personal experiences of soldier-readers. Editors solicited contributions and printed stories, essays, accounts of funny or uncanny incidents, and some fantastically awful poems. Soldiers' newspapers were celebrated as special examples of *Kulturarbeit* in the East, for in addition to providing troops with news and raising morale, they avowed a cultural mission. Instructing troops on the lands and its peoples, they aimed to make troops feel at home, but in the ways most useful to Ober Ost's project. The information was intended to let troops know how to act toward natives. It was an ambitious project of education and "spiritual work."[113]

Military cultural institutions on the Eastern Front encouraged other literary undertakings: field libraries and front bookstores, in the form of book wagons.[114] The chain of field bookstores grew to a hundred. Army press repeatedly highlighted front libraries and bookstores, examples of culture taking to the field in this great war of peoples, German values at the very furthest border: "It was made a priority to push the field bookstores as close up to the front as possible and to provide the entire area with a net of these installations, so important for the soldiers."[115] A book wagon with 1,000 volumes drove near the front to reach divisions there.[116] Pushed up to the limits of the fighting front line, these institutions aimed to strengthen soldiers' national identity, while giving meaning to their presence through German Work.

These ambitions came together most vividly as theatre was mobilized in Ober Ost. Theatre conveyed a message to natives and German soldiers, and functioned as a regulated point of meeting between rulers and ruled. The administration felt the responsibility to present the best products of German culture and to raise its prestige through these achievements.[117] Paul Fussell's classic *The Great War and Modern Memory* explored the extraordinary role of literature and drama in the war: how the Western Front came to conform to expectations of artistic convention and vision, how the war was "literary."[118] Yet even in a war so literary and theatrical, Ober Ost excelled in those qualities. Moreover, Germans of Ober Ost were proud of this. As one writer put it, "To be German is to be literary."[119] The *Tenth Army Newspaper* offered abundant testimony: issue after issue was dedicated to this or that literary figure: Schiller, Goethe, Körner, Cervantes, Shakespeare. A regular section entitled "Mask and Lyre" reviewed local theatre performances. Ober Ost was permeated with this theatricality, itself the deliberate staging of a state, as the administration strove to project a monolithic image.

The uses of theatre were exposed in an article in the *Tenth Army Newspaper*, "Theatre and State."[120] Theatre was culture, social ritual, legitimacy, the measure of a people and its level of civilization. As in so many other spheres, German intellectuals expected war to bring redeeming cultural transformations. War was regarded as the school of the nation, from which the spirit would rise purified. Might one also expect a rebirth in drama, pinnacle of the arts? The state, cultural work, and theatre were all tied up in one German project.

Theatre held a privileged position in the life of Ober Ost. Major cities of the territory operated theatrical houses. Wilna itself had several movie houses, an open-air theatre, and a German city theatre. Judging from enthusiastic descriptions in newspapers and the soldiers' guidebook, the city theatre counted as one of the most important German spiritual landmarks in Wilna: "You must visit it, as soon as you have any time."[121] Opened only three months after the city's capture, its full seasons of plays, operettas, operas, and concerts were eagerly attended.

Theatre in Ober Ost was directed at both Germans and natives. For soldiers, articles insisted, German drama was not only entertainment, but a cultural lifeline to the homeland. Theatre was also a decisive "ethnic interface" culturally, where Germans and natives met, their fraternization otherwise proscribed, while the administration could control and channel their trafficking and relations. At a higher level, officials sought to exercise their function as carriers of *Kultur*. It was explained that "theatre is a very good yardstick for the cultural level of a people." The stage could be the place for national ambitions to act themselves out, instead of politics: "therefore the national stage is also the striving of all the ethnicities, who have only awakened to a cutural-national life in our time." In Ober Ost, the need for critical arbiters was clear, "because here in a relatively narrow space there live next to one another peoples of different cultural levels – in some of them the national idea was already alive early, in others only now awakened." The arbiter stood aloof from natives' childish squabbles, a neutral critic of their development.[122]

Cultural administrators asserted that there had been practically no theatre before the occupation. With rising national consciousness released by German "liberation," energies were let loose, for the occupiers to organize. The program of *Kultur* provided the framework for these efforts:

Thus the ways are made level to the national stage, to the national art of the foreign peoples of Russia; it will depend on the ethnicities themselves, how much they can make the most of their national culture, how far they develop their spiritual life. If the national consciousness is strong enough, then each people will also create for itself a stage of its own and not borrow light and luster from others, if it carries the fire within itself.[123]

Under German tutelage, nationalities competed with one another: the Polish dramatic-musical society "Lutnia"; a Jewish society; Lithuanian and Latvian efforts; the beginnings of Belarusian theatre. All were at different stages of developing *Kultur,* and military drama critics would judge where ethnicities stood. Yet local Germans could not be compared in this cultural gradation. Outside of Ober Ost's laboratory of cultural development, Germans looked down to criticize, evaluate, and instruct it.

Theatre as a cultural meeting place involved two-way traffic. Army newspaper reviewers visited and reported on Yiddish, Lithuanian, and Belarusian performances. Soldiers made up a considerable part of the audiences, understanding little and attracted most by the refreshments and dancing afterwards. The meeting was not always edifying, as more fastidious soldiers complained about native audiences. Locals were ignorant of accepted western etiquette, making themselves obnoxious by keeping their hats on, spitting in the aisles, and talking loudly during performances. Purists preferred all-German audiences.[124] Sometimes meeting natives strengthened earlier prejudices, as soldiers observed those around them: "At Yiddish theatre performances not only the stage is of interest, but also the audience, which is so very different from what one is used to in central Europe." It all gave "opportunity for delightful studies to the impartial observer, who would like to get to know the unique character of eastern Jewry."[125]

The real point of the exercise, however, lay in the arbitration, evaluation, and criticism of performances, so that authorities could steer cultural evolution. Yiddish theatre earned high marks and was taken seriously.[126] A Wilna student group was "at the moment without question the artistically highest-standing native theatre troupe of the entire Ober Ost area." Reviewers announced that it was an advantage that students had no formal training, for what they presented then was the raw stuff of real life for eastern Jews. This was compelling for Germans, seeing a foreign reality: "It is all life and deepest feeling, it is no longer poetry – it is truth, which speaks from the stage."[127] A crucial factor was the fact that

Yiddish was accessible to the German ear. Lithuanian, Latvian, and Belarusian efforts were dubiously received.[128] What Lithuanian performers presented was not true drama, army critics wrote, but rather only "a kind of play, which calls itself drama."[129] This reflected their position on the scale of national evolution: "Theatre occupied a quite wretched position in the spiritual life of Lithuanians and Latvians. Both of the ethnicities are after all made up for the most part of small farmers and workers, with whom one can speak of a spiritual life only in very humble measure at all." In fact, such culture as natives had could supposedly be traced back to earlier German Work. Latvian literature, it was asserted, was "after all not really a Latvian product. It is the German spirit in the Latvian world of thought. German scholars created the foundations from which Latvian literature can now develop itself further." Damningly, Latvians had "not been able to pull themselves together for artistic activity of their own."[130] In all of this, no account was taken of Russification and repression, or of the terrors of the war. The final judgment delivered on Lithuanian and Belarusian performances was that they represented the earliest stages of dramatic sensibility. In both cases, political chief von Gayl judged that their literatures and linguistic coherence were based on pioneering German scholarship.[131] With German Work, natives might eventually produce things worth seeing. This condescending verdict was part of a wider cultural argument: only German stewardship would bring these peoples up from their lower stage of development.[132]

Sometimes, however, an unguarded reviewer was startled by recognition of the real meaning of native performances. Considered from imported German aesthetic criteria, local efforts could clearly not measure up. Yet in fact they addressed another set of standards and needs, the priorities of the peoples themselves:

With the Lithuanians also the results in the area of art are still quite sparse. Amateur performances are all that one had been able to muster. These, however, were received with great interest and show not only the wealth of old folk art in costumes and dances, but also in their songs and dialogue allow the fullness of tone in the old language to come to surprisingly strong effect.[133]

Belarusian art, meanwhile, was rooted in "the unique character and peculiarity of the customs and usages of the rural people, among whom ancient rights and traditions still live on today."[134] In general, however, army reviewers' responses were made up of equal parts of cultural imperialism and interested pleading.

Ober Ost's German cultural mission was to give the best example to the East's primitive peoples. Carrying *Kultur* was a serious business, leading army newspaper reviewers to complain repeatedly about frivolous plays, arguing that this was hardly the face German culture wanted to show to locals and soldiers. As German culture moved east, it should present the best that it had to offer. There was work to be done here, critics sternly reminded themselves:

> One thing must be kept in mind: it does not alone suffice to bring diversion and stimulation to the army at the front and in the rear area, but rather the best must be offered that German artists have to offer. It is not a question of entertainment alone, which is to be solved here, rather it is a great mission of culture [*Kulturmission*], which German art has to fulfill. Now there offers itself a unique opportunity at present, to show the foreign peoples what the nature of German art is, and to educate Germans to a true understanding of art.

The war was seen as a crucial opportunity for culture. Soldiers had to be freed from the trenches' narrow horizon and led to greater things, "since out of the distress and force of the time there has grown out of our people a serious, more deeply founded race." More than this, the East was a possibility and a responsibility:

> And it is not only German soldiers to whom art is to give something. A second mission of culture [*Kulturmission*] must yet be fulfilled here. The saying goes so proudly that the world would be healed by German nature [*am deutschen Wesen die Welt genesen würde*]. Here we finally have for once the opportunity to show by deed that we are capable of bringing salvation to other peoples, to be leaders for them out of the darkness of un-culture [*Unkultur*] and un-education [*Unbildung*] to the light of an ideal existence truly worthy of humans. We have here for once the opportunity to prove that German art is genuine art.

The carriers of *Kultur* were aware of how they were watched by natives, who "all look up to us now as the conquerors . . . but they are also very keen-eyed critics: superiorities as well as mistakes of the German nature do not escape them." One could not let slip the "unique opportunity which offers itself, to bring foreign peoples' sensibility closer to German art and German nature." Authorities made efforts to bring famous actors to the area. Those successful performances "showed also to the foreign inhabitants of the conquered territories, what a magical power lies hidden in genuine German art, has allowed an intuition to dawn for them, that German nature is perhaps after all called to impress on the world a different, German character."[135] The theatre was to present native populations with edifying samples of the best of German culture, when otherwise they might fixate on the regime's severities.

Yet natives' experiences of theatre and its civilizing mission were quite different, as they later claimed they were driven in herds to newly established German theatres by soldiers. Reportedly, locals were crowded into these military temples of art, after being forced to pay to see dramas in a language they did not understand.[136] The result would hardly have been deep appreciation and gratitude. Here was a striking example of the strange primacy which representation had over real actions in the East.

Theatrical performance put a cultural stamp of ownership on the region, each production a "deed of art" driven into the cultural soil.[137] The very fact of the performance was the crucial thing, ritually staging the legitimacy of the occupation, mission and meaning for the German soldier's presence. It was piously hoped that theatre would "have a blessed influence on the diffusion of the German idea in Ober Ost."[138]

Among the hybrid institutions born of Ober Ost's needs and ambitions, the most remarkable was *Fronttheater*, theatre on the front. In trenches on Ober Ost's section of the Eastern Front, *Fronttheater* represented German culture pushing up to the very front lines. One could not get any closer to the outer borders of German influence. Who then could doubt that this was for Germans a war about culture, a true *Kulturkampf?* The scene was a compelling one. Some distance from the fortified front line, set at the edge of a dense forest, a diminutive theatre is dug halfway into the ground. Inside, on rows of close benches made of roughly cut planks, tired ordinary enlisted men and officers sit next to each other, a crowd all in field gray. The blanket curtain before them is drawn aside. On the crude stage, before dim lights, a drama about the Thirty Years' War begins. Perhaps a kilometer away, German and Russian cannon trade explosions, yet these sounds of doom do not distract the actors or audience – they fit too well into the play being performed. In addition to theatre, concerts, chamber music recitals, cabarets, lectures in reading rooms, sports festivals, all pushed up close to the front.[139] *Frontkino*, front cinema, became ubiquitous.[140] By 1917, there were seventy of them on Ober Ost's Eastern front.[141] But above all, newspapers celebrated the front stage.[142] They exhorted soldiers to use war as an opportunity for cultural growth, a raising of standards. Writers deplored the proliferation of *Frontkino*, and praised *Fronttheater*, as a genuine, meaningful, and vital art form.[143] It is unclear how much *Fronttheater* can be traced back to orders or commands. In most cases it seems only to have been encouraged by officialdom, rather than called into existence by superiors. Initiative from below and encouragement from above combined. The very anonymity of the process means that this was a truly general, broad cultural phenomenon "close to the ground." Discussions of front theatre turned technical hardships into virtues: the primitive condition or absence of props, stage machinery, lighting, and female actors. Traditional Bavarian puppet shows harking back to the Middle Ages, or performances of Hans Sachs plays from the seventeenth century seemed all the more authentic.[144] These were the conditions of Shakespeare's time! Making a virtue of necessity, pressed together on benches in the crowded room, watching men from the unit or touring actors, soldiers approached the ideals of Wagner's Bayreuth: *Gemeinschaft*, total community through theatre, and the *Gesamtkunstwerk*, art as a total act transforming the individual, state, and nation.

Performances must have been pleasant diversions, but more important was the very idea of front theatre.[145] This was a ritual of taking possession; settling in at the advanced position showed confidence that there would be no retreat. German Work pressed forward: "the 'Soldiers' Theatre on the Front' is in every sense a German act."[146] Each drama, as an expression of *Kultur*, pushed up to the front, asserted a border, a new limit of control. The institution's true importance lay in its place in the mental geography of the occupiers, as a "German deed of culture" planted in foreign soil.

One drama was singled out, played over and over again, performed on primitive trench-stages, under the rumble of heavy guns; in those saving outposts of German domestic order in unruly lands, "soldier's homes"; and in German theatres of the towns, where the newcomer's high *Kultur* was to astound lowly natives. The one play was performed frequently, as something in it compelled the rapt attention and fascination of audiences in field gray. It was somehow a "perfect fit," expressing the meaning of Ober Ost and what soldiers felt was happening to them there. *The* drama of the military state was Friedrich Schiller's *Wallensteins Lager* (*Wallenstein's Camp*). It became the "theme drama" of the occupation. The choice could not have been more telling.[147] The prelude to the play *Wallenstein*, the *Lager* presents a series of scenes from the encampment of the warlord of the Thirty Years' War. Wallenstein's international band of freebooters around their campfires in Bohemia represent a nation being born, an anarchic, soldierly *Kriegsvolk* – a people of war, or war nation – with no faith or constitution but the iron-plated figure of its leader. Deceptively simple, this ideal play of *Fronttheater* is a drama of identity and the state. Schiller sets his audience down in Wallenstein's encampment, presenting the life and spirit of the *Lager* in a series of tableaux. Above it all, in spirit, sways the superhuman image of Wallenstein. The camp community is wedded to the enormous figure, one with him in moral responsibility: "His camp alone explains his crime."[148] *Wallensteins Lager* is more than an interlude in which Schiller builds up atmosphere for his play, for it presents the social drama of a nation in its genesis, at the moment of formation. Entrance follows on entrance, soldiers added to those already gathered: "there are new peoples arrived." The Watch-Master asks soldiers where they hail from; the army is a mix of nationali-

ties from all Europe, brought together under Wallenstein, gathering into
the *Lager* as one great new nation being born in Bohemia. The tribal
fusion quickly turns to the business of making itself a state: "to establish
an empire of soldiers, / To fire and torch the world." The *Lager* has its
own field school for its young, Wallenstein's own currency, and an ethic
of common property. They are all becoming *Wallensteiner*, as the war
nation turns to its unifying principle: "Who has forged us together so, /
That you will never tell us apart again? / None other than Wallenstein!"
The *Lager* exclaims – "We all stand for *one* man."[149] Successive scenes
show a collapse of identities, smaller units finding themselves in the
larger, in a building intensification. The individual is taken up in the *Volk*,
which submits to the structure of the state, finally vested in one man,
anticipating the formula of "one people, one empire, one leader [*Ein
Volk, ein Reich, ein Führer*]," in the person of Wallenstein, the rearing
cliff-figure. The process has run its course, following a mounting dynamism. With the *Lager*, Schiller has described the world of war, sketched in
the landscape of, as he puts it, this "space in time," unwittingly providing
a model of community based on war, for a war race. *Wallensteins Lager*
was uniquely compelling to the soldiers of Ober Ost, mirroring what they
themselves felt to be happening in the East. A military utopia was being
built, from the supreme commander's will. Out of it, a *Kriegsvolk* was
coming to birth in a land of war. When the play was performed in Kowno
in 1916 to commemorate the city's capture, the writer Eulenberg penned
a new prologue, which claimed the play "today speaks to our interior
more than ever before," as this war gave "new meaning and life" to
Schiller's lines. Through six stanzas, Eulenberg drew parallels between
Ober Ost and the play, which would "touch your souls, rich with connections, because much of that which moved [Wallenstein's] *Lager*-people,
matches our situation, including the Field-Marshal's head as background. The costumes have become different in the world theatre, the
spirit of man has hardly changed, and history still writes today in
blood."[150] In this transmuted vision of the Thirty Years' War, soldiers
found their own historical model and precedent to set against the unfamiliar.[151] Theatre in Ober Ost took on such importance because it paralleled the staging of the state.

The *Kultur* program of Ober Ost projected a compelling vision of the
military state, bracketed native cultures in German institutions, and tried
to give soldiers a sense of their mission. German Work in the East implied
a fundamental division of labor. Under the military state's supervision,
crude and undirected native energies would be gripped by German
organizing, systematizing, rationalizing genius. German Work defined a
people's place and ethnic essence by their function, fixing national ident-

ity. Not only native identities were reduced, for German national identity was also defined, presented, in its essence, as rule. To administer, to wield power, was the national calling in the military state in the East. The army offered a military mission of culture defined as power and control.

The cumulative loss of reality, as ambitions of the state and natives' experience diverged ever more, portended a crisis of rule. The categories and practices growing out of the cultural program were durable, yet precisely that durability created significant problems. In mid 1917 a new situation arose and Germany found it needed a new political course, as the balance of power seemed to be tipping against the Central Powers. Russia's February Revolution fueled calls for self-determination of peoples, adding pressure on Germany's government. Now, visions of outright annexation in the East had to make way for more complicated political arrangements. Natives had to be allowed some voice, enough to legitimate the intended future. The government authorized natives to set up national councils and pursue political activity, yet this was precisely where the *Kultur* program's success yielded a bitter harvest. In a short two years the administration created and propagated a program whose assumptions became so compelling that they impeded the new policies they were to enact. Ultimately, however, the legacy extended beyond failed attempts at accommodation with natives. While *Verkehrspolitik* explained for the soldier in the East the approach to the land, the program of *Kultur* prescribed the approach to the peoples. These, taken together, gave German soldiers on the Eastern Front and in the occupied territories a broader view of the East and the sorts of things which could be done there. That psychological outlook was to be the most unexpected, lasting, and fateful product of Ober Ost.

NOTES

1 Ludendorff, *Kriegserinnerungen*, 138.
2 Klemperer, *Curriculum*, 674.
3 Dehmel, *Zwischen Volk*; Hans Frentz, *Über den Zeiten. Künstler im Kriege* (Freiburg-in-Breisgau: Urban Verlag, 1931).
4 *Das Land*, 133.
5 Ibid., 136.
6 Ibid.
7 Quoted in Bertkau, "Zeitungswesen," 79.
8 BAMA PHD 8/23, *Korrespondenz B*, hereafter *KB*.
9 Schlichting, *Bilder*.
10 *Das Land Ober Ost. Deutsche Arbeit in den Verwaltungsbezirken Kurland, Litauen und Bialystok-Grodno*. The publication was announced in May 1917: BAMA PHD 8/20, "Ziffer 580. Bekanntmachung betreffend Herausgabe des Buches 'Das Land Ober Ost,'" *BUV* 79 (May 26, 1917): 631.

11 Swedish explorer Sven Hedin's *Nach Osten!* (Leipzig: F. A. Brockhaus, 1916); Arthur Feiler, *Neuland. Eine Fahrt durch Ob. Ost* (Frankfurt-on-Main: Frank. Societätsdruckerei, 1917); Fritz Hartmann, *Ob-Ost. Friedliche Kriegsfahrt eines Zeitungsmannes* (Hannover: Gebrüder Jänecke,1917); Ernst Heywang, *Deutsche Tat, Deutsche Saat in russischem Brachland. Eine Frontreise nach Ob.- Ost* (Strasbourg: Strassburger Druckerei und Verlagsanstalt, 1917); Karl Strecker, *Auf den Spuren Hindenburgischer Verwaltung. Erlebnisse und Ergebnisse einer Studienfahrt in Ob. Ost* (Berlin: C. A. Schwetschke & Sohn, 1917); Paul Listowsky, *Neu-Ost. Unser Zukunftsgrenzgebiet um Ostpreussens Ostrand. Fahrten durch Polen und Litauen unter deutscher Kriegsverwaltung* (Königsberg in Preussen: Hartungsche Zeitung, 1917).

12 BA N 1031/2, Gayl, 52, 86; BAMA N 196/1, Heppe, vol. V, 111; Hoffmann, *Aufzeichnungen,* I, 177–78; BAMA N 98/1, Gossler, 69, 83–94.

13 *Das Land,* 147.

14 *Völker-Verteilung in West-Rußland.*

15 *Das Land,* 147.

16 Klemperer, *Curriculum,* 465.

17 *Das Land,* 147.

18 *Sieben-Sprachenwörterbuch. Deutsch / Polnisch / Russisch / Weißruthenisch / Litauisch / Lettisch / Jiddisch.* (n.p. : Presseabteilung des Oberbefehlshabers Ost, [1918]). All quotes that follow are from preface, 5–7.

19 Bertkau, "Zeitungswesen," 132.

20 *Buchprüfungsamt,* or *Bupra.* Häpke, *Verwaltung,* 58; Bertkau, "Zeitungswesen," 156.

21 Dehmel, *Zwischen Volk,* 457.

22 Klemperer, *Curriculum,* 463, 504.

23 Pr. A. nr. 4076, quoted by Bertkau, "Zeitungswesen", 108. These files were destroyed at the Potsdam archive during the Second World War.

24 Ludendorff, *Kriegserinnerungen,* 145–46.

25 "Deutsch im Jiddischen," *ZXA* 284 (June 15, 1917); BAMA PHD 8/20, "Grundlegende Richtlinien zur Wiederbelebung des Schulwesens," *BUV,* supplement to no. 7 (January 28, 1916); Zechlin, *Deutsche Politik,* 224–37. A soldier's letter on commerce testifies to ease of communication: Philipp Witkop, ed., *Kriegsbriefe gefallener Studenten* (Munich: Georg Müller, 1928), 88–97; Klemperer, *Curriculum,* 684.

26 Ludendorff, *Kriegserinnerungen,* 145.

27 LCVIA F. 641, ap. 1, b. 53, "Verwaltungsberichte Rossienie," *Verwaltungsbericht 30. Jan. 1916,* 15; LCVIA F. 641, ap. 1, b. 53, "Verwaltungsberichte Rossienie," *Verwaltungsbericht 29. April 1916,* 14.

28 Klemperer, *Curriculum,* 476, 505.

29 BAMA N 196/1, Heppe, vol. V, 104.

30 LCVIA F. 641, ap. 1, b. 52, *Verwaltungsbericht für Februar 1916. Kreisamt Birsche,* 5.

31 Häpke, *Verwaltung,* 54.

32 (Hoover Institution Archives) Germany. Oberste Heeresleitung. Box 2, folder no. 5, untitled memorandum from Ober Ost (Wilna, May 5, 1916), 109.

33 BA N 1031/2, Gayl, 133.

34 Ibid., 133, 160.
35 BA N 1238/8, Morsbach, Bürgermeister zu Schaulen. Zu Abteilung V. 27 September 1916.
36 BA N 1031/2, Gayl, 239.
37 Ludendorff, *Kriegserinnerungen*, 145.
38 Ibid.
39 BAMA N 196/1, Heppe, vol. V, 72.
40 (Hoover Institution Archives) Germany. Oberste Heeresleitung. Box 2, folder no. 5, untitled memorandum from Ober Ost (Wilna, May 5, 1916), 110b–111b.
41 BAMA N 196/1, Heppe, vol. V, 101.
42 BAMA PHD 8/20, "Ziffer 259. Verwaltungsordnung für das Etappengebiet im Befehlsbereich des Oberbefehlshabers Ost (Ob. Ost)," *BUV* 34 (June 26, 1916): §9, p. 271.
43 BAMA N 196/1, Heppe, vol. V, 100.
44 Ludendorff, *Kriegserinnerungen*, 160.
45 Bertkau, "Zeitungswesen," 127, report on conference of March 20, 1916 in Ober Ost headquarters.
46 Klimas, *Atsiminimų*, 129.
47 Bertkau, "Zeitungswesen," 39–53.
48 Ibid., 124–34.
49 Häpke, *Verwaltung*, 59; Bertkau, "Zeitungswesen," 135–54.
50 Čepėnas, *Naujųjų*, II, 106–11.
51 Zemke, *Schulwesen*; Simas Sužiedėlis, "Mokyklos vokiečių okupacijos laikais (1915–1918)," in *Lietuva*, Lietuvių enciklopedija, vol. XV, ed. Vincas Maciūnas (South Boston, MA: Lithuanian Encyclopedia Press, 1968), 764–67.
52 Sužiedelis, "Mokyklos," 764.
53 LCVIA F. 641, ap. 1, b. 52, *Verwaltungsbericht für März 1916. Kreisamt Birsche*, 19.
54 Ludendorff, *Kriegserinnerungen*, 158–59.
55 Kitchen, *Dictatorship*, 55–63.
56 BAMA PHD 8/20, "Grundlegende Richtlinien zur Wiederbelebung des Schulwesens," *BUV*, supplement to no. 7 (January 28, 1916).
57 BAMA PHD 8/20, "Grundlegende Richtlinien," *BUV*, supplement to no. 7 (January 28, 1916): §5.
58 Sužiedelis, "Mokyklos," 767.
59 BAMA PHD 8/20, "Grundlegende Richtlinien," *BUV*, supplement to no. 7 (January 28, 1916): "Zu nr. 10."
60 Ludendorff, *Kriegserinnerungen*, 158.
61 Sužiedėlis, "Mokyklos," 767.
62 Ibid., 766.
63 BAMA N 98/1, Gossler, 67; BAMA N 98/3, Gossler, 23.
64 LMARS, F. 23–35, "Schulordnung für Litauen," under "§13. Deutschfeindliche Umtriebe," 67.
65 LMARS, F. 23–47, "Vokiečiai Lietuvoje," letter of protest to Prince Isenburg (dated July 10, 1916) from course participants; Gintneris, *Lietuva*, 437.

66 Ludendorff, *Kriegserinnerungen*, 159.
67 Secret orders reprinted in Zemke, *Schulwesen*, 115: order of January 16, 1916. In practice, this often degenerated into germanization after all: BAMA N 196/1, Heppe, vol. V, 144–45.
68 BA N 1031/2, Gayl, 282.
69 Ibid., 173.
70 "Ausstellung der Wilnaer Arbeitstuben," *Scheinwerfer* 25 (August 3, 1916); BAMA N 196/1, Heppe, vol. V, 124.
71 BAMA PHD 8/23, "Ein Jahr Wilnaer Arbeitsstuben," *KB* 40 (July 11, 1917).
72 *Führer durch die Ausstellung Wilnaer Arbeitsstuben 1916* (Wilna: Zeitung der 10. Armee, 1916).
73 Paul Weber, "Die Baudenkmäler in Litauen," in *Kunstschutz im Kriege. Berichte über den Zustand der Kunstdenkmäler auf den verschiedenen Kriegsschauplätzen und über die deutschen und österreichischen Massnahmen zu ihrer Erhaltung, Rettung und Erforschung*, ed. Paul Clemen (Leipzig: E. A. Seemann, 1919), 113.
74 *Führer . . . Ausstellung*, 19.
75 Weber, "Baudenkmäler," 113.
76 Ibid., 112.
77 Clemen, ed. *Kunstschutz*, 13.
78 Weber, "Baudenkmäler," 114.
79 Ibid., 108.
80 Paul Weber, *Wilna, eine vergessene Kunststätte* (Wilna: Verlag der Zeitung der 10. Armee, 1917).
81 Weber, "Baudenkmäler," 102.
82 BAMA N 196/1, Heppe, vol. V, 130.
83 Ibid., 148; Franz Frech, "Vorgeschichtliches aus Kurland," in *Das Land*, 400–402; K. Boneberg, "Die Vorzeit im Schützengraben," in *Das Land*, 403–409; Häpke, *Verwaltung*, 57; Häpke, "Forschung," 19–20.
84 Weber, "Baudenkmäler," 112.
85 BAMA N 196/1, Heppe, vol. V, 126.
86 BAMA PHD 8/23, "Ein germanischer Ringwall in Litauen," *KB* 98 (March 8, 1918).
87 Weber, "Baudenkmäler," 108–109; Walter Jäger, "Die Holzsynagogen des Ostens," *Beobachter* 99 (February 3, 1918).
88 Albert Ippel, *Wilna-Minsk. Altertümer und Kunstgewerbe. Führer durch die Ausstellung der 10. Armee* (Wilna: Zeitung der 10. Armee, 1918); Gefr. Karl Brammer, "Die Ausstellung Wilna-Minsk. Ein Rundgang," *ZXA* 591 (June 8, 1918).
89 Ippel, *Wilna-Minsk*, 12.
90 Ibid., 23.
91 Ibid., 32; see also Uffz. Ippel, "Wilnaer Zunftbücher," *Beobachter* 90 (December 9, 1917).
92 Ippel, *Wilna-Minsk*, 7.
93 BAMA N 196/1, Heppe, vol. V, 33.
94 Šilietis, *Okupacija*, 123.
95 LMARS, F. 23–47, "Vokiečiai Lietuvoje," 3, seventh item in list of grievances.

96 Šilietis, *Okupacija*, 100, incident in Schaulen and elsewhere.
97 *Das Land*, 119–26; police posters in (Hoover Archive) World War I Subject Collection, Box no. 19, folder "Germany. Proclamations. Lithuania," "Hüte dich vor Geschlechtskrankheiten!" (Kowno, January 1916), and "Merkblatt für Männer zur Verhütung von Geschlechtskrankheiten" (Kowno, January 1916).
98 Klemperer, *Curriculum*, 470.
99 Hirschfeld, *Sittengeschichte*, 236, 248–52, 264.
100 BA/MA PHD 8/2, *Merkblatt für den Ausbau von Feldstellungen*. The text (dated May 6, 1916) shows psychological sensitivity for fortification as a factor of war.
101 Marwitz's diary is a prime example of constant concern for "building in": Marwitz, *Stirb*, 52, 57, 82–83, 120–22; *Draussen-daheim. Bilder aus deutschen Soldatenheimen. Kriegstagebuch des Ostdeutschen Jünglingsbundes* (Berlin: Verlag der Buchhandlung des Ostdeutschen Jünglingsbundes, 1916), 12; BAMA N 196/1, Heppe, vol. V, 35, 69.
102 *Draussen*, 12–13, 17.
103 "Das Mannschaftsheim eines Infanterie-Regiments," *ZXA* 64 (April 25, 1916); BAMA PHD 8/23, "Weihe eines Soldatenheimes an der Ostfront," *KB* 35 (June 6, 1917).
104 *Mitau*, 10.
105 Ludendorff, *Kriegserinnerungen*, 144.
106 *Ich Weiß*, 15.
107 Divisionspfarrer Krohn, "Ein Soldatenheim an der vordersten Front," *ZXA* 43 (March 14, 1916); Unteroffz. Kastemacher, "Einweihung eines Soldatenheims," *ZXA* 110 (July 26, 1916); "Soldatenheim der Armierungskompagnie in S.," *ZXA* 430 (December 2, 1917); Fahrer Adolf Sporer, "Einweihung eines Soldatenheimes an der Front," *ZXA* 438 (December 12, 1917); Uffz. Liebe, "Soloquartett Prof. Röhtig im Soldatenheim Schröderwald," *ZXA* 438 (December 12, 1917); "Soldatenheim Grunewald," *ZXA* 498 (February 20, 1918); "Ein neues Soldatenheim," *ZXA* 581 (May 28, 1918); "Eröffnung des Soldatenheims in Polozk," *ZXA* 591 (June 8, 1918); "Eröffnung des Deutschen Soldatenheims in Molodetschno," *ZXA* 693 (October 5, 1918); Karl Rayka, "Im neuen Soldatenheim Molodetschno," *ZXA* 705 (October 18, 1918); LCVIA F. 641, ap. 1, b. 52, *Verwaltungsbericht für Februar 1916. Kreisamt Birsche*, 34.
108 BAMA PHD 23/88, Wilhelm Müller, "Das Soldatenheim beim Oberbefehlshaber Ost," *Unsere Zeit in Wort und Bild* 20 (1916).
109 *Mitau*, 40.
110 Ibid., 41.
111 Ibid.; BAMA PHD 23/88, Müller, "Soldatenheim"; *Draussen*.
112 *Das Land*, 134.
113 Bertkau, "Zeitungswesen," 18; *Das Land*, 135.
114 Ludendorff, *Kriegserinnerungen*, 144.
115 *Das Land*, 140.
116 *Draussen*, 22.
117 *Das Land*, 410–28.

118 Fussell, *Memory*, ix.
119 Gefr. M. Büttner, "Buchgewerbe im eroberten Kurland," *Beobachter* 53 (April 22, 1917).
120 Walter Jäger (Landsturmmann), "Theater und Staat," *Beobachter* 126 (June 6, 1918).
121 *Ich Weiß*, 9.
122 *Das Land*, 410.
123 Ibid., 424–25.
124 Ldstrm. Walter Jäger, "Deutsches Stadttheater Riga. Gastspiele der Dresdner Hofoper," *ZXA* 532 (March 31, 1918).
125 *Das Land*, 424.
126 "Eröffnung des jüdischen Theaters," *ZXA* 32 (February 17, 1916); Curt Winter, "Jüdisches Theater," *ZXA* 34 (February 22, 1916); Curt Pabst, "Jüdisches Theater," *ZXA* 40 (March 7, 1916); Gefr. Breske, "Spektakel," *ZXA* 347 (August 28, 1917) and 348 (August 29, 1917); Erich Weferling, "Jiddisches Theater in Subat," *ZXA* 499 (February 21, 1918) and no. 500 (22 February 1918); BAMA PHD 8/23, Hermann Struck, "Das Jüdische Theater in Wilna," *KB* 5 (November 8, 1916); See also Cohen, *Vilna*, 372–73.
127 *Das Land*, 423–24.
128 "'Naturtheater' in einer weißruthenischen Kinderheim," *ZXA* 353 (September 4, 1917); "Litauischer Abend," *ZXA* 366 (September 19, 1917); "Ein litauisches Dorftheater," *ZXA* 690 (October 2, 1918); "Litauisches Theater," *ZXA* 465 (January 12, 1918) and 467 (January 15, 1918).
129 Kanonier Wöhrle, "Litauischer Abend. Stimmungsbild vom letzten Sonntag," *ZXA* 196 (January 14, 1917).
130 *Das Land*, 417, 418, 422.
131 BA N 1031/2, Gayl, 129, 131.
132 See also Paul Rohrbach, "'Nationale Kultur' im baltischen Gebiet," *ZXA* 543 (April 13, 1918).
133 *Das Land*, 422.
134 Ibid., 423.
135 Ibid., 425–28.
136 In Pašiaušej and elsewhere: Šilietis, *Okupacija*, 108.
137 "Deutsche Konzerte in Wilna," *ZXA* 508 (March 3, 1918).
138 *Das Land*, 428.
139 "Sportfest 5 km hinter dem Schützengraben," *ZXA* 80 (May 27, 1916); "Sportfest am Naroczsee," *ZXA* 125 (August 25, 1916); Jäger, "Kammerspiele 2300m hinter der Front," *ZXA* 227 (March 17, 1917); BAMA PHD 8/23, "Deutsches Ostfront-Theater," *KB* 45 (August 15, 1917); BAMA PHD 8/23, A. Bielefeld, "Deutsche Musik im Rokitno-Sumpf," *KB* 23 (March 14, 1917).
140 Trainsoldat Rosenberg, "Ein Kino an der Front," *ZXA* 191 (January 4, 1917); Uffz. Oppenberg, "Ein Kino hinter der Front," *ZXA* 222 (March 7, 1917); Uffz. Willy Körber, "Frontkino und Fronttheater," *Beobachter* 49 (March 21, 1917).
141 *Das Land*, 428.

142 Landstrm. Heinrich Goldmann, "Soldatentheater an der Front," *ZXA* 34 (February 22, 1916); Leutnant Ficus, "Theater an der Front," *ZXA* 38 (March 2, 1916); Landstrm. Heinrich Goldmann, "Kleines Theater an der Front," *ZXA* 39 (March 4, 1916).

143 Uffz. Willy Körber, "Frontkino und Fronttheater," *Beobachter* 49 (March 21, 1917).

144 Hans Alexander, "Ein Münchener Marionetten-Theater in Pleskau," *ZXA* 693 (October 5, 1918).

145 Ldstrm. Heinrich Goldmann, "Kleines Theater an der Front. Szenen aus 'Goethes Faust,'" *ZXA* 49 (March 26, 1916); Ldstrm. Heinrich Goldmann, "Kleines Theater an der Front. Alt-Heidelberg," *ZXA* 54 (April 5, 1916); *ZXA* 290; Cyrus, "Gedanken beim Besuche eines Fronttheaters," *ZXA* 353 (September 4, 1917); "Unsere Frontbühne," *ZXA* 358 (September 9, 1917); "Theater an der Front," *Scheinwerfer* 14 (May 17, 1916); Hermann Pörzgen, "Das deutsche Fronttheater, 1914–20" (Ph.D. diss., Cologne, 1935); Herbert Maisch, *"Helm ab, Vorhang auf!" Siebzig Jahre eines ungewöhnlichen Lebens* (Emsdetten: Lechte, 1968); Geerte Murmann, *Komödianten fur den Krieg. Deutsches und alliertes Fronttheater* (Düsseldorf: Droste, 1992).

146 "Theater an der Front," *Scheinwerfer* 14 (May 17, 1916).

147 Uffz. P. Mennicken, "Feldtheater. Eindrücken und Vorschläge," *ZXA* 290 (June 22, 1917) and 291 (June 23, 1917); "Deutsches Theater in Wilna. Schillers Geburtstag: 'Wallensteins Lager,'" *ZXA* 413 (Liebesgabe) (November 13, 1917); "Gedenkfeier im Deutschen Theater in Dünaburg am 2.8.," *ZXA* 641 (August 6, 1918). Later, the play was also used in the "Patriotic Instruction" program ordered by Ludendorff once in the supreme command: Kitchen, *Dictatorship*, 61; Klemperer, *Curriculum*, 475, 545.

148 Friedrich Schiller, *Sämtliche Werke*, ed. Gerhard Fricke and Herbert G. Göpert, vol. II, *Dramen II* (Munich: Carl Hanser Verlag, 1958/59): *Wallenstein Prolog*, line 18.

149 *Wallensteins Lager*, line 7; *Auftritt* 11; lines 332–33; 805; 833.

150 Herbert Eulenberg, "Prolog zur Festaufführung von 'Wallensteins Lager,'" *Sonderbeilage zu Nr. 229 der Kownoer Zeitung.*

151 It is hard to overlook images linking scenes of *Wallensteins Lager* with Leni Riefenstahl's propaganda film *Triumph of the Will* (1935) of the 1934 Nazi Party convention in Nürnberg: the communal life of the *Lager*, the review of work troops and their choir call and response. The ritual scenes parallel *Wallensteins Lager*, speaking to its power as a model.

5   The mindscape of the East

The most durable and fateful product of the Ober Ost venture was not a bureaucratic institution or program, but rather a vision: the view of the East it created. A radically changed, apocalyptic German view of the East and what might be done there emerged during the war, formed by the disorienting situation which Germans encountered and the ways in which they sought to deal with it. The eastern front-experience produced in soldiers a specific way of looking out at the East, a German imperialist "mindscape" of the East. By "mindscape" I mean to designate the mental landscape conjured up by looking out over an area: ways of organizing the perception of a territory, its characteristic features and landmarks. This entails much more than a "neutral" description, since it signifies an approach, the posture of advancing into the landscape. A mindscape proposes ways of dealing with land: how to move within it, how to change, appropriate, and order it. Far beyond the merely descriptive, the mindscape is a prescription as well, a vision of the future and what will be expected of the territory. A mindscape, then, yields both a description and prescription of one's relationship to the land, what the mind styles for itself as a typical landscape as it is and ought to be. This outlook would be of great importance, as several million German soldiers of all ranks who shared in the eastern front-experience in greater or smaller measure took in a vision of the East and the meaning of German presence there.

This mindscape presented a land based on enduring first impressions of the 1915 "great advance." Chief among these were the area's vastness and the inner reactions it produced in soldiers who stared out at it, transfixed by empty expanses. A sketch in Ober Ost's public relations journal, entitled "The German Soldier in the Russian Steppe," described this effect:

Steeply the street sprang up out on to the steppe. No transition. It was a small farming town. Far into the farmyards the steppe stretched its fingers, probing. The houses form only small rifts in its sea. If one looks through an open door into the interior of a house, there yawns a further ground: steppe-ground in the middle

151

of the town. And all about the town it surges, like the ocean around a small sea-gnawed, fjord-rich island. Now the soldier went on a narrow, scarcely discernable path. The steppe took him into its spell. He stood still and looked deep into the round. Over there the town slept under few lights – like bright dreams. And to the right there stood now the moon – a bloody half-moon. He went further . . . In the distance, at the horizon, a brighter line now bordered the blackness. There lay the East, the Russian endlessness. He stared into this land, which in its distant expanses makes the eyes wide and yet directs the gaze inwards, which leads people into infinity, and yet leads them back to themselves.[1]

Another official's novel described the oppressive feelings of a train journey through the territory for soldiers, "the pressure which lay upon them, as they looked out into the fleeing vastness." "There is something so destabilizing in this moving and sliding away," one character complained, aching with "the feeling of being without a homeland, of being uprooted. Then life seems to one a negative experience of the soul." These impressions built to an overwhelming reaction:

The sun had risen, and a pale illumination flickered over the plain. As far as the eye could see – nothing but plains, gray, dead, endless, and sad. And the soldiers, who in their journey through the Ukraine . . . had not been able to shake the impression – they felt it vaguely. This was Russia. Like a spectral concept the word stood before their souls. Three days and three nights had passed, and the picture was still the same. Then the uncanny feeling strengthened in them against the land – becoming an unconscious, vague hatred, which blazed up in their hearts, which they felt but did not think. A hatred against the size of the land, which had swallowed them, as a big fish swallows many smaller ones, and which held them here against their will. Only a few thought more clearly. But they, too, felt at this hour only a vague, crippling helplessness, coming from the land and lying on them like fetters, binding them.[2]

As another soldier recorded in his diary, when he was under fire and looked out at the battlefield, he saw emptiness: "Countless farms and entire villages are in flames. One sees not a single human creature in the wide plain, spreading up to most distant eastern heights. And yet, in this frightful vacuum which is only filled with the noise of rumbling artillery and rattle of machine guns, thousands lie in battle."[3] A student seconded this, declaring that the Eastern Front surpassed even the "typical emptiness of the modern battlefield," which here was truly "disconsolate, irretrievable."[4] Images of open spaces riveted artists, like famed expressionist Otto Dix, who arrived in the East as a sergeant in winter 1917, and was inspired to draw abstract sketches of movement across steppes and landscapes of isolated villages.[5] Paintings by war artists recorded similar impressions of expanses.[6] Even the cover of the Tenth Army's songbook showed endless ranks of soldiers marching through snow across empty lands.[7]

Other features disconcerted newcomers, as wild nature brought all of its force to bear on them. Winters of terrible ferocity brought cutting Siberian winds:

Now there came cold such as I have never felt before. The thermometer fell to 38 degrees below zero. Dawn was the coldest. It was so cold that the air shimmered. A little stream, about a meter deep, with quick-flowing water, was frozen to the ground so that we were forced to melt clumps of snow and ice in pots on the stove, if we wanted to make coffee or have water for other purposes. Bread and the other supplies, which were brought by ski, were hard as stone. If a man did not have his head protector pulled over his nose, in five minutes the tip of his nose was yellow-white, all of the blood drained away. Then there came the order that we had to observe one another. Each also received a frost ointment to rub on the frost-bitten spot and to bandage it up. "Man, you have a white nose!," one heard often . . . The nose, ears, the skin on the cheekbones, fingertips, toes, and heels froze most quickly.[8]

Letters from soldiers at the front expressed horror at the land. With spring thaws, lakes appeared out of nowhere, flooding bunkers and positions, and men on watch drowned at their posts or were swept away in icy currents.[9] Hostile nature loomed large during lulls in the fighting as "days passed in monotony. Snow and fog, fog and snow – that was more or less the whole variation."[10] In the trenches, "life took its usual course: standing watch, bad food, and the torment of lice."[11] On the Eastern Front, soldiers found themselves battling nature as much as human enemies, a decisive feature of this front-experience.

While soldiers observed these unfamiliar aspects of the occupied territories, it is important to note that the eastern front-experience was not exclusively a confrontation with romantic strangeness. Indeed, more ordinary but even more unsettling to morale were everyday ordeals of boredom, homesickness, and hopelessness bred of personal losses and the cumulative impact of the horrors seen in this theatre of the war.[12] Long separation from family was an ordeal for many. One official felt wrenched inside when, home for vacation, to his child he was "the foreign man from Russia."[13] Another soldier wrote that he only appreciated the real meaning of homeland, "for the first time now, now that I am in a foreign place in enemy land."[14] Frustration with their dull existence wracked soldiers in quieter sectors. One exclaimed: "we do not fight, we do not starve, we lie in dirt, we kill ourselves through this useless boredom. If only the war would soon end!"[15] These feelings could run together and become identified with this miserable war land, as the same man reflected coldly in a letter:

Is it not the greatest, unknown, holy feeling to have dead friends, who have died heroes' deaths? And so likewise, to see a burned village, empty gables torn up as if by madness, destroyed human habitations, open cadavers and gray heaps of corpses, fires, foreign, foreign faces pressed to the ground, lying as if branches broken by a storm? I have scarcely felt any horror at that. And who has ever seen such pictures with his own eyes? In the face of such things, words fail . . . the life of one or another has become unimportant . . . I felt that those who had passed on were close by me and believe now I'll soon be with them and free of all torment . . . How the world has changed and become empty![16]

Numbed by repeated horrors, soldiers could give way to deep nihilism as they regarded their own lives and surroundings.

The mindscape defined the areas soldiers looked out over as intrinsically lands of war. Soldiers first entered these lands as war raged, with the area on fire. It was also war that gave them free disposition of the lands and peoples: "War is war," went the common excuse during requisitions. As lands of war, the vistas of the mindscape were in motion, since new conquests expanded the area eastwards by leaps and bounds. Ober Ost's state seemed a growing organism. Occupiers could not merely settle in and come to rest. Rather, the mindscape was dynamic, directing their attention and energies ever further East.

In this mindscape, filth was emblematic of eastern lands and peoples. Even after the front passed, an abiding impression was fixed that these lands were unclean, while what soldiers saw and experienced of the roads and displaced peoples heightened the impression. Diseases lurked everywhere in the disorder. Cities overcrowded with sick and starving refugees disturbed a German visitor: "the awful smell of the poor in the ghettos rolled oppressively over the senses and impressions. Horrified, I yelled – 'Bring gas masks!'"[17] In one archetypal moment, Germans claimed that in Wilna, retreating Russians had "dirtied and stunk up [the place] in the most unspeakable way. On the ground floor of City Hall, horse manure lay three-quarters of a meter high. On the upper floor, which horses could not reach, their riders took over the animal act. Today, the rooms are sparkling clean – only the . . . smell of chalk and disinfection reminds one of the dirty business found here."[18] Special aversion was reserved for unfortunate refugees crowded into Wilna's ghetto. Military Administration Lithuania's new chief von Heppe reacted furiously, announcing that it "offended eyes and nose in equal measure . . . probably the wildest example of filth and neglect that I have seen along these lines, in spite of the fact that in over three years I had become used to all sorts of things in this area."[19] Little allowance was made for the fact that war had played its part in reducing the natives to such misery. Parasitic insects and lice soldiers discovered on their own bodies were constant reminders of the dirt and disease they ascribed to the lands and peoples. These omnipresent creatures horrified soldiers and soon became hallmarks of the East.

One soldier quipped, "At first I thought they were some kind of Russian ant." Natives were blamed for this infestation, which they had somehow passed on to Germans. In summer, plagues of flies and gnats appeared.[20]

Filth became symbolic of the lands and peoples before German Work grasped them to change their natures. These areas were also "dirty" and "disorderly" in their complexity, chaotic mixtures of languages, peoples, religions, and histories, as Ober Ost's "Map of the Division of Peoples" so trenchantly pointed out. After first impressions of dirty lands and peoples, the mindscape surveyed an abidingly dirty East.

Further, the mindscape directed attention below the land's surface, to peer into the soil. From their arrival, soldiers remarked on the ground and its qualities, paralleling the military utopia's agricultural fantasies. The soil seemed rich, but undrained and uncultivated, given over to rank growth. It held immense potential, but would have to be won.[21] An economic officer in Kurland recalled the first spring breezes over the "raw land," which under deep snow and ice, he imagined, "dreams of *Kultur*."[22] Its qualities were foreign, as the soldier in the landscape felt: "He went further, ever deeper into the steppe and breathed the strange-smelling air of Russia, which smells so strongly of smoked resin. His eye had accustomed itself to the darkness. He saw now the landscape, this poor, barren land, which trembled underfoot, as mothers tremble, when they want to quiet their child and have no food."[23] For some, ground underfoot was haunted by ghosts and the past: "All around it whispered. The earth here is still blood-soaked, the air pregnant with red atoms, which find no peace yet, which swirl about the nocturnal wanderer. The soil breathes complaints, moans out sighs: in the air sound unsung melancholy hero-songs, unspoken whispering words of fear, withheld wild cries of battle. The landscape speaks its whispering language."[24] This soil was primeval, unworked, but if its strangeness could be overcome, it could be possessed.

The mindscape also revealed the peoples, laying bare their "essences" of irreducible ethnicity, exposing their characteristic powerlessness, misery, poverty, and primitive ways. These peoples had no genuine *Kultur*: their relationship to nature showed them to be incapable of it. All their existence appeared ahistorical and ruled by nature, determined by an environment which they could not resist. In the mindscape, these conclusions were drawn from the land and then read back into the ethnic landscape. The soldier in the steppe listened and found that

the landscape speaks its whispering language. He understood, he reflected: We Germanic people build up – create – the Slav broods and dreams – like his earth.

One feels and understands that in these wide plains, in the monotony of the heath-lands. There is no activity there – only a tired twilight and premonition. There is fate, not will. And as the land, so its poetry. The wide horizon, which loses itself in gray mists: the bleakness of the steppe, which only brightens once in the autumn magic of the heather, grieves in the longing, inconsolable Russian lyric poetry. These poets of Russia are the speaking spirit of this steppe, with . . . limitless gray imagination: they write tragedies over into moments and create out of tiny moments tragedies, which are never forgotten by one who reads them once. And finally their bitterest, bloodiest tragedies affect the Westerner like lyric poetry. Even the animals here take on the landscape's gloomy character. The nightingale, oriole, bittern, all have become the sound out of the plaint of a reticent landscape, sounding inwards. In the epic poetry, however, rears the monumentality of the borderless steppe. The German is powerful in being organized, the Englishman in his trade-political colonization – the Russian in his epics. Who has written more monumentally than Tolstoy, Turgenev, Dostoevsky, to name but a few? . . . One understands them for the first time, understands them in the middle of the steppe at night. This ghostliness, which haunts above the wide plains and heaths on dark nights, lit by no star, is in their works. The daemonic is in their figures as in the nights of the steppe.[25]

The German soldier's reaction was a confusion of contradictory impulses. In seeing these lands, he felt a new understanding for the peoples, a certain new sympathy and closeness, but also repulsion. Their identities seemed not conscious projects or complicated weavings of historical circumstance, choice, and effort. Natives were not agents, actors making choices, but slaves of necessity. Soldiers scanned native "faces" and "visages," trying to discern inner natures, as Jungfer recorded in his novel of life in the rear areas, *The Face of the Occupied Territory*. Ethnicity came to be regarded as race, something immutable, physical, and visible. Natives were sometimes seen as separate nationalities, but since so much about their essential natures was alike, they could also often seem interchangeable, referred to collectively as "Poles" or "Russians" or by mildly derisive labels like *"Panje."* Soldiers looked out at a native scene so varied that there were no clear distinctions to be discerned. Chaos itself seemed characteristic of those lands and peoples.

The dynamic mindscape turned description of the land into a prescription for how it was to be faced, confronted, and approached. Attention was drawn to the East, expressing itself in a fixed eastwards stare: full of tension, a mixture of attraction and desperate repulsion. This stare of the "Watch in the East" was different from that in the West, the defensive "Watch on the Rhine" on the French border. Here, it was energetic and expansive, an occupier's gaze fixed on new horizons, rehearsed to exhaustion in epically bad poems by ordinary soldiers published by front-newspapers:

The Watch in the East

Do you know the street, deep and long?
It comes from the Baltic coast
And leads through hill, valley, and slope
Far away to Hungarian land.
No floods of people, glory of architecture
Enliven its tracks –
There we stand on loyal watch
Before battle-filled plains.
Just as it developed in wild conflict,
In hot, bloody striving,
So it resists the storm of time,
Wants to feel destruction itself.
Because behind the wall of these roads
In the distant German districts,
There all the brothers look up to us
And all the dear women.
And if in nighttimes there surges blind rage –
Then look up high how the stars revolve,
Which above a sea of blood
Show the way into the bright future!
And, listening, look along the street
Where the quails make their song!
There rises the joyful song of the lark
Almost as in peacetime days.[26]

The watch in the East peered into the expanses ahead, ready to ward off threatening nature. As the Tenth Army's theme song announced, "You have swept clean the homeland, / And have opened the way to the East-land! . . . Now you stand, as if formed out of steel / Faithfully holding what has been conquered."[27] Another song, that of "Home Guard Troop Three," also declared:

We stand between mountains and graves and stones,
Between ruins and coffins and dead men's bones!
We keep the watch in the East, tenacious and true;
Always at our posts – We, the Home Guard Troop Three.
Now we are in trenches and foxholes,
The land which we have, we will hold on to it firm.[28]

Once the gaze was fixed, the mindscape then prescribed movement eastwards. While the "wall" which the front represented defended Germany and home, it also strained forward, an aggressive border on the move eastwards. Roads to the East led to apocalyptic landscapes, seas of blood and planes of existence filled with battle and slaughter:

On the Advance March

Like a dark gray coat
The heavy night lowers itself.
Without respite, restless, ever further
Eastwards we carry the battle.
The smell of burning and rubble and corpses.
Pestilence is every pull of breath.
And the jackdaws, hoarsely croaking,
Reel by in heavy flight.
And with wild greed a vulture
Breaks out of the dark realm of clouds.
Horror and terror lie
Over the blood-soaked field.
Let it lie, let it be!
Battle is battle and war is war!
Cheerful and without respite, restless,
Eastwards we carry victory.[29]

The mindscape envisioned German soldiers carrying battle outwards, eastwards into nightmare landscapes. These were lands where limits were broken, in the outside world as well as in the soldier's interior, with "Battle is battle and war is war" the only remaining morality in the East.

Even as the area repelled the occupiers while they ordered the land, their military utopian vision also made them want to possess it forever. Over time, they found themselves coming to feel at home, as a visiting journalist related: "Last year . . . my eldest son was in the field in Lithuania for months. He, too, was shocked at this mix of horror and filth. However, as he saw the blooming, ripening, and gathering of the harvest, he wrote one day: 'And in spite of it all, one becomes fond of this land. What could one not make out of it!' That is the German way."[30] It was supposedly characteristic of Germans that they settled readily in foreign places and soon grew accustomed to them in a way all their own:

The German, however, draws about his surroundings the weaving threads of his sensibility. Even if he should discover after a year that he has settled in an evil swamp area, he is no longer to be removed – because of his character. There is something to this. The German loves work for the sake of work. That which is created is holy to him, because of the feelings out of which he created. It pains him to leave the trench in which he spent the most difficult hours of his life. Best of all, he would like to take it home with him as a memento.[31]

This supposed national characteristic was demonstrated in Ober Ost: "If one claims abroad that we Germans become uprooted quickly, as soon as we leave our native plot, then we may add, with good reason, that we also become rooted very quickly, where duty sets us down. Our soldiers at work at agriculture in the middle of the Lithuanian desolations clearly demonstrate for us the German ability to adapt to difficult conditions."[32] Yet feeling "at home" in foreign lands could be perilous, as soldiers risked "going native" and "going to ground." Officer Victor Jungfer (who himself later went native) depicted life in the rear areas in his novel. Soldiers found themselves sinking in place. In remote areas and towns, they gave themselves over to drinking, card-playing, and exploiting native women. Older men and wounded soldiers succumbed easily to the temptation of lording their power over prostrate native populations. Many soldiers took up with native women in relationships where the women were forced by circumstances to prostitute themselves for food and army issue bread. This was a world apart, dominated by males, standing in absolute authority over subject populations, which were disproportionately female after the forced retreat of native males with the Russians. Some soldiers stopped writing home, losing connection with their families, Jungfer's novel reported.[33] Their manners coarsened, as habits of civility fell away in these lands without limits, while their own sense of interior limits weakened. The official exhortation to "Stay German!" revealed the extent of the danger.[34]

The occupiers would have to ground themselves: they had to change the place, or the place would change them. Moreover, newcomers felt not only danger, but also lust for possession, the lure of future ownership. Men whose work and chances for advancement were cramped in peacetime Germany saw unlimited possibilities. One reporter observed: "I have felt that our men in Ober Ost were glad that they met so much destruction and neglect, because it gave them the opportunity to create something whole. It enabled them to ratchet up primal states to the highest level of development without intermediate steps."[35] Officers hoped for estates after the war, or influential positions.[36] For the mostly Prussian officials, this area promised to be an extension of their nearby home provinces, but with more challenges, freedom of action among non-German populations, and quicker career advancement. In the logic of German Work, the occupiers would change the land to own it, and owned it to change it.

Disorderly, filthy lands and peoples were already being made over by the conqueror's presence, as chaos gave way to a new ordering in the administration's programs. German soldiers moved into the landscape energetically, subduing, subdividing, separating, encapsulating, sealing off, and cleaning. With control secured, they would intensify administration, drain the soil, establish grids of control, and direct all movement, building up the appropriated land. All the while, Ober Ost would expand eastwards, subjecting new territory to the same treatment.

Above all, cleaning was emblematic of German rule, just as filth symbolized the area's tsarist past. Claiming they had first found Wilna's city hall full of Russian excrement, officials equated cleaning with possession: "For fourteen days, sixty cleaning women under German supervision had to keep their hands busy. Then the Head Mayor . . . entered as City Captain. Herein there is also something symbolic. Muscovite character and German character!"[37] It was an archetypal moment of German Work, as natives cleaned under German supervision.[38] In 1916, Schaulen's military mayor ordered Jewish women to clean the market square; soldiers and officers stood by, watching, commenting and photographing them.[39] Across the territory, roads and cities were cleared, while the administration organized programs of public hygiene, built bathhouses and delousing stations, constructed wells, improved sanitation systems and sewers, regulated prostitution, drove natives to the baths and inoculated them by force.

The territory being sanitized was already being drawn into a grid of control: a web of new roads, railroads, telegraph lines, police posts, district borders. This web of communication lines was a constantly recurring symbol in German accounts. The soldier alone on the steppe encountered it on the nighttime plain, a sign that the occupiers were already taking possession: "A noise alarmed him. He stood still in amazement and listened. The noise was in the air. He stared upwards, transfixed – and smiled. He stood next to a telegraph pole. It hummed so loud, that it sounded like a roaring flood. Up there rushed orders which destroyed peoples. Thoughts, plans which overthrew worlds, sang there in the air."[40]

Frontispiece drawings of soldiers' newspapers featured the image. The *Nowogrodek War Newspaper* showed an etching of castle ruins, with telegraph lines leading past it, on to the horizon, a celebration of the modernizing administration's overcoming of the area's history. The masthead of *The East-Watch: Lukow Field Newspaper* showed a helmeted soldier on watch, facing east, while a train steamed past a village with onion-domed church spires, all under tangles of telegraph lines.[41] Zweig's novel depicted the occupied area caught in a mesh of wires and humming lines, a net of control.[42] Painter Otto Dix pictured steppe landscapes with poles and strung wires stretching into the far distance.[43]

The mindscape projected a vista already punctuated by German strong points. "soldiers' homes" dotted cities and towns, while Ober Ost's factories, sawmills, collection points for requisitions and raw materials, and storehouses spread across the area. German theatres rose up to dominate the cultural landscape. Up at the front, institutions of German Work strained towards the most advanced outposts of culture. Each

Fronttheater performance was a deed driven into foreign soil, marking it, keeping it. German soldiers' graves were a part of this overlay, as well, claiming the land, as one poem put it: "In the enemy land, the many graves / Preach voicelessly the honorable goal: / The earth, consecrated by German blood / Must be German forever!"[44] Ober Ost also pinned down native peoples with institutions bracketing native content as their labor was given German form. The mindscape envisioned an East covered with German institutions, spread over the land as a network of strong points, a frame of control.

Ultimately, claims to this territory rested on carrying *Kultur*. German institutions were to save ethnicities from "cultural death by starvation."[45] The versifying Sergeant Max Hamm saw it thus:

> *A Look Backwards*
>
> Even still I hear the pounding of heavy steps
> In the rubble of the cities – hear people pleading.
> Villages moaning, condemned to death in flames.
> All about my eyes still see the misery,
> Which the disgrace of the Russian army inflicted
> On their own land, on works of nature!
> That, which seemed forever lost, was created anew by –
> The German battalions of *Kultur*!
>
> Many thousands of hands I see serving duty,
> The German spirit blows through the poor land;
> And new life rises up out of the ruins,
> Which noble mind snatched from decline.
> The golden bridge of the future is erected,
> Waiting for the spring, field and meadow breathe.
> We have carried eastwards stone upon stone
> We German pioneers of *Kultur*!
>
> Here an unshakable grip writes history,
> The sun turns itself back smiling.
> The henchmen's misdeed, it came to nothing,
> Upon the desolate ruins there blooms a new joy.
> And even if we leave this land one day,
> Many an imperishable monument shows the tracks
> Which we cleared for ourselves through the dirt of the alleys –
> We German battalions of *Kultur*![46]

Another report exulted that German troops were true "pioneers of *Kultur*," and each soldier in fact a teacher in enemy lands.[47] The mindscape showed a land being cultivated: "Everywhere one feels working and striving. The soil has been broken and planted, *Kultur*-seed has been sown, and ripens toward a fateful harvest."[48] The occupied territories were being worked over.

In essence, the mindscape presented the image of a great, aggressive moving border, an entire war state in motion. Even as it drew a new border, a demarcation, it already strained to break that limit and draw another one further east. A frontier thesis of the German East would be radically different from that of America's pioneer West. Instead of myths of individual independence and self-sufficiency, producing democratic views, the collective goal here was ordering, cleaning, and control.

The impressions of the eastern front-experience were reinforced by Ober Ost's propaganda, which worked them over to forge an image of its mission in the East, a structure "built in people's heads" by Ober Ost's press, programs, and institutions. In a striking example of this process, the "Map of the Division of Peoples" amplified an impression to the point where it became a program, suggesting that this was open space without clear ownership, a vacuum to be filled, then presenting maps of splintered ethnicities and allowed readers to draw their own conclusions. Popular journalists took up the chant of open space, *Raum*, stressing the emptiness of these lands.[49] They published wildly enthusiastic travel accounts, entitled *To the East!*, *New Land, German Deed and German Seed in the Russian Badlands*, and *New East: Our Future Borderland on East Prussia's Eastern Rim*.[50] Ober Ost's own propaganda materials demonstrated the "gigantic spiritual conquest" of the occupied territories and the way in which their "unique character" had been caught.[51] Sketchbooks, photographic albums, and postcards recorded faces and places, native "types" and characteristic scenes and landscapes. Meanwhile, Ober Ost's November 1916 Fruit Exhibition in Berlin provided tangible, edible evidence of progress to a Germany threatened by hunger blockade.[52] Other war exhibitions followed. Visitors to the traveling Kurland exhibition in 1917 understood that the central message was that the area already had a German character. The exhibit, which visited Stuttgart, Munich, Dresden, and Berlin, was encouraged by the manager of Stuttgart's Auslandsmuseum. Kurland's chief von Gossler traveled to give speeches at the openings.[53] Perhaps the most effective propagators of the mindscape were those who were possessed by it most completely: officers and administrators, who had vested interests and hopes for the lands and refused to see the contradictory nature of army rule.

In sum, the German imperialist mindscape of the East presented a vast, contradictory complex. Viewing dirty, chaotic lands of war, it produced a volatile and explosive mixture of associations in those who looked through it. Desire for possession contended with revulsion, a tension expressing itself in urges for violent transformation and cleaning. These charges grew out of a distinctive eastern front-experience, where battle against nature, to transform the givens of the landscape, produced lust for possession, especially among officials. The vision of the mindscape, a great wall of war moving eastwards over lands which it pinned down and ordered in its wake, was a potent image.

This mindscape was readily absorbed at home in Germany because there it meshed with other myths and understandings. It connected with a larger popular consciousness in the *Heimat*, guaranteeing for itself a scope much wider even than the consciousness of the multitudes of soldiers on the Eastern Front. Similar images were already prevalent at home, so that it was readily taken up by popular consciousness. The Great War was interpreted for civilians as the culmination of conspiracies of "encircle-ment" by envious great powers seeking to strangle a young and vigorous Germany.[54] While a compelling explanation for many, it missed the fact that the conception of *Einkreisung* had been a self-fulfilling prophecy, driving German foreign policy into precarious isolation. The govern-ment's announcement in August 1914 of a defensive war uniting all Germans was crucial, for it allowed Social Democrats to support what they saw as a struggle against autocratic Russia's aggression, defending German culture and the gains of German workers, while insisting that this was not a war for territory or annexations (though the socialist right wing readily agreed with the need for "strategic corrections" of Ger-many's borders). In the first days of war, the Kaiser proclaimed a *Bur-gfrieden*, the peace within a besieged castle. Soon siege images multiplied, especially as Germany was subjected to a crippling British blockade and economic warfare. Later, when German troops on the Western Front withdrew to more defensible trenches in March 1917, this new "Siegfried Line" was hailed as a barrier against the West. As images of barriers proliferated in the popular siege mentality, the constructions in Ober Ost would also serve as a wall and bulwark against the threatening, unknown East. This was the basis for Ludendorff's plan to restructure the East, building a huge dam from Finland to the Crimea. Popular propaganda literature repeated images of defensive walls, while some accounts, like Wertheimer's *Hindenburg's Wall in the East*, put it front and center.[55] Annexationists took up the image of an eastern wall, pushing ideas of a Polish border strip as a defensive barrier, encapsulating antagonized Poles.[56] Anti-Semites urged closing eastern borders for another reason, to prevent influxes of eastern Jews. Conceptions of the bulwark in the East drew on older popular historical images of "border marches" and war-rior-farmers of Charlemagne's empire. The war held out great promise, even if it was considered defensive. Many intellectuals hoped that the very fact of being surrounded together, pressed from all sides, might forge a

German unity missing in the fragmented *Kaiserreich*. War brought Germans from all parts of the empire to the fronts, showing them new places for the first time. One propagandist shouted, "Germany has already grown within its old borders during the war, because Germans now more than ever see their land as a whole, as a unity, and have gotten to know it."[57] In a paradoxical play of inwardness and outward direction, propagandists hoped that war would give German soldiers a political education, widening their horizons: seeing foreign areas would make them more conscious of what bound them together as Germans. Expansion would produce inner cohesion. While Germany was given over to siege mentality at home, the East presented the other side of the coin. All the nation's energies for break-out could be directed eastwards, where successes like Tannenberg were scored. In the East, armies stood as a wall against another devastation of German lands such as that visited on East Prussia. Yet it was a moving wall, as successes and failed attempts at a grand, crushing encirclement drew the army further into the vast spaces, even as its aggressive front pushed ever further East, taking new territory. Tremendous advances in the East caught the public's imagination at home. Once in the High Command in August 1916, Ludendorff freed discussion of war aims from censorship, "arguing that the promise of vast territorial gains would have a most welcome effect on morale."[58]

Yet even before the Third High Command's encouragement of expansive annexationist aims, there was significant German support for future "rewards" of territory in the war's first years. From the start, nationalist and imperialist pressure groups formulated increasingly ambitious territorial wish lists. In the fall of 1914, Pan-German president Heinrich Class, a disciple of Lagarde's ideas of expansion to the East, created a plan for German mastery in central Europe, supported by influential industrialists. The Catholic Center party's Matthias Erzberger enthusiastically wrote up a September memorandum with far-flung territorial demands. Such ideas were taken into account when the cautious Chancellor Bethmann Hollweg quietly outlined a tentative September Program of war aims in 1914, which ultimately sought to ensure "security of the German Empire against the West and the East for the forseeable future," with western powers weakened and "Russia pushed back, as far as feasible, away from German borders and its rule over the non-Russian vassal-peoples broken."[59] The program revealed the essentials of a *Siegfriede*, a "peace of victory," breaking the encirclement Germany feared in past decades. As hopes for quick victory dimmed, war aims demands perversely grew larger, rather than more modest, since annexationists argued that the very precariousness of Germany's present strategic situation proved the need for these gains, making a return to 1914's demonstrably inadequate dimensions unthinkable.[60] In parliament, a "war aims majority," and in society at large, a "war aims movement" arose to forbid a "weak peace" of renunciation, supported by industrialists and academics, among many others. Industrial interest groups, after consulting with Pan-German leaders, sent the chancellor a petition in May 1915, signed by the Central Association of German Industrialists, League of Industrialists, German Farmers' League, Reich German Middle-Class Association, and Christian German Farmers' Union. This "Memorandum of the Six Economic Organizations" demanded control of industrially important territory in Belgium and northern France, especially Longwy-Briey's ore fields, adding that industrial gains needed to be "balanced" by expansion into agricultural territories in the East. July saw the "Petition of the Intellectuals," organized by Baltic German theologian Seeberg, and signed by 1,347 professionals, university professors forming the largest single group.[61] This memorandum raised similar concrete demands, but emphasized Germany's cultural mission in the East, and the necessity of fighting back against Russian barbarism. While some more tempered voices could be heard in society, support for expansive war aims was broad in the first years of the war, especially among elites and the middle class, for whom expansion and world power represented an "escape into the future," promising to preserve the status quo, while a compromise peace threatened revolutionary turmoil, social disorder, and revenge for unrequited sacrifices.

In the surge of annexationist literature, an important genre demanded a new order in the East. Broederich-Kurmahlen's *The New East-Land* was the most typical and influential example, setting the terms that other pamphleteers followed.[62] A Baltic German landlord from Kurland, Kurmahlen had been in the forefront of prewar colonization efforts there. Now he proposed annexing the Baltic provinces and Lithuania, to be settled by Reich-Germans and ethnic Germans gathered in from Russia. Within fifty years, remaining natives would be assimilated and germanized or moved out in "population exchanges" with Russia. Other propagandists greeted Kurmahlen's plan and agitated the public for it. The mindscape was ensured far-reaching importance, because it connected with aspects of popular consciousness at home in Germany.

The orientations and themes so powerfully fused in the German imperialist mindscape of the East addressed the geographic consciousness of Germans.[63] "Geographic consciousness" may be defined as the collective ways in which a group or culture understands its surroundings and place and relations to other places: the meaning of their own presence in those surroundings, as circumscribed by relations of space. An understanding of this collective geographic consciousness is essential in the German case precisely because geography had always been an existential question for Germany.

It is ironic and yet no coincidence that modern geography was from its inception a "German science," founded at a time when Germany could hardly even be called a "geographical expression," much less a political reality. This preeminence began in the eighteenth century. A "politico-statistical school" of geography put itself at the service of German territorial states; the beginnings of modern geographical science must be sought in the ethos of the "well-ordered police state."[64] Geography held a privileged place in the German academic world from the beginning. Throughout the nineteenth century, it was developed by such giants of geography as Ritter, von Humboldt, and Friedrich Ratzel. The period 1905–1914 was the "Golden Age of German Geography," a time when German fieldwork was of the first rank, while academic scholarship found its dizzying heights at the universities of Berlin, Leipzig, Vienna, and Hamburg's Colonial Institute, celebrated institutions serving as models for the rest of the world. With the outbreak of war in 1914, German geography increased in importance, but not in the hands of scholars. Instead, it became a powerful concern and tool for propagandists.[65]

Geography acquired this sudden prominence because, in the German context, it could never be merely an academic subject of study among others. Instead, its questions were existential ones for any understanding of German national identity, immediately exploding into anguished demands: "What is Germany? Where is Germany? Who is German?" Going far beyond academic geography, there was a longer debate over Germany's "natural borders."[66] Above all, German geographic consciousness fixed on the vital question of borders, uniquely topical in the German case. As a "land of the middle" at Europe's center, Germany conspicuously lacked natural borders. Even in strivings for unification, it was unclear what territories it would involve: a "Smaller" or "Greater Germany," centered on Hohenzollern Prussia or Habsburg Austrian lands? After the Prussian imposition of unity in the Second Reich, regional identities and claims bedeviled the imperial society's claims of cohesion. With non-German minorities, especially in eastern Germany, and Pan-German agitation for a "Drive to the East," questions of borders again arose. The crowning horror to these questions was that Germans' word for border, *Grenze*, was not even German, but borrowed from Slavic, *graniza*. Concerns over borders spoke to larger issues, especially a desire for coherent unities in a fragmented and problematic unit called "Germany."

German geographic consciousness thus occupied a significant place in the popular imagination. Professorial debates were formal, outward expressions of basic foundational myths which a fragmented society had evolved about German identity. Most crucially, the traditions of Romanticism claimed that a specific relation to landscape, an organic "rootedness," was an essential part of German national character: a special trait called *Landschaftsgefühl* (feeling for the landscape) or *Landschaftsverbundenheit* (landscape-connectedness).[67] An enduring collective myth, this perennial conviction even today produces a robust genre of books bearing titles like *The German in the Landscape*. Many peculiarly German phenomena and institutions are part of this overarching conception: the *Wandervogel* youth movement, the national institution of the *Wanderung* hike, traditions of conservation, ecological utopias, the complex of ideas centering on *Heimat*, and study of that home-ground, *Heimatkunde*.[68] Yet this axiom of self-understanding stood in contradiction to another tradition of organization and discipline. Romantic, organic conceptions of harmony with nature had yet to be reconciled with the notion of Germans as systematic, creative "shapers and orderers" (*Gestalter und Ordner*).

The conviction of a special German relation to the land was most effectively articulated by Wilhelm Heinrich Riehl, author of *German Work* and founder of German ethnographic *Volkskunde*. In popularizing works, Riehl aimed to construct a "natural history" of the Germans, based on personal observations from hikes through Germany. In *Land and People*, he proposed that there was an organic connection between people and their land, some reciprocal effect.

Soon after, a concept articulated by Friedrich Ratzel (1844–1904), father of political geography, seemed to resolve the tension between the traditions, in a synthesis of natural and human sciences. This was the idea of the "*Deutsche Kulturlandschaft*," "German *Kultur*-landscape." Ratzel explained, "As Germans in ever-growing numbers bound themselves ever more tightly with their soil, an entirely new landscape emerged, which is full of the signs of the work which a people clears, digs in, and plants into its soil."[69] It was not only people who took their character from the land they inhabited, but their activity also formed the land and made it over in their image. Claims to land rested upon changing it, working changes upon it. Land could become physically German. It could acquire, through cultivation and shaping (*Kultur* and *Bildung*), a German face. A synthesis seemed to have been effected, reconciling Romantic organicism and ordering, rationalizing spirit.

In this formulation, *Kultur*'s imperative united with another tradition of German self-understanding: rationalization and organization in state and society, a tradition rooted in centuries of German "small-statery" predating unification. To compensate for political fragmentation and disunity, the small units strove for internal regimentation with all the more intensity. Since the early modern period, they sought the ideal of comprehensive regulation and oversight called *Polizei*, "policing."[70] This ideal mirrored the authoritarian, paternalistic German household, as principles of state service were internalized by subjects, drilled into them as codes of discipline, ethics of duty, and specialization. This in turn was reinforced by Enlightenment visions of scientific administration, statistics (which bears its *state* origin in its name), regulation, rationalization, and state sciences. As the *Kaiserreich* struggled to accommodate the onrush of industrial modernity, traditions of regulation took on new forms as thinking on *Sozialpolitik* and social reform plans of "academic socialists."

The experience of modern total war altered German geographic consciousness, bringing new ways of looking at land and territory, realizing cherished goals of proponents of German might. From the 1880s, they had called for *Weltpolitik*, an energetic global foreign policy to claim Germany's place among the powers. The policy also promised the internal cohesion Germany lacked, while *Weltpolitik* and colonialism would serve as an outlet for energies of the nation. Cecil Rhodes' encouragement to "think in continents" was cited approvingly. Such goals were shared by imperialist groups founded in the 1880s and 1890s: the Colonial Society, Navy League, Pan-Germans, and League of the Eastern Marches.[71] While these groups envisioned policies differently (setting their sights on overseas possessions, continental empire, or some combination of both) their goal was the same: to give territorial expression to a unified German identity, directed outward.[72] War achieved this, changing geographic consciousness and territorial imagination. Geography was mobilized, both as a discipline and as a way of thinking. Long before the war, the general staff and military establishment cultivated geographic training, intensive concentration on maps and their symbolic thinking.[73] Military mapping was important to the war effort.[74] Intensive surveying of occupied territories during the war itself was meant as a prelude to possible annexation.

But wartime interest in geography was far more general, seizing Germany's public and holding its fascinated attention. In one historian's estimation, "public interest in geography grew as much in three years of war as during the previous half-century."[75] A German geographer remarked, with some surprise, that one saw "everywhere, in the life of these days of war, visible signs of national enthusiasm for everything geographic." Perceptively, he suggested that this was the product of a new kind of war, the "world war": "Why has the world war itself so animated geography? The only answer is: because geography has been assigned the important role of interpreting . . . Geography interprets the war in its causes, theatres of war, and the goals of the war."[76] The public looked to geography to explain titanic events taking place around the country's borders, in a war that mobilized nations and societies as never before. As wireless fed news into rapid, fully developed print media, developments on the fronts and in chancelleries of great states were communicated instantaneously to the masses, whose involvement in international affairs had never been so swift or immediate. In this fundamentally new and bewildering context, the most decisive change which the war brought was in territorial imagination: new ways of looking. A new way of regarding territory was born, as German "War Geography" and "Geopolitics." While overheated annexationists in the press suggested new conquests, war geography proposed something far more radical: new categories for looking out over the world. It cultivated a transformed geographic consciousness. Popular texts entitled "War Geography" explained events and causes of the conflict in geographic terms, and conversely, evaluated geographic givens in military categories, presenting plans for enormous annexations as inevitable.[77] The cornerstone of this new "Geopolitics" was Rudolf Kjellen's *The Political Problems of the World War*. Kjellen, a Swedish disciple of Ratzel, invented the term "*Geopolitik*." In his tremendously popular little book, Kjellen soared above subjective categories of individual morality to view states as "higher personalities," living organisms driven by natural laws and Darwinian necessity. He praised war, because "war speaks the truth," revealing Germany's geographic destiny as a "Reich of the Middle," a position at once vulnerable to encirclement, yet also calling to a glorious career of expansion and consolidation from its perfect center. Pursuing this course, massive resettlement of populations in the borderlands was a thinkable policy. Kjellen ended by casting struggle in the East as another geographical destiny: a battle of exalted German *Kultur* against mere racial identity represented by native peoples.[78] Floods of similar texts echoed Kjellen's formulations, envisaging thorough redrawings of Europe's political map. The most influential was Friedrich Naumann's earlier book *Mitteleuropa*, published in October 1915, the "climax of his career as a political writer" championing ideas for social and economic reform in the Christian-Socialist tradition. His popular work urged creation of a central European economic zone, a natural outgrowth of global consolidation of larger market areas, bound together by a confederation around Germany which would not seek to germanize surrounding peoples, but ensure free, natural development of their own cultural potential. While Naumann's vision was far more generous than that of Pan-German chauvinists, the idea of *Mitteleuropa*, as it gained currency after 1915, quickly picked up a variety of other, more expansive ambitions, "a host of vague and different meanings," until "the more current the expression became in Germany and abroad, the more vague, ambiguous, and emotional was its use." As the slogan was put into action as an indistinctly defined war aim, already anticipated and implicit in Bethmann Hollweg's September Program of 1914, it moved away from Naumann's confederative model. Because of its very indeterminacy, the term was invoked as a compromise between factions in the war aims debate, each able to interpret it in their own fashion.[79] Thus in the course of the war, "precisely because it was perceived as a patent remedy for all the conflicts, contradictions, and rivalries in German society, *Mitteleuropa* never could develop as a coherent policy or programme."[80] All the more, however, it became a common slogan pointing the way to a greater territorial future, encouraging Germans to "think expansively." Youth organizations in particular avowed that their purpose was to create a new generation with a "worldwide outlook."[81] Geopolitics and War Geography presented a new set of categories for understanding the war and German national identity through geography. These categories of thought created a mobilizing, motivating factor with explosive potential in the public at large. A new "territorial imagination" of Germany as an embattled space in the inexorable grip of geographic necessity took hold, as a "map in the mind" of individual Germans.

The most decisive development, however, was a long-term one, in education. New ways of viewing land were instilled in youth, both in schools and outside, where total war necessarily gave an increasingly martial coloring to life. While this was true of all belligerent countries, the German case is especially interesting. In schools, the military turn in education significantly affected the curriculum. A crucial feature was the ever-present map and campaign overview, in newspapers, at school, and at home. Schoolboys followed advances on maps pinned to walls, moving colored pins forward. One teacher related the enthusiasm with which his pupils made little flags to follow the progress of campaigns on maps of the Western and Eastern Fronts (paid for out of their own piggy banks) and the "moment of great suspense when their confidant, the teacher, moves the flags . . . With clear shining eyes they follow the advance of these paper markers and take in retreats with heavy earnestness on their faces."[82] Geography classes discussed attacks and retreats. Schooling increasingly turned to military education, driven by nationalist teachers. Mathematics and science assignments were reformulated in military terms. Word problems referred to the war economy and military technology, in terms most relevant to great issues of the day, as some school ministries urged. Geography classes were to acquaint students with the theatres of the war and the terrain in each, the "type of ground, ground cover, and settlement."[83] Even biology classes showed the "never-ending fight for existence in the animal and plant kingdoms," while humanities were represen-

ted by "war poetry."[84] Pedagogic techniques guided by military imperatives encouraged thinking in terms of military utility. Outside classrooms,
students and other adolescents were organized into "Youth Companies,"
which shot up in fall 1914 throughout Germany to offer premilitary
training from the age of sixteen or even younger.[85] One activity in particular was encouraged to habituate boys to this new martial perspective
fostered by war geography. "Terrain games," *Geländespiele*, were organized for youth as outdoor exercises to inculcate a martial outlook over the
land.[86] They trained to scan terrain for military advantage, to move
forward as units in ordered, planned fashion in games of "capture the
flag," to draw maps for troop movements, assessing the landscape with an
eye to war. In this remarkable way, traditions already strong in Germany
before the war were transformed and redirected. The patriotic gymnastic
movement of *Turnen*, initiated by Friedrich Ludwig Jahn at the beginning
of the nineteenth century, was a nationalistic exercise in the Wars of
Liberation against Napoleon, stressing an individual ethos of prepared-
ness, inner discipline, and firmness in the national cause. After 1914,
these mutated into "*Wehrturnen*," military gymnastics practicing
marching ability, movements of close combat, throwing of grenades, and
sparring with staves as prelude to bayonet fighting (national contests in
these exercises were organized, while courses were made obligatory in
some cities).[87] Terrain games also drew on traditions of the *Wandervogel*
youth movement. After the flawed national unification under the Prussian flag, the "Birds of Passage" incarnated the collective myth of a
special German relationship to the landscape, with their free and easy
hiking through Germany. These two traditions of gymnastics and hiking
merged during war into terrain games, with military instruction and war
geography, transforming categories of practice and perception. Ultimately, this wartime experience at home guaranteed that a new generation,
which had not fought in the war, was receptive to and shared, even at one
remove, in the consequences of the mindscape of the East. The home
front's active participation and intimate involvement in the conduct of
war grew out of the nature of "total war," demanding mobilization of
economies, populations, hearts and minds. Total war's impact could also
be traced in the mobilization of outlooks both among soldiers and civilians, militarizing views of land and territory.

The most portentous outcome of Ober Ost was a far-ranging transformation of outlook, growing out of the eastern front-experience,
marked by struggle with nature, filth, boredom, and inner dislocation in
the difficult work of ruling the occupied territory. A distinctive outlook on
the East evolved from such powerful impressions. This imperialist mindscape surveyed dirty lands and peoples, and saw itself imposing a new

ordering through German Work, behind the advancing, aggressive wall of the front. From the lands it scanned and wanted to own, the mindscape drew conclusions about the national identities of subject peoples and the victorious Germans. The land, whose contours and poor state of cultivation reflected its peoples' relationship to nature, revealed the ethnic "essences" of groups in the East. This was a momentous transformation. Where at the start of the war Germans had suddenly found "places and faces" in distinct lands and peoples, they increasingly saw "spaces and races" subject to war. As this martial outlook on the land evolved, a parallel process was under way in Germany itself, where annexationist propaganda, "War Geography" and "Geopolitics," and military schooling of the young created a new and aggressive geographic consciousness. The mindscape of the East and the martial outlook at home merged readily. The result of this convergence was a new German imagination of territory, given direction eastwards.

NOTES

1 BAMA PHD 8/23, Schirokauer, "Der deutsche Soldat in der russischen Steppe," *KB* 6 (November 15, 1916).
2 Victor Jungfer, *Das Gesicht der Etappe* (Berlin: Fritz Würtz, 1919), 16–19.
3 Marwitz, *Stirb*, 82.
4 Witkop, ed., *Kriegsbriefe*, 67.
5 Linda F. McGreevy, *The Life and Works of Otto Dix: German Critical Realist* (Ann Arbor: UMI Research Press, 1981), 19; Otto Conzelmann, ed., *Otto Dix. Handzeichnungen* (Hannover: Fackelträger–Verlag, 1968), plates 39–40.
6 (Hoover Archives) Dettmann Collection. Ludwig Dettmann, *Von der deutschen Ostfront* (Berlin: Verlag Ullstein & Co., n.d.), plates 4, 7, 11, 14, 21–23.
7 *Vivat, du wackere Armee. Singlieder für Soldaten der 10 Armee* (n.p.: Zeitung der 10. Armee, 1918).
8 Dominik Richert, *Beste Gelegenheit zum Sterben. Meine Erlebnisse im Kriege, 1914–1918*, ed. Angelika Tramwitz and Bernd Ulrich (Munich: Knesebeck & Schuler, 1989), 233–34.
9 Witkop, ed., *Kriegsbriefe*, 220–21.
10 Richert, *Gelegenheit*, 129.
11 Ibid., 237.
12 Hanna Hafkesbrink, *Unknown Germany: An Inner Chronicle of the First World War Based on Letters and Diaries* (New Haven: Yale University Press, 1948), 89.
13 BAMA N 196/1, Heppe, vol. V, 113.
14 Witkop, ed., *Kriegsbriefe*, 64.
15 Marwitz, *Stirb*, 42.
16 Otto Grautoff, ed., *Bernhard von der Marwitz. Eine Jugend in Dichtung und Briefen* (Dresden: Sibyllen-Verlag, 1923), 121–23.

17 Hartmann, *Ob-Ost*, 4.
18 Ibid., 13.
19 BAMA N 196/1, Heppe, vol. V, 133.
20 Fritz Nagel, *Fritz: The World War I Memoir of a German Lieutenant*, rev. edn. (Huntington, VA: Blue Acorn Press, 1995), 74–75; Marwitz, *Stirb und Werde*, 25, 91; BAMA N 196/1, Heppe, vol. V, 15, 56.
21 Hartmann, *Ob-Ost*, 37.
22 Marwitz, *Stirb*, 138.
23 BAMA PHD 8/23, Schirokauer, "Der deutsche Soldat," *KB* 6 (November 15, 1916).
24 Ibid.
25 Ibid.
26 BAMA PHD 8/73, Wehrmann Ernst Henselmann, "Wacht im Osten," *Wacht im Osten. Feldzeitung der 12. Armee* 267 (August 23, 1916). The newspaper's masthead shows a rider, sword brandished, looking to the East, against a background of snow.
27 *Vivat*, 9.
28 Ibid., 35.
29 BAMA PHD 8/73, Gefr. Benny Kippes, "Im Vormarsch," *Wacht im Osten. Feldzeitung der Armee-Abteilung Scheffer* 440 (February 13, 1917).
30 Hartmann, *Ob-Ost*, 96–97.
31 Ibid.
32 Häpke, in *Das Land*, 237.
33 Jungfer, *Gesicht*, 44.
34 *Ich Weiß*, 15.
35 Hartmann, *Ob-Ost*, 98.
36 Thus, Chief of Military Administration Lithuania von Heppe was offered an important position in the occupied territories of the East after the war as an incentive to stay on in the summer of 1918: BAMA N 196/1, Nachlass von Heppe, vol. V, "Im Weltkriege," 152.
37 Ibid., 98.
38 This image recurs elsewhere: *Draussen*, 9, 20.
39 BA N 238/8 Morsbach, Bürgermeister von Schaulen. Zu Abteilung V, 27. September 1916.
40 BAMA PHD 8/23, Schirokauer, "Der deutsche Soldat," *KB* 6 (November 15, 1916); *Draussen*, 10.
41 BAMA PHD 23/87, *Nowogrodeker Kriegszeitung.*; BAMA PHD 23/63, *Ostwacht. Lukower Feldzeitung.*
42 Zweig, *Grischa*, 97.
43 Conzelmann, ed., *Dix*, plate 40.
44 BAMA PHD 8/73, Leutn. Milarch, "Wir halten durch! (Auf der Urlaubsreise durch Polen, Juli 1917)," *Die Wacht im Osten* 625 (August 17, 1917). In this and several other cases, evidence is included from Polish territories which is not specific to those regions, but speaks to the wider eastern front-experience and its impressions. Hartmann, *Ob-Ost*, 12.
45 Hermann Struck and Herbert Eulenberg, *Skizzen aus Litauen, Weissrussland und Kurland* (n.p.: Druckerei des Oberbefehlshabers Ost, 1916), preface.

46 BAMA PHD 8/73, Sergt. Max Hamm, "Ein Rueckblick," *Wacht im Osten* 819 (February 28, 1918).

47 *Draussen*, 8.

48 Hartmann, *Ob-Ost*, 99.

49 Feiler, *Neuland*, 7; Hartmann, *Ob-Ost*, 68 on map.

50 Swedish explorer Sven Hedin's *Nach Osten!*; Feiler, *Neuland*; Hartmann, *Ob-Ost*; Heywang, *Deutsche Tat, Deutsche Saat in russischem Brachland. Eine Frontreise nach Ob.-Ost*; Strecker, *Auf den Spuren Hindenburgischer Verwaltung. Erlebnisse und Ergebnisse einer Studienfahrt in Ob. Ost*; Listowsky, *Neu-Ost. Unser Zukunftsgrenzgebiet um Ostpreussens Ostrand. Fahrten durch Polen und Litauen unter deutscher Kriegsverwaltung.*

51 Struck and Eulenberg, *Skizzen*, preface.

52 *Das Land*, 203.

53 Klemperer, *Curriculum*, 612; BAMA N 98/1, Gossler, 90.

54 Meyer, *Mitteleuropa*, 118–22.

55 Fritz Wertheimer, *Hindenburgs Mauer im Osten*, 3rd edn (Stuttgart: Deutsche Verlags-Anstalt, 1916).

56 Imanuel Geiss, *Der polnische Grenzstreifen. Ein Beitrag zur deutschen Kriegsziel-politik im Ersten Weltkrieg* (Lübeck: Mattheisen, 1960); Fischer, *Griff*, 230–32.

57 Feiler, *Neuland*, 2.

58 Kitchen, *Dictatorship*, 56.

59 Mai, *Ende*, 201; Fischer, *Griff*, 90–95.

60 Mai, *Ende*, 54–55.

61 Craig, *Germany*, 360–61.

62 Silvio Broederich-Kurmahlen, *Das neue Ostland* (Charlottenburg: Ostlan-dverlag, 1915); Colliander, "Beziehungen," 79–88.

63 For fascinating reflections on geography and national identity see: Russell Bermann, "The Geography of Wilhelmine Culture," in *The Rise of the Modern German Novel: Crisis and Charisma* (Cambridge, MA: Harvard University Press, 1986), 1–24.

64 Marc Raeff, *The Well-Ordered Police State: Social and Institutional Change Through Law in the Germanies and Russia, 1600–1800* (New Haven: Yale University Press, 1983).

65 Meyer, *Mitteleuropa*, 244–50.

66 Hans-Dietrich Schultz, "Deutschlands 'natürliche' Grenzen," in *Deutsch-lands Grenzen in der Geschichte*, ed. Alexander Demandt (Munich: Verlag C. H. Beck, 1990), 33–88.

67 For volkish aspect, see Mosse, *Crisis*, 4, 17–21, 42–43, 73, 174–75.

68 Celia Applegate, *A Nation of Provincials: The German Idea of Heimat* (Berkeley: University of California Press, 1990); Jost Hermand, *Grüne Utopien in Deutschland. Zur Geschichte des ökologischen Bewusstseins* (Frankfurt-on-Main: Fischer Taschenbuch Verlag, 1991).

69 Friedrich Ratzel, *Deutschland. Einführung in die Heimatkunde*, 2nd edn (Leip-zig: Fr. Wilh. Grunow, 1907), 255.

70 Gerhard Oestreich, *Neostoicism and the Early Modern State*, trans. David McLintock (Cambridge: Cambridge University Press, 1982); Raeff, *Police State*; Mack Walker, *German Home Towns: Community, State, and General*

Estate, 1648–1871 (Ithaca, NY: Cornell University Press, 1971).

71 Chickering, *We Men*; Wehler, *Kaiserreich*, 93–94.

72 Woodruff D. Smith, *The Ideological Origins of Nazi Imperialism* (Oxford: Oxford University Press, 1986).

73 Whittlesey, *Strategy*, 29–30; Gordon A. Craig, *The Politics of the Prussian Army, 1640–1945* (Oxford: Oxford University Press, 1955), 78.

74 Hermann Cron, *Geschichte des Deutschen Heeres im Weltkriege, 1914–1918* (Berlin: Militärverlag Karl Sigismund, 1937), 219–22.

75 Meyer, *Mitteleuropa*, 245.

76 Bruno Clemenz, *Kriegsgeographie. Erdkunde und Weltkrieg in ihre Beziehungen erläutert und dargestellt nebst Schilderung der Kriegsschauplätze* (Würzburg: Curt Kabitzsch, 1916), v.

77 Ibid.; H. Fischer, *Kriegsgeographie* (Bielefeld: Velhagen & Klasing, 1916); Ernst Oehlmann, *Kriegsgeographie* (Breslau: Ferdinand Hirt, 1916). On use in classroom: Klaus Saul, "Jugend im Schatten des Krieges. Vormilitärische Ausbildung – Kriegswirtschaftlicher Einsatz – Schulalltag in Deutschland, 1914–1918," *Militärgeschichtliche Mitteilungen* 2 (1983): 111.

78 Rudolf Kjellen, *Die politischen Probleme des Weltkrieges* (Leipzig: B. G. Teubner, 1916), 3, 139; 102.

79 Meyer, *Mitteleuropa*, 194–97, 2–3; Mai, *Ende*, 58; Fischer, *Griff*, 90–95.

80 Jörg Brechtefeld, *Mitteleuropa and German Politics: 1848 to the Present* (New York: St. Martin's Press, 1996), 39.

81 *Draussen*, 49–50.

82 "'Der Krieg in der Schule.' Zuschrift eines Lehrers an die Kölnische Zeitung. Oktober 1914," reprinted in Saul, "Jugend," 124. This was fairly common among all the combatant countries. In his memoirs, Mircea Eliade recounts boyhood fascination for the same games.

83 "Verfügung der Schulabteilung der Regierung Stettin, 23.2.1915," reprinted in Saul, "Jugend," 127–28.

84 "'Der Krieg in der Schule.' Zuschrift eines Lehrers an die Kölnische Zeitung. Oktober 1914," reprinted in Saul, "Jugend," 125; "Verfügung der Schulabteilung der Regierung Stettin, 23.2.1915," ibid.

85 Saul, "Jugend," 91, 96. By late 1914, some 600,000 Prussian youths participated in premilitary training.

86 Paul Georg Schäfer, *Geländespiele, den Sohnen unseres Vaterlandes zugedacht* (Leipzig: B. G. Teubner, 1909); Heinrich Leo, *Jungdeutschland. Wehrerziehung der deutschen Jugend* (Berlin-Wilmersdorf: Hermann Paetel Verlag, [1912]); Alfred Berg, *Geographisches Wanderbuch. Ein Führer für Wandervögel und Pfadfinder*, 2nd edn. (Leipzig: B. G. Teubner, 1918); Hermann Rosenstengel, *Leichte Geländespiele für die deutsche Jugend* (Leipzig: B. G. Teubner, 1918); *Draussen*, 50. This tradition, begun before 1914, was continued in the Weimar Republic by settler groups, in the Third Reich by Hitler Youth, and in Germany today by radical right *Wehrsportgruppen*.

87 Saul, "Jugend," 101–103, 109.

6   Crisis

From the first, Ober Ost was a showcase for pathologies of power, which caused the state to seize up just when it seemed that its rule was being made permanent. Interlocking crises overtook the administration's contradictory functioning, the political consciousness and national identity of natives, and the identity of Germans in the East. These emergencies flowed together to seriously affect political developments in Ober Ost in 1917 and 1918, ending with the collapse of the ambitious edifice of power as Imperial Germany itself went down in defeat and revolution. Failure, coming at this highest pitch of ambition, produced lasting consequences for German views of the East.

In 1917, Ober Ost's machinery rumbled on toward a grinding impasse, while more insightful officials looked on helplessly as the administration undermined its own goals: the way in which many policies were executed destroying the aims they were to effect. After Hindenburg and Ludendorff were elevated to the Supreme Command on August 29, 1916, the spirit they had built into the state worked on. Chief of General Staff Falkenhayn had finally been ousted after the unremitting and jealous intrigues of the eastern generals were joined by forces in Germany's political leadership and parliament. By the summer of 1916, Germany's position was seriously embattled, everywhere on the defensive, food in short supply as Britain's blockade intensified, and its allies seeming of little use. When Romania entered the war on the Entente side after seeing the Brusilov offensive's impressive initial gains in June, this setback led to Falkenhayn's removal. In his place, Hindenburg was elevated to Chief of General Staff of the Army, and soon also vested with increased power, as he exercised the Supreme War Command for the Central Powers in the name of the Kaiser (whose real influence shrank as the military heroes ascended), disposing of 6 million men at arms, Germans, Austro-Hungarians, Turks, and Bulgarians.[1] Ludendorff became first quartermaster general, but, remarkably, was made coresponsible with Hindenburg. With the Titans' departure, elderly Prince Leopold of Bavaria was appointed Supreme Commander in the East on August 29, 1916.[2] Since he had little interest in the occupied territories, which he reportedly once called "*Sauland*" ("pig-land" or "filth-land"), Prince Leopold gave a free hand to his chief of staff, Major-General Max Hoffmann.[3] Under his supervision, Ludendorff's policies intensified, often working at cross-purposes with ever-greater efficiency, with added pressure of demands for resources from a strained home front and the Supreme Command. By now, even enthusiastic proponents recognized that Ober Ost showcased "German addiction to over-organization."[4] Von Brockhusen, a high official and advisor to Ludendorff (before the war, a regional governor), conceded that "because of the excessive number of office workers, far too much was being written," producing mountains of paperwork.[5] His response, however, was to pen official memos and admonitions to combat this tendency. One worker noted that in spite of work days from eight in the morning to eight at night, little productive work got done. "The military administrative apparatus," another worker observed, "is of a gruesome formality, because everybody tries to make himself as comfortable as possible in the whole racket process – and the result is that it becomes ever more uncomfortable for everyone involved."[6] Bureaucratic conflicts between offices grew:

On top of everything, no administrative post has real independence – each is coruled by several others . . . and because no one has full responsibility, everyone shirks responsibility. Thus, lower offices proceed with greatest possible severity according to regulations, just so that they would not be reproved from above for their "competence" and thus get involved in a new mess of paperwork.[7]

The state had caught not only natives in its gears, for its administrative apparatus, "a real time-wasting machine, shirk-duty from top to bottom," held Germans captive as well.[8] An official reflected, "I have not spoken to a single one of our men in serious conversation who does not admit the convoluted counter productiveness of our administrative measures . . . but each participates in the madness, because he feels himself helplessly clamped into the paperwork machine."[9] This situation, masked by the outward appearance of military order, could perhaps have continued for some time, but requirements of a new policy from spring 1917 revealed the accumulated contradictions. As it lurched towards a final triumph and the cementing of its rule, the state increasingly broke down.

In 1917, new policies were needed in Ober Ost, calling for an active role for native groups, so that they might ratify permanent German rule. The upheavals in Russia, where the February Revolution was followed by the Bolshevik seizure of power in "Red October," failed policies toward Poland on the part of the Central Powers, and growing discontent in

Germany expressed in the stirrings of parliamentarianism and strikes, meant that the outright annexationism favored by the Supreme Command and far-right groups needed to be replaced with more subtle, indirect forms of domination over a belt of buffer states to Germany's east. Yet, at crucial junctures, the Supreme Command resisted this tactical shift, impeding a more nuanced or veiled approach to supremacy over *Mitteleuropa*. At the same time, within the occupied territory, the cultural programs and nationalities policies undercut the new plans. It was the most consequential example of the conflict between means and ends endemic in Ober Ost.

Economic reality increasingly undermined nationality policies. In this area of malleable national identities, officials insisted that natives were apolitical, and their weak national feelings secondary to economic self-interest.[10] Native loyalty could be bought for Germany if it was demonstrated that this was to their economic advantage. Administration reports claimed that ever more natives began "to reconcile themselves to the thought of Germany. The Latvian is an opportunist through and through. He runs after whoever promises him the best living conditions, and it has become clear to most that they fare better under German administration than under the Russian."[11] Lithuanians, reports judged, were fundamentally apolitical: "The Lithuanians are farmers and workers and are completely docile . . . they have no Great Lithuanian ideas, and will not have these in the future, unless they are artificially awakened in them, through agitation and the press."[12] Military Administration Lithuania's chief reported: "The great mass of the population has reconciled itself to German rule . . . The Lithuanian is only impressed by power. If he sees that he will gain economic advantage through the powerful victorious German Reich, then he will be . . . an easily steered, state-supporting ethnic group in the new, greater Germany."[13]

Alone among native groups, Kurland's Baltic Germans were considered mature and reliable enough to be given official posts. Von Gossler's reports from Kurland lauded them as "German to the core."[14] His policy of ensconcing them in official positions came to be called the "Gossler system." Of his district captains, only one was not Baltic German. His cultural section was led by a born Kurlander, Königsberg professor Seraphim.[15] Yet taking on Baltic Germans was not without its dangers, for in spite of claims of one German identity, their interests could radically diverge from the army's. Their racial fury against natives, "*Undeutschen*," colored the administration's views and actions, while for their part, Latvians could hardly see the new rulers as impartial, when they coopted Baltic Barons. Hoffmann noted that officials alienated Estonians and Latvians by interacting only with Barons, adding, "For years now,

I've warned against such idiocy."[16] Lithuania's chief von Heppe agreed, regretting that German policy had been taken in tow by noble special interests.[17] For their part, Baltic German aristocrats feared that growing parliamentary and democratic pressures in Germany would undercut their position as a privileged caste, and faced the intractable problem of pressing for annexation and union with the Reich, while somehow preserving their exceptional status. Germany's domestic politics spilled over into Ober Ost, complicating already tangled ethnic policies.

This definition of economically determined non-German national identities was fundamental to Ober Ost's project of manipulating and remaking peoples, teaching them to work under German management. Clearly, this would not be easy, for authorities explained that they demanded "from the Lithuanian, who is lazy by nature, a level of work much higher than what he was used to."[18] Yet natives would grow accustomed to "strict but just" rule:

The population is forced to work much more than it was used to before, in order to meet demands made on them. The land produced for them just as much as they needed to live, with a mediocre level of work. To go beyond this, in order to advance and to arrive at better living conditions, was generally foreign to them. Therefore, the Lithuanian finds forced labor burdensome, but will become used to the extra work and will recognize that he is provided for, as conditions allow.[19]

Authorities explained that natives had economic incentives for giving up Lithuanian. Besides, they claimed, no such a language really existed, as it had no standardized form:

Now one notices among many Lithuanians the serious desire to learn German . . . The Lithuanian written language, thus, should only be understood as an auxiliary language, helping to learn German. It is very much in the interest of German rule and position of power if the Lithuanian is helped in his efforts to learn German. He does not understand why the victorious German wants to force on him, instead of German, a language which neither the German nor he understands. He appreciates all the more the necessity of learning German, as he sees that it helps him in his economic advancement.[20]

According to Kurland's chief, the Latvian "is a realistically minded opportunist: whoever offers him the best chances, he will join." Latvians were marked by "unique adaptability . . . If the Latvian sees that he gets further with German than with Latvian, he will very quickly become German. A Latvian Problem, causing special difficulties for Germanization, should hardly arise – a people fragment of one and one-fourth million is not capable of that."[21]

The administration was convinced of the malleability of ethnicity in a land where they found ethnic affiliation so fluid and shifting, yet the result of German policy was the opposite of what was intended. The regime's irrational economics embittered populations and forced natives to see the crisis and their dire future prospects in terms of nationality and conflicting cultural values. In one sphere after another, Ober Ost's drive for control undercut attempts at manipulation.

Another striking example of this was the policy towards religion. From the beginning, the importance of confession in the area had been clear to Germans, noting the high pitch of religious sentiment and observance. Religion's political meaning was underlined by the way in which confession intersected with national identification. Authorities succeeded in establishing amiable relations with higher clergy, but these contacts at upper levels could hardly make up for disastrous impressions created daily abroad in the land. Because most soldiers and officials were Protestants, less-familiar religions heightened the land's strangeness.[22] Their reaction was often not sympathetic and the policies they executed inflamed this volatile religious feeling. *Verkehrspolitik* often hindered parishioners from visiting local churches, across the next area's borders. Soldiers reportedly assaulted priests, hurrying to visit sick parishioners, for not saluting. A popular native source claimed that the district captain of Kedainiai beat a Father Meškauskas, on his way to give last rites to a sick parishioner, carrying the sacrament.[23] Political official von Gayl acknowledged a similar incident, in which the chief of a horse hospital struck the hat from a priest carrying the sacrament. This old officer explained that he had been polite, since "he usually struck the hats from the heads of *Panjes* who met him without greeting with his riding crop, while remembering orders on polite treatment of clergy, he knocked this cap off with his hand." His superiors attested that the soldier "had acted in good faith."[24] Mistreatment of priests, the highest native authorities among Christian groups, bred hatred in even the most passive populations.[25] Natives claimed a range of other outrages, reporting soldiers strolling into masses as loud sightseers, wearing caps and smoking.[26] The army took over churches for its own use, and on occasion native masses were allegedly halted and churches cleared, as in Schaulen, for German services.[27] Lastly, natives claimed troops surrounded churches during mass to catch men for forced labor.[28] Even at the highest levels, there were needlessly provocative measures, such as von Isenburg's refusal to hand out small wheat rations for baking sacramental hosts.[29] Not surprisingly, otherwise conservative clergymen were increasingly driven into opposition and participation in nationalist projects, many priests taking a leading role in the secret school movement. Schaulen's military mayor complained of a pastor Galdikas' activism and explained that policies could only be enacted if he were "transferred or deported [*abgeschoben*]."

Numbers of the more troublesome, of different confessions, were reportedly deported to Germany.[30]

Finally, the administration bankrupted its most minimal claim to native respect: maintenance of order. Even strict enforcement of law and "ordered circumstances," allowing peasants to farm in peace, could have been the basis for a successful occupation. Instead, the administration itself created disorder, with arbitrary rules and requisitions. When gendarmes eased their fight against banditry in 1917, natives recognized that the administration did not even offer them security. Robber bands operated up to the gates of cities, one official reported, and by 1918 there were nearly weekly attacks on police stations or officials.[31] The administration increasingly left natives with nothing to lose.

Popular morale plummeted and reports noted ever-worsening dispositions. Soldiers in the streets met looks of hatred, increasingly open hostility. An ordinary soldier walking in Riga noted, "Because of the desperate situation, a great portion of the population was seized by an unlimited hatred against Germans, so that many times German soldiers were murdered in more out of the way streets. Now we were never allowed to go out at night without a loaded pistol."[32] This was not an auspicious beginning for Ober Ost's attempt to seal its ownership of the region.

As the administration sabotaged its own manipulative policies, it most often blamed the lands and peoples, falling back on generalizations about the disorderly East and intractable ethnic essences. Yet no amount of native collaboration or subservience would have sufficed, for the fatal flaw lay in Ober Ost itself. Its overriding imperative had been control, as one embittered official recognized: "The only purpose of all of these antics is apparently that the foreign population – just like our people at home – learn how to be ruled."[33] Paradoxically, the administration inadvertently created objective conditions for the formation of independent native identities and political consciousness. Its arbitration reinforced differences, producing rebellious consciousness among natives. The clash of cultures with the occupiers compelled natives to articulate values earlier inchoate and implicit in their traditions and ways of life, as an alternative to intolerable present conditions.

The breaking point came when natives felt that German occupation was even worse than Russian rule. As an official observed, natives said, "The Russian knout hurt once in a while – the flat of the Prussian broadsword hurts all the time."[34] This was reflected in a change of native behavior, turning to desperate and undirected resistance.[35] In the winter of 1916/17, authorities worried whether they would be able to feed natives after another disappointing harvest, falling short of exaggerated estimates put about by agricultural experts. Hunger riots and strikes broke out in Bialystok.[36] Troops fanned out through the countryside to seize hidden food, scouring farms. Reports noted the worsening mood and stiffening resistance to requisitions. Earlier characterized by wishful thinking, they now conceded that "in the latest period, heightened unrest and depression are visible."[37] After that admission, things went from bad to worse.[38] Reports doggedly insisted that "the reasons are not political, but economic in nature," overlooking the administration's own formulation of native malleability, as if economic hardship would not eventually be translated into political terms.[39] For the first time, natives resisted horse requisitions in a concerted manner, in Lithuania in the fall of 1917, and troops were sent in to Raczki to force farmers to present horses.[40] The commands and "complete exploitation" became too much for many, who "gnawed themselves inside over the unending orders, but the more they worried, the less they obeyed."[41] The limits of administrative compulsion were reached when it seemed that things got worse whether one obeyed or not. Driven by desperate economic straits, smuggling flourished.[42] In these illegal ventures, peasants cooperated with Jews in towns, who were hit especially hard by *Verkehrspolitik* and the administration's monopoly on trade, as a Lithuanian Jew noted:

Since there's nothing to sell, they have closed their stalls and gone underground. You wouldn't believe it – they dig tunnels under the military cordon around the city to get to the country, where the peasants sell them some potatoes, a bunch of carrots, a dead chicken, which they have hidden from German confiscation. Sometimes the Jews pretend to be dead, let themselves be carried and "buried" at some far corner of the cemetery, and the business is carried on among the graves. And with all that, a quarter of the population has already perished from hunger, and still they hide out so as not to work for the Germans.[43]

Germans in the administration and army also aided smuggling.[44] But von Heppe, chief of Bialystok-Grodno, singled out the Jewish community and threatened their rabbis, assuring them, "I would ruthlessly let them and their people starve" if smuggling were not reined in.[45] Reports indicated that Jews no longer showed friendliness towards Germans, as they had earlier, and urged "serious attention" to their economic activity.[46] At night, in spite of official curfews, country roads teemed with movement in the shadows. Natives flocked to the growing bandit groups. Some marauding groups of Russian soldiers and escaped POWs began to style themselves Bolsheviks.[47]

Native resistance went beyond undirected insubordination, evolving into a political program, as evidenced most clearly in the case of the largest ethnic group, Lithuanians. With other forms of organization banned, officially sanctioned relief committees became centers for political activity. Wilna's Lithuanian Refugee Aid Committee used humanitarian missions as covers for political work. Its executive council wrote memoranda of grievances to the army and civil authorities in Germany and concentrated on schools, preparing educational materials, writing textbooks, and training teachers. In spite of restrictions on movement, it sent spies into the countryside, establishing networks of contacts, and tried to find ties abroad to neutral countries and the Lithuanian diaspora. In the countryside, young people organized leaflet campaigns and secret press activity. These stirrings culminated in late 1916 in unrest in the Geisteriš-kiai village, where local youths circulated proclamations printed on secret presses, and in several instances organized armed resistance. Fearing a wider uprising, the army apparently reacted with panicked ruthlessness, supposedly burning several farmers to death in their homes, while others were rounded up and sent to jail. Several youths implicated in the activities were tortured and shot in military prisons, according to native sources.[48]

This native crisis offers crucial insights into the nature of the nationalist project at these European crossroads in the East. Lithuanian intellectuals arrived first at a personal crisis. For many, the German culture they earlier admired had to be reappraised. This was most wrenching for Prussian-Lithuanians, who saw themselves as participants in German culture. The writer Wilhelm Storosta-Vydūnas described his personal transformation, writing to German author Hermann Sudermann: stories of "the German administration's abuses in Lithuania, I considered to be wartime fictions – as also remarks by Isenburg, Lithuania's ruler, that he would very quickly transform all Lithuanians into Germans. I thought these were just people's fantasies." Yet on learning of the regime's record, he came to the "conviction, that the German administration was in truth preparing to destroy Lithuanian identity." He recognized poignantly that German values still remained dear to him: "But it would be a mistake to consider such convictions as hatred of Germans . . . I view it as a crime on the part of one whom I respected very much – a crime by one who is close to me." That moment was a crisis of identity and action for Vydūnas, who turned from purely cultural work to ethnic politics.[49] Similarly, Prussian–Lithuanian politician Gaigalat-Gaigalaitis, Prussian Land Assembly member, found himself with changed convictions and was seen as increasingly unreliable by authorities. At first timid, he intervened ever more forcefully, carrying memoranda of grievances to civil officials. Within the administration, a dramatic case was the metamorphosis of Bernhard Kodatis.[50] Born in Berlin to Lithuanian immigrants, from 1916 to 1918 he worked in the administration, censoring *The Present Time*, and later in the political section. Kodatis passed important information to

Lithuanian activists. In 1918, he was caught and sent to prison in Tilsit. After the war, Lithuania secured his release, and he moved there, renouncing German citizenship, taking a name with German and Lithuanian traces, Bernardas Kodatis (Kuodaitis). War and experiences in the occupied territories recast his identity, as it did for many others.

More generally, by degrees the occupation regime's hardships called forth a broader nationalist reaction in Lithuanian society at large, radicalizing even peasants earlier indifferent to political programs. Ober Ost's clumsy attempts at ethnic puppetry and manipulation forced natives to view their own predicament ever more in national terms. Their antipathy to German occupation took on the outlines of a cultural clash, bringing into high relief the different values and assumptions held by the occupied and occupier. As one German official blandly remarked, Lithuanian "ethical and moral concepts were fundamentally different from our own."[51] On the Lithuanian side, many of these values were previously inarticulate, part of a seemingly self-evident way of life (refered to as "*būdas*"), but now were recast as constituent parts of a national identity.

Fundamentally, the emerging cultural clash was visible in the contrast between two different concepts of order: German *Ordnung* and Lithuanian *tvarka*. The German concept was incarnated in the administration's policies to enforce "ordered circumstances." Lithuanian *tvarka*, by contrast, did not have the same tie to state power. As was only natural for a peasant people (who had not had an active role in government), the idea of *tvarka* derived from the reality of the farm household. This can even be traced in the word itself, related to words for fencing and enclosure, as well as for creation (*tverti*). In the Lithuanian movement's first secret political manifesto from 1916, concepts of a unique culture, distinctive, ordered economic way of life (*ūkis*), and nascent national consciousness, were held up as home-grown order, an alternative to any outside domination.[52] This model of order also contrasted with the German conception of borders and limits. The Lithuanian conception of limits originated again in the homestead. Its symbol was the hedgerow or "living fence," an image common in folk art, dances, and weaving. The hedgerow's anarchic tangle of natural growth and ceaseless activity, intertwining separate and distinct shoots into one great living whole, seemed to accurately describe the moving, changing, season-driven world in which natives were enmeshed. Lithuanian homesteads were considered incomplete without fences marking them as property, distinguishing landholding here from Slavic traditions of communal agriculture.[53] Yet when this fence marks off a garden plot, it is often a garden which westerners would hardly recognize as such. The scene is strange, for fences separate chaos and untrammeled growth of nature outside from even greater and multihued chaos of life inside the garden. Within the little space, plants grow in profuse color and density, planted closer together than nature alone could manage. A brighter, livelier, amplified chaos is achieved and celebrated there. Where German tradition emphasized forming and channeling, reshaping and cultivating, this native worldview urged a different ideal of "training" the land's growth.

The 1916 proclamation's statement of the people's unique character and values now presented these as national consciousness. Significantly, it refered to the people as a *"tauta,"* an archaic Indo-European term. The common translation of *tauta* as "nation" is an incomplete shorthand rendering, missing its distinctive meaning. "Nation" locates identity in birth (*"natio"*). *Tauta*, however, is different, originally meaning "troop," "crowd," or "a band of riders" (Indo-European *"teuta"*).[54] The unifying principle here, in contrast to "nation," is from the outset voluntaristic, pointing to a common, shared project defining the group.

Since national identity was understood to be rooted not in birth or "blood," but in common resolve, then shared consciousness had to provide the moving spirit, underlined in nationalist exhortations to awareness and conscious commitment, as well as emphasis on education. Individual commitment was crucial because in these lands national identity rested so much on personal decision. At this northern European crossroads of culture, ethnicity, language, religion, and history, there were many possible identifications for individuals to accept. Radical contingency, not clear and inexorable fatality, ruled ethnicity. The national movement's founding intellectuals experienced this themselves in preceding decades, arriving at avowals of Lithuanian identity in dramatic moments of personal conversion.

This snapshot of the development of a national identity, caught in a moment of genesis in the 1916 proclamation, illuminates the distinctive nature of the nationalist project here. The essential point is that this was a deliberate project, aware of itself, creating images of the past and asserting continuities with that past. Western scholarship has often treated nationalism under the rubric of "false consciousness," stressing artifice and manipulation. This misses the dimension of awareness in the project. In fact, models of nationalism current in western scholarship are stood on their heads in this case from the East. Rather than "imagined communities" or "inventions of tradition,"[55] the nationalist project produced here aware "communities of imagination" and deliberate "traditions of invention," a conscious elaboration out of the precarious past, realizing one of many possible projects. Thus, the manifesto declared the need "to become ourselves, with all of the qualities bred in us through the ages."[56]

Scholarly models of nationalism juxtaposing civil, citizenship-based nationalisms of the West with ethnic, birth-based nationalisms of the East, are thus incomplete.[57] Here, "elective ethnicity," nationality as a conscious choice and commitment to creative tradition, was another significant variant. In the final analysis, Ober Ost saw not merely the clash of German and native nationalisms, but something more complex: the collision of markedly different *kinds* of nationalisms and identities, differently understood and motivated, struggling in different directions.

At the same time, in a supreme irony, Ober Ost's administrative practice threw German identity into doubt. German Work defined German identity in the East as systematic rule, but as the administration became entangled in its own contradictions, sending out jets of violence in frustration, reality undermined these pretensions. Left alone, cut off from contact with other Germans, soldiers found themselves lost. As a novelist recalled, "the troops, which hold the land in occupation, are sinking down in the spiritual wasteland."[58] An officer in Kurland commented that his "squadrons are dissolving more and more into large and small businesses," as they were assigned to different tasks in the countryside. In his own residence at the edge of a great forest, he recorded the impact of isolation in his diary:

The loneliness completely dissolves me, or rather confuses me. I must bring myself into balance in this quiet. Here the profound closeness of nature, the deep impressions press in on me of such an immediately and gigantically receptive landscape, which in its details is so impenetrably secretive and unknowable, while as a whole so mightily moved and formed, chasing my senses and all my forces of imagination into such a terrible confusion that I cannot resolve.[59]

Isolated, some soldiers began to turn to the natives. Orders against fraternization lapsed in the face of everyday reality. A hybrid life evolved for troops, prostitution its hallmark, causing outbreaks of venereal disease.[60] Over time, "most of the soldiers became accustomed bit by bit to this ragged life as something normal."[61] An official's novel portrayed the coarsening of their natures:

In the city there were many available women. Their men had either fallen or were in German prisons. They lived, the youngest with children born mostly after losing their men, in poor and cramped conditions. It was no wonder than they sought contact with the occupation troops in the city. They washed clothes for the soldiers, mended their torn possessions and received from them foodstuffs and field kitchen food for the service. The number of women who sold their love . . . grew constantly . . . In the eyes of the soldiers, this prostitution was something so natural that they considered it quite in order to use the opportunities offered. Only a few of the married men remained loyal to their wives at home. They had to endure the ridicule of the others.

The new life became normal as many soldiers lost the feeling of connection to home. The same realistic novel recorded, "the picture of wife and child disappeared from the eyes of some so completely – and became so indistinct as leave was forbidden – that they broke off correspondence and wives often wrote plaintive letters to the company commander, that they had heard nothing from their men for weeks."[62] Surrounded by natives, soldiers might learn smatterings of their languages and take on some of their views. One novel depicted Latvians passing on to German soldiers their hatred for the Baltic Barons.[63] Some, increasingly influenced by socialist ideas, accepted this antipathy for class enemies and resented having to preserve the Barons' social dominance. Reports complained that many could not see that *Balten* were "German to the core" and thus had a right to support.[64] As class lines reasserted themselves, the solidarity of a common ethnic German identity was breached.

These transformations were mixed with soldiers' brutalization, for they were after all still armed representatives of the occupying power. Harsh administrative practices taught troops that order and control sanctioned violence and excused excesses and requisitions with the slogan, "War is war." Limits broke down further when hunger gripped troops, as Germany's supply situation worsened due to the blockade and mistakes in strategic planning by the military dictatorship. As conditions worsened, discipline declined. Ordinary soldiers complained that their miserable fare was "too little to live, too much to die," until they felt freed from moral constraints binding in civilian life.[65] Ober Ost increasingly became a free-for-all of pilfering from military stores, black-market trading, and stealing from impoverished natives. Officials blamed this on the influence of natives, for whom bribery and stealing was a way of life.[66]

German unity buckled as regional identities reasserted themselves. Prussian Poles and Prussian Lithuanians in the ranks caused problems, while the administration's staff was an uneasy mixture of strong Prussian representation with Jewish officials. The High Command considered Alsatians of doubtful loyalty, unreliable on the Western Front. When regiments were transferred west, Alsatians were humiliated, separated from the ranks and left behind. Dominik Richert, a simple Alsatian soldier, described his resentment in an irony-laden memoir. These reactions were not entirely rational, since as fighting in the East quieted down, chances for survival were better here than in the trenches of France. But all the same these acts were insulting: "What swearing there was! Everyone's mood was exactly the same. If the Prussians had been sent where one wished them, they would all have gone to the Devil." In January 1917, as Alsatians were led away from their regiments for reassignment, they reportedly broke out in rebellious shouts of "*Vive la France!*" and sang Alsatian songs. In the spring of 1917, Alsatians were meted out the "same insult as before." As a result of such high-handed policies, their loyalty and sense of German identity were extinguished. Richert reflected, "Sometimes, when I stood thus alone in the cold night, I considered for what or for whom I was actually standing there. In us Alsatians there was no trace of love for the Fatherland or any stuff like that, and sometimes I was gripped by terrible fury when I thought what a comfortable life those who had caused this war were leading." Alsatian soldiers clustered together to speak of the homeland, but by that they meant not Germany, but Alsace. One announced he "could not wait to become a Frenchman."[67] Germany's regional fragmentation was reproduced on the Eastern Front. Many soldiers were united in their resentment of officials and officers, mostly Prussians.

Class conflict among ranks boiled as well. Many official posts were staffed by wounded men or officers too old for front duty. Some older men were intoxicated by their sudden power and an official had earlier observed that "every uniformed self-important personality has thousand-fold opportunities to play the role of dictator."[68] Such despotic authority created deep divisions between officers, pleased with their future prospects in the occupied East, and increasingly miserable men in the ranks. Younger combat soldiers resented superiors all the more when they had not experienced front fighting. Differences in rank were also reflected in the territory's debased life, "in the different living conditions of the prostitutes" in special officers' brothels. There, ordinary soldiers saw scenes which they said made them lose respect for authority. One soldier posted as a guard outside brothels in Mitau recalled:

In the officers' brothel, there were wild scenes. What should we think of our worthy superiors, if we saw how the officers were struck in the face, spit on, and thrown out of the doors with brute force by the girls of the brothel! How much respect could remain, when we saw through a gap in the window, how the officers and prostitutes enjoyed themselves in a strange way in the brothel salon. On one evening in particular things got crazy, at a very late hour. An officer sat at the piano and played some dance piece, while . . . uniformed officers moved about in circles to the music on the floor, on all fours. On the back of each officer sat a buck-naked girl, hitting and spurring on to a quicker pace her partner, who was no longer a *chevalier*, but a *cheval*.[69]

One soldier claimed he recalled a bordello near Wilna's cathedral with the sign, "Only for Officers – Not for Deputy Officers." Reportedly, soldiers hated the German secretaries brought in after 1916 even more than officers, because these women did not socialize with enlisted men, but only with the upper ranks.[70] Open black-marketeering by officers heightened the fury, building to revolutionary rage against a society which allowed such conditions, while "the ordinary soldier had no choice but to starve, scream 'Hurrah!,' allow himself to be tortured by lice, and let himself be shot dead for the 'beloved Fatherland.'" Political interpretations found ready ground. As the Alsatian fumed,

> I had in general a secret fury against all officers from lieutenant on up, who all lived better, had better food and on top of that a nice salary, while the poor soldier had to participate in the whole misery of war, "For the Fatherland and not for money, hurrah, hurrah, hurrah," as the soldier's song went. On top of that, one could not have one's own opinion before an officer. One had to say nothing and only obey blindly.[71]

Radical socialist propaganda made ever stronger inroads. Social Democratic soldiers reportedly helped Lithuanian activists evade *Verkehrspolitik* restrictions, carrying letters to sympathetic Reichstag members. German solidarity, based on a national identity as rulers, broke down.

Among more articulate and thoughtful soldiers, the crisis of identity expressed itself as anxiety over what the regime was doing to German principles and values. Some ordinary soldiers showed a fundamental decency that seems heroic. Locals later gratefully remembered individual soldiers for being kind to the poor, passing food to the starving. Other soldiers and officials were plagued by thoughts on the nature of their occupation, for the tedious life in the occupied territory gave time for such reflections. Simple, uneducated soldiers could not organize their thoughts and some broke down under the stress of their isolation in the press of disturbing circumstances.[72]

A small number of men, especially in the cultural administration's "intellectuals' club,"[73] met the East's new experiences with curiosity and sympathy, or even began to internalize this world. For such men, the true crisis lay in being unable to recognize what had seemed familiar and foundational in themselves. Values which they felt defined their own heritage and identity were being violated, the very "German" values the administration claimed to personify: justice and order, *Bildung* and *Kultur*. Those ideas were debased, becoming crudely literal procedural directives geared toward a sole imperative of control.

Considering this state of affairs, one important figure would have come to mind for educated men: the eighteenth-century thinker Johann Gottfried Herder, whose ideas remained current (even if in foreshortened form), an embodiment of *Kultur* and *Bildung*.[74] As a young pastor in Riga, Herder came to know native peoples, admiring their folk songs, which seemed to realize his ideals of organic culture and authenticity. Herder outlined a mission of *Kultur*, above all educational, insisting all peoples should be free to develop cultures, for the universal good. Herder's romantic vision had crucial effects on Slavs and Balts, letting them conceive of themselves apart from dynasties and states, indeed in opposition to the state: not "national," but rather as "peoples," communities of language and historical experience.[75] Herder's *Ideas Toward the Philosophy of Human History*, which galvanized eastern intellectuals, condemned the Teutonic Knights' crusades. In Herder's view, culture could not be carried by force, a conviction growing not only from instinctive dislike of militarism, but from the certainty that the truest moral power lay in culture itself, not in the force of arms and the state. Where Ober Ost considered ethnicities as primitive "tribes," Herder's folk song collection *Voices of the Peoples* unhesitatingly accorded them the full dignity of *Völker*. Herder's project of culture represented an alternative approach to the East.

Among a handful of educated officials in Ober Ost, tensions between state power and culture created growing unease. Writer Richard Dehmel encountered a crisis of principle. Assigned to the book-checking office in September 1916, he bore the work for only a month. The uselessness of the administration, that "real time-wasting machine," its brutal motives, and what it was doing in the name of German order, education, and culture were intolerable. His disappointment at this "cultural work" was cruel: "Our entire comprehensive administration! My 'Book Checking Office' – God have mercy – turns out to be a suboffice of the censorship police. I had hoped that one could at least encourage distribution of good books here – but it is only a matter of proscribing bad books, and 'bad' not in any pedagogic sense, but only from the military-bureaucratic perspective." German Work was in fact only a "treadmill work" of cataloging and regimentation, with rule and control as ends in themselves. Dehmel's disgusted amazement grew as he saw that realistic officials lacked all conviction and played a vast game of pretend: "There is no one in the office here who does not consider the whole book-checking process a hair-raising mischief." He was disturbed to see natives yoked to the Prussian system. Just as Herder had, Dehmel admired their folk songs and art, but worried that German custodianship was destroying this authenticity. "Unfortunately, our officials are already beginning to 'organize' the artistic sense of this plain little people," Dehmel observed, "This is even more dangerous to genuine popular education than Russian administration, which provoked silent opposition . . . Naive culture goes to the Devil." Above all, Dehmel was disturbed by the implications of this rule for German culture. His verdict was unequivocal and devastating: "What we are doing here is irresponsible, a shameful sin against the German spirit." By November 1916, Dehmel could endure no more, and "so that I would no longer serve as the underling of such gag orders, I requested my transfer, for the specific reason that my *Kultur*-political views could not be reconciled with the duties I was responsible for." Dehmel was changed by his brief tenure in Ober Ost, robbed of the simple patriotism with which he had gone to war. He was left believing that the answer lay in a reform of education which would foster principles.[76]

German-Jewish writer Arnold Zweig experienced another crisis of German principles and came away from Ober Ost with a changed identity. Like Dehmel, Zweig had been torn along by the "Ideas of 1914," exalted by notions of Germany's cultural mission, though his idealism soon sustained terrible blows from what he saw at Verdun, in Belgium, and Serbia. In June 1917, Zweig was recruited into Ober Ost's cultural administration, working in the press section. What he saw of the regime brought on a crisis of principle and identity, driving him to write on the case of a condemned Russian soldier in autumn of 1917, a theme later reworked into the great novel of the Eastern Front, *The Case of Sergeant Grischa*. As Zweig explained:

Then, after two years' work in a reinforcement battalion, I lost my belief in the righteousness of Germany's cause in the war, especially after getting to know life in the occupied territories. But a conviction had remained, nourished from early youth, that in the German army's judicial workings, concepts of justice and humanity were the main criteria, just as they were (as I believed then) in life beyond the military, in state and society. Many "small" incidents gnawed at this conviction, but without shaking it. This only happened when an officer in our Ober Ost judicial administration told me of the case of an escaped and later recaptured Russian prisoner of war, who was shot, even though the commanding general of an army corps had stepped in to assert that justice and right could not be subordinated to any political considerations in the German army . . . This report opened my eyes.[77]

Seeing naked power exulting in injustice changed Zweig's life. In desperation, he committed himself to a personal socialism and a lifetime project of writing about the Great War in utmost fidelity to details, mounting to an indictment of the systems of rule which ground millions of innocents to pieces. His time in the East worked even more fundamental transformations in Zweig's national identity and understanding of his own Jewishness, as he went native in his sympathies. Zweig met *Ostjuden* and found in them unsuspected authenticity and integrity. His articles in *Korrespondenz B* explored their life, traditions, and legends.[78] In another book, *The Face of the Ostjuden*, Zweig announced with convert fervor: "On the earth this is the last part of the Jewish people that has created and kept alive its own songs and dances, customs and myths, languages and forms of community, and at once preserved the old heritage with a vital validity."

For Zweig, *Ostjuden* had a wholeness lost everywhere else, preserved by their refusal to be assimilated, leaving them blessedly immune to the West's cultural "mishmash." Zweig was most impressed that they did not recognize the state based on power, as true reality lay for them in the divine and in universal justice, not in illusions of temporal authority.[79] In them, he saw a *Volk* complete, Jews as a people and nation. His sympathies also extended to other peoples. When Ober Ost's rule collapsed, he stayed on to appeal for better treatment of natives.[80] Ultimately, he made a commitment to Zionism, to realize his ideals in the vision of Israel, and made himself a spokesman for *Ostjuden* in the West.

A different revelation of identity came for Victor Klemperer, the German Jewish soldier in the censorship office. At first shaken by encountering *Ostjuden*, he declared that his own national identity as a German was not based on race but on culture and most of all on his own spiritual choice. Though able to communicate with local Jews, he declared he simply felt no connection to them. The decisive moment for him was a visit to a Wilna Talmud school in 1918. This sight "repelled me as if with fists," for the "swirl of people" in these rooms at prayer or recitation of holy texts represented for Klemperer "repellent fanaticism." He felt his own identity as a liberal German scholar clarified in that instant: "No, I did not belong to these people, even if one proved my blood relation to them a hundred times over . . . I belonged to Europe, to Germany, and I thanked my creator that I was a German." In all his life, he said, he never felt so much a German as in this moment.[81]

There were other recorded instances of such transformations, especially among the translators. The only German soldier able to write in White Ruthenian, one offical claimed, started turning White Ruthenian himself. This translator, Susemihl, "became so ardent a representative of the White Ruthenians, as only a German idealist could be." His activity "was hard to supervise" and he undertook independent political initiatives. Wilhelm Steputat, a Prussian politician of Lithuanian origins (though von Gayl claimed he had no real ethnic ties), was fired to ever more passionate identification with that ethnic group. Two other Prussian Lithuanians were fingered as traitors with double loyalties.[82] These instances underlined the uncertainties of ethnic identifications, heightened in war.

The most radical recorded example of internal transformation was Victor Jungfer.[83] As an officer and then editor in the administration's public relations branch, Jungfer found himself increasingly drawn into Lithuanian culture. Called up for service on the Eastern Front as a student, in 1916–17, he was stationed in Lithuania, where he befriended local pastors. Conversations with Lithuanian priests created and then deepened a fascination for these lands. Sinking himself into the nature and spirit of this place, Jungfer prepared a volume entitled *Culture-Pictures from Lithuania*, published in 1918. When transferred to Kurland, he stayed in contact with Monsignor Jasėnas. Together they translated into German the foundational romantic text of Lithuanian historical writing, Simonas Daukantas' history. Jungfer delved into local stories, songs, and history, publishing articles in Ober Ost's bulletin.

Jungfer gave an intensely personal testimonial in his detailed autobiographical novel, *The Face of the Occupied Territory*, even depicting himself in the figure of Lieutenant Riemann. Riemann came to know all the different aspects of the occupied territory as he was stationed in towns, the countryside, Lithuania and Latvia, and, at one point, was placed in command of a prison camp. The occupation's human misery, in such surreal contrast to the claims of German administration, wore down the sensitive young officer and finally drove him to self-destruction. Riemann looked on helplessly as *Kultur* was brought to the lands and peoples in ways which destroyed that value. Even "work" was corrupted as a moral concept. Yet the most terrible characteristic of being posted here was the time available to meditate on these moral catastrophes. Riemann felt himself disintegrating:

> He lacked something. A man such as he, used to spiritual work and activity all his life, could not endure the tiring, monotonous life of the occupied territory, without eventually being damaged. He felt clearly that something in him began to crumble away, slowly and relentlessly, like leaves falling from a dying tree . . . "It is the aimlessness of the entire existence here," he said to himself frequently, "What is the nature of war? Destruction. And the occupied territory? Propped up as a self-willed state structure over something with quite different conditions of being and vital questions, it creates a disastrous compromise."

Ober Ost's corrupt claims of *Kultur*, order, and *Bildung* soon embittered Riemann until he could not hide his scorn and shame:

> He could often smile quite sarcastically, when talk turned to the care the German Administration took for the land – "It's all a lie . . . We are here to extract from the land the food and raw materials – whatever is possible – for those at home. That is a naked truth and a sober hard fact. Something which is necessary – perhaps – but which should not be put in a rosy light . . . one should learn to keep quiet about things, which may later become painful."[84]

The treatment of natives made Riemann and his friends ashamed of their German uniforms and what they symbolized.

In the moment of this crisis of German identity, Riemann (and Jungfer) discovered the natives' world. A Lithuanian pastor encouraged Riemann to learn their language: "Every people has its special soul, my dear

Lieutenant . . . Do not believe that you will find only dullness and muddle in the East. Something of a people's nature lies in its language." Following Herder's project, Riemann began studying Lithuanian, "without special intent at first – merely to divert himself. But the more progress he made, the more joy he got from his studies. The beauty of sound . . . delighted him, and through his gift for ready apprehension he attained in a brief time an understanding of practical value to him. The people among whom he lived grew up before his soul and took on spiritual content." As Riemann learned Lithuanian, he found himself going native. Indeed, natives accepted him, sensing that he was "not like the others." Riemann entered into their stories and songs, their animistic sense and worldview, transported with wonder: "That is the people, thought the young officer, which we call dull, for some nothing but a herd of animals, which must be led with blows, and in whose soul nature lives with its thousands of wonders – to whom things speak, which for us are voiceless and dead."[85] Riemann discovered his true love among them, a Lithuanian village girl named Domizella (her very name carried portents of "home"). At the same time, Riemann found himself losing his sense of Germany as his home. He could not imagine returning, when so desperately caught in his love for the East's lands and peoples.

Growing homeless and going native, Riemann slid into depression. When revolution and defeat came in November 1918, he felt shattered inside, all his sustaining German values broken. Yet this final breakdown only culminated a longer internal process. Even when the regime was firmly in place, "He thought only about the control to which everything out here was condemned, about the sterility of personal will, which contended with circumstances which were yet stronger, about his rumination which tortured him with thoughts which were useless, about the dead indifference which had gripped him, because life seemed to him repulsive in the extreme." In the end, he was "taken captive by thoughts of the land which he loved and now would have to leave." Unable to bear the inner torment, Riemann packed his bags and shot himself. A close friend explained Riemann's moral crisis:

He lived in convictions, as we all did until now – but for him they were more deeply rooted and interior than for most. His sense of justice rebelled against things which he saw and had to do. But he was too deeply rooted in what he was taught him from his youth . . . As his nation turned away from what he honored as tradition, he saw it as decline . . . He no longer understood the world or himself.

Ober Ost murdered Riemann's German identity, because he had understood it as a commitment to values which the military utopia's power corrupted and mocked. His ethical patriotism was based on values now gone. A fellow officer saw Riemann's extreme case reflecting what had happened to them all in Ober Ost, though they lacked his anguish or moral courage: "He had loved his fatherland in a way, which all the rest of us in the occupied territory had forgotten."[86] In his novel, Jungfer anticipated his own act of going native, as he later moved to Lithuania and became Viktoras Jungferis.

Whether going native or reappraising German values, some men found their understanding of national identity transformed by the catastrophe of trying to carry *Kultur* by force, yet few articulated this lesson. Most were simply caught dumbly in a sense of unease, which a novelist depicted: "Much began to tremble, that had seemed until then to be solid. The dark wave of dissolution, coming from the East, surged more loudly against the strong bulwark which habit had drawn around things, against the structure of self-confident order, which one stressed and felt here even more strongly than in the *Heimat*."[87] Radicalized, troops became unreliable, receptive toward Bolshevism, and could not be shifted to the Western Front, away from this land of transformations.

Ironically, intersecting crises of the military state, the subject populations, and the German army, came to a head when the chance came for Ober Ost's rule to be made permanent. By the spring of 1917, it was clear to the High Command that there were new requirements in the disposition of the occupied territories and decisive action had to be taken now to secure them for Germany. Two events created the new situation: the Central Powers' declaration of the Polish Kingdom and Russia's February Revolution. The Polish declaration of November 5, 1916, made jointly by the German and Austro-Hungarian emperors, promised a future independent kingdom, but defined no borders or sovereign. Ludendorff urged this step to further his dubious plans to recruit Polish soldiers. The result was poor, as few men enlisted, while the Polish problem was exacerbated, expectations raised. Poles scorned this manipulation, Prussian conservatives were alarmed by the very idea of even limited Polish independence, while most crucially, the door slammed on promising possibilities of separate peace with Russia based on the prewar status quo. This has been called "one of the worst political blunders of the war."[88] Soon the 1917 February Revolution altered the entire political situation even more fundamentally. The Petrograd Soviet, expressing Russians' war-weariness, demanded a peace of reconciliation "without annexations or indemnities," a formula then also adopted by the democratic-style Provisional Government. Concessions made to Russia's nationalities by the Provisional Government's liberals and socialists and the Petrograd Soviet threatened German hegemony in the East, fueling native expectations. Calls went up for the "right to self-determination" of small nations, reinforced by Wilsonian rhetoric from across the Atlantic. In Germany, the desire for peace was likewise clear, accompanied by demands for internal reform, expressed in industrial strikes, enlivened radicalism on the socialist party's left wing (culminating in a factional split), and discontent in the Reichstag. Kaiser Wilhelm's Easter message of 1917 attempted to meet some of these demands with promises of political reform in Prussia after the war. Signs of breakdown in the *Burgfrieden*'s social truce alarmed conservatives and annexationists, whose aim of preventing reform through a "Victory Peace" and territorial gains became more urgent. The government now recognized that the East's new ordering had to be ratified in some form, however perfunctory, by natives. Ober Ost's nationality policies shifted into high gear, Ludendorff insisting it was time for Ober Ost "to be given more political content."[89]

In the spring of 1917, the Supreme Command pressed for eastern annexations, asking for directions from the *Reich* chancellor on "nationality policy" in Ober Ost, since earlier "guidelines for neutral treatment of nationality questions and equalization of all nationalities no longer sufficed." It was now clear that "German rule in the area of Ober Ost had to base itself on the Lithuanians and the White Ruthenians," client nationalities forming counterweights to Poles. An important first meeting took place in Bingen on April 5, 1917, with the chancellor's representatives. Ludendorff explained the Supreme Command's ambitions:

The final goal of the Field Marshal General and myself for the future of the lands under the Supreme Commander in the East was a Duchy of Kurland and Grand Duchy of Lithuania. Both of them, in the mutual interest, would be most closely bound to Germany and in personal union with His Majesty, whether as King of Prussia or as Kaiser of Germany. Germany–Prussia would thus gain military security against new attacks from Russia, and also land for feeding our soldiers after the war.[90]

By the time of the Kreuznach war goals conference, on April 23, 1917, matters became even more urgent.[91] The February Revolution's effects demanded clearer policy. At this meeting, Chancellor Bethmann Hollweg acquiesced to the Supreme Command's demands in drafting a war aims' program, all couched in terms of military necessity: in the East, Kurland and Lithuania were to be won, with the rest of the Baltic provinces as a further aim, while Poland remained subject to Germany. On April 30, 1917, guiding principles were outlined: "The Germans were to be privileged, but every appearance of a forced Germanization of all the nationalities was to be avoided . . . Lithuanians were to be won by all means and White Ruthenians . . . were to be brought closer to the Lithuanians."[92] German management could set these new lands against

Poland, lest that country, which they called into existence for their own ends, grow to threaten Germany's domination of Eastern Europe. In these plans, Poland would not only be truncated by confiscation of a frontier strip along its border with Germany, but future satellite states arising in Ober Ost would encircle this rump Poland north and east as well. Bethmann Hollweg, meanwhile, sought to temper the generals' outright annexationist demands, fearing the impression these would cause among Germany's allies and abroad, with suggestions of an "autonomy policy." Demands for German influence and military dominion in the East could be met without scandal, he hoped, by this "middle way" of "dressing up" these countries as independent, while actually binding them to Germany with economic, military, and political treaties. On May 7, 1917, he issued orders to his officials to present the future of the East in terms of autonomy, masking the reality of domination.[93]

Echoing the Soviet's formula and sharing its longing for peace, Germany's Reichstag made a peace resolution on July 19, 1917, calling for peace "without annexations or reparations." Yet this act of parliamentary self-assertion came in the wake of Chancellor Bethmann Hollweg's eviction from office, partly through machinations of the Supreme Command, which considered him irresolute and dangerous in his proposals for domestic reform, to be replaced by the Supreme Command's candidate, Prussian administrator Michaelis. Michaelis undercut the resolution, insisting that his own interpretation would be definitive, knowing that its formulas could be twisted. In opposition to the resolution, right wing forces supporting the Supreme Command's ambitions formed the Fatherland Party, soon numbering over a million members, clamoring for wide annexations and a "peace of victory" associated with Hindenburg's name. Ludendorff also aimed to resist parliamentary pressure by establishing facts on the ground: "The general situation made it ever more urgent to gain a final clarity about our aims in the occupied territories of the East. Slogans, created by enemy propaganda, of 'peace without annexations' and the right to self-determination of small nations, were suited to produce a solution to the Lithuanian question which contradicted German interests." By July's end, the Supreme Command reached agreement with the government on politics to be pursued in the area, approving Ludendorff's "suggestion, to pursue a nationality policy in Kurland and Lithuania, and in Lithuania an emphatically Lithuanian policy. We strove after final realization of our ideas for Kurland and Lithuania."[94] In each land, Ober Ost would call into being a *Landesrat*, regional council, to provide cover for annexation.

Great, comprehensive visions of a new order in the East motivated Ludendorff's plans: a formidable wall of German client states, new lands split off from the Russian empire. Moreover, this new colonial land offered ground for settlement, an agricultural reserve, and new populations for German armies. Ludendorff explained, "Kurland and Lithuania would make our food supply possibilities better, if we were again thrown back on ourselves in a later war . . . This new ordering of the eastern border achieved what seemed necessary for Germany's military and economic security." His ultimate motives were even more expansive: "My hopes went a step further. The inhabitants of Kurland and Lithuania would give Germany new manpower. Every day of this war, I felt that people were power. The great superiority of the Entente lay in its masses of people. Populations of those territories could retain their nationality under the German Reich's protection."[95] To the south, meanwhile, the Polish border strip would be cleared of a part or all of its Poles and Jews.[96] There, and in Ober Ost's depopulated areas, human walls of German settlers would secure the new marches, and thus "the hoped-for large-scale German settlement activity and the collection of Germans abroad in the wide East territories . . . could bring us a further increase in manpower."[97] The great plan realized the German mindscape of the East.

In the fall of 1917, Ober Ost's administration changed its internal structure to further these aims and consolidate centralized control, in defiance of Reichstag demands for civilian oversight. Ober Ost became ever more independent of army offices as well.[98] Subordination of areas to army rear guard areas was lifted, leaving them independent units directly under the Supreme Commander in the East. The new arrangements were not without their problems, as a new administration general, General Graf von Waldersee, was appointed, along with a high civil official, Undersecretary of State Freiherr von Falkenhausen, who was still responsible to the Supreme Commander in the East. This produced more bureaucratic conflicts, as neither would take orders from the other, and an irritated General Hoffmann had to mediate.[99] On February 1, 1918, Military Administration Bialystok-Grodno was incorporated into Military Administration Lithuania, divided into "Lithuania North" and "Lithuania South." According to the new chief von Heppe, formerly chief of Bialystok-Grodno, who replaced the hated Prince Isenburg, Ludendorff's aim in this reorganization was to ensure that none of this area fell to the future Poland.[100] On August 1, 1918 the whole area because "Military Government Lithuania." At long last, Ober Ost was centralized, leaving two large units, Kurland and Lithuania. As Russia's war effort weakened with internal disintegration, after the heroic but ultimately tragic Kerensky offensive spent its force, German armies pushed forward again, storming Riga on September 3, 1917. By mid October, German army and naval forces took the Baltic islands of Oesel, Dagö, and Moon. The sphere of German rule in the East had expanded further.

Projections for the future culminated in plans for this "*Neuland*," organized by the administration by fall 1917, detailing possibilities for the area's development over coming decades.[101] Each administrative department sent in reports on future prospects in its area of activity. Escherich's forestry administration outlined "The Significance of the Primeval Forest Bialowies for the German National Economy."[102] After solving technical problems of *Verkehr* and finding workers, the forestry department achieved an exploitation of this forest which it would be crucial to continue after the war, when this resource would be even more important to Germany as it recovered economically, yet could still expect to be cut off from resources overseas by the economic wiles of its former opponents. Germany's own forests would not suffice, and thus Bialowies must be kept, for it was "the *only* and *last* opportunity" to gain stockpiles of superior timber in Europe.[103] Further reports examined other forests, comparing present income and achievements with future expectations (in some cases, for the next twenty or fifty years).[104] Agricultural prospects and productivity were weighed, anticipating greater returns with more intensive agriculture, scientific drainage, and increased transportation access.[105] Financial experts projected future tax income. The judicial department's income was "extraordinarily generous" compared to that of Prussia's courts, due in part to high fines imposed on transgressions by natives (a measure which should be retained in peacetime, as it "had vindicated itself and encompassed an abundant source of income"). In future, the report noted, salaries of court officials would need to be higher than those in Prussia, to attract talented people to the "occupied territory with its generally still quite primitive conditions." Yet in general, the happy conclusion was that the future judicial administration's finances would be better than those of "Prussia and most other *Kultur* countries."[106] Other reports testified to natural resources in peat, amber, and chalk for future exploitation.[107] Future rationalization of the railroad system was considered.[108] Finally, the schools section gave estimates of future activity and expenditures. In view of the natives' desire for education, establishment of new schools seemed inevitable, and over the long term, the report noted, while "at first it will perhaps be possible to repel the demands for establishment of universities," it would later be necessary to open an academy in Wilna. In general, the report noted, only the "most primitive cultural scale" of improvements was anticipated over the next decade.[109]

As planning for the future progressed, it was necessary to have natives ratify the annexations. In Kurland, under von Gossler, matters moved smoothly. Ignoring other natives, the administration focused on Baltic Barons, for whom German control was crucial, if they were to preserve their traditional privileges.[110] A ceremonial meeting of the Land Assembly convened in Mitau's old Knights' House on September 18, 1917 and resolved to call an expanded Land Assembly. Three days later, the expanded Land Assembly of eighty representatives met in Mitau's palace throne hall, called on the Kaiser for protection, and approved formation of a *Landesrat*, a land council to speak for the country.[111]

By contrast, attempts at political puppetry and manipulation in Lithuania were troubled from the start. In Lithuania, on June 2, 1917, the Supreme Commander in the East announced formation of a "Confidential Council" (*Vertrauensrat*), intended as a collaborationist organ which would simply approve annexation. As a portent of future difficulties, no Lithuanians agreed to participate, though German authorities approached prominent Lithuanians: Samogitia's Bishop Karevičius, Dr. Jonas Basanavičius, "father of the Lithuanian national movement," and Antanas Smetona, leader of the Refugee Aid Committee. All refused to participate, holding out for a legitimate representative body which they hoped could be turned into a provisional government for an independent state. Finally, the military agreed to a national conference to create a *Landesrat*, land council. They also at last allowed Lithuanians to publish their own independent newspaper, *Lithuania's Echo*, after years of declaring that the administration's own periodical sufficed.[112] Beginning publication in September 1917, it was soon involved in one clash after another with Ober Ost. On August 1–4, 1917, the Wilna organizational committee met, with representatives from all classes and political orientations. At the opening session, Ober Ost's spokesman explained that "without annexation to Germany, further negotiations are impossible." To gain room to maneuver, representatives agreed that this would certainly be kept in mind. Because the army would not allow elections, delegates were picked from lists of nominees (later, the army would smugly point out the proceeding's imperfectly democratic character, which it had caused itself). On September 18–23, 1917, the great Wilna conference convened. Under Basanavičius' chairmanship, 214 delegates met, resolving to seek independence and to create a democratic state, electing a Council, the Taryba, of twenty members, with a presidium of five. To the army's annoyance, Lithuanian activists insisted this represented a provisional government. The Taryba encompassed the larger political orientations in Lithuanian society, while conference decisions were taken with large majorities or unanimously, indicating broad social concensus. Provisions were made to coopt minority representatives, but they did not appear (Belarusians and Jews joined only in late 1918). Lawyer Antanas

Smetona, chairman of the Lithuanian Refugee Aid Committee, was elected president of the Taryba (after the war, he became president of the republic and after the 1926 coup, dictator of the authoritarian state).[113]

The Taryba began a complicated game, twisting between the German government, the Reichstag, the Supreme Command, and Ober Ost.[114] Its most important ally was Matthias Erzberger, leader of the Catholic Zentrum party in the Reichstag. After meeting with Lithuanians at a Zurich Catholic conference in August 1917, he made himself a spokesman of their cause. Ober Ost officials resented this interference. Hoffmann called Erzberger a "public menace." His support for Lithuanian independence was dangerous, for in Hoffmann's view, Lithuanians "are as capable of ruling themselves independently as my daughter Ilse is of educating herself independently."[115] Erzberger, officials charged, allowed the Taryba to understand and exploit divisions and clashes between the Supreme Command, chancellor, Foreign Ministry, and Reichstag.[116] The Taryba established ties abroad, securing a measure of legitimacy through the approval of the Lithuanian diaspora. It managed to send representatives to international Lithuanian conferences in neutral countries, which confirmed the Taryba as the people's highest legitimate representative. Through complaints and lobbying in the Reichstag, the Taryba was able to have Prince Isenburg removed as chief of Lithuania.[117] But ultimately, it was not allowed any real power or competence and was cut off from the countryside and countries abroad by *Verkehrspolitik*, which here demonstrated its full political significance. The Taryba was forced to concentrate on floods of memoranda and complaints, seeking to make the military regime milder.[118] When he arrived to take over in February of 1918, new chief of Military Administration Lithuania von Heppe was convinced that "we would never arrive at a lasting ordering of Lithuanian matters in the German interest" by way of the Taryba, which he considered a collection of dreamers, fanatics, adventurers, and ambitious café politicians, without inclination or ability to cooperate in matters of administration. His political adviser Kügler referred to them as his Lithuanian "circus." According to von Heppe, the Taryba's "entire striving was politically directed only towards keeping the future Lithuania free from every tie to Germany and to gain unconditional German recognition." Thus, it was natural that his relations with the Taryba were "in fact only a running chain of partly open, partly hidden conflicts."[119]

As natives pursued their precarious objectives, Ludendorff pressed his own conception of the new East at the November 4, 1917 Berlin meeting at the Interior Ministry with the new chancellor, Count Hertling, and Ober Ost officials: "The guidelines for our policy in Ober Ost aimed, as before, at a clear annexation [*Anschluss*] of Kurland and Lithuania to

Germany in personal union with the house of Hohenzollern. In the interest of our future, I considered it now necessary that the Land Councils make declarations soon." Then, "in both lands the bases for the inner constitutions and for military, economic, and political ties to Germany would be prepared." Ludendorff had intended the councils as mere fronts, not political actors. Frustrated, he complained darkly about Lithuanian democrats and their pretensions, feeling it intolerable that they refused to see "the military administration as the embodiment of German authority," but instead sought support in the Reichstag. Ludendorff referred to the situation as the "Lithuanian mess."[120] Von Gayl presented a more detailed report of the "border state" idea. Because no one contradicted these presentations (though Foreign Secretary Richard von Kühlmann, who sought less direct forms of political domination in the East, was absent, and the chancellor gave no definitive agreement), Ober Ost officials believed they had laid foundations for the "work of the future."[121]

Indeed, von Gayl and his assistants moved to more detailed planning, seizing the initiative for Ober Ost "as the ruler of, and best expert on, the area." Since von Gayl burned the original plans to present their capture in 1918, when Ober Ost collapsed, his memoirs provide the best glimpse of the intended future (written in Nazi Germany, they perhaps stressed affinities to later Nazi plans). According to the "border states" idea, Lithuania would be defined in its ethnographic borders, with southern areas relegated to the future Poland. In brutally realistic terms, the intention was "to create for the German army, outside of our own Reich territory, an expansive, defensible area for deployment against Russia and Poland, as well as a commanding flanking position against Poland in case of a new East war." Strategically, these border states would be Germany's first line of defense, secured by military treaties for "German garrison rights, securely anchoring quartering, troop training areas, airstrips, etc., as well as . . . fortifications." Treaties giving Germany control over transportation and communication (*Verkehr*) served identical military goals. Economically the areas would be bound to Germany by common currency, standards, and a customs union, while giving up independent foreign policies. Their "recompense" would be the "union to the German cultural and economic sphere," while preserving their own national peculiarities. However, because these territories were "considerably below Germany economically and culturally," they would require "strict and goal-oriented" rule for one lifetime, von Gayl estimated: "they needed firm, authoritarian leadership." This rule would be exercised in the emperor's name by a governor who was also supreme commander of German occupation troops. German officials would live in a model

German settlement in Kowno. This authoritarian rule would secure the area against interference by civil authorities in Germany. Von Gayl's assistant, Marburg university's international law scholar Professor Bredt, began to draw up constitutions embodying these ideas, while von Gayl planned organizational structures growing "out of the military administration of Ober Ost." Education was important to these plans, to discipline natives (and perhaps eventually cultivate native officials). Without forcible germanization, learning German language and culture would inevitably draw natives into the German "circle of life." At the same time, it was necessary to avoid creating an "intellectual proletariat" among natives, which would lead to trouble. Young native men could be drafted for two years into a labor force, the *Ordnungsdienst* (order service), to build local infrastructure. Though not yet to be trusted with weapons, they might eventually provide reserves for German forces. For German officials, planners foresaw "small German model settlements everywhere, adapted to the style of the landscape, as examples of domestic culture." Von Gayl ordered an architect on his staff to begin blueprints for Kowno's model settlement – he wistfully planned to use the blueprints to decorate his new home, when his family joined him in the future state. Von Gayl claimed he had been "officially notified that one counted on me for this task in the future," to lead and develop this territory: "only the sad ending of the war choked" this prospective career. Von Gayl regretted that these plans, "not suited for the broad public," leaked out. He was also disappointed that in Germany itself, government agencies did not act with sufficient vigor to realize his plans, but he continued to dream.[122]

But events again turned dramatically, when the Bolshevik October Revolution in Petrograd promised to finally remove Russia from the war. This was the ultimate prize of Germany's long-standing policy of "revolutionizing" the East. Led by Lenin, who in April 1917 was transported to Russia by Germany's Supreme Command, Bolsheviks seized power on November 7, 1917. On November 8, they proclaimed the "Decree of the Termination of the War," and asked for peace negotiations on November 26, 1917. Before negotiations began, the Supreme Command pressed to secure legitimation for territorial demands they would make at the bargaining table, hoping to have declarations from the land councils in their pockets when talks began. Matters went smoothly in Kurland. In Lithuania, military authorities put pressure on the Taryba for a declaration of "permanent union" with Germany, in the form of military and *Verkehrspolitik* conventions, currency and customs union. If the declaration was not made, the army thundered, Lithuania would be regarded purely as a question of military geography, turned into a border zone.[123] Unnerved by this threat, the Taryba made the required declaration on

December 11, 1917, proclaiming independence with "a firm and permanent alliance with Germany." The Taryba was anguished, for it seemed essential to gain recognition for the country before negotiations on the great reordering of the East. Though resisting demands for conventions limiting independence, the Taryba was isolated. Even German parties otherwise supporting Lithuanian demands in the Reichstag viewed "securing of German interests" in the new states as indispensable. Without them, the Taryba would lose all of its support. When a Lithuanian socialist had appealed to SPD leaders to speak out against the army's abuses, for love of shared socialist ideals, Noske reportedly answered: "We are socialists only up to Eydtkuhnen" on the East Prussian border.[124] Clearly, there were limits to the internationalism of German Social Democrats. Moreover, the Entente powers gave no encouragement to natives, instead supporting Russian statehood. The December decision, however, split the Taryba, as four leftist members withdrew in protest.

Negotiations between Germans and Bolsheviks began at German headquarters in the fortress city of Brest-Litovsk on December 22, 1917. After Foreign Secretary Richard von Kühlmann first "agreed in principle" to Bolshevik demands for peace without annexations or indemnities, General Hoffman delivered a smashing blow, cooly informing the Russian delegation that of course Poland, Lithuania, and Kurland had already exercised their right to self-determination, splitting from Russia, and would arrange their futures with German cooperation. As Bolshevik negotiators reeled at that statement, the conference recessed. Signaling the Supreme Command's uncompromising and unsubtle ambitions, the military dictators berated Kühlmann and Hoffmann on their return to Berlin for even the rhetorical concessions they had made, meant to mask domination in the East and still hold open the door for compromise in a general peace settlement. After a furious showdown and direct challenge to the Kaiser's powers of decision, the Supreme Command forced through its uncompromising terms. On January 9, 1918, the Brest conference reopened, Trotsky heading Russia's delegation. Long philosophical arguments ensued over the definition of self-determination. In an amazing spectacle, both sides debated an abstract principle to which neither the German *Reich* nor the Bolsheviks were committed. Trotsky brilliantly stalled for time, desperately hanging on for an expected outbreak of mass strikes and revolution in Germany. Losing patience, and urged on by Austria's desperate need for food supplies from the occupied area, the Germans signed a separate treaty on February 9, 1918 with the Ukrainian delegation, representing a republic. Under this "Bread Peace," the Ukrainian republic undertook to supply Germany with a million tons of bread annually. Yet this settlement immediately produced its own harvest of problems, for Russia's negotiators objected, while the apportionment of Chelm province to Ukraine infuriated Poles, who claimed this area for a larger future Poland, resulting in riots and demonstrations in Lublin, where the Kaiser's portrait was burnt, and even the more cooperative Regency Council installed by the Central Powers in 1917 protested against a "new partition" of Poland. Russian reaction was even more dramatic on February 10, 1918, when Trotsky stormed out after announcing his revolutionary formula of "No peace, no war." Lenin's misgivings concerning this tactic were confirmed, as the Germans simply responded by attacking. On February 16, 1918, Hoffman broke the armistice, and German troops were ordered to push ahead on February 18, 1918. A million troops moved East, as Hoffmann looked on with pleasure, professing to believe that if the Bolsheviks were allowed to have their way, they would wipe out the peoples of Eastern Europe and threaten the continent. Now was the right time to strike, for in his view, "All of Russia is nothing but a great pile of maggots: all rotten, all swarming together without order."[125] Speeding onward by rail, German armies made huge conquests, meeting almost no resistance. Hoffmann laughed at the "most comical war I have ever seen," conducted by rail and automobile, racing from one train station to the next. It had, he said, "at least the thrill of novelty."[126] The rest of Latvia, Livonia, Estonia, Belarus, and Ukraine were conquered. Units moved northwards from Riga to Dorpat and Reval in February. The armies moved relentlessly eastwards, taking Narwa in early March. During the Russian evacuation of Reval, as Estonian army units fought retreating Bolsheviks in the streets before the German arrival, the Committee of Elders of the Estonian *Maapäev* (provincial assembly) emerged to declare independence. The German army refused to acknowledge them and set about establishing its own regime.

Amid these dramatic events, Lithuania's Taryba saw its position worsening and a moment of decision approaching, as Germany refused to allow Lithuanian delegates to Brest-Litovsk, and they were even forbidden to publicize the December declaration. The Taryba now decided on a desperate move. Members who had withdrawn in protest returned, and by unanimous vote, on February 16, 1918, the Taryba declared Lithuania's complete independence, without ties to any foreign powers. A democratic, independent Lithuanian state was to be established within ethnographic boundaries, with Vilnius (Wilna) as its capital. A constituent assembly was to be elected to determine the state's constitution and future ties with foreign countries. German reaction to this step was swift. Issues of *Lithuania's Echo* with the declaration were confiscated by military police, the paper shut down, and censors rushed to stop the news from circulating. However, the announcement reached newspapers in Germany, carried (it was later claimed) by German soldiers sympathetic to Lithuanians.[127] Because of this embarrassment, Germany's chancellor communicated that now recognition was impossible. As the Taryba refused to withdraw the declaration, nervous stalemate settled in. Hoffmann blamed the Reichstag and especially Erzberger for making a mess in Lithuania, encouraging the Taryba to the point where German civilians had made them "go crazy on us."[128]

At the end of February 1918, the Bolsheviks were forced to return to the table at Brest-Litovsk, choosing to lose much, rather than everything, to save the revolution. The final sessions produced the notorious dictated settlement, the Treaty of Brest-Litovsk, signed on March 3, 1918.[129] Its terms established a new political structure for Eastern Europe, carving off huge sections of the Tsar's empire to create German client states. Russia gave up control of Estonia, Latvia, Lithuania, Russian Poland, and most of Belarus, also ceding districts in the south to Turkey, and recognized independent Finland and Ukraine. The Russian empire lost a million square miles and 50 million inhabitants. With these, it lost 90% of its coal mines, 54% of its industry, 33% of its rail system, 32% of its agricultural land, 34% of its population, and almost all of its oil and cotton production.[130] Russia shrank down to its borders of the days before Peter the Great. To many in Germany it seemed that the war in the East had been won. In spite of some anxieties and strike unrest, the Reichstag supported the treaty, with only Independent Socialists opposing. The Treaty of Bucharest signed with defeated Romania on May 7, 1918, ensured German economic domination, and deliveries of much needed oil and food. It seemed that hopes of a *Mitteleuropa* of economic satellites ranged around a powerful Germany were realized, while a nearly exhausted Germany could now turn to the West, hoping for decision there as well.

After Brest-Litovsk, Ober Ost's military command could settle in to its occupation. Russia further renounced sovereignty over Livland and Estonia in supplementary treaties on August 24, 1918. German "police action" in newly occupied territories was severe. Ober Ost's model of rule was extended to Latvia and Estonia, where the army suppressed all political activity, almost all newspapers, and introduced comprehensive censorship. Schools geared toward rapid germanization of natives were established (though some officials worried about the ethnic friction this would cause), and Ober Ost's cultural policies extended, with the founding of "work rooms" in Riga.[131] The army placed Baltic Germans at the head of local administrations, returning to conditions of the Old Regime, while native political figures were arrested and sent to concentration camps. Jüri Vilms, member of the Estonian Maapäev's Rescue Commit-

Map 4 The fullest extent of the German advance on the Eastern Front
by 1918

tee, was caught by German troops while crossing to Finland to join
Estonian delegations looking for diplomatic recognition abroad, and
summarily executed. Under the occupation regime, workers and peasants
were hardest hit, with a drastic deterioration in their economic situation,
already difficult before. Official reports noted that under the pressure of

requisitions, the economy worsened from month to month, and were amazed that massive hunger deaths were somehow avoided.[132] As earlier in Lithuania and Kurland, this was a decisive development. When German occupation was seen as even worse than Russian rule, natives had no choice but to think in terms of independence. Military policies intended to pave the way for incorporation of these lands instead provided a decisive impetus and direction for native desperation and mobilization.[133] Reports recognized, for the first time, an increasing attention to politics on the part of the masses in Lithuania.[134] Elsewhere, they noted "ill will and passive resistance of a larger part of the population."[135] In May 1918, officials in Dünaburg arrested sixty people for planning a conspiracy against German rule, encouraging assassination of officers, and urging peasants to revolt.[136]

After the triumph of Brest-Litvosk, authorities moved to give permanent form to rule in the East. Repressing or ignoring Latvian and Estonian demands, they established governments based on the traditional authority of *Balten* knights and barons. On March 8, 1918, Kurland's land council invited the Kaiser to take the grand ducal crown, which he graciously accepted. The land council also requested that all Baltic provinces be united into one administration. Meanwhile, preparations for German settlement in Kurland proceeded, establishing a colonization union. To strengthen their ethnic base, Baltic Barons agreed to cede a third of their land for German settlement.[137] While requests from Germany for settlement had to be deferred by authorities, by the summer of 1918 waiting lists were begun in Ober Ost's offices.[138]

In the northern Baltic provinces, land assemblies convened in April 1918, again dominated by *Balten*. The land assemblies of Livonia, Estonia, Riga, and Oesel then met together in Riga as the United Land Council of Baltic Lands. Sensing that native voices had to be added to the German initiatives to lend them international credibility, the Barons and army made unsuccessful attempts to bully Estonian and Latvian elders into participating in the request. The natives resisted stubbornly. Konstantin Päts, as "ringleader" of Estonian resistance, was sent to a camp. Finally, seeing that it would have to do without native approval, on April 12, 1918, the United Land Council asked for personal union with Kaiser Wilhelm, who accepted on April 21, 1918. Even after this declaration, authorities sensed that it lacked legitimacy. Native "support" had to be documented, in the form of coerced native petitions. Using "economic, military, and psychological pressure," German authorities and native collaborators collected signatures. Armed officials "canvassed" populations. Some peasants could not get their grain milled without signing petitions.[139] The military government vigorously suppressed native political activity. Estonian council members were sentenced to fifteen years in prison for unauthorized meetings. Latvia's Democratic Bloc met in secret in Riga, dodging vigilant authorities.[140] Ignoring natives, the army pressed forward to consolidate German gains. On May 14, 1918, a commissar meeting already considered constitutional projects for annexation of these territories.[141] In the summer of 1918, Estonia and Livonia were united with Kurland into a common Baltic military administrative unit, the "Baltikum."[142]

In Lithuania, German plans were checkmated by an obstinate Taryba, which refused to withdraw or annul the February independence declaration, while insisting (in a victory over logic) that it did not injure the earlier December declaration. Finally, on March 23, 1918, Kaiser Wilhelm officially recognized Lithuanian independence on the basis of the December declaration. Even this could not resolve problems, for the administration did not change, and Lithuania was burdened with the obligation to sign conventions on economics and *Verkehr* to guard Germany's interests in the country, and to help pay Germany's war expenses once peace arrived. Hoffmann mistrusted even this incomplete sovereignty, insisting again that "Lithuania can only become something if it is tightly joined to Prussia, not through independence." Speculation continued concerning Lithuania's future and Hoffmann complained in his diary that "so many authorized and unauthorized people are mucking about in this Lithuanian mess that no one knows what will actually come of it."[143] Once again, the Taryba was driven to desperation and independent action, since military administration in Lithuania was not removed, but became stricter. The council saw that it was in danger of being compromised in the eyes of the people it had undertaken to represent, since its cooperation yielded no real German concessions. Requisitions reached a new pitch of harshness and Wilna schools were shut down in June for not teaching German from the first grade.[144] Even after the Kaiser's formal recognition of independence, authorities continued to make plans without regard for promised Lithuanian statehood. Germany's press discussed possibilities for union with Prussia, Saxony, or another German state. As in Estonia and Livland, officers in northern Lithuania tried to coerce peasants into signing petitions for German plans, but with little success.[145] Independent action by the Taryba was again called for. Since April 1918, Erzberger had been looking for solutions to the Lithuanian problem. To head off plans for dynastic union with Saxony or Prussia, the Taryba, at his urging, precipitated a second crisis. In a stormy all-night session on July 13, 1918, over objections by socialists and republicans, the Taryba elected Duke Wilhelm von Urach, of the Catholic line of the house of Württemberg, as king of Lithuania, with the title of Mindaugas II.[146] Urach was selected on Erzberger's advice; because the duke was not in Württemberg's line of succession, he was more likely to devote himself to Lithuania's interests alone. Conditions were outlined for the intended monarch: the state was to be a democratic constitutional monarchy, with a Lithuanian government, and the king and his family had to become Lithuanians, speaking the language at court.[147] In essence, Lithuanians demanded a feat of "elective ethnicity" from the future ruling house, as the children were to be educated in Lithuania, becoming Lithuanian. Gentle, democratically minded Urach accepted, and spent the summer learning Lithuanian. At the same time, the Taryba declared itself the State Council of Lithuania. These insubordinate moves raised an uproar in Germany's press, though von Gayl tried to suppress the news (he blamed Erzberger for its dissemination).[148] Months of tense struggle followed, as officials refused to deal with the Taryba and ignored the Kaiser's recognition of Lithuanian independence. When *Lithuania's Echo* refused Ober Ost's order to publish an article denouncing the Taryba's move, the intractable newspaper was shut down for a month.[149] Politically, the game ground to a halt. The chief of Military Administration Lithuania noted that the mood of Lithuanians did not improve, while "Bolshevik elements streaming in from the East, in intimate union with Poles and Jews, increased anti-German sentiment."[150] In spring and summer 1918, returning refugees from Russia added to the administration's woes, even as food riots erupted in Wilna. Three to four million civilians streamed back across the border into Poland and Ober Ost.[151] According to officials, they brought with them "disorder of every kind," as well as diseases, including spotted fever. Reports blamed this onslaught for increases in banditry, "Bolshevik influences," "social revolutionary ideas," and the population's radicalization, visible in increased resistance to orders. Officials also claimed that noticeably greater political involvement and self-assertion of the Jewish population was in part caused by the impact of Bolshevik ideas on young Jews.[152]

Yet failed attempts to manipulate natives seemed entirely insignificant compared to the look of the new map of the East, which showed tremendous gains. Finland was secured by German troops, and Ludendorff could even weigh in his mind a possible "Operation Cap-Stone," an attack against Petrograd to crush the weak Bolshevik regime. Ukraine was occupied by German armies, the Crimea was in German hands, and the Caucasus lay open. It seemed that Ludendorff and Hindenburg's vision of a great wall in the East was realized. Yet at this peak of success, the same process was taking place which marked Ober Ost's military utopia: the abstraction of the map obscured reality on the

ground. New conquests turned into dangerous disappointments, particularly in Ukraine.[153] The republican *Rada* council was overthrown in
a coup engineered by the leader of the conservative League of Land-
owners, General Skoropadsky, in cooperation with German officers.
Skoropadsky took over as *Hetman* of Ukraine in late April 1918, promising to continue sending food and agreeing to complete German military
control. As Germans introduced their regimes of requisition, peasants
resisted violently, culminating in the assassination of General Eichhorn
in Kiev on July 30, 1918. Ober Ost officials reacted by tightening control of movement in town streets, where they felt German troops and
officers to be in most danger.[154] Moreover, occupation did not secure
the promised foodstuffs, while the masses of troops needed to hold
down the vast territories were increasingly revolutionized. Soon, the
army was afraid to move these troops back to the West and kept them
out in the East, since they were infected with revolution.[155]

But these developments did not intrude on the supreme command's
mental pictures of a great new order in the East, a chain of German
protectorates, land for settlement, agriculture, and a vast parade ground
which Hindenburg blithely indicated he needed to maneuver his left
wing when the next war against the East began.[156] On August 1, 1918,
by order of the Supreme Command, Ober Ost's rule was fundamentally
reorganized. As its policies increasingly came under fire in Reichstag
debates, the central administration was shut down, its powers divided
into two units, Military Administration Lithuania, to be headed by General Harbou, and Military Administration of the Baltic Lands, headed by
Major von Gossler, former head of Kurland. General Hoffmann was
pleased with the simplified reorganization, but troubled by the personalities in charge, sighing that "we seem to have an unlucky hand in personnel matters."[157] He feared the new administrators would soon be committing "idiocies." Yet the move still seemed to represent progress,
giving clearer definition to the East's emerging order. The culminating,
symbolic act of eastern policy was a "deed of culture," the September
1918 reopening of the University of Dorpat headed by Baltic German
professor Theodor Schiemann. Blithely ignoring the fierce aspirations of
native peoples all around, instruction there would only take place in
German, at the furthest outpost of German *Kultur* in its mission in the
East.[158]

Despite the apparent success and triumph of Brest-Litovsk, decision in
this war would still have to come on the Western Front, as Hindenburg
and Ludendorff understood. At the start of 1917, they gambled that
unrestricted submarine warfare would bring England to the breaking
point before America entered the war, an inevitable side effect of such a

policy, and tipping the balance of forces in the West. While the United States indeed declared war on Germany on April 6, 1917, the U-boat campaign failed to choke off "perfidious Albion." Before American troops arrived *en masse* as fresh reserves of manpower in France, Ludendorff gambled again, staking everything on one last throw he had decided upon in November 1917: the spring and summer offensives of 1918. Code-named Operation Michael, his plan foresaw concentrating all available troops for a breakthrough in the West, now that the eastern war had been won. Launched on March 21, 1918, Operation Michael gained considerable ground, again threatening Paris, before grinding to a halt, a reverse marking German defeat in the "Second Battle of the Marne." Reserves were lacking to exploit gains in the West, and Ludendorff was criticized for having left masses of troops and three cavalry divisions in the East and Ukraine. Even less able troops transferred from the East could have freed up other units to throw into battle and perhaps tip the precarious balance.

Yet this in turn pointed to the unhappy state of troops left in the East. Since the armistice there, Ludendorff withdrew troops from other fronts to strengthen his gamble in the West, but the quality of these troops was doubtful, for some were already influenced by revolutionary events in Russia. After the February Revolution, Russian and German soldiers fraternized along quieter stretches of the Eastern Front.[159] A gunner's letter of September 5, 1917 reported disapprovingly that his unit imitated Russian revolutionaries in organizing a soviet: "That socialism has already gained the upper hand in everything is characterized in our battery by the fact that a so-called soldiers' council has its hand in everything. All the doings of an officer which are not free from objection are most sharply criticized by the noncommissioned officers and men. But in doing this everyone is most cunningly serving his own interest."[160] Nonetheless, since December 1917, thirty-three divisions from other fronts were moved west, while many units received special instruction in storm-troop tactics (which had proven themselves in the attack on Riga) to break the trench stalemate. When Operation Michael began, soldiers left behind in the East numbered over a million men. Yet as divisions were transferred west, they exchanged older men for younger ones, and the divisions remaining sent men under thirty-five to the West to replace the wounded and killed. As a result, batallions in the East were far below strength, staffed by older men. In the months that followed, as Ludendorff's last offensive surged and then ebbed in the West, divisions continued to be pulled from the eastern territories, until by October 1918, twenty-six divisions remained on the Eastern Front, totaling just over half a million men.[161]

The mood among the soldiers of the East certainly was flagging. The 1918 Tenth Army song book contained a multitude of ballads written by troops in the East on the theme of soldiers' graves in Russia and the omnipresent possibility of meeting one's end in these foreign lands, carrying titles like "The Soldier's Death," "Today Or Tomorrow We Die," and "Farewell."[162] Marked tones of despair and exhaustion could be heard. When these soldiers were collected for the transports to the Western Front, mutinous incidents began. Many understood orders for transfer as punishment of their units. As their trains moved off west, troops chalked bitter messages on the wagons: "Cattle for slaughter in Flanders" or "Criminals from the East."[163] Cannier soldiers used the train ride through Germany as an opportunity to desert, escaping home. As early as mid 1917, authorities noted that transports lost ten percent of their men *en route*. Various expedients were ordered: closer supervision of smaller transport units, arrest of suspected ringleaders, disarming soldiers so they would not fire from the windows while moving, and intensive guarding of more restive trains.[164] These measures of compulsion further worsened morale. By 1918, 5,000 soldiers in Dwinsk refused to obey transport orders and had to be disciplined, while in October, 2,000 men due for transport mutinied in Charkow.[165] Searching for reserves, the Supreme Command also moved to the West former German prisoners of war released from Russian captivity, until they were often discovered to be unreliable and sympathetic to Bolshevik ideas they had encountered in Russia.[166] Troops now left behind in the East were older reservists and Home Guardsmen, along with Alsatians and Prussian Poles.[167] The contact these men had with natives was damaging, it seemed to officials, who claimed to see its consequences in increased taking of bribes and receptivity to Bolshevik ideas, blamed later on local Jews who supposedly had "great opportunities to influence soldiers" while engaging in trade.[168] Army officials tried to direct their own propaganda toward troops, opposing Bolshevism from Russia and socialist and democratic influences from the home front. In the spirit of "Patriotic Instruction," the Tenth Army's press published pamphlets denouncing democratic trends in Germany. In spite of this, close police surveillance of suspicious political activity among troops in the East apparently revealed in August 1918 the existence of secret associations in Kowno "whose task it was to canvass for German soldiers who were to distribute several thousand leaflets among the troops as quickly as possible." There were even disturbing incidents of violent altercations between enlisted men and officers.[169]

While utopian visions unfolded in the East, masking a precarious state of affairs, in the West came unmistakable portents of German collapse.

The futility of continued struggle was revealed on August 8, 1918, the "Black Day of the German Army," when lines by Amiens were overrun by British forces with hundreds of tanks. German resolve broke and 16,000 surrendered. Amiens was not immediately strategically decisive, yet nonetheless shattering because it revealed the exhaustion and declining morale of German soldiers. Retreating troops shouted abuse at reserves moving up to hold the line, labeling them "strike-breakers" intent on prolonging war. Ludendorff blamed the crisis on soldiers from the Eastern Front, infected with revolutionary ideas. It now seemed clear that the war could no longer be won. The Supreme Command pressed for an armistice, accompanied by a "revolution from above," introducing parliamentary government in Germany the better to negotiate with President Wilson. Civilian authorities would also provide the Supreme Command with a scapegoat for their failures in politics, for the new government would preside over this desperate time. New Chancellor Prince Max von Baden at first resisted Ludendorff's insistence on suing for peace immediately, but at last, on October 4, 1918, Germany asked for an armistice. Under Baden's new government, with supporters of Lithuania in the cabinet (Erzberger and Scheidemann as secretaries of state), the situation changed for the East. As impending collapse became ever more evident, officials made moves to allow local governments. On October 20, 1918, the chancellor tersely informed Lithuanians that state power was being handed over to them and they would be left to their own affairs. He explained that Germany would not intervene in questions of borders, an implicit threat that Wilna would be left to the Poles. Ludendorff recovered sufficiently from his earlier mental prostration to begin intriguing against the new chancellor. He denounced Wilson's answer and without authorization sent out orders to the army to fight to the end. Coming at a time when it was imperative for German leaders to demonstrate civilian control over the army, this was at last too much. The order, though recalled, was secretly forwarded to the Berlin leaders of the Independent Socialist party by a wireless operator in Kowno.[170] In the last showdown with the Kaiser, Ludendorff, who so often had used the threat of his own resignation and that of Hindenburg as the greatest weapon of their silent military dictatorship, now found himself dismissed on October 26, 1918. The architect of Ober Ost was overthrown. Finally, a cabinet order signed by the Kaiser officially ended military administration of the occupied territories on November 3, 1918, replaced by a civil government responsible to civilian authorities.[171] The occupation's "unique character," its military monopoly, was officially ended. Ober Ost's military utopia lasted four years, before collapsing in what had seemed to be its moment of triumph.

Released from Ober Ost's control, native peoples now took action. On November 2, 1918, the Lithuanian Taryba withdrew its invitation to Urach, the future Mindaugas II. It drafted a democratic provisional constitution and began forming a government. On November 5, 1918, Dr. Zimmerle of the German Ministry of Justice was named "Plenipotentiary of the German Reich for Lithuania," to manage affairs until the evacuation. Still not understanding events, the Baltikum's baronial United Land Assembly elected a Regency Council on November 7, 1918, as a provisional government. It held its constituent sitting on November 9. But events quickly voided the resolutions of Baltic Barons. That same day, revolution broke out in Germany.

The turmoil of the German revolution of November 9, 1918 finally snapped the order of the occupied territories. News traveled quickly of unrest in Germany, with revolt in garrison towns, navy ports, insurrection in Munich, and the declaration of both a radical socialist republic and a majority socialist republic in Berlin. In the East, Reval was first to be seized by disturbances, as mobs of striking factory workers crowded around city hall square and German forces began to lose their discipline. On the evening of November 9, restive troops elected a sailors' and soldiers' council on the Russian model and the next day declared they would not shoot at the local population. Over the days that followed, the council began negotiations with Estonian leaders. The frightened German commander allowed the Estonian provisional government to meet on November 11, 1918. Next evening, in a stormy meeting, the soldiers' council demanded that the government immediately be handed to Estonians. Two officers sent to observe the meeting returned grim and shaken, feeling that officers and officials were now in personal danger.[172] In the confused circumstances, power changed hands quickly, handed over by the land captain, though his distant chief in Riga tried to prevent it. The Estonian provisional government assumed control and began forming a national army to hold off the Bolsheviks again pressing in from the East. With the administration chief at hand in Riga, events in Latvia moved more slowly, though here too soldiers' councils demanded that the govermenment be handed to the natives. On November 28, 1918, the Latvian Republic was declared, and negotiations followed for orderly transfer of authority. When General Commissar for Lithuania Zimmerle arrived on the day of the revolution to oversee the change in government, he found that the Lithuanians had not waited for him. Yet native proclamations were acts of desperate hope, rather than expressions of confidence. On November 11, 1918, with the signing of the Armistice at Compiègne, the war was formally ended, but fitful aftershocks of conflict continued in the East. The lands were aswarm with confused, terrified, and mutinous German troops.

Native governments had no armies or resources beyond an unreasonable inner determination. And now there loomed another great threat from the East, for on November 13, 1918, the Soviets annulled the Treaty of Brest-Litovsk and set their armies in motion. By geographical fate, Ober Ost was the bridge for the revolution, as Bolsheviks moved to link up with uprisings in Germany. If radical socialist upheavals of Russia and Germany could be joined, they might ignite world revolution. German industry and discipline, fused with popular forces unleashed in Russia, promised the dawn of a new age of triumphant socialism. Looking to Ludendorff's "war socialism" in Germany, Lenin urged, "Yes: learn from the Germans!," observing that by a historical anomaly, German imperialists had come to "embody the principle of discipline, of organization, of solid working together, on the basis of the most modern machinery, of strict accounting and control," the very things Bolsheviks lacked. Their political socialist achievement would only be fully realized when joined to Germany's inadvertent economic socialism.[173] The Red Army began to advance, attacking German positions at Narwa in the northeast.

Ober Ost's structures of rule, which only yesterday seemed such permanent and powerful embodiments of self-confident authority, came crashing down. According to his memoirs, von Gayl burned all his papers, including secret plans for the future of Ober Ost.[174] Thrown into confusion, German troops milled about, deeply disturbed and agitated by news and rumors. A novelist recalled: "A great inner insecurity oppressed the troops, like the effect of a mass-suggestion. Everyone felt only the collapse which now came from the homeland, hardly anyone understood the power at work here, and only a few thought of building something up out of the existing chaos." The discipline which had kept the great engine of the war state working disappeared, exposing conflict between ranks:

The officers had lost their authority. In this instant one saw clearly that their influence in the occupied territory had long since vanished, that no living force bound them to the soldiers anymore, that they had long since become nothing more than pistons in a machine, which had until then worked mechanically and suddenly seized up, now that an overwhelming power pushed itself into the gears. No one trusted them anymore.

Some officers fled to Germany, leaving their troops behind in a state of mutiny. After military defeat, the threatening East all around them, the foreignness which Ober Ost had sought to contain pressed in on soldiers:

One was in hostile land. Suddenly, this thought came to the troops. Until then, one had felt self-confident and hadn't given it a thought. Suddenly, everyone felt the idea as something terrible. Men leaned over their maps and calculated the distance which separated them from Germany. The hundreds of kilometers which they measured out seemed to them all at once as a terribly real specter which lurked for them and threatened to hold them up here in wide Russia – one had to escape, if one did not want to go down. The feeling of being soldiers here, tens of thousands strong, with weapons in hand, disappeared. Perhaps they had never had it. And the thought which now animated them was only this: they were out here, exposed, a mass of men, rear guard troops, who had never fought, who were too old to offer resistance, who because of illness or infirmity could only be used for office work or, at most, watch duty, who were lost, if they were attacked by an energetic will.[175]

Seized by terrifying thoughts, this account recalled, troops suffered a "complete nervous breakdown."[176] One official recorded that every night, sentries fired volleys over the rooftops in fear.[177] Wild rumors circulated of chaos back home in Germany and the advancing Red Army. Others feared a Polish attack or a right-wing coup by officers. Discipline eroding, soldiers sold everything they could lay hands on. In the streets, weapons, uniforms, military horses, and army stores were openly sold to natives. In Reval, soldiers of the sea-plane base sold or destroyed almost all the planes, equipment, and gasoline they were supposed to be guarding.[178] The military storehouses of Ober Ost's spoils were emptied. For former servants of the war state, "the concept of state property had disappeared," while some officials blamed local Jews for bribing and corrupting Germans over the past years. Von Gayl deplored soldiers' public drunkenness, robberies, and the sexual looseness of Ober Ost's German secretaries.[179] As cohesion fell apart, units melted away. Individual soldiers did not wait for demobilization and slipped off discretely, bound for home.

In the German Republic's chaotic first days, revolutionary soldiers' councils formed on the model of Russian soviets. In Kowno, Ober Ost's headquarters, communications troops were the avant-garde, as they had been constantly following events back in Germany. Yet as Grodno, Minsk, Riga, Kowno, and Kiev also elected councils, they increasingly came into conflict with one another over questions of preeminence, until a Central Council for the Eastern Front was established on November 30, 1918 in Kowno, holding stormy meetings where anyone and everyone could speak up from the various councils, though Kiev's council jealously guarded its independence.[180] While outwardly resembling soviets, and announcing Marx as the war's true victor, these councils (seemingly permanently in session) represented a curious, desperate compromise between order and revolution, declaring themselves anti-Bolshevik. They banned compulsory salutes to officers, but insisted all decent soldiers would still salute out of politeness.[181] At the same time, the council tried to keep order in the ranks and cooperated with the command to ensure organized evacuation. On November 10, 1918 General Hoffmann had a long conversation with the council's president, finding him to be "honestly striving for quiet and order."[182] Hoffmann noted that, oddly enough, one of the greatest fears of ordinary soldiers was that their officers would leave without them, while rumors circulated that on the day of the revolution officers began leaving in rail cars, but were stopped by the troops.[183] Some officers, hated by the troops, were reportedly sent home by their superiors. One high police official, fearing that troops would murder their officers, reportedly walked about armed to the teeth.[184] In this environment, certain soldiers tried to repair relations with the native populations around them.[185] Arnold Zweig was elected to the soldiers' council in Wilna, where hundreds of soldiers met in the former "work rooms." Zweig pleaded that judicial abuses against natives by military courts be examined and redressed, but found little sympathy.[186]

The strange tension between chaos and order, built into the Ober Ost state, also marked its end. By mid November 1918, a German army in the process of disintegration, carrying red flags back home, began to pull out of the territories that had been Ober Ost. Even though the Allies insisted at the armistice that German troops remain in the East to hold off the Bolshevik advance, the feelings of German soldiers were too strong, for they had, as a realistic novel reported, "one single thought: the Bolsheviks are coming – we want to go home – Home!"[187]

Hoffmann faced the difficult task of arranging an ordered withdrawal, complaining in his diary, "I cannot hold our people – they want to go home." The transformation of authority, he explained, confused many soldiers, shaking their earlier reliable bearing, since many assumed their military oath was now canceled and they could head home on their own. The soldiers' council did all it could to preserve order, yet remaining troops had been winnowed of the best forces. The majority were older men straining to leave and that leftover mass of disgruntled Alsatians. In Hoffmann's judgment, "in general, discipline and order have gone to the devil." The Supreme Command issued confusing orders, urging evacuation to proceed as slowly as possible, while matters were scarcely under control. Soon, Hoffmann had added worries: "Our situation with the troops grows somewhat more difficult. Everyone strains towards home and in spite of the most sensible address of completely calm and reasonable Soldiers' Councils, people cannot be held any longer. The worst is, that if people here in the rear go away, our troops up front, especially in Ukraine, will be left hanging." Everyone was possessed, he reported, by one thought to the exclusion of all else: "to go home." The result was that the men "were stupid and incapable being taught anything." In Hoffmann's view, his East army had degenerated into an "East mob."[188] As order disintegrated among regular troops, Germany's War Ministry and Supreme Command called for volunteers, both from armies in the East and men back in Germany, to defend eastern borders and to guard the retreat.[189] In spite of these improvisational efforts, the situation on the front with the Bolsheviks grew threatening, for the troops, losing the will to fight, did not resist the Red advance. As a result, evacuation grew even more disordered. Soon, Hoffmann thought, Riga would fall. His last bitter words in his diary were: "our troops no longer want to fight."[190]

In spite of this chaos, Hoffmann and his officers continued to work for a minimum of order, and on January 2, 1919 the headquarters were moved to Königsberg in East Prussia to be dissolved.[191] Troops embarked on trains steaming back towards Germany, with revolutionary red flags rolled up and stowed away once aboard, as the soldiers' council pleaded that if they were allowed to flutter from open windows, they would confuse train engineers, for whom the signal meant emergency braking.[192] To the very last, the troops of Ober Ost displayed a characteristic mix of order and chaos.

Ober Ost's military utopia was a failure. Internally, it was wracked by incompatible ends and means. Its regime and ambitions left natives with nothing to lose and forced them into a new understanding of national identity, a conscious struggle for survival. Consequently, the German identity and mission in the East which Ober Ost promised to build was frustrated. How Ober Ost failed was crucial, for it collapsed just when triumph seemed secured. This disappointment blinded many to this military state's contradictory nature. Instead, the occupiers drew from this failure lessons about the East. If the cause of failure was not some fatal flaw in Ober Ost, then the fault must lie in the material it worked with: the lands and peoples. Back in Germany, a political myth was being elaborated to explain defeat. Prepared by Ludendorff, the "Stab in the Back" legend asserted that brave German troops were betrayed by those at home, especially socialists, democrats, and Jews. In considering the East, a parallel legend arose, with the East as the treacherous party contaminating Germany. Forgetting the hand their own leaders had in "revolutionizing" Russia's tottering empire, publicists surmised a secret invasion of spies and agitators from the East.[193] Ober Ost's earlier planners now furiously rejected the East, seeing a dangerous, uniform, hulking, dirty East of dirty populations. Four years took the occupiers from relative ignorance of the East to an awareness of its complexity and difference, then back again to willed ignorance, now infused with humiliation and hatred. Earlier the object of future plans, the East now stood as the very opposite of German spirit. A realistic novel of Ober Ost closed with one character's verdict: "In the soul of the East there lives chaos – but in the soul of even the most simple of our countrymen, faith in development."[194] The East appeared as an area of races and spaces, which could not be manipulated, but could only be cleared and cleaned. Failures, not only successes, have historical consequences, and Ober Ost was a failure of momentous importance for German views of the East.

NOTES

1 Wheeler-Bennett, *Wooden Titan*, 80; Herwig, *First World War*, 215.
2 Hans-Michael Körner and Ingrid Körner, eds., *Leopold Prinz von Bayern, 1846–1930. Aus den Lebenserinnerungen* (Regensburg: F. Pustet, 1983), 302.
3 BA N 1031/2, Gayl, 64; Karl Friedrich Nowak, ed., *Die Aufzeichnungen des Generalmajors Max Hoffmann* (Berlin: Verlag für Kulturpolitik, 1929), I, 174–75.
4 Brockhusen, *Menschenleben*, 258, 242.
5 Ibid., 258.
6 Klemperer, *Curriculum*, 473; Dehmel, *Zwischen Volk*, 448.
7 Dehmel, *Zwischen Volk*, 458.
8 Ibid., 454.
9 Ibid., 461.
10 BAMA N 196/1, Heppe, vol. V, 103; GSTA PK, I. HA. Rep. 84a, nr. 6211, 6. *Druckbericht. Verwaltungsbericht der Militärverwaltung Litauen für die Zeit vom 1. Oktober 1916 bis 31. März 1917*, 45; GSTA PK, I. HA. Rep. 84a, nr. 6211b, *Verwaltungsbericht der Militärverwaltung Bialystok-Grodno für die Zeit vom 1. April bis 30 September 1917*, 38; GSTA PK, I. HA. Rep. 84a, nr. 6212, *Verwaltungsbericht der Militärverwaltung Suwalki für die Zeit vom 1. Oktober 1917 bis 31. März 1918*, 36.
11 BAMA PHD 23/31, *Verwaltungsbericht Kurland* (October 1915), 25.
12 BAMA PHD 23/45, *Verwaltungsbericht Litauen* (January 1916), 30; GSTA PK, I. HA. Rep. 84a, nr. 6211b, *Verwaltungsbericht der Militärverwaltung Litauen für die Zeit vom 1. April bis 30 September 1917*, 42.
13 BAMA PHD 23/46, *Verwaltungsbericht Litauen* (May 1916), 46.
14 BAMA PHD 23/31, *Verwaltungsbericht Kurland* (October 1915), 27.
15 Ibid.; BAMA N 98/1, Gossler, 65–66.
16 Nowak, ed., *Aufzeichnungen des Generalmajors Max Hoffman*, I, 216.
17 BAMA N 196/1, Heppe, vol. V, 150.
18 BAMA PHD 23/47, *Verwaltungsbericht Litauen* (August 1916), 22.
19 BAMA PHD 23/48, *Verwaltungsbericht Litauen* (November 1916), 33–34.
20 BAMA PHD 23/46, *Verwaltungsbericht Litauen* (May 1916), 45.
21 BAMA N 98/3, Gossler, 25, 29.
22 Jungfer, *Gesicht*, 40–41.
23 Šilietis, *Okupacija*, 119.
24 BA N 1031/2, Gayl, 238–39.
25 LMARS, F. 23–47, "Vokiečiai Lietuvoje," list of complaints, 9.

26 Šilietis, *Okupacija*, 104; Gintneris, *Lietuva*, 373.

27 Šilietis, *Okupacija*, 105. In one novel, soldiers scoff at religious processions and drunken gendarmes stumble into services: Jungfer, *Gesicht*, 42.

28 Šilietis, *Okupacija*, 94.

29 Linde, *Deutsche Politik*, 49.

30 Sužiedelis, "Mokyklos," 767; Šilietis, *Okupacija*, 106; BA N 1238/8, Morsbach, *Tätigkeitsbericht des Bürgermeisteramtes Schaulen von Mitte August bis 30. September 1916*. On deportation of Polish and Orthodox priests: BAMA N 196/1, Heppe, vol. V, 101, 105; BA N 1031/2, Gayl, 271.

31 BA N 1031/2, Gayl, 278–9.

32 Richert, *Gelegenheit*, 275. Riga was captured September 3, 1917.

33 Dehmel, *Zwischen Volk*, 461.

34 Ibid.; Klimas, *Atsiminimų*, 155.

35 Klimas, *Atsiminimų*, 122.

36 BAMA N 196/1, Heppe, vol. V, 96–97.

37 BAMA PHD 23/48, *Verwaltungsbericht Litauen* (November 1916), 33.

38 Later reports noted the trend intensifying: BAMA PH 30 III/5, *Verwaltungsbericht der Militärbezirksverwaltung Litauen Süd in Bialystok für die Zeit 1. April bis 30. September 1918*, 45; BAMA PH 30 III/3, *Verwaltungsbericht 3. April 1918. Militärverwaltung Litauen, Militärkreis Podbrodzie*, 34; BAMA PH 30 III/3, *Verwaltungsbericht 30. September 1918. Militärverwaltung Litauen, Militärkreis Nowoswenzjany*, 72.

39 BAMA PHD 23/33, *Verwaltungsbericht Kurland* (April 1917), 40.

40 GSTA PK, I. HA. Rep. 84a, nr. 6212, *Verwaltungsbericht der Militärverwaltung Suwalki für die Zeit vom 1. Oktober 1917 bis 31. März 1918*, 36.

41 BAMA PHD 23/33, *Verwaltungsbericht Kurland* (April 1917), 40; Klimas, *Atsiminimų*, 66.

42 Klimas, *Atsiminimų*, 52.

43 Josef Buloff, *From the Old Marketplace*, trans. Joseph Singer (Cambridge, MA: Harvard University Press, 1991), 258.

44 Jungfer, *Gesicht*, 184–89. Natives asserted requisitioned goods appeared on the black market: Šilietis, *Okupacija*, 85.

45 BAMA N 196/1, Heppe, vol. V, 97.

46 GSTA PK, I. HA. Rep. 84a, nr. 6212, *Verwaltungsbericht der Militärverwaltung Suwalki für die Zeit vom 1. Oktober 1917 bis 31. März 1918*, 36; GSTA PK, I. HA. Rep. 84a, nr. 6213, *Verwaltungsbericht der Militärverwaltung Suwalki für die Zeit vom 1. April bis 30. September 1918*, 15.

47 A report of 1917 noted that bands were ever more made up of local youths: LCVIA F. 641, ap. 1, b. 53, "Verwaltungsberichte Rossienie," *Verwaltungsbericht für die Zeit 1. Oktober bis 31 Dezember 1917. Georgenburg*. Genovita Raudeliūnienė, "Lietuvos gyventojų pasipriešinimas vokiečiu okupantams pirmojo pasaulinio karo metais (1915–1918)" (Diss., Lithuanian SSR Academy of Sciences, Vilnius, 1969).

48 Klimas, *Atsiminimų*, 46; 73, 91.

49 Jurgėnas Storosta, "Apie Vydūno ir Zudermano santykius," *Literatūra ir menas* (27 March 1993): 4.

50 *Lietuvių enciklopedija*, s.v. "Kodatis, Bernardas."

51 BAMA N 196/1, Heppe, vol. V, 124.
52 Klimas, *Atsiminimų*, 84. Later accounts repeated concerns for order: Valentinas Gustainis, "Nepriklausoma Lietuva: Kaimiecių ir jaunimo valstybė," *Proskyna kultūros almanachas Jaunuomenei* 3.6 (1990): 170–71, 181.
53 Geroid Tanquary Robinson, *Rural Russia Under the Old Regime* (London: Longmans, Green & Co., 1932), 35.
54 Irish mythology's *"Tuatha de Danaan"* – "Diana's Troop," and kingdoms, *tuath*, share this root, related to *"Teutsch,"* which meant "common people" before signifying "German." Konstantīnas Karulis, ed., *Latviešu etimoloģijas vārdnīca* (Riga: Avots, 1992), II, 380–81.
55 Benedict Anderson, *Imagined Communities: Reflections on the Origin and Spread of Nationalism*, rev. edn (London: Verso, 1991); Eric Hobsbawm and Terence Ranger, *The Invention of Tradition* (Cambridge: Cambridge University Press, 1983); Eric Hobsbawm, *Nations and Nationalism Since 1780: Programme, Myth, Reality* (Cambridge: Cambridge University Press, 1990).
56 Klimas, *Atsiminimų*, 78.
57 William Pfaff, *The Wrath of Nations: Civilization and the Furies of Nationalism* (New York: Simon & Schuster, 1993).
58 Jungfer, *Gesicht*, 140.
59 Marwitz, *Stirb*, 143; 133.
60 Gintneris, *Lietuva*, 306, 371, 373.
61 Richert, *Gelegenheit*, 279.
62 Jungfer, *Gesicht*, 44.
63 Ibid., 158.
64 BAMA PHD 23/31, *Verwaltungsbericht Kurland* (January 1916), 30.
65 Richert, *Gelegenheit*, 247.
66 *Die Rückführung des Ostheeres*, vol. I, *Darstellungen aus den Nachkriegskämpfen Deutscher Truppen und Freikorps* (Berlin: Verlag E. S. Mittler & Sohn, 1936), 5.
67 Richert, *Gelegenheit*, 224, 239, 228, 245; Klemperer, *Curriculum*, 678.
68 Dehmel, *Zwischen Volk*, 458.
69 Hirschfeld, *Sittengeschichte*, 249–50.
70 Oskar Wöhrle, *Querschläger. Das Bumserbuch. Aufzeichnungen eines Kanoniers* (Berlin: Verlagsbuchhandlung J. H. W., 1929), 312; Klemperer, *Curriculum*, 678.
71 Richert, *Gelegenheit*, 256, 228.
72 Ibid., 265; Jungfer, *Gesicht*, 70, 175.
73 Klemperer, *Curriculum*, 477.
74 BA N 1031/2, Gayl, 129; Walter Horace Bruford, *The German Tradition of Self-Cultivation: "Bildung" from Humboldt to Thomas Mann* (Cambridge: Cambridge University Press, 1975).
75 Isaiah Berlin, *Vico and Herder: Two Studies in the History of Ideas* (London: Hogarth Press, 1976); Franz Schnabel, *Deutsche Geschichte im neunzehnten Jahrhundert* (Freiburg im Breisgan: Herder Verlag, 1964), 229–51; Lehmann, "Herder"; Petras Jonikas, *Lietuvių kalba ir tauta amžių būvyje* (Chicago: Lituanistikos instituto leidykla, 1987), 19.
76 Dehmel, *Zwischen Volk*, 453–67.
77 Georg Wenzel, ed., *Arnold Zweig, 1887–1968. Werk und Leben in Dokumenten und Bildern* (Berlin: Aufbau-Verlag, 1978), 88.

78 As an example, BAMA PHD 8/23, Arnold Zweig, "Gedenktag der Juden," *KB* 44 (8 August 1917).

79 Arnold Zweig, *Das ostjüdische Antlitz* (Berlin: Welt-Verlag, 1920), 42; 28.

80 Wenzel, ed., *Zweig*, 82.

81 Klemperer, *Curriculum*, 484, 684, 687.

82 BA N 1031/2, Gayl, 180; 175; 155, 157.

83 *Lietuvių enciklopedija*, s.v. "Jungfer, Victor."

84 Jungfer, *Gesicht*, 34–36.

85 Ibid., 73, 102, 106.

86 Ibid., 229; 320–21.

87 Ibid., 197–98.

88 Wheeler-Bennett, *Wooden Titan*, 85; Broszat, *Polenpolitik*, 189.

89 Ludendorff, *Kriegserinnerungen*, 374.

90 Ibid., 374–75.

91 Fischer, *Griff*, 289–92; Kitchen, *Dictatorship*, 102.

92 Ludendorff, *Kriegserinnerungen*, 376.

93 Fischer, *Griff*, 230–39; 316–19.

94 Ludendorff, *Kriegserinnerungen*, 376.

95 Ibid., 417.

96 Fischer, *Griff*, 230–32; Geiss, *Grenzstreifen*.

97 Ludendorff, *Kriegserinnerungen*, 417.

98 BAMA N 196/1, Heppe, vol. V, 95.

99 Hoffmann, *Aufzeichnungen*, I, 184.

100 BAMA N 196/1, Heppe, vol. V, 119.

101 Aba Strazhas first found and examined plans in Vilnius' Lithuanian Central State Historical Archives (LCVIA). Strazhas, *Ostpolitik*, 246–53.

102 LCVIA, F. 641, ap. 1, b. 971, "Die Bedeutung des Urwaldes von Bialowies für die deutsche Volkswirtschaft," 3–6v.

103 Ibid., 5v; 6.

104 LCVIA, F. 641, ap. 1, b. 971, "Übersicht über die zu erwartenden Erträge aus den Staatsforsten des Verwaltungsgebietes Ob. Ost," 15, 21, 33.

105 LCVIA, F. 641, ap. 1, b. 971, untitled document (October 21, 1917), 27.

106 LCVIA, F. 641, ap. 1, b. 971, "Die voraussichtliche Gestaltung des Etats der Justizverwaltung" (October 20, 1917), 41–41v, 43v; 42v; 44.

107 LCVIA, F. 641, ap. 1, b. 971, "Bericht über die im besetzten Gebiet lagernden Werte am Torf, Bernstein und Kalk und deren Nutzbarmachung," 45–46.

108 LCVIA, F. 641, ap. 1, b. 971, "Eisenbahnen im Ob. Ost-Gebiete," 48.

109 LCVIA, F. 641, ap. 1, b. 971, "Betrifft Veranschlagung der Einnahmen und Ausgaben der Kultusverwaltung Oberost für die Zukunft," 68–70.

110 Karl-Heinz Janßen, "Alfred von Goßler und die deutsche Verwaltung im Baltikum, 1915–1918," *Historische Zeitschrift* 207 (1968): 42–54; Karl-Heinz Janßen, "Die baltische Okkupationspolitik des deutschen Reiches," in *Von den baltischen Provinzen zu den baltischen Staaten. Beiträge zur Entstehungsgeschichte der Republiken Estland und Lettland, 1917–1918*, ed. Jürgen von Hehn, *et al.* (Marburg/Lahn: J. G. Herder-Institut, 1971), 217–54.

111 *Das Land*, viii.

112 *Lietuvos Aidas*. Klimas, *Atsiminimų*, 128–34.

113 Petras Klimas, "Lietuvos valstybės kūrimas 1915–1918 metais Vilniuje," in *Pirmasis nepriklausomos Lietuvos dešimtmetis, 1918–1928* (Kaunas: "Spindulio" B-vės spaustuvė, 1928), 6–7.

114 Senn, *Emergence*, 27.

115 Hoffmann, *Aufzeichnungen*, I, 177.

116 BAMA N 196/1, Heppe, vol. V, 139–40.

117 Ibid., 109–10, 118–19; BAMA FC 1179 N and FB 1180 N, Nachlass Franz Joseph Fürst Isenburg-Birstein.

118 BAMA N 196/1, Heppe, vol. V, 139.

119 Ibid., 139–40.

120 Ludendorff, *Kriegserinnerungen*, 427–28.

121 BA N 1031/2, Gayl, 222.

122 Ibid., 223–34, 332.

123 Klimas, "Lietuvos," 9.

124 Klimas, *Atsiminimų*, 110–11.

125 Hoffmann, *Aufzeichnungen*, 1, 185–86.

126 Ibid., 187.

127 Klimas, *Atsiminimų*, 119.

128 Hoffmann, *Aufzeichnungen*, 1, 190.

129 John W. Wheeler-Bennett, *Brest-Litovsk: The Forgotten Peace, March 1918* (New York: William Morrow & Co., 1939); Winfried Baumgart, *Deutsche Ostpolitik 1918. Von Brest-Litowsk bis zum Ende des Ersten Weltkrieges* (Vienna: R. Oldenbourg Verlag, 1966).

130 Kitchen, *Dictatorship*, 183.

131 (Hoover Library) *Verwaltungsbericht der Zivilverwaltung der baltischen Lande. 15. August bis 15. Dezember 1918*, 5; BAMA PHD 8/23, "Rigaer Arbeitsstuben," *KB* 109 (May 8, 1918).

132 *Verwaltungsbericht der Zivilverwaltung der baltischen Lande. 15. August bis 15. Dezember 1918*, 6.

133 Raun, *Estonia*, 106.

134 GSTA PK, I. HA. Rep. 84a, nr. 6212, *Verwaltungsbericht der Militärverwaltung Litauen, Bezirk Süd in Bialystok für die Zeit vom 1. Oktober 1917 bis 31. März 1918*, 42

135 (Hoover Library) *Verwaltungsbericht der Zivilverwaltung der baltischen Lande. 15. August bis 15. Dezember 1918*, 10.

136 Hoffmann, *Aufzeichnungen*, I, 197.

137 Rauch, *Geschichte*, 52; Stupperich, "Siedlungspläne"; Raun, *Estonia*, 106; (Hoover Library) *Verwaltungsbericht der Zivilverwaltung der baltischen Lande. 15. August bis 15. Dezember 1918*, 7.

138 LCVIA, Fondas 641 (Lietuvos karinės valdybos viršininkas), aprašymas 1, byla 54.

139 Page, *Formation*, 106.

140 Ibid., 106–107.

141 Fischer, *Griff*, 529.

142 Ludendorff, *Kriegserinnerungen*, 532.

143 Hoffmann, *Aufzeichnungen*, I, 190; I, 192.

144 Klimas, *Atsiminimų*, 137; Colliander, "Okkupation," 178.

145 BA N 1031/2, Gayl, 261; Demm, "Ropp," 36.
146 Klimas, "Lietuvos," 18; Senn, *Emergence*, 36.
147 Klimas, *Atsiminimų*, 141.
148 BA N 1031/2, Gayl, 269–70; Fischer, *Griff*, 531.
149 Klimas, *Atsiminimų*, 142; Klimas, "Lietuvos," 19.
150 BAMA N 196/1, Heppe, vol. V, 141.
151 Hoffmann, *Aufzeichnungen*, I, 194
152 BAMA N 196/1, Heppe, vol. V, 146; GSTA PK, I. HA. Rep. 84a, nr. 6213, *Verwaltungsbericht der Militärverwaltung Litauen-Süd in Bialystok für die Zeit vom 1. April bis 30. September 1918*, 45–46.
153 Oleg S. Fedyshyn, *Germany's Drive to the East and the Ukrainian Revolution, 1917–1918* (New Brunswick: Rutgers University Press, 1971).
154 Hoffmann, *Aufzeichnungen*, I, 203.
155 Kitchen, *Dictatorship*, 237.
156 Wheeler-Bennett, *Wooden Titan*, 126.
157 Hoffmann, *Aufzeichnungen*, I, 202.
158 (Hoover Library) *Verwaltungsbericht der Zivilverwaltung der baltischen Lande. 15. August bis 15. Dezember 1918*, 5–6; BAMA PHD 8/23, "Wünsche für Dorpat," *Baltisch-Litauische Mitteilungen*, 128 (September 11, 1918); Fischer, *Griff*, 532.
159 Kitchen, *Dictatorship*, 104–105.
160 Quoted in Ralph Haswell Lutz, ed., *The Causes of the German Collapse in 1918*, trans. W. L. Campbell (Stanford: Stanford University Press, 1934), 126–27.
161 Mai, *Ende*, 143; Lutz, ed., *Collapse*, 53–55; *Die Rückführung*, 3.
162 *Vivat.*
163 Friedrich Altrichter, *Die seelischen Kräfte des Deutschen Heeres im Frieden und Weltkriege* (Berlin: E. S. Mittler & Sohn, 1933), 122.
164 Ibid.; Klemperer, *Curriculum*, 639.
165 Ulrich Kluge, *Soldatenräte und Revolution. Studien zur Militärpolitik in Deutschland 1918/19* (Göttingen: Vandenhoeck & Rupprecht, 1975), 95; *Die Rückführung*, 4.
166 Altrichter, *Kräfte*, 160–62.
167 Ibid., 180; *Die Rückführung*, 5.
168 Altrichter, *Kräfte*, 181.
169 Lutz, ed., *Collapse*, 149; Kluge, *Soldatenräte*, 95.
170 Wheeler-Bennett, *Wooden Titan*, 174.
171 (Hoover Library) *Verwaltungsbericht der Zivilverwaltung der baltischen Lande. 15. August bis 15. Dezember 1918*, 7.
172 Ibid., 13.
173 Quoted in Paul Johnson, *Modern Times: The World from the Twenties to the Nineties*, rev. edn (New York: HarperCollins, 1991), 90.
174 BA N 1031/2, Gayl, 300.
175 Jungfer, *Gesicht*, 299–301.
176 Ibid. A soldiers' council's proclamation warned that "we are surrounded on all sides by dangers" and only unity offered safety: BAMA PHD 23/70, *Die neue Zeit. Organ des Soldatenrates Kowno* 1.8 (November 19, 1918).

177 BA N 1031/2, Gayl, 326.
178 Klemperer, *Curriculum*, 696, 699; *Die Rückführung*, 19.
179 Jungfer, *Gesicht*, 309; Altrichter, *Kräfte*, 181; BA N 1031/2, Gayl, 279, 314; 316, 325, 320; Klemperer, *Curriculum*, 703. The soldiers' council banned passing weapons or matériel to Bolsheviks: BAMA PHD 23/70, *Die neue Zeit. Organ des Soldatenrates Kowno* 1.38 (December 27, 1918).
180 BAMA PHD 23/70, *Die neue Zeit. Organ des Soldatenrates Kowno*, 1.2 (November 13, 1918); ibid., 1.18 (December 2, 1918); BAMA PHD 8/29, "Kowno zum Gruß," *Mitteilungsblatt des Großen Soldatenrates der Heeresgruppe Kiew* 1 (November 23, 1918).
181 Klemperer, *Curriculum*, 701, 703; BAMA PHD 8/29, "Dem Sieger," *Mitteilungsblatt des Großen Soldatenrates der Heeresgruppe Kiew* 1 (November 23, 1918); BAMA PHD 23/70, "An Alle!," *Die neue Zeit. Organ des Soldatenrates Kowno* 1.1 (November 12, 1918).
182 Hoffmann, *Aufzeichnungen*, I, 218.
183 Ibid., 218, 220–21; Kluge, *Soldatenräte*, 100; *Die Rückführung*, 115.
184 BA N 1031/2, Gayl, 295.
185 BAMA PHD 23/70, *Die neue Zeit. Organ des Soldatenrates Kowno* 1.4 (November 15, 1918); ibid., 1.5 (November 16, 1918); BAMA PHD 8/29, "Die zweite Versammlung," *Mitteilungsblatt des Großen Soldatenrates der Heeresgruppe Kiew* 1 (November 23, 1918).
186 Klemperer, *Curriculum*, 693, 704–706; Wenzel, ed., *Zweig*, 82.
187 Jungfer, *Gesicht*, 305.
188 Hoffmann, *Aufzeichnungen*, I, 218–23.
189 BAMA PHD 23/70, *Die neue Zeit. Organ des Soldatenrates Kowno* 1.38 (December 27, 1918); Wheeler-Bennett, *Wooden Titan*, 214.
190 Hoffmann, *Aufzeichnungen*, I, 220–24.
191 Cron, *Geschichte*, 60.
192 BAMA PHD 8/29, *Mitteilungsblatt des Grossen Soldatenrates der Heeresgruppe Kiew. Herausgegeben vom Propaganda-Ausschuß* 2 (December 1, 1918).
193 W. Nicolai, *Geheime Mächte. Internationale Spionage und ihre Bekämpfung im Weltkrieg und heute*, 2nd edn (Leipzig: K. F. Koehler, 1924).
194 Jungfer, *Gesicht*, 314.

7   Freikorps madness

The search for a German identity in the East launched by Ober Ost did not end with the military state's collapse in November 1918, but was revived in the form of a wild adventure by bands of German freebooters, the *Freikorps*. In defeat, many a soldier felt that "everything within him was broken."[1] As traditions and authority were swept away, collapse and defeat exacerbated the difficulties of "psychological demobilization," leaving many soldiers unable to return to peacetime normalcy, which younger recruits had indeed never known as adults. As the fronts around Germany buckled and civil unrest gripped the unstable new Republic's cities, individual soldiers looked to action, any action, to redeem this inner crisis. They organized themselves into hundreds of "Free Corps" units, each owing alliegance only to its commander. New National Defense Minister Gustav Noske authorized the units on January 4, 1919, impressed by a volunteer formation he reviewed at a camp outside Berlin, underwriting a process already far advanced. These Freikorps, together with the conservative officer caste, would become the embattled Republic's defenders, helping Noske quell the radical socialists. This fratricidal duty earned Noske his nickname – "Bloodhound." Such odd cooperation began the night after the events of November 9, when Ludendorff's successor Groener called the Republic's new president. His pledge that the army would support the government by keeping order was exchanged for implicit promises that the officer class's status and the army's structure would not be remade or abolished in revolutionary reforms. Reassured, the army worked for a retreat in good order back from the fronts. In the East, volunteers were called for "border guard" units to shield the evacuation of troops. In the months that followed, some hurried to conflicts erupting on Germany's borders, while other Freikorps units took to the cities, crushing workers' revolts. The most driven and desperate men refused to put themselves in service to democracy at home and instead trekked beyond the borders out to the "Eastland," leaving the new Germany far behind. They were joined by German students and other adolescents too young to have served in the army during the war.

In marching to the "Baltikum," as Germans called the lands along the Baltic, these adventurers also left reality behind. Naming themselves "*Baltikumer*," they launched a brutal adventure and search for an identity in Ober Ost's former areas. Very rough contemporary estimates of their numbers ranged from 20,000 to 40,000 men.[2] While Germany's government and army tried to use Freikorps in the East for their own political purposes, these attempts at direction from above masked terrible, senseless frenzy in the ranks below. The Freikorps adventure in the Baltikum recapitulated Ober Ost's trajectory, but now in more extreme and spontaneous form. While freebooters arrived hoping to find an identity here, they were thrown into confusion and madness instead, as the mission in the East turned into a rampage, which changed the *Baltikumer*. They returned to Germany brutalized, scarred by a failure they could not accept or explain, and filled with intense hate for the East which had transformed them.

The confused vacuum of power left behind by Ober Ost created opportunities for many competing political projects at this European crossroads. With Germany's defeat, native peoples were freed from control and hurried to establish republics. Polish activists sought to win the area for a larger Poland, resurrected in the old Polish–Lithuanian Commonwealth's borders. Yet these projects immediately faced a new threat from the East, when the Red Army invaded to link up with revolutionary unrest in central Europe. On November 13, 1918, the Bolsheviks denounced Brest-Litovsk and began to push west. Their march was directed by the Red Army's Latvian Commander-in-Chief, Jukums Vācietis (whose name, testimony to the ethnic confusion, actually means "the German" in Latvian), former leader of the Fifth Latvian Rifles Regiment. Bolshevik troops followed close behind withdrawing Germans and though poorly equipped and organized, at first met little resistance from exhausted natives. Attacks began in the north against Narwa on November 22, 1918. In the captured territories, local communists declared the Estonian Workers' Commune (later the Soviet Republic of Estonia) on November 29, 1919. Red forces pressed westward, taking Dorpat and capturing Riga on January 3, 1919. After losing most of Latvia in a few weeks, President Ulmanis' government fled to Libau on the coast. Of the Soviet governments declared in the Baltic region, Latvia's found most support among the population, which sympathized with the Latvian Rifles regiments, the Red Army's most trusted units. Yet over the next months of Bolshevik terror and worsening economic conditions, popular support evaporated.[3]

To the south, between sporadic clashes in the streets with Polish legionnaires, the Germans evacuated Wilna in the early hours of January 4,

1919. The next day, the Red Army entered and a Soviet government was declared, under Lithuanian communists Kapsukas-Mickevicius and Angarietis, advised by Joffe from Soviet Russia. In Lithuania, a rural country lacking large industrial development and a proletariat, Bolsheviks found less support than in Latvia or Estonia.[4] In addition, Ober Ost's regime had for a long time cut the country off from the radical wave of late 1917 and Bolshevik organization inside the Russian empire. Because support was so limited, the communists made plans to unite Lithuania with Belarus in a Soviet Republic named Lit-Bel, its proclamations promising a new socialist order for natives.[5] The Lithuanian government fled to Kowno, where German forces still held the line and, in spite of the dire situation, tried to marshal support throughout the land. In the countryside, farmers organized local councils, which came to the Lithuanian government's support.[6] The Taryba's promise of land reform rallied the population. Formation of an army began and as Lithuanian volunteers gathered, units of mercenaries from Saxony were hired to bolster them.

All across the Baltic countries, the situation in the winter of 1919 was desperate. At first, this "battle of weakness against weakness" favored the Red Army, so that by late February Latvia and much of Lithuania were overrun. Yet events soon took a decisive turn in Estonia, where officers organized an improvised army out of fragments of Estonian regiments disbanded by the Germans in the spring of 1918. These forces, with units of schoolboys, rallied to defend the capital, Tallinn (Reval). The Allies provided weapons and supplies, and Estonian efforts were soon reinforced by a thousand Finnish volunteers ferried across the Baltic. Ferocious combat marked this turning point, until at last Estonians had cleared the land by February 24, 1919, the republic's first anniversary of independence.

Alarmed by the situation in the East, as the Red Army drew ever closer to Prussia, Germany's government and Supreme Command prepared to take action, aware also that involving German forces in these territories offered possibilities for again securing influence over the area.[7] Such thoughts were made possible by irresolute Allied policy in the Baltic region. While concerned about Soviet expansion, the Allies could not spare troops or much material support for the struggling republics. Moreover, they backed the anti-Bolshevik White forces, aiming at restoration of the Russian empire. Only Britain took a more active role, with Admiral Sinclair's naval squadron representing its interests in the area. The ambivalent Allied stand was written into the Armistice, as article 12 ordered German troops to remain in the East, holding off Bolshevik invaders, until the Allies permitted their withdrawal. Article 14 ordered an end to requisitions and forbade removal of supplies. Neither order was obeyed fully, but Allied sanction for German military presence was used as cover for a new Baltic campaign. The German Supreme Command organized the Northern Border Defense High Command to coordinate efforts in the East.[8] At the same time, diplomatic representatives put pressure on the republics, to bring them under German influence. Plenipotentiary August Winnig negotiated with Latvia's government to allow formation of a Baltic German armed force, the *Baltische Landeswehr*. As he later declared in his memoirs, Winnig saw himself paving the way for a new *Ostpolitik*, securing land for German expansion and settlement, in hopes of opening a new sphere of action for Germany, now that the West was closed.[9] Backed into a corner, Latvia signed a treaty negotiated by Winnig on December 29, 1918, in which every German volunteer who fought for four weeks in Latvian service would be given citizenship. Winnig kept pushing the Latvians to offer grants of land, but got no concessions. In spite of this, recruitment offices springing up in Germany promised estates to prospective volunteers.

In Germany, individual commanders organized armed bands, luring desperate men. Noske, who authorized the Freikorps, said he had no control over these "little Wallensteins."[10] Baltic Germans stood at the forefront of recruitment, including Silvio Broederich, the wartime propagandist and author of the influential booklet on eastern war aims, *The New Eastland*.[11] Though presented as a crusade against Bolshevism, the venture's real attraction lay even more in the possibility of a new departure, a chance for German policy to nullify negotiations under way at Versailles with new victories. Leaving a shattered Germany behind, the Freikorps went East.

To coordinate these efforts, the army sent General Count Rüdiger von der Goltz, who had commanded German troops intervening in Finland's civil war in the spring of 1918. He arrived in Libau in February 1919 to take command of German forces there, including the *Landeswehr* and the Iron Division Freikorps. Immediately, Goltz set about weakening the Latvian army, to make the republic more dependent on German forces. He weeded out Latvian soldiers from mixed units and obstructed Latvian recruitment efforts, insisting that natives were unreliable and would be a threat behind his lines. Instead, he accelerated the recruitment of Germans with wild promises of future settlement, even establishing a soldiers' newspaper, *The Drum*, to discuss colonization. *Balten* landholders offered soldiers lectures and courses on agriculture.[12] Latvians looked on with growing distrust and worry. Under Goltz's command, the spring offensive against the Red Army was launched in mid February. Moving briskly out from Libau, German units and the Latvian Balodis Brigade soon took Goldingen, Windau, and Mitau. By early March, the Baltic coast was cleared of Bolshevik forces and the Germans and Latvians prepared for an assault on Riga.

At just this point, however, the *Baltikumer* felt confident enough to seize power in Latvia with the Libau putsch of April 16, 1919. When the Latvian government arrested a German soldier on charges of preparing a coup, Freikorps Pfeffer rushed in to capture 500 Latvian officers, the army's entire staff. Baron von Manteuffel, young commander of the *Landeswehr*'s elite Shock Troop, arrested the Latvian government, though Premier Ulmanis escaped to a British battleship. Goltz, who had discreetly gone for a long walk while these events unfolded, returned from his stroll to declare martial law. The Germans attempted to convince Colonel Balodis to join a military directorate, but he refused. Instead, a puppet government was established under Pastor Niedra, a pro-German Latvian and political opponent of Ulmanis. Niedra's government was transparently a German tool and had no support in the radicalized population. When Britain angrily demanded the recall of German troops, Germany's government pointed out that this would give Bolsheviks a free hand in the area. Britain backed down, assured that there would be no further offensive action (which then promptly took place). For the moment, the factions put aside their differences to continue the advance. A multinational force made up of the Balodis Brigade, White Russian units under Count Anatol Lieven, and German Freikorps moved on Riga, with the *Landeswehr* leading the assault. On May 23, 1919 the city was taken, after the Shock Troop stormed the Düna bridge.

Paradoxically, this victory sealed the fate of the Baltikum adventure. Afterwards, the Iron Division's leader, Bischoff, declared, "We've won ourselves to death!"[13] For the extent of the success alarmed the Allies, who now protested loudly. Equally, brutal treatment of natives by Freikorps in captured towns precipitated resistance. In Mitau, Freikorps reportedly shot 500 Latvians suspected of Bolshevik sympathies without a trial, 200 in Tukkum, and 125 in Dünamunde. When Riga was taken, it was reported 3,000 died in the terror that followed.[14] After the Red Army withdrew from the entire Baltic area in late May, natives turned on the Freikorps and German forces. A new kind of fighting followed, embittered and without mercy on either side. Combined Estonian and Latvian forces bore down on the *Landeswehr* from the north, defeating them at Wenden on June 22. The Iron Division was dispatched to help their comrades and to teach natives a lesson, but was also repulsed as the Estonians fought with great ferocity fueled by centuries of national antagonism and class hatred.

The Allies at last took matters in hand and, on May 23, dispatched an Allied military mission to help natives organize regular armies and evacuate German forces. The mission, under General Sir Hubert Gough, arrived in mid June and quickly deposed Niedra, reinstated Ulmanis, and put the *Landeswehr* under British command. German forces were ordered to withdraw from Riga and Goltz was compelled to sign an agreement accepting evacuation. However, the duplicitous policy of Germany's government and army command prolonged their presence there by months, as another plan was put into effect, to have German soldiers go over to the anti-Bolshevik "White" Russian forces. Losing patience, the Allies finally delivered an ultimatum: either the troops would be withdrawn, or blockade would be reimposed on an already emaciated Germany. Faced with these threats, President Ebert recalled the forces on August 5, but as the Iron Division prepared to board trains for Germany in Mitau on August 24, their commander Bischoff mutinied. His troops, already alienated from the Republic by its signing of the Versailles Treaty in late June, cheered and celebrated their renegade status with torchlight processions. The next day, officers met and established a German legion made up out of a dozen Freikorps, counting in all 14,000 men and boasting 64 airplanes, 6 cavalry units, 56 field pieces, armored sections, a field hospital, and 156 machine guns. Feeling called upon to justify their mutiny, the officers issued a declaration, motivating their actions by a crusade against the Bolshevik East, supposedly out of their "fear for the culture of the entire world."[15] This vicious rabble-at-arms styled itself as a champion of *Kultur*, while in fact it was driven by nihilistic aimlessness bred of defeat, revolution, and years of total war.

These German forces went over to the western White Russian army, under a Russian adventurer, the self-styled General Prince Avalov-Bermondt, a bizarre character who "liked to think of himself as a dashing adventurer, a great – if syphilitic – lover, and a brilliant military leader."[16] While Bermondt struck heroic poses in his Caucasian warlord costume, in reality Goltz was the effective commander. "Official transfer" of troops began on September 17, 1919. Bermondt claimed that he commanded 55,000 men, 40,000 of them German volunteers. In one of those bewildering transformations of national identity common to this land, Freikorps men "became" Russians, as they changed German insignia on their caps for the Russian Whites' cockades, tried to get used to drinking vodka, and reportedly marched singing both German and Russian anthems.[17] Bermondt now undiplomatically announced that he ruled the Baltic lands in the name of the Tsar of Holy Russia and prepared to take Riga.

Real political developments mattered less to the Freikorps, however, than the inner convulsions driving their rampage, adding fuel to its increasing brutality. The central, burning issue was a new direction for

German identity, broken by defeat. As the Great War ended, lost on the Western Front (though seemingly won in the East), the first thought of many men who were to become Freikorps fighters was that ties which had held Germany to the West were now broken and Germans had to turn elsewhere in search for their destiny.[18] It was then that "there awoke a vague hope in the East" for Freikorps fighters.[19] Germany itself was consumed by revolutionary chaos within, while "round about the boiling land, the borders were glowing."[20] A border war, it seemed to some, would be much clearer than the civil war in Germany's cities, where German fought German. Out there, it would be far easier to understand who "they" and "we" were. The direction of march would be more obvious: ever outwards, ever forwards. Distant borders called: "while in the homeland, bullets whipped through the cities, while confused comrades carried the red flag of a utopian Internationale through the streets, a secret murmuring went through the grey front of the genuine warriors: *Off to the Baltikum!*"[21] The scenes of the mindscape, propagated by Ober Ost and now reinvigorated by desperation, invited Freikorps men to landscapes of destruction in the East.

Adventurers who made their way to the Baltikum entered a world in which "everything appeared fantastic to the sober observer."[22] The new Baltikum fighters reached what often seemed to them a magical landscape. In their strange physical appearance and qualities, land and nature here were of a different world. Even the sun seemed unfamiliar, as the rising sun's light mixed itself with the rays of the descending one, while on marches and before battles, it appeared through ominious mists, a "threatening, symbolic sphere."[23] The land itself was an expanse of wilderness, its forests mysterious, impenetrable, and threatening: "we were taken in by seemingly endless dark pine forest." One soldier remembered, "these forests make a tremendous, gloomy impression." From isolated positions along indistinct front lines, Freikorps men could see "up to the dark forests, where 'they' were hidden," an unknown enemy.[24] As winter came and winds brought Siberian cold and heavy snow, the landscape was subjected to the terrors of the season: brief days, hunger, unfamiliar rules of warfare. Then the landscape was most fantastic, as "black nights, in which wind and ice create ghostly noises, slowly drag away the hours."[25]

Freikorps men had to master this fantastic landscape, a difficult and vital task, since "every change of location was a question of life and death . . . and created tension."[26] Yet fighters looked forward to eventually settling here, for by degrees the landscape grew familiar. They became attached to it, for all its exotic nature, and even felt an erotic charge. One man recalled:

With every pull of breath, a special, acerbic smell filled the lungs. It forced its way through the entire body with an almost painful spiciness. This exhalation of Kurland's earth allowed me to sense in a dull way, what the land had to offer us. I thrust my finger into the rich earth, which seemed to pull me in. We had conquered this ground. Now it challenged us; suddenly, it had become a committing symbol.

The Baltikum was beautiful and dangerous, "a landscape of gentle and treacherous loveliness," forming the backdrop for violent fun and games, the "carefree activity" of a bloody Baltikum adventure.[27]

The foreign physical landscape acted upon the new arrivals, triggering other sets of associations from distant pasts. The Freikorps fighter so powerfully affected by the smell of the soil, Ernst von Salomon (later a political terrorist and popular author), explained,

I still knew quite exactly, how this smell had then seemed for me to unite everything in itself, the hope and danger which had moved me in Kurland. I was transported by the dangerous foreignness of this land, to which I stood in a peculiar relationship. Precisely the feeling, in this lovely landscape always in fact to be standing on swaying swamp-ground, which unceasingly sent up its bubbles, had given the war up here the moving, constantly changing character, which may have already communicated to the Teutonic Knights that roving restlessness which always drove them out of their secure castles anew to daring expeditions.[28]

Just as in Ober Ost, the landscape prompted historical "memories" from the German past. While growing up, future Freikorps fighters took in popular understandings of German history, even if only in caricatured form. Now, scenes from that past seemed to be resurrected, pictures and voices filtered through into the fragmented present, and Freikorps men eagerly seized these evocations. To discover that they were playing historical roles from their nation's past gave meaning to their adventuring. Ernst Jünger, preeminent author of Germany's front generation, recognized how the past invaded the present in turbulent times, reminding that "we ourselves had experienced, after all, how in such moments all the dormant forms and shapes to be found in time and space become living. All of history awakes at the same moment; each of the past conditions knocks once again on the gates of the present."[29] Even the name *Freikorps* demonstrated history's role in the identity they were patching together. Their chroniclers pointed out that "this name came to them of itself. It flew to them out of the past."[30] The original Freikorps were famous volunteer units fighting against Napoleon. Beginning with their name, the Freikorps depicted their often sordid experiences with a romanticizing historical sense.

Freikorps fighters found a landscape full of historical references. German place-names and romantic ruined castles reminded them of the crusading Teutonic Order. The very act of passing "castles with German names, like Marienhausen, Kreuzburg, and Dünaburg," names which sounded familiar in territory with otherwise strange names, invited adventurers to compare their campaigns with those remoter ones. A Freikorps man recalled,

The remains of fortifications from the times of the Order, Cremon, Treiden, and Segewoldt, looked down upon us. Were they surprised at the little flag with the black cross, which snapped up and down below them? Did they recognize the badge on our caps, which they had once seen on the white cloaks of their inhabitants? Our destination was Wenden. There, more than four hundred years ago, the knights, vassals with their ladies, and German yeomen had blown themselves up in the air. It was the last heroic act of the declining Order.[31]

The conditions of this war recalled past times as well. Hostile natives used secret swamp trails unknown to the Germans, just as pagans had against the Knights.[32] In the persons of Baltic Germans among them, adventurers saw living descendants of distant German history. The imaginations of Freikorps fighters could not resist the roles which were being offered them and eagerly let themselves be overpowered, as epochs flowed together: "Behind the commander rode, on a huge stallion, a six-foot tall courier in a steel helmet, bearer of an old name, well-known in Baltic history. The wind played with the white pennant on his lance, on which the black cross was clearly to be seen. I had to think of the past. A Knight of the Order, who had come back to life. It seemed to me as if all the intervening ages had been extinguished."[33] The Freikorps took up the invitation to see themselves dressed in roles from the past. They characterized their adventure as the "*Ritt gen Osten*," the ride against the East, the battle cry of the Teutonic Knights. Reveling in a high "crusading spirit," the Freikorps wrapped themselves in the costume of the Knights, drank themselves sick in ancient baronial manor halls, and considered their own victories "worthy of the battles of the Knights of the Order against Poles and Tartars."[34] Other historical dressing rooms were also at their disposal; the dim and distant prehistory of the Dark Ages' great migrations of tribes and the Goths beckoned, as did more recent heroes of the young Prussian state, like the rebel Yorck.[35]

As roles taken from popular German history were tried on and then exchanged for others, the Baltikum took on the aspect of a giant, violent costume party. Anachronism raged, as resurrected Teutonic Knights brushed shoulders with self-styled Germanic tribesmen. As Baltikum fighter von Salomon related, in spite of this confusion of identities, "out of the mass, which rolled to the East from the collapsed front in the West, similar ones sorted themselves out. We found our way to each other as if by a secret sign." He described units carrying *Bundschuh* flags of the Reformation's Peasant War, and troops from Hamburg following the old Hansa flag, singing pirate songs, and letting their beards grow out. Before battles, a friend doffed a beret like that of *Wandervögel* or minstrels of the high Middle Ages.[36]

But of all the roles that came to them out of the past, one in particular fit perfectly the restless times and their wild doings. This was the Thirty Years' War, which had already risen to mind for soldiers of Ober Ost. Now that model from popular imagination was let loose in the real world. In the unlimited Freikorps adventure, it came fully to life, leaping to the stage of the present. A typical character rose out of the Thirty Years' War, standing tall in German imagination: the figure of the *Landsknecht*, the German freebooter mercenary. The profound impression the *Landsknecht* left on German popular historical imagination was a result of his position in cultural history. He had been such a flamboyant character in outrageous costumes of slashed cloth in many colors, puffed sleeves, hats with streaming plumes, that printmakers and genre painters could not resist such a subject and the *Landsknecht* entered German cultural history as the first figure from the common people (along with rustic farmers) to find such popularity in all levels of art. The carefree freebooter left an impression on German historical memory, so that images of *Landsknechte* were featured in the historical romances of romantics. As with other roles, Freikorps men acted out a "memory" with great abandon. Von Salomon declared, "thus, the stragglers gave the used-up, derogatory word a new content, proudly called themselves *Landsknechte*, and gave their wars a form fitting *Landsknechte*."[37] They worked over their experiences, shaping them to fit their assumed role, until occupied cities recalled the bustle of Wallenstein's encampments, and their long wagon trains were said to resemble his mercenary armies on the move.[38] Wars along the border were called repetitions of the "Wallenstein drama."[39] Sometimes, this associative urge to make historical connections was carried to extremes, so that, picking images closest to mind, a Freikorps man compared an exploded mine thower to a *Landsknecht*'s fluted pants. The role and name of *Landsknecht* fitted Baltikum fighters too well to be resisted, so they seized upon it and called themselves *Landsknechte* over and over again.[40]

When old forms of Imperial German society were broken, such historical role-playing by Freikorps men was part of their attempt to grasp an identity. They counted their historical fascinations a strength and looked down on natives for their "complete lack of historical thought."[41] It would later be a badge of pride for them that "when we explore the elements which gave the German Freikorps fighter spiritual bearing . . . we can find traces of all the elements that have worked in German history,"[42] a multiplicity of available archaic German roles. Emerging from the Great War, which launched modernity, they marched straight into remembered pasts: "only so far did the affair resemble war of the twentieth century. What then followed were pictures from the German past."[43] This desperate urge to find connections, ransacking storehouses of popular historical memory, showed how intolerable the present was to some Germans, as they tried to recast a shattered national identity.

Even so, while Baltikum fighters had come out to lands beyond Germany's farthest border in search of a new German identity, what they encountered ultimately only heightened their uncertainties. Instead of forging a stable sense of self and purpose, in the end the rampage left them as nothing more than representatives of violence and power without limit or restraint in the East. Soldiers wandering up from the Western Front rediscovered martial glory in the Baltikum, played at historical roles, but they sensed that a great personal price was paid for this. Outlawed by Weimar for the international embarrassment they were causing, the adventurers still felt themselves to be Germans, and yet were no longer Germans like those at home. One reported, "soldiers in the Baltikum sang a marching song, whose first verse began, 'We are the last Germans, who stayed opposite the enemy.' Now we felt ourselves to be the last Germans, period."[44] They felt great uncertainty about their Germanness, not least because, as soldiers of fortune, they fought under different citizenships, first as Latvians against Bolshevism, then as Russians in the imperial cause, wearing both German and Russian insignia.[45] This newest masquerade could go to absurd lengths. Confused natives looked on, a popular source claimed, as Germans tried to sing "God Save the Tsar," though uncertain of the words and needing help from their new adoptive countrymen; asserting that they were Russians, even though they did not speak the language, some Freikorps men supposedly avoided using German in front of natives and communicated using sign language.[46] In Riga, a note of anguish escaped one Freikorps man who ironically declared, "we are German soldiers, who are nominally not German soldiers, and are protecting a German city, which nominally is not a German city."[47] When the Freikorps found fellow Germans fighting on the Bolshevik side or in the service of the native republics, national designations became even more doubtful.[48]

The Freikorps men were involved in wild plans, as they cast about for a mission from which a coherent identity might grow. They were already in the Baltikum when they heard of the signing of the Versailles Treaty. Without much sense of broader political and military realities, they had hoped negotiations would be broken off, allowing Germany to resume the war. They reacted to the signing with shame, grief, and anger, finally simply rejecting the news: "After all, what has that got to do with us?"[49] If their sense of the realities of the world had been weak before, ties with the outside were now broken off entirely. Germany became "a land without reality" to them.[50] Freikorps men saw themselves as a "people without a homeland on campaign."[51] Germany had to be replaced, somehow. Some suggested that it was really here with the fighters, in their midst, while others began to equate the nation with its borderlands, affirming, "Germany was at the frontier."[52] They hatched grandiose schemes to give some reality to ideas of a new martial Germany. These fantastic plans were important and attractive for the Freikorps and much of their attention was devoted to them, from generals down to volunteeers.[53] They talked of "reinforcement of military Germany from the East."[54] A new German state would rise up east of its earlier borders and again take up the war against the Allies (Ober Ost's political official von Gayl in Prussia hatched similar abortive plans for a nationalist uprising, forming a new German "East-state").[55] Fighting to conquer the Baltikum, Freikorps men could already see themselves as "governors of this province for the as yet unborn nation."[56] As the Allies continued to press for their removal, these castles in the air were not so much scaled down as moved to another cloud, for once in the White Russian army, new dreams appeared before them. They would restore the Russian empire, to be reconstructed and administered by a ruling class of German nobility. When these plans crumbled, Freikorps fighters returning to Germany wondered where they had made their mistake. Their unrealistic and crazed regret was, "if only we had attacked Poland instead!"[57]

Such different pipe dreams all had in common a central vision taken over from Ober Ost's ambitions. Freikorps men strove for "battle and settlement . . . the two guiding stars of the campaign now beginning."[58] In the Baltic Germans, they had found the "seed of a *Herrenvolk*," with a 700-year tradition of domination in these lands.[59] The men could readily imagine themselves helping to continue settler traditions, for no sooner had they arrived in the East than the "ten thousand German soldiers already saw themselves as free farmers sitting on their heights . . . a new race of military farmerhood, a battle-ready chain of colonizers, which believed that it had a Teutonic Knight mission to fulfill."[60] The vision of settlement was a powerful one, promising a permanent and stable identity. Here and there, reportedly, settlement actually began.[61] Freikorps fighters saw themselves as embodiments of "an eternal soldierhood and onward-pressing spirit of colonization."[62]

The very nebulousness of such plans makes clear that specifics were of little concern. What really mattered to Freikorps fighters was drawn in broad outline and general terms – the idea of "German possibilities" for the men themselves and for the nation they had lost. The Baltikum now "appeared as a magical center, as a new German field of power."[63] It "was now . . . a German possibility. We wanted to use it." For all the exotic features of landscape, historical associations, and colorful natives, the Baltikum was most fantastic and magical for being a possibility, a gate by which to escape into new vistas of heroism. A freebooter thrilled, "That was possible in the Baltikum; there everything was possible."[64]

The image and word around which this longing for German possibilities revolved was the notion of "*Aufbruch*," an evocative term describing an army breaking camp and surging into motion. Allied to it was the word "*Vormarsch*," the advance. Together, these words recur among *Baltikumer*, with a transcendental, mystical meaning. The impulse was similar to that of Ober Ost's mindscape of the East, but now violence alone took pride of place, displacing ideas of ordering and cleaning. Even in defeat, the very "word *Vormarsch* had . . . a meaning that was deep and made one happy."[65] Von Salomon shared this feeling and avowed, "the word *Vormarsch* had for us . . . a mysterious, delightfully dangerous meaning. In the attack, we hoped for the last, satisfying increase of powers, we craved to confirm the consciousness that we were up to any fate, we hoped to learn the real values of the world in ourselves."[66] *Vormarsch* was less a directed, useful military action than a nihilistic end in itself.[67] In the "Riga Marching Song," the elemental notions of *Aufbruch* and *Vormarsch* were presented as the Baltikum venture's entire meaning.[68] Implicit in them was the bursting of borders, earlier central to Ober Ost's mindscape. These borders also were internal, making the Baltikum adventure a destructive spiritual exploration, as one freebooter recalled: "these Freikorps marched off into the beckoning distance, whose borders lay beyond every calculation and prudent reason."[69] Paradoxically, attempts to build identity involved both drawing and bursting of inner borders for *Baltikumer*, also expressing itself in an explosion of sexual anxieties and violence among the Freikorps men, documented by Theweleit's study, *Male Fantasies*.[70]

The Baltikum landscape was a stereotyped, colonial world in which the Baltic Freikorps identity moved, playing historical roles, seeking redemption through military metaphors. This *Baltikumer* identity was concerned with German possibilities and the idea of the borderland. Identity was vested in the frontier, discovered and articulated there. Since it was committed to dynamism, as a frontier identity, it lived in a love–hate relationship with borders, which were to be drawn so that they might be exploded to create new borders. Baltikum fighters cut themselves off from the outside world, both politically and psychologically, so that von Salomon could cry out, looking death in the face, "There is nothing in the world besides me . . . I am really quite alone. There has never been anything outside of me."[71] This radical self-absorption expressed itself in the drive of the identity, the structured self, to shape the outside world in its own image. Freikorps men focused on borders as metaphysical concepts as much as physical and political realities, announcing, "no border for Germans is conceivable, which is not exclusively formed through the consciousness of Germans: up to here and no further."[72] *Baltikumer* wanted to "break open a door through the surrounding wall of the world" and to march out into open, apocalyptic eastern landscapes of destruction.[73] Borders between classes and traditions burst, "suddenly erased without a trace in the instant of engagement."[74] The only real border was represented by fighting Germans. Von Salomon captured this obsessive relationship to borders:

We lay here now in crackling darkness; we searched for the entrance into the world, and Germany lay somewhere way back there in the fog, full of confusing pictures; we searched for the soil, which would give us the power, but this soil did not give itself over voluntarily; we searched for the new, the last possibility, for Germany and for us, and there in the secret darkness lay that unknown, that formless power . . . half admired by us and half hated.[75]

That elusive power was the East and the exploding of borders directed eastward, as with each step away from the West, Freikorps men "lost a bit of inherited ballast," growing lighter.[76] For them, the *"Drang nach Osten,"* the supposedly inevitable historic German surge into the East, was joined to concepts of attack and mobilization. In contrast to Ober Ost's slogans, Baltikum Freikorps could not be used to impose order: "here there were no units fighting for order."[77] They identified themselves with expanding borders, announcing, "We traveled, to protect the border, but there was no border there. Now we were the border, we held the ways open."[78] Recasting Ober Ost's mindscape of the East, *Baltikumer* identity was violent, expansive, obsessively at play with historical roles, fixated on borders, looking for fulfillment in mobilization, and committed to German possibilities to the East.

Baltikumer identity, founded on violence directed against the East, confronted a threatening, overwhelming foreignness and met it with a ferocious, merciless kind of fighting, mirroring that of the natives. The Baltic war was called a "small war," but had "a wild and generous character."[79] It could not be compared to any other European war of recent times, Freikorps men insisted. In describing it, they fell back on comparisons to frontier ventures. It seemed a "small-scale war of Indian-style wildness, accompanied by a Wild West romanticism." Another insisted it "was much more comparable to an expedition in the interior of

Africa," with a style of fighting at first difficult to absorb.[80] The Germans abandoned both their own military practice and preconceptions of how wars had to be fought, a classical story of colonial conflict, as they found treacherous and savage warfare: "suddenly, shadows are everywhere. Ambush, surprise attack."[81] The Freikorps adapted, and lost the vaunted German discipline, but seeing themselves as mercenary *Landsknechte*, they were glad to imitate storied, informal brutalities of the Thirty Years' War.

The enemy, even when met, was a hazy concept for them (it was the person of the Freikorps fighter, asserting his identity outwards, that was at the heart of the matter). The figure of the enemy was compounded from many images, until an indistinct, stereotyped figure eventually emerged. Bolsheviks were said to have distinctive hairstyles, a "Bolshevik lock" above "animal-like, satanic faces." The enemy was synthesized from so many other figures that soon everything flowed together, as "everything which happened in this land took on a Bolshevik face."[82] Many enemies were collapsed into an indistinct idea of "them": German POWs fighting for the Russians, Bolshevik women's battalions, "Chinese" Red Guards, and Latvians gifted "with oriental slyness."[83] All the varied foreign peoples seemed a uniform enemy – the East.

War here was of incredible ferocity and frightening intensity, as the terrible things they did and saw brutalized Freikorps fighters. This colonial war was a pivotal experience for freebooters who went on to join the Nazis, notably Rudolf Höss, later commandant of Auschwitz. In his trial after the Second World War, Höss recounted decades later the jarring transformation he underwent in the East, searing his nature:

The fighting in the Baltikum was of a wildness and grimness, which I had experienced neither before in the World War nor afterwards in all the Freikorps fighting. There was hardly an actual front, the enemy was everywhere. And when it came to a clash, it became a slaughter to the point of complete destruction. The Latvians especially distinguished themselves in this. There I saw for the first time horrors visited on the civilian population. The Latvians took gruesome revenge on their own people who had taken in or provided for German or Russian soldiers of the White Army. They set their houses on fire and allowed those dwelling within to be burned alive in the house. Countless times I saw the horrible pictures with the burned-out huts and the charred or smeared corpses of women and children. When I saw this for the first time, it was as if I had been turned to stone. Back then I believed that a further intensification of human destructive madness was not possible. Even though I later had to see incessantly far more gruesome pictures, today still there stands clearly before my eyes the half-burned hut with the entire family which had perished inside, there at the edge of the forest on the Düna. Back then I could still pray and I did so![84]

In these lands without borders, Freikorps men lost limits inside. With interior barriers broken, they raged in landscapes of destruction, aimless and desperate. The *Baltikumer*'s increasing brutalization crested with their defeat, as Bermondt's fantasies ended in failure. Some of Bermondt's plans seemed to mimic Ober Ost in strange ways. To finance his schemes and pay his soldiers, he issued worthless currency, supposedly drawn on crown forests.[85] When this proved impractical, he proposed using natives for slave labor at sawmills, to cut wood for shipment to Germany.[86] Bermondt's troops in Latvia and northern Lithuania behaved with extravagant cruelty, according to native sources. They were infuriated by the sight of Lithuanian soldiers and officials, who symbolized a competing claim to the land. In Schaulen and Kowno, freebooters attacked town garrisons and killed several soldiers. Native policemen were waylaid. In many places, Freikorps seized school buildings for their own uses, as casinos or hospitals, expelling students and teachers. On September 30, 1919, Freikorps Diebitsch emptied Schaulen's gymnasium, reportedly injuring forty teachers and pupils. Testifying to freebooters' mental instability, in March a soldier ran amok in Schaulen's marketplace, shooting at shoppers and killing three, including a young girl. Popular native sources claimed the Freikorps staged massive acts of arson, turning parks and orchards into enormous bonfires for recreation, pouring gasoline on trees and setting them alight.[87] *Baltikumer* surrendered to pathological anger and lust for annihilation. One announced, "We did not know what we wanted, and what we knew, we did not want. War and adventure, riot and destruction, and an unknown, torturing drive which whipped us on from every corner of the heart!"[88]

These events steeled native determination and amateur armies readied for a decisive blow. Bermondt tried to gain the initiative by laying siege to Riga on October 8, 1919, but Latvians held the line and were soon reinforced by two armored trains sent by Estonia. Bombardment by Britain's naval squadron forced Bermondt's abject withdrawal. Bermondt's fantasies proved to have very real political consequences on a larger scale, for his defeat at Riga ruined plans for a concerted assault on a broad front by all White forces. Without this support, Yudenich's Northwest Army attacked Petrograd and at first made impressive gains, only to peter away. For Bermondt, a protracted retreat followed. At one point, the Iron Division was trapped near Thorensberg and threatened with annihilation until rescued by Freikorps Rossbach, in an epic forced march from Berlin. In late November retreating troops pulled out of Mitau, leaving it in flames, and headed for Lithuania. Eberhardt, Goltz's successor, tried to negotiate withdrawal, but here as well native troops let loose their fury, defeating them at Radviliškis, on November 21–22, in an unremitting day-long attack, culminating in close combat with bayonets. From Riga to East Prussia's border, even in retreat, the adventurers pillaged and plundered, leaving a trail of destruction: "The soldiers of the Iron Division and the German Legion unloaded all their despair and fury in one wild power blow" against the Latvians, as "villages burst into flames, prisoners were trampled under foot . . . chaotic revenge and destructive joy. The leaders were powerless, or else looked on with grim approval."[89] The bloody end of the Baltic rampage made beasts of the adventurers, producing a nihilistic identity exulting in destruction and advance. The same conflict also had decisive results for natives, as these 1919 wars of liberation were viewed as baptisms of fire for independence.

On December 13, 1919, the last Freikorps units in Lithuania were thrown back on to Prussian territory, their year-long rampage brought to an end. Pulled together into disciplined formation by their officers as they crossed into Germany, their return made a powerful impression. The Baltikum fighter "carried with his flags the symbols of a singular world, the signs of a terrible and grandiose landscape, into the flatlands of bourgeois forms of imagination."[90] In his identity and memory, the Baltikum Freikorps man took some of that world and landscape back with him. In real terms the adventure was a failure, but *Baltikumer* hoped that their new spirit might become a meaningful force back home.[91] This was precisely what Germany's government feared, and in mid March the formations were demobilized.[92] Freikorps leaders tried to keep their men from drifting apart, organizing *Lager* camps for agricultural work and settlement.[93] The Freikorps cast about for political direction, eventually forming a small but important part of the support for the Nazis, whose program reflected their aims of expansion and war in the East. The last verse of a marching song, "The *Balten* Flag," announced that the banner would force Germans "to carry it against the East-land / It wants, it must go that way."[94] Vaguely, they sensed that their identity would again be directed against the East.

The Freikorps rampage in the Baltikum speedily recapitulated in accelerated, extreme, and savage forms many of the developments in Ober Ost. The adventure was a continuation of the military utopia by other means. The Freikorps saw the East as a place with no limits, where the only order was violence. While they had hoped that the adventure would produce a stable identity, honor, and settlement for German soldiers, it pitched them into unreality and madness. The rampage brutalized *Baltikumer*, leaving them with a greater hatred for what they saw as a monolithic, threatening East, which had first changed and then defeated them.

NOTES

1 "Offizier 1918," in *Deutscher Aufstand: Die Revolution des Nachkrieges*, ed. Curt Hotzel (Stuttgart: Verlag W. Kohlhammer, 1934), 20.
2 Hagen Schulze, *Freikorps und Republik, 1918–1920*, Militärgeschichtliche Studien, vol. VIII (Boppard am Rhein: Harald Boldt Verlag, 1969), 185–86; Robert G. L. Waite, *Vanguard of Nazism: The Free Corps Movement in Postwar Germany, 1918–1923* (Cambridge, MA: Harvard University Press, 1952), 125–26; Edgar von Schmidt-Pauli, *Geschichte der Freikorps, 1918–1924* (Stuttgart: R. Lutz, 1936). This account also draws on Rauch, *Geschichte*, Senn, *Emergence*, and Page, *Formation*.
3 Rauch, *Geschichte*, 65.
4 Ibid., 58; Page, *Formation*, 131.
5 (Hoover Institution Archives) Lithuanian Subject Collection, box no. 1, "Revolutionary Proclamations"; Rauch, *Geschichte*, 58–59; Page, *Formation*, 132.
6 Gintneris, *Lietuva*, 358; Gustainis, "Nepriklausoma," 171–73.
7 Charles Sullivan, "The 1919 German Campaign in the Baltic: The Final Phase," in *The Baltic States in Peace and War, 1917–1945*, ed. V. Stanley Vardys and Romuald J. Misiunas (University Park: Pennsylvania State University Press, 1978), 31.
8 Ibid., 31.
9 August Winnig, *Am Ausgang der deutschen Ostpolitik. Persöhnliche Erlebnisse und Erinnerungen* (Berlin: Staatspolitischer Verlag, 1921); Waite, *Vanguard*, 101.
10 Waite, *Vanguard*, 135.
11 Sullivan, "Campaign," 33.
12 Ibid.
13 Waite, *Vanguard*, 118.
14 Ibid., 118–19.
15 Ibid., 125–27.
16 Ibid., 123.
17 Sullivan, "Campaign," 34; Šilietis, *Okupacija*, 165–66, 178–79.
18 Franz Nord, "Der Krieg im Baltikum," in *Der Kampf um das Reich*, ed. Ernst Jünger (Essen: Deutsche Vertriebsstelle "Rhein u. Ruhr" Wilh. Kamp, [1929]), 63.
19 Ernst von Salomon, *Die Geächteten* (Berlin: Rowohlt Verlag GmbH, 1930), 107.
20 Ernst von Salomon, "Hexenkessel Deutschland," in *Kampf*, ed. Jünger, 35.
21 Friedrich Wilhelm Heinz, "Der deutsche Vorstoß in das Baltikum," in *Aufstand*, ed. Hotzel, 47.
22 Georg Heinrich Hartmann, "Aus den Erinnerungen eines Freiwilligen der baltischen Landeswehr," in *Deutsche Revue* (Stuttgart: Deutsche Verlagsanstalt, 1921), 75.
23 Nord, "Krieg," 75, 82.
24 Hartmann, "Erinnerungen," 44, 142, 43.
25 Nord, "Krieg," 88.
26 Hartmann, "Erinnerungen," 67.

27 Salomon, *Geächteten*, 65, 115; "Ein wilder Ritt. Patrouillenunternehmen – 150 Kilometer hinter die feindliche Front. Nach dem Tagebuch des Rittmeisters W. von Engelhardt, ehem. Führer der Kav.-Abtlg. von Engelhardt," in *Das Buch vom deutschen Freikorpskämpfer. Herausgegeben im Auftrage der Freikorpsgesellschaft 'Der Reiter gen Osten,'* ed. Ernst von Salomon (Berlin: W. Limpert, 1938), 183. This volume, like the one edited by Jünger, is a collection of first-hand accounts and memoirs by former Freikorps fighters.

28 Salomon, *Geächteten*, 115.

29 Ernst Jünger, "Vorwort," in *Kampf*, ed. Jünger, 5. Similar thoughts are also expressed in Remarque's *All Quiet on the Western Front*.

30 Schmidt-Pauli, *Freikorps*, 26.

31 Hartmann, "Erinnerungen," 72, 260.

32 Schmidt-Pauli, *Freikorps*, 102.

33 Hartmann, "Erinnerungen," 259.

34 Nord, "Krieg," 70, 79, 49, and Heinz, "Vorstoß," 60.

35 Von Zeschau, "Streiflichter aus den Kämpfen um Litauen. Von Major von Zeschau, ehem. Führer des Sächsischen Freiwilligen-Infanterie-Regiments 18," in *Freikorpskämpfer*, ed. Salomon, 142; Hartmann, "Erinnerungen," 150; Schmidt-Pauli, *Freikorps*, 124.

36 Salomon, *Geächteten*, 72, 116, 69, 71.

37 Ernst von Salomon, "Die Versprengten," in *Kampf*, ed. Jünger, 114.

38 Hartmann, "Erinnerungen," 74; Zeschau, "Streiflichter," 142.

39 Schmidt-Pauli, *Freikorps*, 300.

40 Nord, "Krieg," 71; Erich Balla, *Landsknechte wurden wir. Abenteuer aus dem Baltikum* (Berlin: W. Kolk, 1932).

41 Hartmann, "Erinnerungen," 155.

42 "Vorwort," in *Freikorpskämpfer*, ed. Salomon, 14.

43 Zeschau, "Streiflichter," 142.

44 Salomon, *Geächteten*, 111.

45 Nord, "Krieg," 81.

46 Šilietis, *Okupacija*, 178–79.

47 Salomon, *Geächteten*, 92.

48 Waite, *Vanguard*, 120.

49 Salomon, *Geächteten*, 110.

50 Ibid.

51 Hartmann, "Erinnerungen," 143.

52 Ibid., 68; Salomon, *Geächteten*, 64.

53 Rüdiger von der Goltz, *Meine Sendung in Finnland und im Baltikum* (Leipzig: K. F. Koehler, 1920).

54 Schmidt-Pauli, *Freikorps*, 39.

55 BA N 1031/2, Gayl, 345.

56 Salomon, *Geächteten*, 112.

57 Heinz, "Vorstoß," 68.

58 Ibid., 51.

59 Nord, "Krieg," 69.

60 Heinz, "Vorstoß," 51.

61 Goltz, *Sendung*, 219–20.

62 Heinz, "Vorstoß," 48.
63 Nord, "Krieg," 63.
64 Salomon, *Geächteten*, 108, 69.
65 Nord, "Krieg," 63.
66 Salomon, *Geächteten*, 69, in a chapter entitled "Vormarsch."
67 Nord, "Krieg," 64.
68 Heimdall, "Riga-Marschlied," in *Freikorpskämpfer*, ed. Salomon, 414.
69 Heinz, "Vorstoß," 52.
70 Klaus Theweleit, *Male Fantasies*, trans. Stephan Conway (Minneapolis: University of Minnesota Press, 1987). On sociological implications and fixation on borders: Shannee Marks, *Die Grenze der Schuld. Soziologische Strukturen der faschistischen Ideologie*, Beiträge zur sozialwissenschaftlichen Forschung, 77 (Opladen: Westdeutscher Verlag, 1987).
71 Salomon, *Geächteten*, 84.
72 Ernst von Salomon, "Die Gestalt des deutschen Freikorpskämpfer," in *Freikorpskämpfer*, ed. Salomon, 12.
73 Salomon, *Geächteten*, 72.
74 Salomon, "Die Versprengten," 115.
75 Salomon, *Geächteten*, 66.
76 Nord, "Krieg," 64.
77 Salomon, *Geächteten*, 72; Salomon, "Hexenkessel," 17.
78 Salomon, *Geächteten*, 66.
79 Nord, "Krieg," 66.
80 Schmidt-Pauli, *Freikorps*, 68; Heinz, "Vorstoß," 57; Hartmann, "Erinnerungen," 48.
81 Nord, "Krieg," 77.
82 Hartmann, "Erinnerungen," 42, 148, 264.
83 Ibid., 46; Heinz, "Vorstoß," 53; Hartmann, "Erinnerungen," 161, 162.
84 Rudolf Höß, *Kommandant in Auschwitz. Autobiographische Aufzeichnungen von Rudolf Höß*, (Stuttgart; Deutsche Verlags-Anstalt, 1958), 34–35.
85 Sullivan, "Campaign," 38.
86 Waite, *Vanguard*, 130.
87 Šilietis, *Okupacija*, 156, 171, 155, 183; Puzinas, *Rinktiniai*, 273–80.
88 Salomon, *Geächteten*, 72–73.
89 Quoted in Waite, *Vanguard*, 131.
90 Nord, "Krieg," 92.
91 Hartmann, "Erinnerungen," 163.
92 Sullivan, "Campaign," 41.
93 Waite, *Vanguard*, 137–39.
94 Baron von Manteuffel-Katzdangen, "Die Baltenfahne," in *Freikorpskämpfer*, ed. Salomon, 214.

8   The triumph of *Raum*

The experience of the Eastern Front in the First World War and the ambitions expressed in Ober Ost left a fateful legacy for German views of the East after the war. In the Weimar Republic, certain conclusions were drawn from the experience and given durable form in political agitation and propaganda, and after the Nazis seized power in 1933, they put a radicalized myth of the East into violent action as an integral part of their ideology and foreign policy aims.

The front experience of the East and its perceived "lessons" are crucial to any estimation of Germany's loss in the First World War. Most basically, events there touched great numbers of people. Besides 2 or 3 million men at the Eastern Front or working in occupied territories, many more at home participated vicariously through the propaganda of Ober Ost and annexationists. After the war, veterans at local taverns and family gatherings shared their memories with others. In the decades that followed Ober Ost administrators met in Berlin for reunions, often attended by Hindenburg and at first by Ludendorff, remembering their "war work."[1] Experiences were also reworked in print, as veterans wrestled with the meaning of what had happened to them, producing a whole genre of "soldierly literature."[2] Countless writers held up the Great War as a transformative experience, with a "new man" forged in the trenches of the West, under the pounding of mechanized warfare.[3] Jünger's popular writings gave heroic interpretations to the slaughter: *In Storms of Steel* (1920) and *Battle as an Inner Experience* (1922). Remarque's *All Quiet on the Western Front* (1928), though in far more equivocal terms, also announced a new, transformed, and damaged generation and a new age. Writers mythologizing the trenches were of widely different political orientations, but they shared a myth, using the experience to develop generational politics, whether of the right or left.

Just as the eastern front-experience was distinct from that of the West, the way in which it was understood and mythologized afterwards also showed great contrasts. In comparison, literature on the eastern front-experience was curiously muted. The most acclaimed novel was Arnold

Zweig's *The Case of Sergeant Grischa* (1927), drawing directly on his experiences in Ober Ost's administration. It condemned the structures of state power, extending their domination over individuals under cover of war.[4] The novel was very popular in Germany and internationally, and was even made into a movie. If Zweig's novel was an eastern parallel to Remarque's work, then Jünger's impulse to mythologize and celebrate combat was echoed by Walter Flex's *The Wanderer Between Both Worlds*, but with significant differences.[5] While Jünger exulted in the new storm trooper, radiating vitality and steely definition, Flex's experience was more ambiguous. His popular book (first published in 1917, it went through thirty-nine editions, selling a quarter of a million copies in less than two years) was dedicated to his comrade Ernst Wurche, an idealistic *Wandervögel* killed in the East.[6] Its theme was the wandering between natural and supernatural worlds, in which the East appeared as a ghostly landscape haunted by loss. Where Jünger in the end reasserted brutal vitality, Flex's book was given a different moral by the death of the author himself in the storming of the Baltic island of Oesel in 1917. Flex was buried in "German earth" near a castle of the Teutonic Knights, far in the East, like his friend Wurche. Thus, while the western front-experience found meaning in the creation of a new man of steel, any redemptive value of the eastern front-experience was lost in the confusion of distant lands, historical memories, unfulfilled visions of settlement and *Kultur*.

Ultimately, however, works of literature were less authoritative than the memoirs of Hindenburg and Ludendorff (though unacknowledged fiction was a strong element here too), in presenting compelling versions of what the venture in the East meant. Ludendorff's instant memoirs, published in 1919, were crucial. Printed in large editions, they were reworked into condensed "people's editions" for wider circulation.[7] After depicting the effort armies invested in chaotic lands and ungrateful peoples, Ludendorff proclaimed, in what seemed his definitive verdict on "German Work" in the East, "The work has not been in vain. It had at least been useful to the homeland, army, and the land itself during the war. Whether seeds remain in the ground and later will bear fruit, that is a question of our hard fate, which only the future can answer."[8] If mythologizing of the Eastern Front was more ambivalent than in the West, it was in part because its conclusions were held in abeyance, awaiting later political developments and possible revisions.

War in the East lacked the West's sense of "closure," yet the German public drew a set of specific conclusions or "lessons" from the experience of the East. The most obvious conclusion was the popular perception that Germany had in fact won the war in the East. Only later did

incomprehensible events rob Germany of its eastern conquests. Wartime annexationist fantasies made this conclusion even more enormously bitter. As Golo Mann points out, "Brest-Litovsk has been called the
forgotten peace, but the Germans have not forgotten it. They know that
they defeated Russia and sometimes they look upon this proudly as the
real, if unrewarded European achievement of the war."[9] If war in the
East was won, how to explain the eventual loss? The same question was
asked on the Western Front, where German leaders welcomed troops
home as "undefeated on the battlefield." The result was the myth of
the "Stab in the Back," claiming that the home front's weakness and
perfidy caused Germany's defeat. This same society supposedly met
returning soldiers with abuse rather than gratitude (the reality was in
fact different).[10] In thinking about the East, Germans assimilated a
similar legend at one remove. After the war, those natives who had been
(it was believed) so generously cultivated stood in a very different relation to the defeated Germans.[11] Now independent and asserting their
own statehood, they provoked shame and fury in their erstwhile custodians. Afterwards, one Ober Ost official considered that the real mistake
had been Germans' "addiction to being schoolmasters in their treatment of foreign peoples."[12] Von Gayl declared that "in the area of
culture, in fact, too much of a good thing was done."[13] Officials doubted the newly independent states' viability. The former chief of the
Baltic administration called them "people with little cultural development" who must gravitate towards Germany, since "what culture Latvians and Estonians have is of German origin."[14] All this implied that
natives somehow bore responsibility for what happened, a resentful intuition worsened by the fact that the order which the army sought to
carry eastwards was lost at home in the November Revolution, when it
seemed that the East's contagion flooded Germany, as the army disintegrated. By one post war account, the "humiliating collapse of the
Eastern army is the darkest chapter of the entire war," ascribing it in
part to the demoralizing effect on soldiers of working at nonmilitary
duties in occupied territories and the influence of natives (Jews were
singled out for special blame) and Bolshevik ideas soldiers picked up
from them.[15] Germany had also been stabbed in the back by the dangerous occupied East, it seemed.

The second lesson, following from the first, was that the East was
threatening. The view eastwards was now even more charged by fear of
Bolshevism. Revolution in Germany, street-fighting and unrest on the
Bolshevik model, seemed to be a deluge of eastern chaos. Bolshevism
represented a competing model for ordering of lands and peoples to the
East, a different blueprint for the future. A new element was thus added

Map 5 Postwar Eastern Europe in the 1920s

to the earlier complex of German popular pictures of Russia, laid along-side traditional images of repression, filth, and chaos. After the war, this fear was seconded elsewhere in Western Europe, and given concrete form in diplomatic ventures of building a "*Cordon Sanitaire*" around the Soviet Union, to contain its spreading revolutionary internationalism.

A third lesson emphasized the importance of borders. The wartime obsession with borders returned in a new form. In the Weimar Republic it became a central topic in political agitation. *Irridenta*, "unredeemed" territories, were crucial issues all across a new Europe of redrawn states, stranded minority populations, and new boundaries. In Germany, the issue of frontiers and "bleeding borders" was used in education and politicized, Germans urged never to forget that they had been stripped of 10 percent of their population and 13 percent of their territory by a settlement ostensibly enshrining national self-determination. Across social and political divisions, a broad consensus among Germans rejected the new borders. The continuity of this revisionist striving ran all through Weimar foreign policy.[16] A renewed feeling of "encirclement" became current, so that some historians of the period speak of a "mass claustrophobia" in Weimar Germany. In journalism and popular literature, Germany's condition was depicted as stifling narrowness produced by the loss of territories. A study of political map-making shows how geographers and activists grew skilled in producing maps illustrating the wrongs of the Paris settlement, as "the discourse of German self-determination became thoroughly cartographic." The propaganda methods of these maps, often attributed to the Nazis, were in fact inherited from this earlier nationalist mobilization, reflecting how "much of the expansionism of the Nazi state had been made palatable and convincing to the public as early as the 1920s," laying the groundwork for later aggression.[17] Yet concern for borders applied not only to provinces split off from Germany, but extended beyond to former occupied territories, where German soldiers had fought, died, and were buried. A "cult of the dead soldier" grew up in all combatant countries, expressed in tending of war graves and the institution of the Tomb of the Unknown Soldier.[18] But the German variant was different, not only because of its doubly sorrowful intensity following on defeat, but also because Germans had fought the Great War on enemy soil, where countless graves of their young dead now lay. The idea was tried out that now Germany extends as far as her cemeteries, to lands soaked with the blood of German soldiers. This argument originated during the war, in annexationist slogans, when propagandists cried that territories in which Germans bled must come to Germany; otherwise their sacrifices had been meaningless. It now took on a life of its own. In an elaboration of the mindscape of the East, some monument planners imagined a ring of what came to be called *Totenburgen*, huge memorial "Castles of the Dead" around Germany's territories and fronts (a tradition taken up by the Nazis).[19] These fantastic projects were inspired by the national monument to Tannenberg, which seemed a gigantic haunted castle of the Teutonic Knights. Dedicated in a symbol-laden nationalist ceremony in 1927, this fortress-like structure of stark towers and high walls (with a large arena for military reviews) was intended to serve as final resting place of the battle's hero, now Reich president, von Hindenburg (he was indeed buried there in 1935), surrounded by the graves of his soldiers in the East.[20] Obsession for borders and this cult fused in the Weimar Republic. Earlier claims to "owning" land were now also based on the dead there. Walter Flex's story of paladins lying in "German ground" far to the East presented unredeemed promises. Already powerful concerns, borders and the cult of the war dead together acquired even more emotional significance.

Above all, one central lesson was learned from failed plans for structuring, framing, and ordering the East: instead of planning for cultural development of lands (as was done in Ober Ost, for all the cynical calculation involved in those projects), the East was to be viewed more objectively and coldly, in terms of *Raum*, "space." At first, conquest in 1915 brought awareness of how variegated these "lands and peoples" were, but defeat produced a visceral opposite reaction. With the failure of plans to "manage" that variety, the East's diversity collapsed in popular imagination as well. Defeat and humiliation led to rejection of the earlier awareness, until the East was no longer a complicated, varied pattern of languages, ethnicities, histories. It now seemed an undifferentiated East, a chaotic and dirty expanse where unmanageable, intrinsically backward, and unclean populations lurked, all part of some vast, threatening presence: the "*Ost*." A crucial transformation was completed, as the terms of "*Land und Leute*," "lands and peoples," for regarding the East were overthrown, while new operative terms took their place, another resonant pairing: "*Volk und Raum*," "race and space." "*Volk*," now intoned to stress the term's racial sense, reduced "foreign peoples" to carriers of unchangeable ethnic essences. Their territories, meanwhile, were no longer understood as "lands," areas with history and internal coherence, organization, and meaning all their own. Instead, the category of "*Land*" was replaced by a stark, "neutral" concept of *Raum*. Emptied of historical content, *Raum* was triumphantly ahistorical, biological, and "scientific." Empty *Raum* stretched to the eastern horizon, dotted only by scattered races.

A decisive conceptual barrier was broken by this formulation of "*Volk und Raum*." Now the lands and peoples were stripped of any legitimate claim to independent existence and stood bare as objects and numbers, resources to be exploited and exhausted. This fateful conceptual breakthrough yielded the central lesson of the experience of war in the East. The imperative of the future had to be: leave out the peoples and take the spaces. The flaw in the project of German Work in the East lay not in its planning or the terms of the occupation. Rather, the fault had to be found in the nature of foreign populations which the occupiers had so generously taken under their tutelage. "*Raum*" was the crucial concept here in understanding how to again move to encounter the East, providing a program in one word. "*Raum*" itself is in some sense untranslatable, because of the crucial charge and associations it carries in German.

To translate it as "space" in English misses the ways in which the word acts. It is simultaneously expansive and yet delimiting. It also has the meaning "to clear," "to clean," "evacuate" – "*räumen.*" This semantic shift was crucial, as thinking in terms of *Raum* was not just a description, but yielded a program of clearing and cleansing. *Raum* opened a whole new horizon of possibilities, as the word made terrible options "thinkable."[21]

Raum became an important concern in the Weimar period, soon ubiquitous in literature and thought. Popularizing geographer Ewald Banse's *Space and Race in the World War* (1932) attempted to draw out the lessons of the war in these terms (and provoked international furor over its publishing).[22] The political mystic Moeller van den Bruck's writings, among them *The Third Reich*, a culmination of conservative cultural pessimism, envisioned the West's collapse and a new German destiny linked with the East's *Raum und Volk.*[23] Of greatest impact, however, was Hans Grimm's best-selling novel, *Volk ohne Raum*, "The Race Without Space," going through large editions (first published in 1926, five years later more than quarter of a million copies had appeared).[24] In it, the German hero escapes Germany's narrow confines for the colonies, in search of space. Yet he discovers that the British control the space there as well, and returns to Germany, in despair over the *Raum* problem (only to be killed by a Social Democrat, as he tries to spread the gospel of space at home). Using the title as a slogan, Germany's right wing found in *Raum* a way to bring together under one heading a host of modern anxieties: the effects of industrialization, urbanization, class fragmentation, and Germany's weakness in world politics. Indeed, the book's title itself had more impact than the narrative, a potent catchphrase entering common usage.

These concerns and conclusions found institutional expression in two new "sciences" of the Weimar period, geopolitics and "*Ostforschung,*" "East research." Geopolitics treated peoples and states as organisms, absolutely subject to Darwinian laws. It grew out of geography, and may be dated from the 1896 publication of Friedrich Ratzel's article "The Laws of the Spatial Growth of States." The state was to be regarded as an organism, subject to natural laws. Ratzel isolated seven laws for the natural expansion of states. As mere expressions of these dynamic laws, boundaries were neither permanent nor formal political demarcations. Rather, they were lines and fields of force along which states grew or shrank, according to their health. To be healthy, states needed expansive geographic, or "spatial," consciousness. While Ratzel intended the state-organism image as a metaphor, rather than as literal truth, his personal caution counted for little. The idea caught on in a cruder form, as did his term *"Lebensraum,"* "living space," describing the area a race or state needed to survive or grow.

Other geopolitical conceptions were abroad at the turn of the century and found eager reception in Germany. American Alfred Mahan emphasized the decisive dynamics of modern sea power. From England, Halford Mackinder's deterministic "new geography" was summed up in his famous later aphorism, that control of Eastern Europe was the key to the Heartland (central Eurasia), which in turn dominated the World Island (Eurasia). Mahan and Mackinder both seemed to Wilhelmine *Weltpolitik* publicists to ratify German claims for international influence commensurate with their economic strength, providing sanction for energetic *Weltpolitik*. Swedish political scientist Rudolf Kjellen synthesized these ideas of geopolitics (indeed coining the term) at the beginning of the new century. They now came into their own, seized upon by a Germany seemingly on the threshold of domination of *Mitteleuropa*. During the conflict, war geography promoted new, expansive geographical consciousness, but was left at loose ends with defeat and German territorial losses. In the Weimar period, geopolitics sought to adapt this outlook to changed circumstances.

The prophet of the new geopolitics was Karl Haushofer. Major General Haushofer taught geography at the University of Munich after the war, launching an energetic campaign for his views. An Institute of Geopolitics was announced there, and the popularizing *Zeitschrift für Geopolitik* began publication in 1924. In 1931 the Working Group for Geopolitics was established, encouraged by Haushofer's pupil Rudolf Hess and Nazi agricultural expert Walter Darré. Haushofer spoke at public gatherings and on the radio about once a month between 1922 and 1939, while also publishing a constant stream of books. Building on Ratzel, Mackinder, and Kjellen, Haushofer flatly asserted that one-fourth of all reality was geographic. According to him, "Geopolitics wants to be, and must be, the geographic conscience of the state." Geopolitics, then, was the study of *Raum* for the state.

With such effective self-promotion, geopoliticians sought to secure a place of influence in the service of the coming total state, making expansive claims for their field's future. It offered ready-made justifications for aggressive foreign policy and a strategic emphasis on war was at the very core of its discipline, as *"Wehr-Geopolitik,"* a transmuted version of "War Geography." Geopolitics promised not only rhetorical arguments, but also crucial information, as geopoliticians concentrated on two goals: massive collection of information for planning, and propaganda to promote their interpretive tool. Their efforts spoke to Germany's present condition and how it might be changed. Haushofer's *Borders and Their*

Geographical and Political Significance (1927) captured the postwar obsession with borders, emphasizing that they were changeable, shaped by political forces and geographic consciousness.[25] Geopolitics was uniquely successful at capturing themes of discontent in the Weimar Republic, giving them territorial expression.

The intellectual influence of geopolitics on the German public was out of all proportion to its institutional or academic importance. It seemed to give a technical, scientific seal of approval to strivings for territorial revision and more expansive plans. *"Raum"* and *"Raum* consciousness" turned into powerful mobilizing concepts. Perhaps the most striking propaganda success lay in the innovative use of maps pioneered by Haushofer. He outlined new conventions for political maps, drawn boldly to emphasize a single aim. Whereas geographers traditionally sought objective renderings of conditions on the ground, geopoliticians' maps, full of dynamic arrows, stark contrasts of blocks of color, and simplified symbols, were programs. With such drawings, geopolitics transformed the terms by which Germans considered their political situation. Geopoliticians, journalists, and activists for ethnic Germans living abroad cultivated a geographic hysteria, a mass claustrophobia in the Weimar Republic, by which resentment for both the humiliating Versailles settlement and Germany's democratic government associated with it were given territorial expression and directed outwards.[26]

Another "science" turned its attention to the East: *Ostforschung*, "East research."[27] Supposedly impartial multidisciplinary academic work on ethnography, archaeology, and history was placed in the service of revision of borders in the East and claims to land. University institutes of *Ostforschung* and study associations used "ethnocentric geopolitical and cultural-geographical concepts" to build larger arguments for continuing the German mission in the East. An extensive interdisciplinary effort of important sections of academia aimed at "little more than supplying the detailed evidence to substantiate the political claims represented by these concepts."[28]

A key idea uniting geopolitics, "East research," and their popularized versions in right-wing politics was *"Boden,"* "ground" or "soil." A *"Boden"* vocabulary grew up in the sciences, first articulated by Albrecht Penck, professor of geography at the University of Berlin. Drawing on Ratzel's formulation of the "German *Kultur* landscape," land shaped to a "German character," Penck defined different kinds of land: *"Staatsboden," "Volksboden,"* and *"Kulturboden."*[29] Each term represented claims to land shaped by German Work in those territories which Germany had lost after the First World War. *"Boden"* became a central concept or slogan in these "sciences."[30] For the public of a defeated

Germany, geopolitics offered the key concept of "space" for understanding its current situation, while *Ostforschung* pointed towards efforts to change the situation eastwards.

The mindscape of the East brought home from the First World War and reworked in Weimar was an important legacy for the Nazis and their ideological goals of transforming the German people. Historians have looked for the roots of Nazism in intellectual history and pedigrees of "völkish" thought. Yet the number of concerns Nazism claimed to address seemed endless and often mutually contradictory. In some sense, indeed, this was a conscious strategy, for the movement's welter of statements drew in discontented people by seeming to address one of their particular concerns. Thus, Hitler's own *Mein Kampf* was not so much a consistently and coherently argued treatise, but rather a jumble of pronouncements most easily read from the index backwards (some mass editions, in fact, began with the index for ease of reference).[31] Yet Nazis claimed to be a "movement," distinguished by a worldview. This claim needs to be taken literally (in spite of the skepticism of Golo Mann and others) in its crassest sense.[32] While the movement lacked a totally systematic, coherent internal content, it propagated particular categories of perception and practice: ways of looking at the world. Among those categories of perception and practice, important ones were inherited from the eastern front-experience. Ober Ost's categories and practices were taken up again and radicalized: the gaze toward the East, cleansing violence, planning, subdivision and "intensification of control," forced labor. Chief among them was the lesson of *Raum*.

Obviously, there were many other central elements to the Nazi program, some born of the First World War, others with much older pedigrees: anti-Semitism, mystical German völkisch nationalism, a Social-Darwinist outlook on the world as an arena of never-ending struggle, biological racism, leader worship, hatred of Communism, the militarization of politics, irrationalism, and facist ideas of revitalized national communities. These elements were all part of the Nazi message – in the teleology of the Nazi worldview, the East was where many of these ideas would be realized, determining the future.

War for living space in the East was half of Hitler's program from the first, and stood in intimate relation to the other half, his anti-Semitism and racism.[33] After the 1923 Beer Hall Putsch, Hitler systematized his views in writing *Mein Kampf* while in prison, where Haushofer visited him, bringing a copy of Ratzel's *Political Geography*. Haushofer and his pupil, Hess, provided Hitler with geopolitical concepts, including the central concern of "living space," *Lebensraum*, as a tool to explain Germany's failure in the First World War, its perilous present situation, and future possibilities. Hitler opened *Mein Kampf* with a statement of his long-term goals. He believed that destiny had determined his birth in a border town in Austria, a periphery where issues of national identity were present in all their immediacy. This gave him his mission of uniting Germans in one state, and then seeking living space beyond its borders: "after the Reich's borders include the last German, and no longer can offer a secure food supply, the need of the *Volk* gives the moral right to gain foreign land and soil. The plow is then the sword, and from the tears of war will grow daily bread for the world to come."[34] Borders were not natural or given, but merely temporary limitations set on "living space."[35] With a view to "military-geographical considerations," the state's borders and *Raum* had to be expanded: "ground and soil are the goals of our foreign policy."[36] Internal consolidation in Germany would be followed by imperialist expansion.[37] For this expansion, Hitler rejected overseas colonization, instead looking east: "If one wanted ground and soil in Europe, then this could happen, by and large, only at Russia's expense – then the new Reich would have to set itself to march on the road of the Knights of the Teutonic Order of yore – with the German sword for the German plow, for the Nation, however, to gain daily bread."[38] The coming Nazi regime would "direct the gaze toward the land of the East. We finally close the politics of colonialism and trade and go over to the politics of soil of the future."[39] It initiated an "*Ostpolitik* in the sense of gaining the necessary land for our German *Volk*."[40] The target of Nazi *Ostpolitik* was above all the Soviet Union. Russia, Hitler claimed, had been built by a "racial core" of "Germanic organizers and lords," since the "lower races" of the East were incapable of such work on their own (this argument had already surfaced in Ober Ost's programs). For Hitler, the Bolshevik state represented the final dissolution of Russia's Germanic racial core, replaced by a ruling class of Jewish revolutionaries. Since they did not possess German genius for organization, but were instead a "ferment of decomposition," the "giant empire in the East is ripe for collapse."[41] Scholars practicing psychological history make a compelling case that the impetus behind Hitler's eastward orientation was part of a widely shared popular urge to reenact the First World War, with a new ending in place of the disaster and shame that followed.[42] Yet even as Hitler harnessed this public will, his own plans extended far beyond the goal of "correcting" the outcome of the last war, passing instead to the vision of a racial utopia. In Hitler's brutal biological conception of life as war, permanent war in the East was both inevitable and desirable. It would speed the way for the larger plan in his *Ostpolitik*, which Hitler expressed in 1932:

Our great experimental field is in the East. There the new European social order will arise, and this is the great significance of our Eastern policy. Certainly we shall admit to our new ruling class, members of other nations who have been worthy in our cause . . . In fact, we shall very soon have overstepped the bounds of the narrow nationalism of today. World empires arise on a national basis, but very quickly they leave it far behind.[43]

War in the East was to transform German national identity itself in a fundamental way, leading it away from earlier conceptions to a stark racial definition. In place of Herder's national criteria of language and accumulated folk tradition, Hitler set the destiny of biology.

Hitler's disposition toward the East (though it should be noted that he himself only fought on the Western Front) was both shared and influenced by other Nazis from the movement's first days. Over time, that program evolved out of the ambiguous relationship of radical conservatives to the East, a mixture of fear and traditional Russophilia, evidenced in their brief flirtation with National Bolshevism. In *Mein Kampf*, Hitler vigorously condemned this tepid "East orientation," insisting instead on his own "*Ostpolitik*." The case of Moeller van den Bruck was a prime example of this radicalizing process. During the war, van den Bruck fought in the East. Afterwards, in his work *The Third Reich*, he called for a turn toward the East and the unlimited possibilities latent in its "spaces and races." Early Nazis took up his concepts (as well as his book's title), but turned them to a different program. The former architect of Ober Ost, Ludendorff, lent the movement his support in its early days. Other contributions were made by Baltic Germans, who played important roles in the beginnings of the Nazi party. Above all, Hitler admired them for their clannishness and air of superiority over others, "as if the rest of humanity were composed exclusively of Latvians."[44] Most notable in this group was Alfred Rosenberg, the young movement's leading philosopher, who energetically pushed a mission in the East, arguing from his personal experience of growing up in those lands. Rosenberg was born in Estonia and studied in Riga and Moscow. He asserted that such culture as the East had was created by those of Germanic race. Bolshevism, under Jewish leadership, represented the collapse of those achievements and now threatened Germany, Rosenberg believed. A fellow Baltic German, Max Erwin von Scheubner-Richter, called by one historian "the great mystery man of early Nazi history," also played a role in the earliest stages of Nazi *Ostpolitik*.[45] During the war, he headed Ober Ost's press section in Riga. Scheubner-Richter, with his extensive social and political connections and ties to Ludendorff and the new army, helped the fledgling movement to the beginnings of respectability. Another historian surmises that it was through Scheubner-Richter, who also served as vice-consul in

Turkey, that Hitler learned of the Armenian massacres. Years later, during the Second World War, Hitler would disdainfully demand, "Who remembers the Armenian Massacres? Thus, it will be the same with the Jews."[46] Scheubner-Richter was killed between Hitler and Ludendorff during the failed 1923 putsch, which he is believed to have organized. Another Baltic-German friend of his and Rosenberg's, Arno Schickedanz, who served under Scheubner-Richter in Ober Ost, went on to become a Nazi ideologist and administrator in the occupied East.[47] Baltic-German views on the East found echoes in other important party personages. The Nazi spokesman on agriculture, Richard Walter Darré, later head of the SS Race and Settlement Office, cultivated the mysteries of "*Blut und Boden,*" "blood and soil," another coinage expressing the idea of race and space, in his writings in the late 1920s, and later in practice. The most important case was that of SS chief Heinrich Himmler. In 1921, after hearing a talk by General von der Goltz, leader of the Baltikum adventure, he was converted to ecstatic visions of war in the East.[48] Because of their shared first name, Himmler came to believe that he was a reincarnation of Henry of Saxony, the medieval leader of the German *Drang nach Osten.*[49] During the Second World War, Himmler moved from theory to practice, expanding his own SS empire in the East, where he could realize the utopias of the regime.

After coming to power in 1933, official Nazi propaganda and education aimed to instill a sense of mission in the *Raum* of the East. Scholarship on propaganda points out that indoctrination proves most effective when building on a set of already established predispositions, views, and prejudices.[50] Nazi propaganda built on a consensus in public opinion rejecting the borders drawn in the East at Versailles, a sense of Germany's threatened geographical position, and ideas about the East formed during the First World War. Hitler's foreign policy moves abrogating the Versailles Treaty were broadly welcomed. However, the Nazis sought more than acceptance of modest revisions; they aimed at a larger agenda under the slogan of *Lebensraum.*

Nazi propaganda pressed the case for expansion in the East. As was their peculiar talent, the Nazis were perhaps most successful in turning language to their uses, channeling it into the categories which they defined (as was recognized by philologist Victor Klemperer, a former Ober Ost soldier, in his study *LTI*). The mission in the East was written into the language itself.[51] An entire vocabulary grew up around the "*Ost*" concept: *Ostraum, Ostarbeit, Osteinsatz, Osthilfe, Ostarbeiter.* Most of all, *Lebensraum* became a firmly established key word. It is testimony to the durability of such semantic "achievements" that some of these words retain their currency today, although with altered meanings (thus, German magazines today carry advertisements referring to *Lebensraum*, but now referring to designs for spacious family living rooms). Some propaganda explicitly looked back to the advances in Eastern Europe in the past war. Especially telling is a booklet of the "League of the German East," emblazoned with a map of Germany's eastern borders (with revisions marked with dotted lines) and a swastika superimposed on a Teutonic black and white cross coat of arms. Entitled "German Work in Poland and Lithuania During the World War," it announced that states now existing to Germany's east were in fact creations of German wartime policies, when it was necessary to "create out of nothing," except insofar as German colonists and culture had influenced these lands in previous centuries.[52] Ober Ost's rule blessed the area through its economic policies, construction projects, and *Kulturarbeit* of custodianship (which astonishingly revealed traces of "German *Kultur* influence of bygone days"). Further, the booklet emphasized German health measures in an area which "even in peacetime was infected with all varieties of disease, above all smallpox, spotted fever, and typhus." The health policies were a "great deed of German organizational work." Their "cleansing actions were directed on the one hand at the streets and houses, on the other hand at the people." It was noted that this "forced cleaning, i.e. the delousing of the population" displeased some natives (the booklet singled out eastern Jews). The pamphlet concluded that chances of a "German ordering of the East-space [*Ostraum*]" slipped away because of irresolute German national policy, leaving benefits of German Work to fall to foreign states. The "German task" of the future would be to achieve this ordering, now that Germans were a "race united in National Socialism."[53]

Seeking to instill ideas of a mission in the East, Nazis concentrated on youth. A new generation could more easily be won for that goal than those who still remembered the Great War's suffering. In schools, traditional subjects were rewritten and instrumentalized, with history and geography, in particular, turned to Nazi purposes. A complicated and multifaceted historical phenomenon like the "Drive to the East" of medieval settlement and emigration was twisted out of context to suit the Nazis' more aggressive vision, presented as a biological phenomenon.[54] Geography lessons cultivated new ways of looking at land, as "*Erdkunde*" focused on *Raum* and invoked "Blood and Soil." Word problems in subjects were again set in military terms.[55] The Nazi Teachers' League established study groups to prepare teachers in geopolitical instruction. Teaching guides outlined new requirements, bringing in geopolitics, terrain games, and "patriotic instruction."[56] School educational films stressed these themes. In its reports on the morale of the country, the Nazi Security Service (SD) noted successes in this area.[57]

In Nazi youth organizations, indoctrination on *Raum* and the East intensified. Youth organizations and schools took up trends in the curriculum of the First World War and war geography. Renewed "terrain-games" were of special importance for Hitler Youth.[58] Boys "learned camouflage and how to write combat messages (when, where, who, how), use a compass, and read maps. These exercises culminated a few times a year in the so-called *grosse Geländespiele*," including hundreds of boys.[59] In schools, it was noted that a special merit of such exercises was that "reading material on the Great War is put into action."[60] At the same time, films and books pressed the regime's views of the First World War. Boys accepted the "Stab in the Back" legend, read avidly Jünger's *Storm of Steel* and Edwin Erich Dwinger's Freikorps novel, *The Last Riders*. Meanwhile, Zweig's novel, *The Case of Sergeant Grischa*, was thrown onto bonfires, along with Remarque's *All Quiet on the Western Front*. As during the First World War, boys played grandiose "map games." One recalled later that "we cultivated this popular game of map reading also on a global scale." During the first years of the Second World War, that game continued with even more earnest enthusiasm. With huge conquests in the East, a former Hitler Youth recalled, the future of these lands was a "frequent subject of discussion among us." Utopian visions of soldier-farmer settlements "in the Ural mountains two thousand miles east of their homeland" and new German living space offered in Nazi magazines left strong impressions.[61]

Much youth activity centered on the institution of the *Lager*, the camp. It was a crucial institution on the Eastern Front, a German strong point in foreign surroundings for men realizing Wallenstein's "empire of soldiers." After their return to Germany, Freikorps leaders tried to keep their men together in work groups and agricultural camps, antecedents to the Nazi Work Service (*Arbeitsdienst*). The *Lager* offered a model of social organization for the *Volk* community which the dictatorship aimed to create. The regime took young people away from their families to the *Lager*. One former Hitler Youth afterwards reflected:

Many years later in conversations with friends and acquaintances, I sometimes said jokingly that our generation spent more of its formative years from the age of ten to eighteen in camps, tents, and barracks than in the bourgeois surroundings of our parents' homes. In examining this statement now more closely and seriously, it becomes clear to me that it was not just a joke, that it comes fairly close to the truth. When I add up the months and years . . . I arrive at the astounding number of approximately thirty-six months of "camps" in less than eight years.[62]

Youth were taken up by the "*Lager* experience," a world apart. At a later age, the Work Service continued the institution of the *Lager*, celebrating its collective psychological effect.[63]

At their camps, Hitler Youth and German Maidens sang hymns to the "Drive to the East," poems new and old. Former members testify that these songs were among the most important parts of the indoctrination process, but are often overlooked by historians because they are so intangible, largely missing in the historical record.[64] The repertoire of East songs was considerable. Turning history to their own purposes, Nazis set up genealogies for their own modern program of expansion. By singing old songs and repeating older slogans, they asserted historical continuities. Old traditions of Flemish colonists were placed in a new context:

Ostland Song

1. To the Ostland we want to ride, we want to come along to Ostland – Well over the green heath, fresh over the heath, there is a better place for us.
2. When we come into the Ostland, into the house high and fine – There will we be let in, fresh over the heath, one bids us welcome.[65]

The archaic song of Flemish settlers, however, had to be rewritten, reading doctrines of "plow and sword" back into it in a new version:

The Ostland trekkers

Now the wide land grows too narrow, the ground too hard.
There the morning dawns like a fire for a good journey.
To the Ostland travels the wind! Therefore, wife and child and bonds-man and household,
Onto the wagons and to horse! We hunger for fresh earth and sense the good wind.
The home country burns bright and strong in our blood.
We will build her a new *Mark* [border land] for good protection.
The foreign wilderness does not frighten us with falseness and deceit –
We will give it a German face with sword and plow! To the East blows the wind!

Other new songs hit all of the themes of the mindscape of the East which grew out of the eastern front-experience of the First World War:

In the East Wind Raise the Flags

1. In the East wind raise the flags, for in the East wind they stand well – Then they command to break camp, and our blood hears the call. For a land gives us the answer, and it bears a German face – Many have bled for it, and therefore the ground cannot be still.
2. In the East wind raise the flags, let them go along new streets, Let them draw new streets, that they may see old homeland. For a land gives us the answer, and it bears a German face – Many have bled for it, and therefore the ground cannot be still.

3. In the East wind raise the flags, for they flutter for a new journey. Make yourselves strong! He who builds in the East is spared no trouble. But a land gives us the answer, and it bears a German face – Many have bled for it, and therefore the ground cannot be still.
4. In the East wind raise the flags, for the East wind makes them full – There there is an act of building, which is greater than time. And a land gives us the answer, and it bears a German face – Many have bled for it, and therefore the ground cannot be still.

The song raised all the themes of *Verkehrspolitik*, building in the East, transformation of the landscape through German Work. This particular song, written by Nazi poet Hans Baumann, was part of a much larger creation of his entitled "The Call From the East," of alternating choruses, typical of Nazi theatre productions called *Thingspiele*. His larger work spoke of a new march to the East by a reinvigorated German race taking up the "gaze towards the East" to "build a road into the new land" (which, however, the poem claimed had been German in ages past), fighting to extend the Reich's borders as far as their desire extends, settling and shaping the good earth "which has never borne seeds." Germany's future rose like the sun in the East, dedicated to the drive to the East, directed there like a great flood coursing along its "riverbed into immortality."

Other songs presented the East, without bothering with such specific aims, as an elemental, spiritual goal:

To the Ostland Goes Our Ride

1. To the Ostland goes our ride, high waves the banner in the wind, the stallions tramp swiftly.
    Up, brothers, forces tensed – we ride out into new land.
2. Away with care and grief! Out of narrowness and mugginess!
    The wind swirls about us cool, blood hammers in the veins, we trot with joyful courage.
3. The storm rages loudly out there, we ride despite wailing and complaint,
    we ride by night and by day, a house gathered together, to the Ostland goes our ride!

Advancing eastwards was presented as a possibility for release from confinement at home, while pledging alliegance to the movement leading Germany's youth there.

Education to "spatial consciousness" and the mission in the East reflected the wider triumph of *Raum* as a concept of the regime. Ultimately, these exercises and practices did more than provide a program or set of aims. They did something far larger, building categories in people's heads, organizing ways of thinking and looking, those categories through which the world was perceived, understood, and approached. The professed aim of this reeducation was empowering *"Raum* thinking." Such as it was, then, the Nazi movement's intellectual coherence was to be found not only in doctrines, but also in categories of practice and perception. Perhaps the best illustration of this is the paradoxical situation of the "science" of geopolitics and its fortunes in the Nazi state. Geopolitical thinking took on enormous significance as a mode of thinking, providing concepts which became current in popular thought. Yet at the same time, the "scholars" who eagerly provided those concepts remained locked in institutional impotence, their concrete advice ignored (for instance, geopoliticans' warnings against war on Russia). After providing crucial concepts, geopoliticians had little influence on policy built with those concepts. While at first Haushofer seemed to exert considerable intellectual influence, he was reduced to a pawn in deadly Nazi bureaucratic politics, passing from the patronage of Hess to Himmler, finally ending in Dachau concentration camp by war's end. The true significance of geopolitical thought lay not in institutional forms, but in its coherence as a theme in the movement's worldview. Its "scientific" authority could convince people otherwise skeptical of Nazi slogans and make aggressive foreign policy seem inevitable. *"Raum* thinking" was reflected in the image the regime sought to present of itself, especially in monolithic architectural programs, which constructed outsize spaces, dwarfing individuals.[66] Himself a failed architect, Hitler noted, "A sense of spaciousness is important, and I am delighted to see our architects planning on broad and spacious lines."[67]

Raum thinking peaked in a specific "science" and practice of the regime, *Raumordnung*.[68] This "spatial ordering" carried on ambitions implicit in *Verkehrspolitik*. Its aim was to create a comprehensive collection of information [*Raumforschung*] on population, settlement, movement, and land, paving the way for systematic planning all through Germany. The Reich Office for *Raum* Ordering (Reichstelle für Raumordnung) was created in 1935 by a Führer decree and was directly subordinated to Hitler. Among those active in *Raum* ordering, Konrad Meyer stands out.[69] Originally a professor of agriculture, he was pivotal in putting the "science" into practice. He was the author of the infamous "General Plan for the East," laying out the new ordering of the occupied territories.[70] An important subset of Nazi *Raum* ordering was *Verkehrspolitik*, echoed in the fascist cliché "making the trains run on time," Hitler's *Autobahn* program and unrealized visions of huge highways extending east, to the Crimea and Greater Germany's new territories. Within Germany, plans for total registration and classification of the population got underway.[71] *Raum* ordering implied total planning.

But the true triumph of the idea of *Raum* came with the advent of the Second World War in 1939, which fused the ideological concepts of war, space and race, and the East. The Nazi orientation toward the East determined the nature of the new war there, following precedents set down by the imperialist mindscape of the East, influencing how the war itself was conceived. Nazis saw the war in the East not as a traditional war, not something limited, circumscribed by realistic calculations of success. Instead, their vision was apocalyptic in the extreme: war in the East as a process of permanent radicalization. Furious energies were to be unleashed, clearing and cleaning the space for a new order and settlement. Where Ober Ost's slogan had been "German Work," that of the Nazis was simpler and more total, "*Aufbau im Osten*" – "Building in the East."

At a November 1937 conference at the Reich Chancellery, recorded in the "Hossbach Memorandum," Hitler outlined the solution he was preparing for Germany's *Raum* problem. The long-range goal was conquest of living space to the East. Dividing up the East between Germany and Russia was the first step, defining spheres of interest and eliminating states which had arisen in this region between the two powers. On August 23, 1939, the Molotov–Ribbentropp Pact was signed, pledging nonaggression, but fortified with secret clauses carving up Eastern Europe. Germany launched its *Blitzkrieg* attack on Poland on September 1, 1939. Sections of western Poland were split off from the rump General-Gouvernement, and added to Germany as "Incorporated East Territories." On October 7, 1939, Hitler appointed SS chief Himmler as Reich Commissar for the Fortification of Germandom.[72] In this capacity, he would oversee deportations, resettlements, and other measures to consolidate the East's ethnic ordering. Baltic Germans, now in the expanded Soviet sphere of interest, were evacuated and resettled in the East Territories. Jews were targeted for expulsion and concentration in ghettos, awaiting Nazi future plans for their elimination. An epoch of the moving, expulsion, and shuttling of entire ethnic populations began in earnest. Not only the ethnic make-up of newly annexed areas was to be changed, however. The landscape was also to "become German." Himmler promulgated "Landscape Rules," stating that displacing natives with Germans would not suffice, but that "the space must also receive a character corresponding to our way of being so that . . . German man feels at home, becomes sedentary, and is ready to love and defend this his new *Heimat*."[73] While natives had allowed this area to resemble steppe, the new masters would transform it into a "designed *Kultur* landscape," giving it German forms and importing plants considered to be "German." The expansion of Himmler's duties in the East began a long process by which the SS "state within a state" tried to make these areas its preserve for realizing a racial utopia. While Nazis consolidated their control in Poland, Stalin occupied and annexed the Baltic states of Estonia, Latvia, and Lithuania. Caught between these regimes, native peoples at first congratulated themselves bitterly on at least having fallen to the Russians, not to the Germans. Remembering Ober Ost's regime, people contrasted Russian rule, brutal but unsystematic, with the comprehensive, efficient severity of German occupation. The following year of intensifying Stalinist terror and deportations, turned this cold comfort into a crueler joke. New ideological energies abroad in Europe upset calculations based on earlier precedents.

Nazi ambitions for a "final settlement" in the East were set in motion with the largest military campaign in history, Operation Barbarossa. Nearly 4 million German troops massed in preparation for the assault, launched on June 22, 1941, a campaign against what Hitler understood to be a "rotting empire," ripe for defeat in three months. Declared a "war of ideologies," the conflict took on a character very different than the western campaigns. Hitler's "Commissar Order" defined homogenized categories for liquidation: "all Bolshevik agitators, partisans, saboteurs and Jews found behind Russian lines." Combat was ferocious, fueled by and reinforcing Nazi propaganda among German troops.[74] Germans were welcomed as liberators by some civilians in the Ukraine and the Baltic states, where the first great Soviet deportations had taken place only a week before. In the Baltics, German advance was preceded by native uprisings against retreating Soviets. Natives began to establish provisional governments, hoping to repeat the political formula which had allowed them to find room to maneuver towards a final goal of independence during the First World War, but it quickly became clear that they had not understood the intervening changes in the occupiers' ideology. Later attempts to coopt native societies as a whole (rather than finding individual collaborators) as the war turned against the Nazis, met with considerable resistance (for instance, Lithuanian refusal to form a legion under the SS or army led to arrests and executions).[75]

As German soldiers invaded the lands of the Soviet Union, scenes they confronted were in many ways similar to those encountered by their fathers' generation in Ober Ost. Landscapes of devastation again showed hauntingly desolate, dirty, and war-ravaged lands. Again, nature turned out to be as formidable an opponent as enemy troops. For many *Landser*, ordinary foot soldiers, a recent study points out, "Russia seemed less a place than a series of natural disasters."[76] The ferocity of increasingly precarious battles led to "demodernization of the front," preparing the way for increasing Nazi political indoctrination and brutalization of German soldiers, in an effort to compensate for material inferiority.[77] Seen through Nazism's ideological filter, the nature of the fighting, its desperation, and the brutality of their own occupation paradoxically reinforced soldiers' assumptions about the nature of these races and spaces already impressed upon them before the campaign. Jewish populations and other native groups appeared powerless, at the mercy of soldiers, just as propaganda about "subhumans" of these lands announced. Letters home echoed themes heard in Ober Ost: travel through flat and featureless wastelands, meeting subject populations, and expounding above all on the East's dirtiness. Yet, as a recent study points out, there was a significant semantic shift in these letters of the Second World War, when compared to those of the First. Now, dirtiness was much more firmly identified with native populations, in explosions of abusive language. In the Nazi invasion, "no longer were conditions mostly noted, but rather people were denounced," their degraded present state judged an essential part of their character.[78] This fighting in the East, the "climax of the Nazi regime," was, as Omer Bartov notes, a vast "self-fulfilling prophecy" of self-reinforcing ideology and accelerating barbarism.[79] Away from the fighting, behind the lines, SS *Einsatzgruppen*, mobile killing squads, began the Nazi program of genocide against the Jews of Eastern Europe, killing over 1 million in the two-year span of their operation, through mass shootings.

Most territories taken in the great offensive were divided into new Reich Commissariats of Ukraine and a territory named "Ostland," encompassing Estonia, Latvia, Lithuania, and western Belarus. Alfred Rosenberg, named Reich Minister for Occupied Eastern Territories on July 17, 1941, was nominally in command but proved spectacularly ineffective, and the areas became entangled in a chaos of competing offices and branches typical of the Nazi regime. Hinrich Lohse was named Reich Commissar for Ostland in November 1941. His Riga office looked back to Ober Ost and its materials for information, as it also prepared atlases and statistical overviews.[80] Some officials had been active there during or after the First World War, making for continuity in personnel.[81] Like its predecessor, Ostland was soon "celebrating orgies of economic over-organization."[82] Yet, unlike Ober Ost, apart from plans for establishing a German Ostland university to replace native institutions, this new regime paid scant attention to "politics of culture."[83] Since the areas were to be cleared and settled by Germans later, there was little need for such policies, apart from censorship. Ukraine's regime was harsher, under Reich Commissar Erich Koch, who closed down schools and practiced policies infused with hatred for people he saw as "*Untermenschen*." As harsh as immediate measures in the East were, they were merely a first step in a larger plan for a "new ordering."

Outlines of the future envisioned by Nazis for the East emerged in the blueprint of the General Plan for the East (*Generalplan Ost*, or GPO), written by noted *Raum* expert Dr. Konrad Meyer, from the SS Planning Office of the Reich Commissar for the Fortification of Germandom. Himmler reviewed the draft on June 12, 1942. Produced in collaboration with Rosenberg's East Ministry and the Party's Office for Racial Policies, the plan represented the sanctioned Nazi vision of the future East. In administrative language and statistics, it delivered an apocalyptic proposal. Twenty-five years after the war, 31 million in the area were to have been removed to Siberia and decimated. Fourteen million natives of "better racial qualities" were to remain, serving as slave labor for colonists. The occupiers would build a network of German strong points to hold down the territory, pinned by thirty-six settlement hubs of 20,000 inhabitants, each protected by a surrounding ring of villages and connected by military roads. The German racial border would thus be pushed 500 kilometers to the East.[84]

This blueprint, produced under SS direction, also portended the advance of the SS empire in the East. In the chaos of administration, SS encroachments continued and its growth intensified as the military situation worsened. The SS asserted its dominance most clearly by making itself the executor of the Final Solution, the program of genocide against the Jews. The program was outlined at the January 20, 1942 Wannsee Conference, where representatives of the agencies involved met to consider implementation of the program. Europe's Jews were to be shifted to the East, worked to death at road building, and survivors exterminated.[85] But the program of racial annihilation in fact took precedence over economic and construction plans, and centered on the factories of the death, the "destruction *Lager*." Himmler outlined his further plans for developments in the East. Ultimately, native populations were not to be subjugated and preserved. Now, the purpose was to conquer lands, not peoples. In 1942, Himmler insisted, "Our duty in the East is not germanization in the former sense of the term, that is, imposing German language and laws upon the population, but to ensure that only people of pure German blood inhabit the East."[86] There was no need for edicts on education such as Hindenburg had issued. In fact, lavishing German Work on natives was dangerous: "It is a crime against our blood to worry about them and give them ideals," as this would make later rule more difficult.[87] For the immediate future, native populations were only to be taught obedience to the *Herrenvolk* master race. Himmler declaimed, "We are not bringing these people civilization," and said that it would be enough if "children learn to read the traffic signs so that they do not run under vehicles," how to write their names and count up to twenty-five.[88]

Natives would merely provide labor to build a racial utopia in the East, for as Himmler explained coldly, "Whether nations live in prosperity or starve to death interests me only insofar as we need them as slaves for our *Kultur*: otherwise it is of no interest to me."[89] In Himmler's vision, a radicalized mindscape of the East, this would be a "perpetual eastern military frontier which, forever mobile, will always keep us young."[90] As the Nazi elite envisioned it, the occupied East would serve as a laboratory for a greater experiment in identity, dwarfing the conceptions of Ober Ost. German identity, no longer national, would be superceded by racial engineering, in programs of breeding, domination, and extermination.

Once war raged in the East, Hitler sketched the future he imagined there, in a series of emotional outbursts while speaking privately with associates at his eastern headquarters in East Prussia and Winnitza in the Ukraine. These "secret conversations" were transcribed and preserved by his aides. Hitler's nightmarish visions reveal both continuities with the preceding Ober Ost venture of the First World War and significant differences. For Hitler, the East was to be a "magnificent field of experiment" and an "unqualified field of action," giving Germans work for the coming era of their race. What was unfolding in the East was the recovery of the purest form of war, war for space. Yet Germans had claims to these far-off lands, for according to Hitler these were originally German lands, again made familiar during the First World War: "The points we have reached are dotted along areas that have retained the memory of Germanic expansion. We've been before at the Iron Gates, at Belgrade, in the Russian space." The memory of the First World War on the Eastern Front had special significance because it included what he considered the great victories of war, Tannenberg and the Masurian Lakes. The East would provide work for Germans for hundreds of years, while some demanding tasks could also be subcontracted to Germanic racial allies in Europe, as common work in the East to cement Hitler's unified Europe. Hitler saw himself giving the crucial gift of space to Germans, for it was essential to a race's greatness to have vast spacial consciousness. He mused, "If only I can make the German people understand what this space means for our future!" It was important for all Germans to "acquire a feeling for the great, open spaces. We must arrange things so that every German can realise for himself what they mean." For now, the essential task in the East was to conquer, secure these areas, and later administer them.[91]

Since "the beginnings of every civilization express themselves in terms of road construction," the first task of the Germans in the East would be to build roads. The new territories would be bound to the Reich by *Autobahn*: "just as the autobahn has caused the inner frontiers of Germany to disappear, so it will abolish the frontiers of Europe." Ordinary highways would be inadequate, however, so Hitler envisioned roads eleven meters wide, carrying three lanes of traffic. These "roads will open the country for us," while strong-point villages punctuating their course would also break the roads' monotony through the open spaces, Hitler judged. Space would be overcome, and "problems of distance, which worry us a little today, will cease to exist." The space in the East, moreover, could keep on growing and expanding. No peace need be established in the East, nor definitive borders drawn. Hitler explained, "in case of necessity, we shall renew our advance wherever a new center of resistance is formed." He attached no importance to "a formal, juridical end to the war on the Eastern Front," for continuing fighting would provide the army with constant training. The real frontier, he announced, is that separating Germans and Slavs, and must be moved whenever Germans require it. The furthest advance would be marked by an East Wall.[92]

The new territories would be colonized by soldier-farmers, their settlements and spacious farms forming a living wall in the East. Noncommissioned officers would serve as teachers for children. Besides land for settlements, the area would also function as a gigantic plain for military maneuvers and deployment for future war. The land itself, meanwhile, would be made over to give it a German character: "In comparison with the beauties accumulated in Central Germany, the new territories in the East seem to us like a desert . . . This Russian desert, we will populate it. The immense spaces of the Eastern Front will have been the field of the greatest battles in history. We'll give this country a past. We'll take away its character of an Asiatic steppe, we'll Europeanise it." The spaces were to be changed, thus giving Germans title to the areas that now bore their imprint.[93]

With regard to natives, Hitler broke with the ideas that motivated Ober Ost's venture. He warned, "it is not our mission to lead the local inhabitants to a higher standard of life." They were not to be reshaped or cultivated or ordered, since "we must in no circumstances repeat the mistakes of excessive regimentation in the Eastern territories." Hitler would allow only a minimum of administration in the East. Natives were only to be exploited, not improved, as in any case, "delousing infuriates the inhabitants, as does our fanatical desire to civilise them." In the East, Hitler saw no place for the Jews, who were to be eliminated, though he characteristically veiled the way in which they were to be done away with. In future, German settlers would remain totally separate from natives, to prevent any fusion with locals. Natives were to be isolated "in their own pig-sties; and anyone who talks about cherishing the local inhabitant and civilising him, goes straight off into a concentration camp!" Hitler stressed again and again that "it is not by taking over the miserable Russian hovels that we shall establish ourselves as masters in the East. The German colonies must be organised on an altogether higher plane."[94]

In contrast to Ober Ost's occupation regime and *Kultur* program, Hitler insisted that "above all, nobody must let loose the German schoolmaster on the Eastern territories!," for "nothing could be a worse mistake on our part than to seek to educate the masses there. It is in our interest that the people should know just enough to recognise the signs of the roads." Echoing the lessons learned from the East after the First World War, Hitler declared, "The German has made himself detested everywhere in the world, because wherever he showed himself he began to play the teacher. It's not a good method of conquest." Germans had no obligation to "play at children's maids," for Slavs were born slaves, he explained, and teaching natives would only produce resistance.[95]

Further, Hitler announced, "in the field of public health there is no need whatsoever to extend to the subject races the benefits of our knowledge. This would only result in an enormous increase in local populations, and I absolutely forbid the organisation of any sort of hygiene or cleanliness crusades in these territories. Compulsory vaccinations will be confined to Germans alone." Instead of being given inoculations, natives were to be convinced that they were dangerous. No transplanting of "German ideas of cleanliness" was to take place, but natives were to remain as before in their dirty huts, surrounded by their own filth. In the great scheme of things, it was wrong to try to bring cleanliness, for in Hitler's view, Slav peoples were "not destined to live a cleanly life. They know it, and we would be wrong to persuade them of the contrary." Immediately, Hitler continued, "It was we who, in 1918, created the Baltic countries and Ukraine. But nowadays we have no interest in maintaining Baltic States, any more than in creating an independent Ukraine." Above all, those peoples must be denied any political organization which might eventually challenge German rule. Unlike in Ober Ost, the Nazis would not "struggle against hovels, chase away the fleas, provide German teachers, bring out newspapers – very little of that for us!" No higher education would be allowed, and indeed no "enlightenment nonsense, propagated by an advance guard of parsons!" Natives were not to be entrusted with work requiring thinking, but had only "one justification for existence – to be of use to us economically." Only enough German would be taught so natives could not pretend they misunderstood orders. As the biological and racial laws of Hitler's universe wore down native populations, their numbers declining, the closed society of German colonists would come into their own, inheriting in these new lands a "magnificent field of experiment." Such was Hitler's view of the future of the East, revealed in his private conversations as war raged.[96]

In Nazi expansionism into the spaces of the East, the "*Ostraum,*" the whole question of the character of the regime debated by historians, whether "reactionary" or "progressive," "conservative" versus "forward-looking," "antimodern" or "modernizing," finds its resolution.[97] The regime used modern techniques for the goal of a terrible future utopia which classical modernity would not recognize, seeking space, rather than development. While the Soviets retreated, "trading space for time,"[98] the Nazis gave up time to gain space – seeking an everlasting, timeless present of destructive expansion in their vision of the Ostland. As the tide of events turned in the East, Hitler refused to give up the spaces conquered and forbade withdrawal again and again, producing military disasters. The ideological primacy of *Raum* was fatal in its consequences in the East. At long last, this was brought home to Germans as the Red Army invaded their territory by 1945, turning the utopia of *Raum* into a nightmare of the advancing East.

Between the world wars, Ober Ost's military utopia and the eastern front-experience of the First World War passed an important legacy to ordinary Germans, shaping the terms of their understanding of the East and what one might do there. In defeat, specific conclusions were drawn from the failed mission in the East. The most crucial development came in the form of new categories for viewing those "lands and peoples" which Ober Ost had tried to shape. They were now seen as "spaces and races" to be cleaned and cleared. Nazi ideology built on these conceptions to "direct the gaze eastwards," where it envisioned a "*Raum* without *Volk*" for a "*Volk* without *Raum*," to be created by genocide, enslavement, and deportation. In the Nazi program, however, war in the East was also a means for transforming the German *Volk*. The *Raum* of the East became yet again the setting for a project in German identity, as national identity was to be reengineered into racial identity. The Nazis' racial utopia in the East was geared toward aims far more total than those of Ober Ost, but Nazi ends evolved in part from the means used by Ober Ost, its categories of perception and practice in trying to transform lands and peoples in the East. In this case, practice had preceded theory: earlier practice conditioned ideas about the East, now drawn upon to promote a radicalized program elaborated from earlier experience. The line of continuity between the military utopia and Nazi plans can be traced in the way in which Ober Ost's practices and assumptions were radicalized and then put into action in renewed war in the East. The vicious outlook of the Nazis as they surveyed the East, seeing their own future in its conquest, was built upon a prior experience in the First World War and the lessons it seemed to yield.

NOTES

1 BAMA N 196/1, Heppe, vol. V, 112; BAMA N 98/1, Gossler, 128–29.
2 Karl Prümm, *Die Literatur des Soldatischen Nationalismus der 20er Jahre (1918–1933)* (Kronberg Taunus: Scriptor Verlag GmbH, 1974); Eksteins, *Rites of Spring*, 275–99.
3 Hüppauf, "Langemarck," 70–103; Winter, *Sites*, 199.
4 Zweig, *Grischa* .
5 Walter Flex, *Der Wanderer zwischen beiden Welten. Ein Kriegserlebnis* (Munich: C. H. Beck'sche Verlagsbuchhandlung, 1917).
6 Wohl, *Generation*, 50.
7 Ludendorff, *Kriegserinnerungen*.
8 Ludendorff, *Kriegserinnerungen*, 161.
9 Golo Mann, *The History of Germany Since 1789*, trans. Marian Jackson (Harmondsworth: Penguin, 1974), 561.
10 Richard Bessel, "The Great War in German Memory: The Soldiers of the First World War, Demobilization, and Weimar Political Culture," *German History* 6.1 (April 1988): 20–34.
11 As late as the 1960s, general surveys by noted German historians highlighted cultural policies in the East: Walther Hubatsch, *Germany and the Central Powers in the World War, 1914–1918* (Lawrence: University of Kansas Press, 1963), 66.
12 BAMA N 196/1, Heppe, vol. V, 145.
13 BA N 1031/2, Gayl, 283, 149.
14 (Hoover Library) *Verwaltungsbericht der Zivilverwaltung der baltischen Lande. 15. August bis 15. Dezember 1918*, 17.
15 Altrichter, *Kräfte*, 180.
16 Detlev J. K. Peukert, *The Weimar Republic: The Crisis of Classical Modernity*, trans. Richard Deveson (New York: Hill & Wang, 1993), 201.
17 Guntram Henrik Herb, *Under the Map of Germany: Nationalism and Propaganda, 1918–1945* (London: Routledge, 1997), 2, 4.
18 Mosse, *Fallen Soldiers*; Winter, *Sites*.
19 Siegfried Scharfe, ed., *Deutschland über Alles. Ehrenmale des Weltkrieges* (Königstein-in-Taunus: Karl Robert Langewiesche, 1938); Mosse, *Fallen Soldiers*, 85–86; Meinhold Lurz, *Kriegerdenkmäler in Deutschland*, vol. V, *Drittes Reich* (Heidelberg: Esprint, 1986), 123–33, 356–58; Sabine Behrenbeck, *Der Kult um die toten Helden. Nationalsozialistische Mythen, Riten und Symbole, 1923 bis 1945* (Vierow bei Greifswald: SH-Verlag, 1996).
20 Jay W. Baird, *To Die For Germany: Heroes in the Nazi Pantheon* (Bloomington: Indiana University Press, 1990), 5–6; Mosse, *Fallen Soldiers*, 97; Wheeler-Bennett, *Wooden Titan*, 315–16.
21 Evidencing increasing use: BA N 1031/2, Gayl, 117–18, 284.
22 Ewald Banse, *Raum und Volk im Weltkriege. Gedanken über eine nationale Wehrlehre* (Oldenburg: G. Stalling, 1932).
23 Stern, *Politics of Cultural Despair*, 239.
24 Francis L. Carsten, "'Volk ohne Raum': A Note on Hans Grimm," *Journal of Contemporary History* 2.2 (April 1967): 221–27.

25 Karl Haushofer, *Grenzen in ihrer geographischen und politischen Bedeutung* (Berlin: Kurt Vowinckel Verlag, 1927).

26 Klaus Kost, *Die Einflüsse der Geopolitik auf Forschung und Theorie des Politischen Geographie von ihren Anfängen bis 1945* (Bonn: Ferd. Dümmlers Verlag, 1988).

27 Burleigh, *Germany*; Christoph Klessmann, "Osteuropaforschung und Lebensraumpolitik im Dritten Reich," in *Wissenschaft im Dritten Reich*, ed. Peter Lundgreen (Frankfurt-on-Main: Suhrkamp, 1985), 350–83; Mechtild Roessler, *Wissenschaft und Lebensraum. Geographische Ostforschung im Nationalsozialismus. Ein Beitrag zur Disziplingeschichte der Geographie* (Berlin: Dietrich Reimer Verlag, 1990).

28 Burleigh, *Germany*, 25.

29 Albrecht Penck, "Deutscher Volks- und Kulturboden," in *Volk unter Völkern*, ed. Karl Christian von Loesch (Breslau: F. Hirt, 1925), 62–73.

30 Burleigh, *Germany*, 25–29; Herb, *Map*, 55–64.

31 Adolf Hitler, *Mein Kampf* (Munich: Zentralverlag der NSDAP Frz. Eher Nachf., 1939).

32 Mann, *Germany*, 733–35.

33 Eberhard Jäckel, *Hitlers Weltanschauung. Entwurf einer Herrschaft* (Tübingen: R. Wunderlich, 1969), 140.

34 Hitler, *Mein Kampf*, 1.

35 Ibid., 740.

36 Ibid., 728, 735.

37 Ibid., 1.

38 Ibid., 154.

39 Ibid., 742.

40 Ibid., 757.

41 Ibid., 742–43.

42 For psychohistorical interpretation of Hitler's eastward orientation, see Rudolph Binion's *Hitler Among the Germans* (New York: Elsevier, 1976), "Hitler Looks East," *History of Childhood Quarterly* 3.1 (summer 1975): 75–102, and "Hitler's Concept of *Lebensraum*: The Psychological Basis," *History of Childhood Quarterly* 1.2 (fall 1973): 187–258.

43 Quoted in Alan Bullock, *Hitler: A Study in Tyranny*, rev. edn (New York: Bantam Books, 1961), 274.

44 *Hitler's Secret Conversations, 1941–1944* (New York: Octagon Books, 1972), 527.

45 Laqueur, *Russia and Germany*, 70.

46 Imanuel Geiss, "The Civilian Dimension of the War," in *Facing Armageddon: The First World War Experience*, ed. Hugh Cecil and Peter H. Liddle (London: Leo Cooper, 1996), 19.

47 Laqueur, *Russia and Germany*, 72.

48 Richard Breitman, *The Architect of Genocide: Himmler and the Final Solution* (Hanover, NH: Brandeis University Press, 1991), 15–16.

49 On Henry of Saxony, ibid., 39. On the belief in reincarnation, Robert Wistrich, *Who's Who in Nazi Germany*, s.v. "Himmler, Heinrich" (London: Weidenfeld & Nicolson, 1982).

50 David Welch, ed., *Nazi Propaganda* (London: Croom Helm, 1983).

51 Heinz Paechter, ed., *Nazi-Deutsch: A Glossary of Contemporary German Usage With Appendices on Government, Military, and Economic Institutions* (New York: Frederick Ungar Publishing, 1944); Victor Klemperer, *Die unbewältigte Sprache. Aus dem Notizbuch eines Philologen "LTI,"* 3rd edn (Darmstadt: Joseph Melzer Verlag, n.d.).

52 Hans Nithack, *Deutsche Arbeit in Polen und Litauen während des Weltkrieges* (Berlin: Bund Deutscher Osten, n.d.), 3–4.

53 Ibid., 19, 13–14, 28–29.

54 Wippermann, *"Drang,"* 104–16.

55 Geert Platner *et al.*, eds. *Schule im Dritten Reich- Erziehung zum Tod? Eine Dokumentation* (Munich: Deutscher Taschenbuch Verlag GmbH & Co. KG, 1983), 229–36; Gregor Ziemer, *Education for Death: The Making of the Nazi* (Oxford and London: Oxford University Press, 1941), 158–59.

56 Franz Schnass, *Nationalsozialistische Heimat- und Erdkunde mit Einschlu, der Geopolitik und des vaterländischen Gesamtunterrichts* (Osterwieck am Harz: A. W. Zickfeldt Verlag, 1934); Gert Gröning, "The Feeling for Landscape – a German Example," *Landscape Research* 17.3 (1992): 108–15.

57 David Welch, "Educational Film Propaganda and the Nazi Youth," in *Nazi Propaganda*, ed. Welch, 71.

58 *Kriegsausbildung der Hitler-Jugend im Schieß- und Geländedienst. Ausgabe 1941.* (Berlin: Verlag Bernard & Graefe, 1941); Gerhard Rempel, *Hitler's Children: The Hitler Youth and the SS* (Chapel Hill: University of North Carolina Press, 1989), 182; Platner *et al.*, eds., *Schule*, 59, 198–99; Ziemer, *Education for Death*, 72, 164–65 (with some terrain games lasting ten days in all).

59 Willy Schumann, *Being Present: Growing up in Hitler's Germany* (Kent, OH: Kent State University Press, 1991), 24.

60 Platner *et al.*, eds., *Schule*, 199.

61 Schumann, *Present*, 45–47, 103.

62 Ibid., 35, 63, 104.

63 Hellmut Petersen, *Die Erziehung der deutschen Jungmannschaft im Reichsarbeitdienst* (Berlin: Junker & Dünnhaupt Verlag, 1938).

64 Schumann, *Present*, 25.

65 The songs are from a collection for the League of German Maidens, *Wir Mädel singen. Liederbuch des Bundes Deutscher Mädel. Herausgegeben von der Reichsjugendführung*, 2nd edn (Wolfenbüttel: Reichsjugendführung, 1941), 173–76. "The Call From the East" is from Hans Baumann, *Wir zünden das Feuer* (Jena: Eugen Diedrichs Verlag, 1940), 5–14.

66 Robert R. Taylor, *The Word in Stone: The Role of Architecture in the National Socialist Ideology* (Berkeley: University of California Press, 1974).

67 *Hitler's Secret Conversations*, 365.

68 Mechthild Roessler, "Applied Geography and Area Research in Nazi Society: The Central Place Theory and its Implications, 1933 to 1945," *Environment and Planning D, Society and Space* (December 7, 1989): 419–31; Mechthild Roessler, "Die Institutionalisierung einer neuen 'Wissenschaft' im Nationalsozialismus: Raumforschung und Raumordnung, 1935–1945," *Geographische Zeitschrift* 75.3 (1987): 177–94; Roessler, *Wissenschaft und Lebensraum*;

Akademie für Raumforschung und Landesplanung, *Handwörterbuch der Raumforschung und Raumordnung*, 2nd edn (Hannover: Gebrüder Jänecke Verlag, 1970).

69 Konrad Meyer, *Bodenordnung als volkspolitische Aufgabe und Zielsetzung nationalsozialistischen Ordnungswillens* (Berlin: Verlag Walter de Gruyter & Co., 1940).

70 After the war, Meyer went on to occupy important positions in the Federal Republic, continuing *Raumordnung* and *Raumforschung*.

71 Götz Aly and Karl Heinz Roth, *Die restlose Erfassung. Volkszählen, Identifizieren, Aussondern im Nationalsozialismus* (Berlin: Rotbuch Verlag, 1984).

72 Robert L. Koehl, *RKFDV: German Resettlement and Population Policy* (Cambridge, MA: Harvard University Press, 1957).

73 Quoted in Gröning, "Feeling for Landscape," Gert Gröning and Joachim Wolschke-Bulmahn, *Die Liebe zur Landschaft. Teil III: Der Drang nach Osten*, Arbeiten zur sozialwissenschaftlich orientierten Freiraumplanung (Munich: Minerva Publikation, 1987).

74 Bartov, *Eastern Front*.

75 Vardys and Sedaitis, *Lithuania*, 58.

76 Stephen G. Fritz, *Frontsoldaten: The German Soldier in World War II* (Lexington: University Press of Kentucky, 1995), 119.

77 Bartov, *Hitler's Army*, 12–28.

78 Klaus Latzel, "Tourismus und Gewalt. Kriegswahrnehmungen in Feldpostbriefen," in *Vernichtungskrieg: Verbrechen der Wehrmacht 1941 bis 1944*, ed. Hannes Heer and Klaus Naumann (Hamburg: Hamburger Edition, 1995): 447–59; Bartov, *Hitler's Army*, 147–78.

79 Bartov, *Hitler's Army*, 182, 107.

80 Reichskommissar für das Ostland. Abt. II Raum, *Strukturbericht über das Ostland* II (Riga, Reichskommissar für das Ostland, 1942), preface lists as information Ober Ost materials. Further accounts presented experiences of the First World War as a basis to build upon: Butz, "Die kriegswirtschaftliche," 224–29.

81 Hans-Heinrich Wilhelm, "Personelle Kontinuitäten in baltischen Angelegenheiten auf deutscher Seite von 1917/19 bis zum Zweiten Weltkrieg?," in John Hiden and Aleksander Loit, eds., *The Baltic in International Relations Between the World Wars*, Acta Universitatis Stockholmiensis, Studia Baltica Stockholmiensia 3 (1988): 157–70.

82 Alexander Dallin, *German Rule in Russia, 1941–1945*, 2nd rev. edn, (Boulder, CO: Westview Press, 1981), 187.

83 Hans-Dieter Handrack, *Das Reichskommissariat Ostland. Die Kulturpolitik der deutschen Verwaltung zwischen Autonomie und Gleichschaltung, 1941–1944* (Hann. Münden: Gauke Verlag, 1981); Raun, *Estonia*, 166–68.

84 Wolfgang Benz, "Der Generalplan Ost. Zur Germanisierungspolitik des NS-Regimes in den besetzten Ostgebieten, 1939–1945," *Die Vertreibung der Deutschen aus dem Osten. Ursachen, Ereignisse, Folgen*, ed. Wolfgang Benz (Frankfurt-on-Main: Fischer Taschenbuch Verlag, 1985), 39–48.

85 Klaus P. Fischer, *Nazi Germany: A New History* (New York: Continuum, 1995), 505–506.

86 Quoted in Dallin, *German Rule*, 279.
87 Quoted in Bullock, *Hitler*, 627.
88 Quoted in Burleigh, *Germany*, 8.
89 Ibid.
90 International Military Tribunal, *Trials of the Major War Criminals* (Nuremburg: International Military Tribunal, 1949), vol. XXXVIII, 523.
91 *Hitler's Secret Conversations, 1941–44*, 29, 36; 43; 30, 34; 43; 20, 500, 576; 29; 28.
92 Ibid., 436, 467; 4, 469; 469; 30, 436; 469; 4–5; 76, 78; 23; 469.
93 Ibid., 13, 21; 79; 21, 78; 56.
94 Ibid., 478; 479; 479; 500; 57; 467; 501; 501.
95 Ibid., 287, 13. Later, he considered traffic safety no concern, as native victims did not matter much: 478. Ibid., 20; 57, 28.
96 Ibid., 344–45; 477, 467; 29; 343; 57; 478; 288, 343; 478; 29.
97 Cf. Michael Burleigh and Wolfgang Wippermann, *The Racial State: Germany, 1933–1945*. (Cambridge: Cambridge University Press, 1991), 7–22.
98 Richard Grunberger, *Germany, 1918–1945* (London: Batsford, 1964), 165.

Conclusion

Under the impact of modern war from 1914 to 1918, German views of the East underwent a fundamental transformation with far-reaching cultural and political consequences. Millions of German soldiers were directly involved in the eastern front-experience, marked by fighting significantly unlike that of the West and colored by the realities and impressions of occupation. A different face of "total war" was exposed in the East. While in the trenches of the West, soldiers cowered under relentless bombardments of industrial modernity and faced battle against machines, German soldiers in the East instead directly confronted hostile nature, an insistent past all around them in a theatre of war that seemed ever less modern, and cultural clashes with surrounding native groups. Soldiers on the Eastern Front were changed by this distinctive combat and the day-to-day practice of executing the duties of occupation and the military utopia's orders, while bombarded by Ober Ost's motivational propaganda about their cultural mission. One officer summed up his experience of the Eastern Front in a catalog of hateful features, spitting out disturbing images that he recalled. It was, he said, "Deepest Russia, without a glimmer of Central European *Kultur*, Asia, steppe, swamps, claustrophobic underworld, and a godforsaken wasteland of slime."[1] Paradoxically, such sweeping antipathy could combine with ambitions for colonization, determined to overcome the *Unkultur* of conquered lands and peoples. Thus, another report exulted that the troops were true "pioneers of *Kultur*," and "thus, whether aware of it or not, the German soldier becomes a teacher in the enemy land," on a mission of bringing order and development.[2] Both of these views arose out of the eastern front-experience, in the context of war. The East was feared even as it was exploited and readied for plans to transform it. These disparate elements came together in a vision of the East growing out of that front experience and the realities, practice, and illusions of German occupation policy in Ober Ost.

The First World War's eastern front-experience was of decisive importance in shaping German views of the East in the next decades of the violent twentieth century. The encounter which took place there over four years, lit by the flames of war, fundamentally transformed German understandings of the region. While earlier German views had been based on second-hand generalizations and literary images in the popular imagination, meeting the East as it really was and trying to come to terms with its newly revealed complexity yielded new terms and categories of understanding, based this time on real experience and practice. Clearly, Eastern Europe was not utterly unknown to a good many soldiers, who had experience of Germany's Polish minorities or the border provinces, but the war presented even these men with a new set of experiences of greater immediacy and lasting impact. Above all, seeing these lands for the first time in war had a disastrous effect. It is tantalizing to speculate that different circumstances for this first meeting might have yielded a different long-term result. Yet the devastation of "scorched earth" and the helplessness of natives facing German armies alike seemed to be permanent facts and characteristics of the East. Phenomena like the "elective ethnicity" and fluidity of national identifications were taken as further proof of the East's essential disorder. This putative disorder, in turn, formed a springboard for the ambitions of the Ober Ost state, which sought to organize the occupied lands through its "movement policy" and to control the area's ethnicities through a program of *Kultur*. The new German view of the East produced fateful consequences, as it set the terms for Germany's difficult relationship with the lands and peoples to its East for decades to come. This process can be traced in the semantic shift from the descriptive term "lands and peoples" to "spaces and races." The "lessons" of the Eastern Front were eventually taken up by the Nazi movement and fused with the vile energies of their anti-Semitism, to produce a terrible new plan for the East, which they would launch with the coming of the Second World War.

The geographical fantasies of the East born in the eastern front-experience and launched in practice by Ober Ost came to a definitive end as the war unleashed by the Nazi regime turned back on to German territory. In the period between the end of the Second World War and the present, the "*Ost*" meant something different again. Rather than referring to non-German borderlands and Russia's interior, in the Federal Republic, "East" now meant the "other Germany" of the Soviet zone, the DDR. During the Cold War, "*die Mauer*" walled off Berlin and the halves of the country, dividing West from East, borders now drawn through Germany rather than beyond. Over the years, this separation grew into a "wall inside people's heads" as well, as many became resigned or reconciled to permanent division, while the Federal Republic was tied in to its Western European community and identity. But with the unexpected fall of the wall in 1989 came the discovery of new horizons and an enlarged homeland. Political commentators ventured the announcement that for Germany "the center lies to the East." A new relationship had to be negotiated in a new Europe, itself now suddenly unclear in outline. Significantly, notions of *"Aufräumen"* and *"Aufbau,"* clearing and constructing, once slogans of the Nazi Ostland, are instead used today in reference to the challenges of integrating the new lands of the Federal Republic. The next decades will show how the new horizons of Germany's future relationship with the East will be understood. The history of that relationship contains both happier precedents and cautionary examples, but it is clear that the relationship itself is unavoidable, a necessary neighboring, inescapable for Germany as a European "realm of the middle."

The anatomy of a modern occupation presented here underlines the tendency of war to realize the worst in those caught in its toils, affecting their cultures as well. Values like *Kultur* and *Bildung*, used as slogans of German Work, were distorted in the East. New terms for understanding the lands and peoples were forged, which would have disastrous consequences. This momentous change in outlook, coming from real experiences and practice, opened new horizons of terrifying political possibilities which before had not been thinkable. Here, ideology was built upon real experiences. Observing how the consequences spanned whole decades, one sees war's continuing evil effects in the lives of peoples. In place of history's frequent bias in favor of recording successes, it is necessary to note that failure also has consequences. After Ober Ost's failure gave a venomous twist to the eastern front-experience, the Nazis' failure at last extinguished many of these ideas. This cautionary example reveals how occupations are damaging for both occupiers and occupied. The corrosive effect of violent power exercised over others was demonstrated as the values of *Kultur* were affected, redefined as control over others, until in a final obscenity, Himmler could speak of needing "slaves for our *Kultur*." That Germany's relationship with the peoples and lands to its East is not preordained to inevitably course along these lines is proved by the protests of those conscientious Germans in Ober Ost's administration who warned against this perversion of their cultural values. Their stance testifies to more positive models of neighborly relations and understanding.

In the last decades, struggling to account for the wrong turn into the nightmare of Nazi dictatorship, historians engaged in a *"Sonderweg* debate" concerning Germany's "unique road" to the present. Was Germany always a great exception? Disputes raged over the alleged "late" development or "failed modernization" of Germany as compared to an ideal type of the liberal West. Yet comparisons and investigations limited only to the West remain one-sided, especially for the "country of the middle," inevitably interacting with the lands to its East as well. This was the insight of a great European, Goethe, who judged that "he who knows himself and others" knows that the old divisions of East and West are no longer tenable, and announced: "To balance oneself thoughtfully between both worlds, thus to move between East and West, I avow – that is best." The future of Europe's center would be a fortunate one if guided by the spirit of the *Kultur* of Goethe and Herder, rather than the spirit of Ober Ost's ambitions.

NOTES

1 Marwitz, *Stirb*, 147.
2 *Draussen*, 8.

Select bibliography

ARCHIVAL SOURCES

Bundesarchiv (BA), Koblenz, Germany
Nachlässe (N)
N 1031   Nachlass von Gayl
N 1238   Nachlass Morsbach

Bundesarchiv-Militärarchiv (BAMA), Freiburg-in-Breisgau, Germany
Preußen-Heer (PH)
PH 30/III   Militärverwaltungen
Amtsdrucksachen Preußen-Heer (PHD)
PHD 23   Militärverwaltungen
PHD 8   Oberkommandos
Nachlässe (N)
N 98   Nachlass von Gossler
N 196/1   Nachlass von Heppe, vol. V ("Im Weltkriege")
FC 1179 N, FC 1180 N   Nachlass Franz Joseph Fürst Isenburg-Birstein

Geheimes Staatsarchiv Preussicher Kulturbesitz (GSTA PK), Berlin, Germany
I. HA. Rep. 84a   Verwaltung, deutsche, für die im Weltkrieg 1914/
                          18 besetzten feindliche Gebiete

Hoover Institution, Archives, Stanford University, Stanford, California
Dettmann, Ludwig
Germany. Oberste Heeresleitung
Lithuanian Subject Collection
World War I Subject Collection

Lietuvos Centrinis Valstybinis Istorijos Archyvas (LCVIA), Vilnius, Lithuania
Fondas 641   Lietuvos karinės valdybos viršininkas

Lietuvos Mokslų Akademijos Rankraščių Skyrius (LMARS), Vilnius, Lithuania
Fondas 9, BF-3117   Ob. Ost ir jo štabo įvairūs įsakymai
Fondas 23   Vokiečių okupacija Lietuvoje 1914–1918 m.m.

University of Pennsylvania, Philadelphia, Special Collections, Van Pelt Library

Zeitung der 10. Armee, no. 1 (December 9, 1915) – no. 753 (December 6, 1918), with supplements *Der Beobachter. Beilage zur Zeitung der 10. Armee* and *Scheinwerfer. Bildbeilage zur Zeitung der 10. Armee*. Wilna: Druck & Verlag Zeitung der 10. Armee, 1915–18.

PRIMARY SOURCES

Balla, Erich. *Landsknechte wurden wir. Abenteuer aus dem Baltikum*. Berlin: W. Kolk, 1932.

Banse, Ewald. *Raum und Volk im Weltkriege. Gedanken über eine nationale Wehrlehre*. Oldenburg: G. Stalling, 1932.

Baumann, Hans. *Wir zünden das Feuer*. Jena: Eugen Diedrichs Verlag, 1940.

Berg, Alfred. *Geographisches Wanderbuch. Ein Führer für Wandervögel und Pfadfinder*. 2nd edn Leipzig: B. G. Teubner, 1918.

Bialowies in deutscher Verwaltung. Herausgegeben von der Militärforstverwaltung Bialowies. Berlin: Verlagsbuchhandlung Paul Parey, 1919.

Brockhusen-Justin, Hans-Joachim von. *Der Weltkrieg und ein schlichtes Menschenleben*. Greifswald: Verlag Ratsbuchhandlung L. Bamberg, 1928.

Broederich-Kurmahlen, Silvio. *Das neue Ostland*. Charlottenburg: Ostlandverlag, 1915.

Buloff, Josef. *From the Old Marketplace*. Translated by Joseph Singer. Cambridge, MA: Harvard University Press, 1991.

Butz, Werner. "Die kriegswirtschaftliche Nutzung des besetzten Ostraums im Weltkrieg 1914–1918." *Wissen und Wehr* 23 (1942): 224–29.

Clemen, Paul, ed. *Kunstschutz im Kriege. Berichte über den Zustand der Kunstdenkmäler auf den verschiedenen Kriegsschauplätzen und über die deutschen und österreichischen Massnahmen zu ihrer Erhaltung, Rettung und Erforschung*. Leipzig: E. A. Seemann, 1919.

Clemenz, Bruno. *Kriegsgeographie. Erdkunde und Weltkrieg in ihre Beziehungen erläutert und dargestellt nebst Schilderung der Kriegsschauplätze*. Würzburg: Curt Kabitzsch, 1916.

Conzelmann, Otto, ed. *Otto Dix. Handzeichnungen*. Hannover: Fackelträger-Verlag, 1968.

Das Land Ober Ost. Deutsche Arbeit in den Verwaltungsbezirken Kurland, Litauen und Bialystok-Grodno. Herausgegeben im Auftrage des Oberbefehlshabers Ost. Bearbeitet von der Presseabteilung Ober Ost. Stuttgart: Verlag der Presseabteilung Ober Ost, 1917.

Das Litauen-Buch. Eine Auslese aus der Zeitung der 10. Armee. Wilna: Druck & Verlag Zeitung der 10. Armee, 1918.

Daugirdas, Tadas. *Kaunas vokiečių okupacijoje*. Kaunas: Spindulio B-vės spaustuvė, 1937.

Dehmel, Richard. *Zwischen Volk und Menschheit. Kriegstagebuch*. Berlin: S. Fischer Verlag, 1919.

Dettmann, Ludwig. *Von der deutschen Ostfront*. Berlin: Verlag Ullstein & Co., n.d.

Draussen-daheim. Bilder aus deutschen Soldatenheimen. Kriegstagebuch des Ostdeutschen Jünglingsbundes. Berlin: Verlag der Buchhandlung des Ostdeutschen-Jünglingsbundes, 1916.

Dreyer, J. *Die Moore Kurlands nach ihrer geographischen Bedingtheit, ihrer Beschaffenheit, ihrem Umfange und ihrer Ausnutzungsmöglichkeit. Herausgegeben mit Unterstützung der Verwaltung des Oberbefehlshabers Ost.* Veröffentlichungen des geographischen Institutes der Albertus-Universität zu Königsberg, 1. Hamburg: L. Friedrichsen & Co., 1919.

Dwinger, Edwin Erich. *Die letzten Reiter.* Jena: Eugen Diedrichs Verlag, 1935.

Elias, Norbert. *Reflections on a Life.* Translated by Edmund Jephcott. Cambridge, MA: Polity Press, 1994.

Feiler, Arthur. *Neuland. Eine Fahrt durch Ob. Ost.* Frankfurt-on-Main: Frank. Societätsdruckerei, 1917.

Fischer, H. *Kriegsgeographie.* Bielefeld: Velhagen & Klasing, 1916.

Flex, Walter. *Der Wanderer zwischen beiden Welten. Ein Kriegserlebnis.* Munich: C. H. Beck'sche Verlagsbuchhandlung, 1917.

Frentz, Hans. *Über den Zeiten. Künstler im Kriege.* Freiburg-in-Breisgau: Urban Verlag, 1931.

Friedrichsen, Max. *Landschaften und Städte Polens und Litauens. Beiträge zu einer regionalen Geographie. Auf Grund von Reisebeobachtungen im Dienste der "Landeskundlichen Kommission beim Generalgouvernement Warschau."* Berlin: Gea Verlag GmbH, 1918.

Führer durch die Ausstellung Wilnaer Arbeitsstuben 1916. Wilna: Zeitung der 10. Armee, 1916.

Gäbert, Karl and Hans Scupin. *Bodenschätze im Ostbaltikum,* Die Kriegsschauplätze 1914–1918 geologisch dargestellt, 10. Berlin: Gebr. Borntraeger, 1928.

Gintneris, Antanas. *Lietuva caro ir kaizerio naguose. Atsiminimai iš I Pasaulinio karo laikų* 1914–1918 m. Chicago: ViVi Printing, 1970.

Goltz, Rüdiger von der. *Meine Sendung in Finnland und im Baltikum.* Leipzig: K. F. Koehler, 1920.

Grautoff, Otto, ed. *Bernhard von der Marwitz. Eine Jugend in Dichtung und Briefen.* Dresden: Sibyllen-Verlag, 1923.

Gustainis, Valentinas. "Nepriklausoma Lietuva: kaimiečių ir jaunimo valstybė." *Proskyna. Kultūros almanachas Jaunuomenei* 3. 6 (1990): 169–92.

Häpke, Rudolf. *Die deutsche Verwaltung in Litauen 1915 bis 1918. Der Verwaltungschef Litauen. Abwickelungsbehörde Berlin.* Berlin: Reichsdruckerei, 1921.

Hartmann, Fritz. *Ob-Ost. Friedliche Kriegsfahrt eines Zeitungsmannes.* Hannover: Gebrüder Jänecke, 1917.

Hartmann, Georg Heinrich. "Aus den Erinnerungen eines Freiwilligen der baltischen Landeswehr." *Deutsche Revue* (Stuttgart: Deutsche Verlagsanstalt, 1921).

Haushofer, Karl. *Grenzen in ihrer geographischen und politischen Bedeutung.* Berlin: Kurt Vowinckel Verlag, 1927.

Hedin, Sven. *Nach Osten!* Leipzig: F. A. Brockhaus, 1916.

Heinz, Friedrich Wilhelm. "Der deutsche Vorstoß in das Baltikum." In Hotzel, ed., *Deutscher Aufstand.*

Heywang, Ernst. *Deutsche Tat, Deutsche Saat in russischem Brachland. Eine Frontreise nach Ob.-Ost.* Strasbourg: Strassburger Druckerei & Verlagsanstalt, 1917.

Hindenburg, Paul von. *Aus meinem Leben*. Leipzig: S. Hirzel, 1920.

Hitler, Adolf. *Mein Kampf*. Munich: Zentralverlag der NSDAP. Frz. Eher Nachf., 1933.

Hitler's Secret Conversations, 1941–1944. New York: Octagon Books, 1972.

Hoffman, Max. *Die Aufzeichnungen des Generalmajors Max Hoffman*. Ed. Karl Friedrich Nowak. 2 vols. Berlin: Verlag für Kulturpolitik, 1929.

Höß, Rudolf. *Kommandant in Auschwitz. Autobiographische Aufzeichnungen von Rudolf Höß . Eingeleitet und kommentiert von Martin Broszat*. Quellen und Darstellungen zur Zeitgeschichte, 5. Stuttgart: Deutsche Verlags-Anstalt, 1958.

Hotzel, Curt, ed. *Deutscher Aufstand: Die Revolution des Nachkrieges*. Stuttgart: Verlag W. Kohlhammer, 1934.

Ich Weiß Bescheid. Kleiner Soldatenführer durch Wilna. Wilna: Verlag Armeezeitung AOK 10, 1916.

Ippel, Albert. *Wilna-Minsk. Altertümer und Kunstgewerbe. Führer durch die Ausstellungder 10. Armee*. Wilna: Zeitung der 10. Armee, 1918.

Johann, Ernst, ed. *Innenansicht eines Krieges. Bilder, Briefe, Dokumente, 1914–1918*. Frankfurt-on-Main: Verlag Heinrich Scheffler, 1968.

Jünger, Ernst. *Der Kampf als inneres Erlebnis*. Berlin: E. S. Mittler & Sohn, 1922.

In Stahlgewittern. Aus dem Tagebuch eines Stosstruppführers. Leipzig: R. Meier, 1920.

Jünger, Ernst, ed. *Der Kampf um das Reich*. Essen: Deutsche Vertriebsstelle "Rhein u. Ruhr" Wilh. Kamp, [1929].

Jungfer, Victor. *Alt-Litauen. Eine Darstellung von Land und Leuten, Sitten und Gebräuche*. Berlin: G. Neuner, 1926.

Das Gesicht der Etappe. Berlin: F. Würtz, 1919.

Mit der schlesichen Landwehr in Ruß land. Sieben Monate am Feinde. Heilbronn: E. Salzer, 1915.

Kjellen, Rudolf. *Die politischen Probleme des Weltkrieges*. Leipzig: B. G. Teubner, 1916.

Klemperer, Victor. *Curriculum Vitae. Erinnerungen, 1881–1918*, vol. II. Berlin: AufbauTaschenbuch Verlag, 1989, 1996.

Klimas, Petras, ed. *Der Werdegang des Litauischen Staates von 1915 bis zur Bildung der provisorischen Regierung im November 1918. Dargestellt auf Grund amtlicher Dokumente*. Berlin: Paß und Garleb GmbH, 1919.

Is̆ mano atsiminimų. Vilnius: Lietuvos enciklopedijų redakcija, 1990.

Körner, Hans-Michael, and Ingrid Körner, eds. *Leopold Prinz von Bayern, 1846–1930. Aus den Lebenserinnerungen*. Regensburg: F. Pustet, 1983.

Kriegsausbildung der Hitler-Jugend im Schieß - und Geländedienst. Ausgabe 1941. Berlin: Verlag Bernard & Graefe, 1941.

Leitner, Wilhelm. *In den Rokitno-Sümpfen. Kriegserfahrungen eines Geographen*. N.p.: Stellv. Generalkommando I. Armeekorps, Abt. K., [1917].

Leo, Heinrich. *Jungdeutschland. Wehrerziehung der deutschen Jugend*. Berlin and Wilmersdorf: Hermann Paetel Verlag, 1912.

Listowsky, Paul. *Neu-Ost. Unser Zukunftsgrenzgebiet um Ostpreussens Ostrand. Fahrten durch Polen und Litauen unter deutscher Kriegsverwaltung*. Königsberg-in-Preussen: Hartungsche Zeitung, 1917.

Ludendorff, Erich. *Meine Kriegserinnerungen, 1914–1918.* Berlin: E. S. Mittler & Sohn, 1919.

Maisch, Herbert. *"Helm ab, Vorhang auf!" Siebzig Jahre eines ungewöhnlichen Lebens.* Emsdetten: Lechte, 1968.

Marwitz, Bernhard von der. *Stirb und Werde. Aus Briefen und Kriegstagebuchblättern des Leutnants Bernhard von der Marwitz.* Breslau: Wilh. Gottl. Korn Verlag, 1931.

Meyer, Konrad. *Bodenordnung als volkspolitische Aufgabe und Zielsetzung nationalsozialistischen Ordnungswillens.* Berlin: Verlag Walter de Gruyter & Co., 1940.

Mitau. Bilder aus deutschen Soldatenheimen. Ausschu, für Soldaten- und Eisenbahnerheime an der Ost- und Südfront. Berlin: Furche Verlag, 1917.

Monty, Paul. *Wanderstunden in Wilna.* Wilna: Verlag der Wilnaer Zeitung, 1916.

Mueller, Ernst Ferdinand. *Statistisches Handbuch für Kurland und Litauen nebst Übersichten über Livland und Estland. Mit einem bibliographischen Anhang zur Wirtschaftskunde Ruß lands.* Schriften des Instituts für ostdeutsche Wirtschaft an der Universität Königsberg, 4. Königsberg: G. Fischer, 1918.

Nagel, Fritz. *Fritz: The World War I Memoir of a German Lieutenant.* Rev. edn Huntington, VA: Blue Acorn Press, 1995.

Nicolai, W. *Geheime Mächte. Internationale Spionage und ihre Bekämpfung im Weltkrieg und heute.* 2nd edn Leipzig: K. F. Koehler, 1924.

Nithack, Hans. *Deutsche Arbeit in Polen und Litauen während des Weltkrieges.* Berlin: Bund Deutscher Osten, n.d.

Nord, Franz. "Der Krieg im Baltikum." In Jünger, ed., *Der Kampf um das Reich.*

Oehlmann, Ernst. *Kriegsgeographie. Bearbeitet von Herausgebern der E. von Seydlitz'schen Geographie (Dr. E. Oehlmann und Dr. R. Reinhard).* Breslau: F. Hirt, 1916.

Penck, Albrecht. "Deutscher Volks- und Kulturboden." In *Volk unter Völkern,* ed. Karl Christian von Loesch. Breslau: F. Hirt, 1925.

Petersen, Hellmut. *Die Erziehung der deutschen Jungmannschaft im Reichsarbeitdienst.* Berlin: Junker & Dünnhaupt Verlag, 1938.

Petkevičaitė-Bitė, Gabriele. *Karo meto dienoraštis.* Vilnius: Vaga, 1966.

Ratzel, Friedrich. *Deutschland. Einführung in die Heimatkunde.* 2nd edn Leipzig: Fr. Wilh. Grunow, 1907.

Reichskommissar für das Ostland. Abt. II Raum. *Strukturbericht über das Ostland II.* Riga: Reichskommissar für das Ostland, 1942.

Remarque, Erich Maria. *Im Westen nichts Neues.* Berlin: Kiepenheuer & Witsch, 1928.

Richert, Dominik. *Beste Gelegenheit zum Sterben. Meine Erlebnisse im Kriege, 1914–1918.* Edited by Angelika Tramwitz and Bernd Ulrich. Munich: Knesebeck & Schuler, 1989.

Riehl, Wilhelm Heinrich. *Die deutsche Arbeit.* Stuttgart: J. G. Cotta'scher Verlag, 1861.

Land und Leute. Stuttgart: Cotta, 1854.

Rosenstengel, Hermann. *Leichte Geländespiele für die deutsche Jugend.* Leipzig: B. G. Teubner, 1918.

Rümker, Kurt von. *Bevölkerungs- und Siedelungsfragen im Land Ob. Ost.* Berlin:

Verlagsbuchhandlung Paul Parey, Verlag für Landwirtschaft, Gartenbau und Forstwesen, 1918.

Rümker, Kurt von and R. Leidner. *42 Sortenanbauversuche im Verwaltungsgebiete des Oberbefehlshabers Ost.* Berlin: Verlagsbuchhandlung Paul Parey, Verlag fürLandwirtschaft, Gartenbau und Forstwesen, 1918.

Ruseckas, Petras, ed. *Lietuva didžiajame kare.* Vilnius: Vilniaus žodis, 1939.

Salomon, Ernst von, ed. *Das Buch vom deutschen Freikorpskämpfer. Herausgegeben im Auftrage der Freikorpsgesellschaft "Der Reiter gen Osten."* Berlin: W. Limpert, 1938.

Die Geächteten. Berlin: Rowohlt Verlag GmbH, 1930.

Sanitätsbericht über das Deutsche Heer (Deutsches Feld- und Besatzungsheer) im Weltkriege 1914/1918 (Deutscher Kriegssanitätsbericht 1914/18). Bearbeitet in der Heeres-Sanitätsinspektion des Reichskriegsministeriums, vol. I, *Gliederung des Heeressanitätswesens.* Berlin: E. S. Mittler & Sohn, 1935.

Sanitätsbericht über das Deutsche Heer (Deutsches Feld- und Besatzungsheer) im Weltkriege 1914/1918 (Deutscher Kriegssanitätsbericht 1914/18). Bearbeitet in der Heeres-Sanitätsinspektion des Reichs kriegsministeriums, vol. II, *Der Sanitätsdienst im Gefechts- und Schlachtenverlauf im Weltkriege 1914/1918 und Stichwortverzeichnis für I., II. und III. Band.* Berlin: E. S. Mittler & Sohn, 1938.

Sanitätsbericht über das Deutsche Heer (Deutsches Feld- und Besatzungsheer) im Weltkriege 1914/1918 (Deutscher Kriegssanitätsbericht 1914/18). Bearbeitet in der Heeres-Sanitätsinspektion des Reichswehrministeriums, vol. III, *Die Krankenbewegung bei dem Deutschen Feld- und Besatzungsheer.* Berlin: E. S. Mittler & Sohn, 1934.

Schäfer, Paul Georg. *Geländespiele, den Sohnen unseres Vaterlandes zugedacht.* Leipzig: B. G. Teubner, 1909.

Scharfe, Siegfried, ed. *Deutschland über Alles. Ehrenmale des Weltkrieges.* Königstein-in-Taunus: Karl Robert Langewiesche, 1938.

Schell, Adolf von. *Battle Leadership.* Columbus, GA: Benning Herald, 1933; reprinted, Quantico, VA: Marine Corps Association, 1988.

Scheller, Thilo. *Geländespiele für die deutsche Jugend.* Bücherei für Leibesübungen und körperliche Erziehung. Leipzig: Verlag Quelle & Meyer, 1928.

Schiller, Friedrich. *Sämtliche Werke.* Edited by Gerhard Fricke and Herbert Göpert. Vol. II, *Dramen II.* Munich: Carl Hanser Verlag, 1958/59.

Schlichting, R. *Bilder aus Litauen. Im Auftrage des Chefs und unter Mitarbeit zahlreicher Herren der Deutschen Verwaltung Litauen.* Kowno: Kownoer Zeitung, 1916.

Schnass, Franz. *Nationalsozialistische Heimat- und Erdkunde mit Einschluß der Geopolitik und des vaterländischen Gesamtunterrichts.* Osterwieck am Harz: A. W. Zickfeldt Verlag, 1934.

Schumann, Willy. *Being Present: Growing up in Hitler's Germany.* Kent, OH: Kent State University Press, 1991.

Sieben-Sprachenwörterbuch. Deutsch/Polnisch/Russisch/Weißruthenisch/Litauisch/ Lettisch/Jiddisch. Herausgegeben im Auftrage des Oberbefehlshabers Ost. N.p.: Presseabteilung des Oberbefehlshabers Ost, [1918].

Šilietis, J. *Vokiečių okupacija Lietuvoje, 1915–1919 m. paveikslėliuose ir trumpuose jų aprašymuose.* Kaunas: "Varpo" B-vės spaustuvė, 1922.

Skalweit, Bruno. *Die Landwirtschaft in den litauischen Gouvernements, ihre Grundlagen und Leistungen.* Schriften des Instituts für ostdeutsche Wirtschaft an der Universität Königsberg, 3. Königsberg: G. Fischer, 1918.

Strecker, Karl. *Auf den Spuren Hindenburgischer Verwaltung. Erlebnisse und Ergebnisse einer Studienfahrt in Ob. Ost.* Berlin: C. A. Schwetschke & Sohn, 1917.

Struck, Hermann. *Ostjüdische Typen.* Berlin: Welt-Verlag, 1922.

Struck, Hermann and Herbert Eulenberg. *Skizzen aus Litauen, Weissrussland und Kurland.* N.p.: Druckerei des Oberbefehlshabers Ost, 1916.

Tiessen, Ernst. *Die Geographie des östlichen Kriegsschauplatzes.* Berlin: Concordia, 1914.

Vivat, du wackere Armee. Singlieder für Soldaten der 10 Armee. N.p.: Zeitung der 10. Armee, 1918.

Völker-Verteilung in West-Ruß land. Kowno: Verlag der Kownoer Zeitung, 1916.

Völkerverteilung in West-Ruß land. 2nd edn. N.p.: Druckerei des Oberbefehlshabers Ost, 1917.

Weber, Paul. *Wilna, eine vergessene Kunststätte.* Wilna: Verlag der Zeitung der 10. Armee, 1917.

"Die Baudenkmäler in Litauen." In Clemen, ed., *Kunstschutz im Kriege.*

Wenzler, Josef. *Mit Draht und Kabel im Osten. Aus dem Tagebuch eines Telegraphisten.* Karlsruhe: Badenia, 1918.

Wertheimer, Fritz. *Hindenburgs Mauer im Osten.* 3rd edn. Stuttgart: Deutsche Verlags-Anstalt, 1916.

Wicker, Konrad. "Der Weltkrieg in Zahlen." In Walter Jost and Friedrich Felger, eds., *Was wir vom Weltkrieg nicht wissen,* 2nd edn. Leipzig, H. Fikentscher Verlag, 1938.

Winnig, August. *Am Ausgang der deutschen Ostpolitik. Persöhnliche Erlebnisse und Erinnerungen.* Berlin: Staatspolitischer Verlag, 1921.

Wir Mädel singen. Liederbuch des Bundes Deutscher Mädel. Herausgegeben von der Reichsjugendführung. 2nd edn. Wolfenbüttel: Reichsjugendführung, 1941.

Witkop, Philipp, ed. *Kriegsbriefe deutscher Studenten.* Gotha: Verlag Friedrich Andreas Perthes A.-G., 1916.

Kriegsbriefe gefallener Studenten. Munich: G. Müller, 1928.

Wöhrle, Oskar, *Querschläger. Das Bumserbuch. Aufzeichnungen eines Kanoniers.* Berlin: Verlagsbuchhandlung J. H. W., 1929.

Zechlin, Erich. "Litauen und seine Probleme." *Internationale Monatsschrift für Wissenschaft, Kunst und Technik* 10.3 (December 1, 1915): 257–86.

Zeschau, von. "Streiflichter aus den Kämpfen um Litauen. Von Major von Zeschau, ehem. Führer des Sächsischen Freiwilligen-Infanterie-Regiments 18." In Salomon, ed., *Freikorpskämpfer.*

Zweig, Arnold. *Das ostjüdische Antlitz.* Berlin: Welt-Verlag, 1920.

Der Streit um den Sergeanten Grischa. Potsdam: Gustav Kiepenheuer Verlag, 1927.

SECONDARY SOURCES

Afflerbach, Holger. *Falkenhayn. Politisches Denken und Handeln im Kaiserreich.* Munich: R. Oldenbourg Verlag, 1994.

Akademie für Raumforschung und Landesplanung. *Handwörterbuch der Raumfor-schung und Raumordnung.* 2nd edn. Hannover: Gebrüder Janecke Verlag, 1970.

Aleksandravičius, Egidijus. "Political Goals of Lithuanians, 1863–1918." *Journal of Baltic Studies* 23. 3 (fall 1992): 227–38.

Altrichter, Friedrich. *Die seelischen Kräfte des Deutschen Heeres im Frieden und Weltkriege.* Berlin: E. S. Mittler & Sohn, 1933.

Aly, Götz and Karl Heinz Roth. *Die restlose Erfassung. Volkszählen, Identifizieren, Aussondern im Nationalsozialismus.* Berlin: Rotbuch Verlag, 1984.

Anderson, Benedict. *Imagined Communities: Reflections on the Origin and Spread of Nationalism.* Rev. edn London: Verso, 1991.

Applegate, Celia. *A Nation of Provincials: The German Idea of Heimat.* Berkeley: University of California Press, 1990.

Aschheim, Steven E. *Brothers and Strangers: The East European Jew in German and German Jewish Consciousness, 1800–1923.* Madison: University of Wisconsin Press, 1982.

"Eastern Jews, German Jews and Germany's Ostpolitik in the First World War." *Leo Baeck Institute Year Book* 28 (1983): 351–65.

Asprey, Robert B. *The German High Command at War: Hindenburg and Ludendorff Conduct World War I.* New York: William Morrow, 1991.

Atamukas, Solomonas. *Žydai Lietuvoje. XIV-XX amžiai.* Vilnius: Akcinė bendrovė Lituanus, 1990.

Baird, Jay W. *To Die For Germany: Heroes in the Nazi Pantheon.* Bloomington: Indiana University Press, 1990.

Bartov, Omer. *The Eastern Front, 1941–1945: German Troops and the Barbarisation of Warfare.* New York: St. Martin's Press, 1986.

Hitler's Army: Soldiers, Nazis and War in the Third Reich. Oxford: Oxford University Press, 1991.

Basler, Werner. *Deutschlands Annexionspolitik in Polen und im Baltikum.* Berlin: Rütten & Loening, 1962.

Baumgart, Winfried. *Deutsche Ostpolitik 1918. Von Brest-Litowsk bis zum Ende des Ersten Weltkrieges.* Vienna: R. Oldenbourg Verlag, 1966.

Behrenbeck, Sabine. *Der Kult um die toten Helden. Nationalsozialistische Mythen, Riten und Symbole 1923 bis 1945.* Vierow bei Greifswald: SH-Verlag, 1996.

Benz, Wolfgang. "Der Generalplan Ost. Zur Germanisierungspolitik des NS-Regimes in den besetzten Ostgebieten, 1939–1945." In *Die Vertreibung der Deutschen aus dem Osten. Ursachen, Ereignisse, Folgen,* ed. Wolfgang Benz, Frankfurt-on-Main: Fischer Taschenbuch Verlag, 1985.

Berlin, Isaiah. *Vico and Herder: Two Studies in the History of Ideas.* London: Hogarth Press, 1976.

Bermann, Russell. *The Rise of the Modern German Novel: Crisis and Charisma.* Cambridge, MA: Harvard University Press, 1986.

Bertkau, Friedrich. "Das amtliche Zeitungswesen im Verwaltungsgebiet Ober-Ost. Beitrag zur Geschichte der Presse im Weltkrieg." Ph.D. diss., University of Leipzig, 1928.

Bessel, Richard. "The Great War in German Memory: The Soldiers of the First World War, Demobilization, and Weimar Political Culture." *German History*

6. 1 (April 1988): 20–34.

Bienhold, Marianne. *Die Entstehung des Litauischen Staates in den Jahren 1918–1919 im Spiegel Deutscher Akten.* Bochum: Studienverlag Dr. N. Brockmeyer, 1976.

Bilmanis, Alfred. *A History of Latvia.* Princeton: Princeton University Press, 1951.

Binion, Rudolph. *Hitler Among the Germans.* New York: Elsevier, 1976.

"Hitler Looks East." *History of Childhood Quarterly* 3.1 (summer 1975): 75–102.

"Hitler's Concept of *Lebensraum*: The Psychological Basis." *History of Childhood Quarterly* 1.2 (fall 1973): 187–258.

Blau, Friedrich. *Die deutschen Landsknechte. Ein Kulturbild.* 3rd edn. Kettwig: Phaidon Verlag, 1985.

Bramwell, Anna. *Blood and Soil: Richard Walther Darré and Hitler's "Green Party."* Abbotsbrook, Bucks: Kensal Press, 1985.

Brechtefeld, Jörg. *Mitteleuropa and German Politics: 1848 to the Present.* New York: St.Martin's Press, 1996.

Breitman, Richard. *The Architect of Genocide: Himmler and the Final Solution.* Hanover, NH: Brandeis University Press, 1991.

Broszat, Martin. *Zweihundert Jahre deutsche Polenpolitik.* Rev. edn. Frankfurt-on-Main: Suhrkamp, 1972.

Bruford, Walter Horace. *The German Tradition of Self-Cultivation: "Bildung" from Humboldt to Thomas Mann.* Cambridge: Cambridge University Press, 1975.

Bullock, Alan. *Hitler: A Study in Tyranny.* Rev. edn. New York: Bantam Books, 1961.

Burleigh, Michael. *Germany Turns Eastwards: A Study of "Ostforschung" in the Third Reich.* Cambridge: Cambridge University Press, 1988.

Burleigh, Michael and Wolfgang Wippermann. *The Racial State: Germany, 1933–1945.*Cambridge: Cambridge University Press, 1991.

Campbell, Joan. *Joy in Work, German Work: The National Debate, 1800–1945.* Princeton: Princeton University Press, 1989.

Canetti, Elias. *Crowds and Power.* Translated by Carol Stewart. London: Victor Gollancz, 1962.

Carsten, Francis L. "'Volk ohne Raum': A Note on Hans Grimm." *Journal of Contemporary History* 2.2 (April 1967): 221–27.

Čepėnas, Pranas. *Naujųjų laikų Lietuvos istorija*, vol. II. Chicago: M. Morkūno spaustuvė, 1976.

Chickering, Roger. *Imperial Germany and the Great War, 1914–1918.* Cambridge: Cambridge University Press, 1998.

We Men Who Feel Most German: A Cultural Study of the Pan-German League, 1886–1914. London: Allen & Unwin, 1984.

Churchill, Winston S. *The Unknown War: The Eastern Front.* New York: Scribner's Sons, 1931.

Cohen, Israel. *Vilna.* Philadelphia: Jewish Publication Society of America, 1943.

Colliander, Börje. "Die Beziehungen zwischen Litauen und Deutschland während der Okkupation, 1915–1918. " Ph.D. diss., University of Åbo, 1935.

Conze, Werner. *Polnische Nation und deutsche Politik im ersten Weltkrieg*. Cologne: BöhlauVerlag, 1958.

"Nationalstaat oder Mitteleuropa? Die Deutschen des Reichs und die Nationalitätenfragen Ostmitteleuropas im ersten Weltkrieg." In *Deutschland und Europa. Historische Studien zur Völker- und Staatenordnung des Abendlandes. Festschrift für Hans Rothfels*, ed. Werner Conze. Düsseldorf: Droste Verlag, 1951.

Craig, Gordon A. *Germany, 1866–1945*. Oxford and New York: Oxford University Press, 1978.

The Politics of the Prussian Army, 1640–1945. Oxford: Oxford University Press, 1955.

Cron, Hermann. *Geschichte des Deutschen Heeres im Weltkriege, 1914–1918*. Berlin: Militärverlag Karl Sigismund, 1937.

Dallin, Alexander. *German Rule in Russia, 1941–1945: A Study of Occupation Policies*. 2nd rev. edn. Boulder, CO: Westview Press, 1981.

Davies, Norman. *God's Playground: A History of Poland*. New York: Columbia University Press, 1982.

Demandt, Alexander, ed. *Deutschlands Grenzen in der Geschichte*. Munich: Verlag C. H. Beck, 1990.

Demm, Eberhard. "Friedrich von der Ropp und die litauische Frage (1916–1919)." In *Zeitschrift für Ostforschung* 33 (1984): 16–56.

Die Rückführung des Ostheeres, vol. I, *Darstellungen aus den Nachkriegskämpfen Deutscher Truppen und Freikorps*. Berlin: Verlag E. S. Mittler & Sohn, 1936.

Dorpalen, Andreas. *The World of General Haushofer: Geopolitics in Action*. New York: Farrar & Rinehart, 1942.

Ekdahl, Sven. "Tannenberg/Grunwald – Ein politisches Symbol in Deutschland und Polen." *Journal of Baltic Studies* 12.4 (winter 1991): 271–324.

Eksteins, Modris. *Rites of Spring: The Great War and the Birth of the Modern Age*. Boston: Houghton Mifflin, 1989.

Ellis, John. *Eye-Deep in Hell: Trench Warfare in World War I*. New York: Pantheon Books, 1977.

Elsner, Lothar. "Ausländerbeschäftigung und Zwangsarbeitspolitik in Deutschland während des Ersten Weltkrieges." In *Auswanderer – Wanderarbeiter – Gastarbeiter. Bevölkerung, Arbeitsmarkt und Wanderung in Deutschland seit der Mitte des 19. Jahrhunderts*, ed. Klaus J. Bade. Ostfildern: Scripta Mercaturae Verlag, 1984.

Fedyshyn, Oleg S. *Germany's Drive to the East and the Ukrainian Revolution, 1917–1918*. New Brunswick: Rutgers University Press, 1971.

Feldman, Gerald D. *Army, Industry and Labor in Germany, 1914–1918*. Princeton: Princeton University Press, 1966.

Fischer, Fritz. *Griff nach der Weltmacht. Die Kriegszielpolitik des kaiserlichen Deutschland 1914/1918*. Düsseldorf: Droste, 1961; 3rd rev. edn 1967.

Fischer, Klaus P. *Nazi Germany: A New History*. New York: Continuum, 1995.

Fritz, Stephen G. *Frontsoldaten: The German Soldier in World War II*. Lexington: University Press of Kentucky, 1995.

Fussell, Paul. *The Great War and Modern Memory*. Oxford: Oxford University Press, 1975.

Gay, Peter. *Weimar Culture: The Outsider as Insider.* New York: Harper & Row, 1968.

Geiss, Imanuel. *Der polnische Grenzstreifen. Ein Beitrag zur deutschen Kriegsziel-politik im Ersten Weltkrieg.* Lübeck: Mattheisen, 1960.

"The Civilian Dimension of the War." In *Facing Armageddon: The First World War Experience,* ed. Hugh Cecil and Peter H. Liddle. London: Leo Cooper, 1996.

Goodspeed, D. J. *Ludendorff: Genius of World War I.* Boston: Houghton Mifflin, 1966.

Greimas, Algirdas Julius and Saulius Žukas. *Lietuva Pabaltijy. Istorijos ir kultūros bruožai.* Vilnius: Baltos lankos, 1993.

Gröning, Gert. "The Feeling for Landscape – a German Example." *Landscape Research* 17.3 (1992): 108–15.

Gröning, Gert and Joachim Wolschke-Bulmahn. *Die Liebe zur Landschaft. Teil III: Der Drang nach Osten.* Arbeiten zur sozialwissenschaftlich orientierten Freiraumplanung. Munich: Minerva Publikation, 1987.

Grunberger, Richard. *Germany, 1918–1945.* London: B. T. Batsford, 1964.

Hafkesbrink, Hanna. *Unknown Germany: An Inner Chronicle of the First World War Based on Letters and Diaries.* New Haven: Yale University Press, 1948.

Handrack, Hans-Dieter. *Das Reichskommissariat Ostland. Die Kulturpolitik der deutschen Verwaltung zwischen Autonomie und Gleichschaltung, 1941–1944.* Hann. Münden: Gauke Verlag, 1981.

Häpke, Rudolf. "Die geschichtliche und landeskundliche Forschung in Litauen und Baltenland, 1915–1918." *Hansische Geschichtsblätter* 45 (1919): 17–34.

Hellmann, Manfred. *Grundzüge der Geschichte Litauens und des litauischen Volkes.* 4th edn. Darmstadt: Wissenschaftliche Buchgesellschaft, 1990.

Herb, Guntram Henrik. *Under the Map of Germany: Nationalism and Propaganda, 1918–1945.* London: Routledge, 1997.

Herbert, Ulrich. *A History of Foreign Labor in Germany, 1880–1980: Seasonal Workers / Forced Workers / Guest Workers.* Translated by William Templer. Ann Arbor: University of Michigan Press, 1990.

Hermand, Jost. *Arnold Zweig.* Reinbek bei Hamburg: Rohwohlt Taschenbuch Verlag, 1990.

Grüne Utopien in Deutschland. Zur Geschichte des ökologischen Bewusstseins. Frankfurt-on-Main: Fischer Taschenbuch Verlag, 1991.

Herwig, Holger. *The First World War: Germany and Austria-Hungary, 1914–1918.* London: Edward Arnold, 1997.

Hirschfeld, Magnus. *Sittengeschichte des Ersten Weltkrieges.* Rev. 2nd edn. Hanau: Schustek, 1966.

Hobsbawm, Eric. *Nations and Nationalism Since 1780: Programme, Myth, Reality.* Cambridge: Cambridge University Press, 1990.

Hobsbawm, Eric and Terence Ranger. *The Invention of Tradition.* Cambridge: Cambridge University Press, 1983.

Howard, Michael. *War in European History.* Oxford: Oxford University Press, 1976.

Hubatsch, Walther. *Germany and the Central Powers in the World War, 1914–1918.* Lawrence, KS: University of Kansas Press, 1963.

Hüppauf, Bernd. "Langemarck, Verdun, and the Myth of the *New Man* in Germany After the First World War." *War and Society* 6.2 (September 1988): 70–103.

Jäckel, Eberhard. *Hitlers Weltanschauung. Entwurf einer Herrschaft.* Tübingen: R. Wunderlich, 1969.

Janßen, Karl-Heinz. "Alfred von Goßler und die deutsche Verwaltung im Baltikum, 1915–1918." *Historische Zeitschrift* 207 (1968): 42–54.

"Die baltische Okkupationspolitik des deutschen Reiches." In *Von den baltischen Provinzen zu den baltischen Staaten. Beiträge zur Entstehungsgeschichte der Republiken Estland und Lettland, 1917–1918,* ed. Jürgen von Hehn, Hans von Rimscha, and Hellmuth Weiss. Marburg/Lahn: J. G. Herder-Institut, 1971.

Jeserich, Kurt G. A., *et al.,* eds. *Deutsche Verwaltungsgeschichte,* vol. III, *Das Deutsche Reich bis zum Ende der Monarchie.* Stuttgart: Deutsche Verlagsanstalt, 1984.

Johnson, Paul. *Modern Times: The World from the Twenties to the Nineties.* Rev. edn. New York: HarperCollins, 1991.

Jonikas, Petras. *Lietuviu kalba ir tauta amžių būvyje. Visuomeniniai lietuvių kalbos istorijos bruožai.* Chicago: Lituanistikos instituto leidykla, 1987.

Karulis, Konstantīnas, ed., *Latviešu etimologijas vārdnīca.* 2 vols. Riga: Avots, 1992.

Keegan, John. *The Face of Battle.* New York: Viking Press, 1976.

The Second World War. Hammondsworth: Penguin, 1990.

Kern, Stephen. *The Culture of Time and Space, 1880–1918.* Cambridge, MA: Harvard University Press, 1983.

Kitchen, Martin. *A Military History of Germany from the Eighteenth Century to the Present Day.* Bloomington: Indiana University Press, 1975.

The Silent Dictatorship: The Politics of the German High Command Under Hindenburg and Ludendorff, 1916–1918. London: Croom Helm, 1976.

Klee, Ernst and Willi Dressen, eds. *'Gott mit uns.' Der deutsche Vernichtungskrieg im Osten, 1939–1945.* Frankfurt-on-Main: S. Fischer Verlag, 1989.

Klemperer, Victor. *Die unbewältigte Sprache. Aus dem Notizbuch eines Philologen "LTI."* 3rd edn. Darmstadt: Joseph Melzer Verlag, n.d.

Klessmann, Christoph. "Osteuropaforschung und Lebensraumpolitik im Dritten Reich." In *Wissenschaft im Dritten Reich,* ed. Peter Lundgreen. Frankfurt-on-Main: Suhrkamp, 1985.

Klimas, Petras. "Lietuvos valstybės kūrimas 1915–1918 metais Vilniuje." In *Pirmasis nepriklausomos Lietuvos dešimtmetis, 1918–1928.* Kaunas: "Spindulio" B-vės spaustuvė, 1928.

Kluge, Ulrich. *Soldatenräte und Revolution. Studien zur Militärpolitik in Deutschland 1918/19.* Göttingen: Vandenhoeck & Rupprecht, 1975.

Kocka, Jürgen. *Klassengesellschaft im Krieg. Deutsche Sozialgeschichte, 1914–1918.* Göttingen: Vandenhock & Ruprecht, 1973.

Koehl, Robert Lewis. *RKFDV: German Resettlement and Population Policy.* Cambridge, MA: Harvard University Press, 1957.

Koetzle, Hermann. *Das Sanitätswesen im Weltkrieg, 1914–18.* Stuttgart: Bergers Literarisches Büro & Verlagsanstalt, 1924.

Kossmann, E. H. *The Low Countries, 1780–1940.* Oxford: Oxford University Press, 1978.

Kost, Klaus. *Die Einflüsse der Geopolitik auf Forschung und Theorie des Politischen Geographie von ihren Anfängen bis 1945. Ein Beitrag zur Wissenschaftsgeschichte der Politischen Geographie unter besonderer Berücksichtigung von Militär- und Kolonialgeographie.* Bonner Geographische Abhandlungen, 76. Bonn: Ferd. Dümmlers Verlag, 1988.

Kramer, Alan. "'Greueltaten': Zum Problem der deutschen Kriegsverbrechen in Belgien und Frankreich 1914." In *"Keiner fühlt sich hier als Mensch." Erlebnis und Wirkung des Ersten Weltkriegs,* ed. Gerhard Hirschfeld, *et al.* Frankfurt: Fischer Taschenbuch Verlag, 1996.

Kuebart, Friedrich. "Zur Entwicklung der Osteuropaforschung in Deutschland bis 1945,"*Osteuropa* 30 (1980): 657–72.

Langer, Herbert. *Kulturgeschichte des 30 jährigen Krieges.* Stuttgart: W. Kohlhammer, 1978.

Laqueur, Walter. *Russia and Germany: A Century of Conflict.* London: Weidenfeld & Nicolson, 1965.

Latzel, Klaus. "Tourismus und Gewalt. Kriegswahrnehmungen in Feldpostbriefen." In *Vernichtungskrieg: Verbrechen der Wehrmacht 1941 bis 1944,* ed. Hannes Heer and Klaus Naumann. Hamburg: Hamburger Edition, 1995.

Leed, Eric J. *No Man's Land: Combat and Identity in World War I.* Cambridge: Cambridge University Press, 1979.

Lehmann, Ulf. "Herder und die Slawen. Probleme des Geschichtsbildes und Geschichtsverständnisses aus historischer Perspektive." *Jahrbuch für Geschichte der sozialistischen Länder Europas* 22.1 (1978): 39–50.

Lietuvių enciklopedija. Ed. Vaclovas Biržiška. 36 vols. South Boston, MA: Lietuvių Enciklopedijos Leidykla, 1953–69.

Lincoln, W. Bruce. *Passage Through Armageddon: The Russians in War and Revolution, 1914–1918.* New York: Simon & Schuster, 1986.

Linde, Gerd. *Die deutsche Politik in Litauen im ersten Weltkrieg.* Wiesbaden: Otto Harrassowitz, 1965.

Lurz, Meinhold. *Kriegerdenkmäler in Deutschland.* Vol. V, *Drittes Reich.* Heidelberg: Esprint, 1986.

Lutz, Ralph Haswell, ed. *The Causes of the German Collapse in 1918.* Translated by W. L. Campbell. Stanford: Stanford University Press, 1934.

Maclean, Pam. "Control and Cleanliness: German–Jewish Relations in Occupied Eastern Europe during the First World War." *War & Society* 6.2 (September 1988): 47–69.

Mai, Günther. *Das Ende des Kaiserreichs. Politik und Kriegführung im Ersten Weltkrieg.* Munich: Deutscher Taschenbuch Verlag, 1987.

Mann, Golo. *The History of Germany Since 1789.* Translated by Marian Jackson. Harmondsworth: Penguin, 1974.

Marks, Shannee. *Die Grenze der Schuld. Soziologische Strukturen der faschistischen Ideologie.* Beiträge zur sozialwissenschaftlichen Forschung, 77. Opladen: Westdeutscher Verlag, 1987.

McGreevy, Linda F. *The Life and Works of Otto Dix: German Critical Realist.* Ann Arbor: UMI Research Press, 1981.

Meyer, Henry Cord. *Mitteleuropa in German Thought and Action, 1815–1945*. The Hague: Martinus Nijhoff, 1955.

Milosz, Czeslaw. *Native Realm: A Search for Self-Definition*. Translated by Catherine S. Leach. Garden City, NY: Doubleday, 1968.

Misiunas, Romuald and Rein Taagepera. *The Baltic States: Years of Dependence, 1940–1990*. Rev. edn. Berkeley: University of California Press, 1993.

Mommsen, Wolfgang J. "The Debate on German War Aims." *Journal of Contemporary History* 1.3 (July 1966): 47–72.

Mosse, George L. *The Crisis of the German Ideology: Intellectual Origins of the Third Reich*. New York: Schocken Books, 1981.

Fallen Soldiers: Reshaping the Memory of the World Wars. Oxford and New York: Oxford University Press, 1990.

Murmann, Geerte. *Komödianten fur den Krieg. Deutsches und alliertes Fronttheater*. Düsseldorf: Droste, 1992.

Oestreich, Gerhard. *Neostoicism and the Early Modern State*. Translated by David McLintock. Cambridge: Cambridge University Press, 1982.

Paechter, Heinz, ed. *Nazi-Deutsch: A Glossary of Contemporary German Usage With Appendices on Government, Military, and Economic Institutions*. New York: Frederick Ungar Publishing, 1944.

Page, Stanley W. *The Formation of the Baltic States: A Study of the Effects of Great Power Politics Upon the Emergence of Lithuania, Latvia, and Estonia*. Cambridge, MA: Harvard University Press, 1959.

Parkinson, Roger. *Tormented Warrior: Ludendorff and the Supreme Command*. New York: Stein & Day, 1979.

Peukert, Detlev J. K. *The Weimar Republic: The Crisis of Classical Modernity*. Translated by Richard Deveson. New York: Hill & Wang, 1993.

Pfaff, William. *The Wrath of Nations: Civilization and the Furies of Nationalism*. New York: Simon & Schuster, 1993.

Plakans, Andrejs. *The Latvians: A Short History*. Stanford: Hoover Institution Press, 1995.

Platner, Geert, *et al.*, eds. *Schule im Dritten Reich- Erziehung zum Tod? Eine Dokumentation*. Munich: Deutscher Taschenbuch Verlag GmbH & Co. KG, 1983.

Pörzgen, Hermann. "Das deutsche Fronttheater, 1914–20." Ph.D. diss., Cologne, 1935.

Pounds, Norman J. G. *Eastern Europe*. Chicago: Aldine Publishing, 1969.

Prümm, Karl. *Die Literatur des Soldatischen Nationalismus der 20er Jahre (1918–1933)*. Kronberg Taunus: Scriptor Verlag GmbH, 1974.

Puzinas, Jonas. *Rinktiniai rastai*, vol. II. Chicago: Lituanistikos Instituto Leidykla, 1983.

Raeff, Marc. *The Well-Ordered Police State: Social and Institutional Change Through Law in the Germanies and Russia, 1600–1800*. New Haven: Yale University Press, 1983.

Rauch, Georg von. *Geschichte der baltischen Staaten*. 3rd edn. Munich: Deutscher Taschenbuch Verlag, 1990.

Raudeliūnienė, Genovita. "Lietuvos gyventojų pasipriešinimas vokiečių okupantams pirmojo pasaulinio karo metais (1915–1918)." Diss., Lithuanian SSR

Academy of Sciences, Vilnius, 1969.

Raun, Toivo U. *Estonia and the Estonians.* 2nd edn. Stanford: Hoover Institution Press, 1991.

Rempel, Gerhard. *Hitler's Children: The Hitler Youth and the SS.* Chapel Hill: University of North Carolina Press, 1989.

Robinson, Geroid Tanquary. *Rural Russia Under the Old Regime: A History of the Landlord–Peasant World and a Prologue to the Peasant Revolution of 1917.* London: Longmans, Green & Co., 1932.

Roessler, Mechthild. *Wissenschaft und Lebensraum. Geographische Ostforschung im Nationalsozialismus. Ein Beitrag zur Disziplingeschichte der Geographie.* Hamburger Beiträge zur Wissenschaftsgeschichte, 8. Berlin: Dietrich Reimer Verlag, 1990.

"Applied Geography and Area Research in Nazi Society: The Central Place Theory and its Implications, 1933 to 1945." *Environment and Planning D, Society and Space* (December 7, 1989): 419–31.

"Die Institutionalisierung einer neuen 'Wissenschaft' im Nationalsozialismus: Raumforschung und Raumordnung, 1935–1945." *Geographische Zeitschrift* 75.3 (1987): 177–94.

Rothfels, Hans. "The Baltic Provinces: Some Historic Aspects and Perspectives." *Journal of Central European Affairs* 4.2 (July 1944): 117–46.

Saul, Klaus. "Jugend im Schatten des Krieges. Vormilitärische Ausbildung – Kriegswirtschaftlicher Einsatz – Schulalltag in Deutschland, 1914–1918." *Militärgeschichtliche Mitteilungen* 2 (1983): 91–184.

Schama, Simon. *Landscape and Memory.* New York: Alfred A. Knopf, 1995.

Schmidt-Pauli, Edgar von. *Geschichte der Freikorps, 1918–1924. Nach amtlichen Quellen, Zeitberichten, Tagebüchern und persöhnlichen Mitteilungen hervorragender Freikorpsführer dargestellt.* Stuttgart: R. Lutz, 1936.

Schmitt, Bernadotte E. and Harold Vedeler. *The World in the Crucible, 1914–1919.* New York: Harper & Row, 1984.

Schnabel, Franz. *Deutsche Geschichte im neunzehnten Jahrhundert. Die Grundlagen der neueren Geschichte.* Freiburg im Breisgau: Herder Verlag, 1964.

Schultz, Hans-Dietrich. "Deutschlands 'natürliche' Grenzen." In *Deutschlands Grenzen in der Geschichte,* ed. Demandt.

Schulze, Hagen. *Freikorps und Republik, 1918–1920.* Militärgeschichtliche Studien, 8. Boppard-on-Rhein: Harald Boldt Verlag, 1969.

Schwarte, M., ed. *Der grosse Krieg.* 10 vols. Leipzig: Barth, 1923.

Senn, Alfred Erich. *The Emergence of Modern Lithuania.* New York: Columbia University Press, 1959.

Smith, Woodruff D. *The Ideological Origins of Nazi Imperialism.* Oxford: Oxford University Press, 1986.

Politics and the Sciences of Culture in Germany, 1840–1920. Oxford: Oxford University Press, 1991.

Stern, Fritz. *The Politics of Cultural Despair: A Study in the Rise of the Germanic Ideology.* Berkeley: University of California Press, 1961.

Stökl, Günther. *Osteuropa und die Deutschen. Geschichte und Gegenwart einer spannungsreichen Nachbarschaft.* 3rd edn. Stuttgart: S. Hirzel Verlag, 1982.

Stone, Norman. *The Eastern Front, 1914–1917.* New York: Scribner's Sons, 1975.

Storost-Vydūnas, Wilhelm. *Sieben Hundert Jahre deutsch-litauischer Beziehungen.*
    Kulturhistorische Darlegungen. Tilsit: Ruta-Verlag, 1932.
Storosta, Jurgėnas. "Apie Vydūno ir Zudermano santykius." *Literatūra ir menas*
    (March 27, 1993): 4.
Stražas, A. "Die deutsche Militär-Verwaltung 'Oberost' – Prototyp der geplanten
    Kolonialadministration 'Neuland' (1915–1918)." *Wissenschaftliche Zeit-
    schrift der Pädagogischen Hochschule "Dr. Theodor Neubauer," Erfurt-Mü-
    hlhausen, Gesellschafts- und sprachwissenschaftliche Reihe* 8 (1971): 39–44.
Strazhas, Aba. *Deutsche Ostpolitik im Ersten Weltkrieg. Der Fall Ober Ost, 1915–
    1917.* Wiesbaden: Harrassowitz Verlag, 1993.
    "The Land Oberost and its Place in Germany's Ostpolitik, 1915–1918." In
    Baltic States in Peace and War, ed. Vardys and Misiunas.
Stromberg, Roland. *Redemption by War: The Intellectuals and 1914.* Lawrence:
    The Regents Press of Kansas, 1982.
Stupperich, Robert. "Siedlungspläne im Gebiet des Oberbefehlshabers Ost
    (Militärverwaltung Litauen und Kurland) während des Weltkrieges." *Jom-
    sburg* 5 (1941): 348–67.
Sukiennicki, Wiktor. *East Central Europe During World War I,* 2 vols. Boulder,
    CO: East European Monographs, 1984.
Sullivan, Charles. "The 1919 German Campaign in the Baltic: The Final Phase."
    In *Baltic States in Peace and War* , ed. Vardys and Misiunas.
Sužiedėlis, Simas. "Mokyklos vokiečių okupacijos laikais." In *Lietuva,* Lietuvių
    enciklopedija, 15, ed. Vincas Maciūnas, South Boston, MA: Lithuanian
    Encyclopedia Press, 1968.
Tatham, George. "Geography in the Nineteenth Century." In Taylor, ed., *Ge-
    ography in the Twentieth Century.*
Taylor, Griffith, ed., *Geography in the Twentieth Century: A Study of Growth, Fields,
    Techniques, Aims and Trends.* New York: Philosophical Library, 1951.
Taylor, Robert R. *The Word in Stone: The Role of Architecture in the National
    Socialist Ideology,* Berkeley: University of California Press, 1974.
Theweleit, Klaus. *Male Fantasies.* Translated by Stephan Conway. Minneapolis:
    University of Minnesota Press, 1987.
Thielecke, Albert. "Deutsche landeskundliche Arbeit im Weltkriege. An der
    europäichen Ost- und Südost-Front und in den anschliessenden Etappen-
    gebieten." Ph.D. diss, Friedrich-Schiller University, Jena, 1936.
Urbšienė, M. *Vokiečių okupacijos ūkis Lietuvoje.* Kaunas: Spindulio B-vės spaus-
    tuvė, 1939.
Vakar, Nicholas P. *Belorussia: The Making of a Nation.* Cambridge, MA: Harvard
    University Press, 1956.
Van Valkenburg, Samuel. "The German School of Geography." In Taylor, ed.,
    Geography in theTwentieth Century.
Vardys, V. Stanley and Romualdas J. Misiunas, eds. *The Baltic States in Peace and
    War, 1917–1945.* University Park: Pennsylvania State University Press,
    1978.
Vardys, V. Stanley and Judith B. Sedaitis, *Lithuania: The Rebel Nation.* Boulder,
    CO: Westview Press, 1997.
Vondung, Klaus, ed. *Kriegserlebnis. Der erste Weltkrieg in der literarischen Gestaltung*

und symbolischen Deutung der Nationen. Göttingen: Vandenhoeck & Ruprecht, 1980.

Waite, Robert G. L. *Vanguard of Nazism: The Free Corps Movement in Postwar Germany 1918–1923.* Cambridge, MA: Harvard University Press, 1952.

Walkenburg, S. van, "The German School of Geography." In Taylor, ed., *Geography in the Twentieth Century.*

Walker, Mack. *German Home Towns: Community, State, and General Estate, 1648–1871.* Ithaca, NY: Cornell University Press, 1971.

Weeks, Theodore R. *Nation and State in Late Imperial Russia: Nationalism and Russification on the Western Frontier, 1863–1914.* DeKalb: Northern Illinois University Press, 1996.

Wehler, Hans-Ulrich. *Das Deutsche Kaiserreich, 1871–1918.* Göttingen: Vandenhoeck & Ruprecht, 1973.

Weigert, Hans W. *Generals and Geographers: The Twilight of Geopolitics.* Oxford and New York: Oxford University Press, 1942.

Welch, David. "Educational Film Propaganda and the Nazi Youth." In Welch, ed., *Nazi Propaganda.*

Welch, David, ed. *Nazi Propaganda: The Power and Limitations.* London: Croom Helm, 1983.

Wenzel, Georg, ed. *Arnold Zweig, 1887–1968. Werk und Leben in Dokumenten und Bildern.* Berlin: Aufbau-Verlag, 1978.

Wheeler-Bennett, John W. *Brest-Litovsk: The Forgotten Peace, March 1918.* New York: William Morrow, 1939.

Wooden Titan: Hindenburg in Twenty Years of German History, 1914–1934. New York: William Morrow, 1936.

Whittlesey, Derwent. *German Strategy of World Conquest.* New York: Farrar & Rinehart, 1942.

Wilhelm, Hans-Heinrich. "Personelle Kontinuitäten in baltischen Angelegenheiten auf deutscher Seite von 1917/19 bis zum Zweiten Weltkrieg?" In John Hiden and Aleksander Loit, eds., *The Baltic in International Relations Between the World Wars,* Acta Universitatis Stockholmiensis, Studia Baltica Stockholmiensia 3 (1988): 157–70.

Williams, Robert C. "Russians in Germany, 1900–1914." *Journal of Contemporary History* 1.4 (October 1966): 121–49.

Winter, J. M. *The Experience of World War I.* Oxford and New York: Oxford University Press, 1989.

Winter, Jay. *Sites of Memory, Sites of Mourning: The Great War in European Cultural History.* Cambridge: Cambridge University Press, 1995.

Wippermann, Wolfgang. *Der "Deutsche Drang nach Osten." Ideologie und Wirklichkeit eines politischen Schlagwortes.* Darmstadt: Wissenschaftliche Buchgesellschaft, 1981.

Wistrich, Robert. *Who's Who in Nazi Germany.* London: Weidenfeld & Nicolson, 1982.

Wohl, Robert. *The Generation of 1914.* Cambridge, MA: Harvard University Press, 1979.

Zaprudnik, Jan. *Belarus: At a Crossroads in History.* Boulder, CO: Westview Press, 1993.

Zechlin, Egmont. *Die deutsche Politik und die Juden im Ersten Weltkrieg.* Göttingen: Vandenhoeck & Ruprecht, 1969.

Zemke, Hans. *Der Oberbefehlshaber Ost und das Schulwesen im Verwaltungsbereich-Litauen während des Weltkrieges.* Schriften der Kriegsgeschichtlichen Abteilung im historischen Seminar der Friedrich-Wilhelms-Universität Berlin, 14. Berlin: Junker & Dünnhaupt Verlag, 1936.

Ziemer, Gregor. *Education for Death: The Making of the Nazi.* Oxford and London: Oxford University Press, 1941.

Zunkel, Friedrich. "Die ausländischen Arbeiter in der deutschen Kriegswirtschaftspolitik des 1. Weltkrieges." In *Entstehung und Wandel der modernen Gesellschaft. Festschrift für H. Rosenberg zum 65. Geburtstag,* ed. Gerhard Ritter. Berlin: n.p., 1970.

Index

agriculture, 61, 65–71, 72
  estates, 66, 69
  exhibitions, 69, 162
  experiments, 96
  German plans for, 68–69, 199
  problems, 68–69
  soil reports, 94
  surveys, 94
Allies, assistance to Baltic republics, 229, 231–32, 242
Alsace-Lorraine, 35, 95
  Alsatian soldiers, 187–89, 213, 218
Angarietis, Zigmas, 228
anti-Semitism, 58, 61, 120, 132, 163
  Nazi, 256, 265, 267, 268, 270
archaeology, 37–38
Armenians, 259
Armistice, 229–30
August Wilhelm of Prussia, Prince, 58
Auschwitz, 241
Austria, 16, 204, 257
autarchy, 64–65
Auxiliary Service Law, 55
Avalov-Bermondt, Pavel, 232, 242

Baden, Max von, 214
Balodis, Jānis, 231
Balodis Brigade, 230
Baltic countries, see Estonia; Latvia; Lithuania
Baltic Germans, 24, 33, 165, 208
  administration includes, 57, 178, 206
  Barons, 31, 33, 187, 208, 215
  ethnic conflict and, 33, 178–79
  Freikorps and, 230, 238
  Landeswehr volunteer force, 230, 232
  national identity of, 33, 187
  Nazis and, 258–59, 265
Baltikum administrative unit, 209, 215
Baltikumer, see Freikorps
bandits, 33, 74, 78–79, 181
  measures against, 78–79, 91

Banse, Ewald, 253
Barbarossa, Operation, 266
Bartov, Omer, 5, 267
Basanavičius, Jonas, 200
Baumann, Hans, 263
Bavaria, 35
Bebel, August, 24
Belarus and Belarusians, 31, 62, 132, 192
  art, 139
  German views of, 120–21
  language, 118
  newspaper for, 123
  schools and, 125
  Soviet Lit-Bel, 229
Belgium, 56, 95, 100, 165
  Louvain, 129
Below, von, 17
Bermondt, see Avalov-Bermondt
Bertkau, Friedrich, 115
Bethmann Hollweg, Theobald von, 23, 164, 170, 196–97
Bialowies forest, 20, 27, 72, 199
Bialystok-Grodno, 21
  administration of, 55, 58, 61–62, 198
  riots, 69
  schools, 124
Bingen, 196
Bischoff, Josef, 231, 232
Bismarck, Otto von, 23
blockade, British naval, 64, 72, 163, 176, 213, 232
Bolsheviks, 177, 182, 195, 203, 210, 216, 218, 241, 249
  Red Army, 228–29, 231
borders, 166, 240, 250–51
  geopolitics and, 253, 254–55
Bredt, Johann Victor, 203
Brest-Litovsk
  German capture of, 17, 20
  Treaty of, 95, 204–6, 216, 228, 249
bridges, 97–98
Britain, 229, 231, 242

Brockhusen-Justin, Hans-Joachim von, 61, 177
Broederich-Kurmahlen, Silvio, 165, 230
Brody, 21
Brusilov Offensive, 21, 176
Bug river, 98–99

Calvinists, 33
Carpathian mountains, 17
Caucasus, 210
census, 94
Center Party, 164, 201
Central Association of German Industrialists, 165
Charkow, 213
Chelm, 205
Christian German Farmers' Union, 165
Churchill, Winston, 3
cleanliness, 19, 80–81, 105–6
   cleaning, 154, 160
clash of cultures, 181, 184–86
Class, Heinrich, 164
Clemen, Paul, 130
Cologne, 117
colonial experience, German, 78, 240–41
Colonial Institute, Hamburg, 166
Colonial Society, 168
colonization, see settlement
Cossacks, 15, 19, 22, 30
Courland, see Kurland
Cracow, 16
Crimea, 210
"cultural gradient," 25
cultural mission, 140, 165
   cleanliness and, 105
   East and, 70–71, 97
   Freikorps and, 232
   German Work and, 45–46, 94, 113
   culture, German views of, 29, 31
   Herder's view of, 190
   juxtaposed with civilization, 29
   juxtaposed with "Unkultur," 29, 70, 140, 155, 278
   Nazi views of, 267
"culture landscape," 167, 255, 265
cultural program, 89
   aims of, 113–14
   art historical catalogs, 129–32
   beginnings of, 113
   German traces and, 130–31
   structure of, 115
   Wilna-Minsk exhibition, 132

Dabartis, see Present Time, The
Dagö (Hiiumaa), 199

Damaschke, Adolf, 95
Danzig, 117
Darré, Richard Walter, 254, 259
Dehmel, Richard, 115, 119, 190–91
delousing, 43, 80, 160
   certificates of, 92
   natives and, 106
   rail cars for, 92
deserters, 79
disease, 22, 42, 80–81, 186, 210, 260
   control at border, 92
   German fear of, 81, 105
   workers and, 74
Dix, Otto, 152, 160
Drang nach Osten, "Drive to the East," 25, 39, 166, 240, 260, 262–63
Dwinger, Edwin Erich, 261
Dwinsk, 213
dogs, 65, 80, 102
Döblin, Alfred, 41
Dorpat (Tartu), 205, 211, 228
Dresden, 117
Düna river (Daugava), 20
Dünaburg (Daugavpils), 208
Dvinsk (Daugavpils), 19

"Easterners," 16
"East Research," see Ostforschung
Eberhardt, Magnus von, 242
Ebert, Friedrich, 232
economic officers, 66
economy, 61, 64–65
   gains in, 73
   political importance of, 178–79
   problems with, 75, 207
   quotas, 66
   statistics, 66–67
education
   failure of policy, 127–28
   future plans for, 199, 203
   German language, 125–26, 203, 209
   German teachers, 126
   Germanization, 126, 127
   ideas of Bildung, 114, 122, 135, 167
   monopoly, 124
   native schools, 78, 123–24, 206
   Nazi views of, 260–61, 268–71
   policy, 123–27, 206
   teachers' courses, 126
   universities, 127, 199, 211, 267
Eichhorn, Hermann von, 19, 211
Eisenhart-Rothe, General von, 60
Eksteins, Modris, 4
Elias, Norbert, 2, 25, 96
Engels, Friedrich, 24

Erzberger, Matthias, 201, 206, 209–10,
    214
  war aims of, 164
Escherich, Georg, 72, 199
espionage, 91, 92
Estonia (*Estland*) and Estonians, 33, 205,
    208
  army, 229
  Assembly, 205, 206, 209, 215
  Freikorps and, 231, 242
  Nazi occupation of, 266
  Soviet, 228
  Soviet occupation of, 266
Eulenberg, Herbert, 115, 143
exhibits, traveling, 117

Falkenhausen, Freiherr von, 198
Falkenhayn, Erich von, 16, 17, 55
  ousted, 176
  rivalry with Hindenburg and
    Ludendorff, 16, 20, 21
famine, 69, 75, 182
Fatherland Party, 197
Finland, 210, 230
  Finnish volunteers, 229
Fischer, Fritz, 3
Flex, Walter, 41, 248, 252
forestry, 72, 98, 199, 242
Frankfurt on the Oder, 95
Frantz, Constantin, 23
Freikorps
  Baltic *Landeswehr* volunteer force, 230,
    232
  culture and, 232
  Diebitsch, 242
  disbanded, 243
  German "East state" and, 238
  German Legion, 232, 243
  historical memory and, 234–37
  identity defined, 237–40
  Iron Division, 230, 231, 232, 242–43
  Libau Putsch, 231
  Nazis and, 243
  numbers of, 228, 232
  origins of, 227
  Pfeffer, 231
  reported atrocities of, 231, 242–43
  Rossbach, 242
  settlement and, 230
  songs, 239, 243
  White Russians and, 232, 237
front, Eastern, German, 12, 152
  area of, 89
  boredom, 153
  cemeteries, 161, 251

disease, 22
experience compared to Western, 14,
    21, 22, 135, 247–49, 278
fortification and, 21, 134
losses, 22
numbers of soldiers, 14, 212
perceived post-war lessons of, 247–53,
    262
revolutionized, 212–14
"Stab in the Back" Legend of, 249
uniformity of natives, 156
front, Western, German
  experience, 12, 247
  strategic importance, 16
frontier thesis, German, 162
Fussell, Paul, 4, 136

Gaigalat-Gaigalaitis, Wilhelm, 183
Galicia, 17, 21
Gayl, Wilhelm Freiherr von, 61, 64, 127,
    180, 192, 202, 210, 216–17, 249
  German "East state" and, 238
  Jews and, 120
  on native literature, 139
  settlement activity, 94–95, 202–3
gendarmes, *see* police
geography
  borders and, 166, 250–52, 253, 254–55
  German culture and, 165–68
  maps and, 92, 93, 95
  military, 93
  Nazis and, 260
  schools and, 171
  surveys, 93
  war geography, 169–71, 254
  Weimar Germany and, 253–56
geopolitics, 169, 253–55, 264
German Academic Exchange Service, 57
German Army
  bearing of, 44
  collapse of, 212, 213–19, 249
  conflict in ranks, 64, 187–89
  Eighth Army, 15, 17
  fraternization with natives, 43, 44, 133,
    135, 138, 186–87, 213
  General Staff, 95
  "Great Advance" of 1915, 17, 22,
    151
  guidebooks to cities, 43–44
  High Command, 16, 21, 176, 195
  Ninth Army, 16
  Njemen Army, 17, 19
  Northern Border Defense, 230
  Russian army compared to, 19
  Tenth Army, 19, 21, 213

German Farmers' League, 165
"German Work," 45–47, 58, 96, 116, 132, 133
  division of labor in, 114
  movement policy and, 105
  origin of term, 45
  work rooms and, 129
Germany and Germans
  Eastern European studies in, 24
  eastern provinces, 23
  Foreign Ministry, 95
  German Jews, 41–42, 57, 58, 77
  Interior Ministry, 95
  Jews, attitudes towards, 119–20, 182
  leftist views of Russia, 24
  national identity, 35, 39, 46, 59
  natives and, 42–43, 44, 133
  Polish minority, 23, 25, 35, 61, 187
  present-day, 279–81
  prewar views of Russia, 22–25, 35
  regionalism, 35, 59, 187–88
  seige mentality, 163
  "Stab in the Back" legend, 219, 249
  university fraternities, 57
  war aims, 95, 164–65, 196–97
  Weltpolitik, 23, 168, 254
  women, 134, 188, 217
Goltz, Count Rüdiger von der, 230–31, 232, 259
Gorlice, 17
Gossler, Alfred von, 62, 64, 117, 162, 178, 199, 211
Gough, Sir Hubert, 232
Gumbinnen, Battle of, 15
Grimm, Hans, 253
Grodno, 17, 55
  administrative area, 61–62
  captured by Germans, 19
  Grodnoer Zeitung, 115
Groener, Wilhelm, 227

Hague conventions, 65, 75
Hakatisten, *see* League of Eastern Marches
Harbou, General von, 211
Hasse, Ernst, 23
Haushofer, Karl, 254–55, 256, 264
health measures
  Nazis on, 271
  sanitary measures, 80, 106
  vaccines, 106
Hedin, Sven, 117
Heimatkunde, 167
Henry of Saxony, 259
Heppe, Theodor von, 62, 154, 182, 198, 201

Herder, Johann Gottfried, 24, 189–90, 258
  effect on Eastern Europe, 36, 190
Hertling, Georg von, 201
Hess, Rudolf, 254, 264
Himmler, Heinrich, 259, 264, 265, 268–69
Hindenburg, Paul von, 16, 211, 247
  education and, 125, 127
  High Command, 21, 176
  Hindenburg Program, 55
  Ludendorff and, 16
  post-war activities of, 248, 251
  statues of, 41
  as Supreme Commander in the East, 15, 16, 21
  Wallenstein and, 41, 143
Hitler, Adolf, 256–58, 259, 265, 266
  Mein Kampf, 256–57, 258
  on *Raum* and East, 264, 265, 266, 269–72
Hoffmann, Max, 15, 177, 198, 201, 211
  at Brest-Litovsk, 204–5
  on Lithuanians, 201, 206, 209
  revolution and, 218–19
Holy Alliance, 23
Höss, Rudolf, 241
Hugenberg, Alfred, 117
Hungary, 17

industry, 72, 165
Isenburg-Birstein, Prince Franz Joseph zu, 62, 180, 183, 198, 201

Jahn, Friedrich Ludwig, 171
Jews
  economic role, 68
  German Jews, 41–42, 57, 58, 77, 191–92
  Hassidim, 41
  Karaite sect and, 33
  Litvaks, 32, 131
  Nazi genocide of, 265, 267, 268, 270
  in Ober Ost, 62, 67, 68, 119–20, 160, 182, 210, 217, 249
  Ostjuden, 32, 191–92
  Russian expulsion of, 20
  schools and, 126
  synagogues, 131–32
  theatre, 138–39
  translators, 32
  Zionism, 41, 192
  see also anti-Semitism; Yiddish
Joffe, A. A., 229
Jünger, Ernst, 2, 12, 234, 247, 248, 261

Jungfer, Victor, 156, 159, 192–95
    Face of the Occupied Territory, 156, 159,
        193–95

Kapsukas-Mickevičius, Vincas, 229
Karaites, 33
Karevičius, Bishop Pranciškus, 200
Kaunas, *see* Kowno
Keegan, John, 4
Kern, Stephen, 4
Kiev, 211, 217
Kjellen, Rudolf, 169, 254
Klemperer, Victor, 58, 115, 119, 120, 192,
    259
Koch, Erich, 267
Kodatis-Kuodaitis, Bernhard, 183
Königsberg, 219
Korrespondenz B, 46, 116, 191
Kowno, 80, 97, 213, 214, 217
    German capture of, 17
    German impressions of, 27
    Kownoer Zeitung, 115
Kratzenberg, 61
Kreuznach conference, 196
Krupp works, 117
Kühlmann, Richard von, 202, 205
Kultur, see culture
Kurland, 20, 21, 31, 33, 42, 155, 196–200
    administrative area, 57, 61–62, 198
    depopulated, 20
    German settlement plans, 33, 95, 165,
        208
    Land Council, 200, 208
    language problems in, 121
    schools in, 126
    traveling exhibition, 162
    workers in, 73
    see also Latvia

labor
    battalions dissolved, 74
    forced labor, 66, 72–74, 180
    future plans for, 203
    gangs, 98
    movement policy and, 101
Lagarde, Paul de, 23, 164
"*Land und Leute,*" 22, 26, 35, 116, 119
    Riehl's formulation, 46
    shift away from, 107, 252, 272
Landsknecht, 40, 236
landscape, impact of, 26–29, 151–56, 167
    Freikorps and, 233
    Nazis and, 265
Lange, Friedrich, 23
Latvia and Latvians, 31, 187, 208–9

army of, 230
art, 139
Freikorps and, 230–32, 241, 242–43
German perception of, 179, 241, 258
Latvian Rifles Regiment, 228
Lutheranism, 31
Nazi occupation of, 266
Soviet, 228
Soviet occupation of, 266
    see also Kurland
League of the Eastern Marches, 23, 168
League of Industrialists, 165
Lebensraum, see Raum
Leipzig, 117, 119
Lemberg, 21
Lenin, Vladimir, 203, 216
Leopold, prince of Bavaria, 20, 91, 176–77
Libau (Liepāja), 17, 97, 230, 231
lice, 105–6, 154–55
    see also delousing
Liebknecht, Wilhelm, 24
Lieven, Count Anatol, 231
Lit-Bel, 229
Lithuania and Lithuanians, 30–31,
        196–200, 208
    administrative area in Ober Ost, 55, 57,
        61–62, 198
    art in work rooms, 128
    concepts of order, 185
    diaspora, 37, 183, 201
    education, 37
    Freikorps in, 242, 243
    German perceptions of, 30–31, 158–59,
        179, 184
    Grand Duchy of, 17, 31, 32, 36
    independence declarations, 204, 205, 209
    language, 31, 118, 179
    Lithuania Minor, 59
    Lithuania's Echo, 123, 200, 205, 210
    Mindaugas II, 209–10, 215
    national identity of, 31, 37, 184–86
    Nazi occupation of, 266
    newspapers, 118, 123
    Prussian Lithuanians, 59, 123, 187, 192
    Russification, 36–37
    schools and, 125
    Soviet Lit-Bel, 229
    Soviet occupation of, 266
    Taryba (Land Council), 200–6, 209–10,
        215
    tauta, 185
    theatre, 139
    volunteers, 229
Litvaks, 32, 131
Litzmann, 17

Livland, 33
Livonians, 33
Lutherans, 20, 31
Lohse, Hinrich, 267
Lomza, 17
Longwy-Briey, 165
Lübeck, 57, 99, 117
Ludendorff, Erich, 15, 19, 212, 214
  authority in Ober Ost, 21
  cultural program of, 113
  depicted by Zweig, 77
  dismissed, 214
  education and, 124–25
  High Command and, 21, 176
  Hindenburg and, 16
  Operation Cap-Stone and, 210
  plans of, 38, 46–47, 54, 94–95, 96, 163,
    195, 196, 197–98, 201–2
  post-war activities, 247, 248, 258, 259
  war aims debate and, 164

Mackensen, August von, 20
Mackinder, Halford, 254
Mahan, Alfred, 254
Mann, Golo, 249, 256
Mann, Thomas, 24
Manteuffel, Baron Hans von, 231
"Map of the Division of Peoples," 94, 117,
    155, 162
Marx, Karl, 24, 217
Masuren, winter battle of, 17
Masurian Lakes, battle of, 16, 269
Memel, see Njemen
Mennonites, 33
Meyer, Konrad, 264, 268
Michaelis, Georg, 197
Milosz, Czeslaw, 5
Mindaugas, Grand Duke, 36
mindscape, 151, 154–63, 240, 256
Minsk, 20
Mitau (Jelgava), 17, 37, 231
Mitteleuropa, 169–70, 178, 206, 254
Moeller van den Bruck, Arthur, 253, 258
Molotov-Ribbentropp Pact, 265
Moltke, Helmuth von, 15, 16
money, 242
  East money, 65, 67
monopolies, 65
monuments
  graves, 251
  preservation efforts, 130–32
  Russian removal of, 19
Moon (Muhu), 199
Morsbach, Adolf, 73, 104
Mosse, George, 4

movement policy (Verkehrspolitik), 61, 201,
    202, 203, 209, 211
  changes, 91
  cleanliness and, 105
  control of communication, 99
  defined, 89–90
  enforcement, 103–4
  German language and, 99–100
  inner movement, 102
  native perception of, 93
  Nazi variants of, 263, 264
  section, 91
  streets, 104
museums, 129

Napoleon, 26, 33
Narwa (Narva), 205, 216, 228
National Bolshevism, 258
national identity, 33–35, 114
  education and, 125
  elective ethnicity, 34, 51 n86, 121,
    185–86, 210
  ethnic confusion in, 33–34, 121
  geography and, 166
  German views of, 119, 122, 156, 178–80
  Lithuanian views of, 185
  religion and, 32, 34, 59, 120–21
  scholarship on, 185–86
nationality policy
  aims of, 127
  Ludendorff and, 127, 196–98
Naumann, Friedrich, 169
Nazis, 243, 247, 251
  Baltic Germans and, 258–59
  camps, 261
  Commissar Order, 266
  concentration camps, 264, 268
  General Plan for the East, 264, 268
  Hitler Youth, 261–63
  ideology, 256, 272
  Jews, policies towards, 267, 268, 270
  Ober Ost officials in, 258–59, 267
  Ostland territory, 267
  propaganda on East, 259, 262–65
  SD, 260
  SS, 259, 265, 266, 267, 268
  use of language, 259
  Wannsee Conference, 268
  World War II and, 264
"New Land" company, 95
newspapers, 129, 116
  army, 38, 44, 130, 132, 135–36, 213
  German local, 115–16
  mastheads, 99, 160
  native language, 123

Nicholas Nikolaevich, Grand Duke, 20
Niedra, Andrievs, 231–32
Nietzsche, Friedrich, 24
Njemen (Memel) river, 17, 97–98
Northwest Territory, 19, 21, 36
Noske, Gustav, 204, 227, 230

Ober Ost
  Baltic Germans in, 57
  central administration, 55, 60–61
  changes in administration, 62, 198–99,
    206–8, 211
  church policy, 61
  culture policy, 61, 113–44
  death sentences, 76, 79
  end of, 214
  ethnic composition of, 30–35
  exclusively German, 58
  forests, 27–28
  future plans, 71, 199, 202–3
  history of, prewar, 35–8
  inner conflict, 64, 177, 198
  intelligence officer, 92
  isolated, 92, 101
  justice system, 61, 75–77, 199, 218
  landscape of, 26–30
  male nature of, 57–58, 159
  military utopia in, 21, 198
  neutrality toward ethnic groups, 122
  officials, 56–58
  "Order of Rule," 55, 58, 63, 66, 73, 75,
    122
  population of, 21, 30
  rapes reported, 63
  revolution in, 215–19
  settlement plans, 96, 199
  size of administration, 56
  subdivision, 61–62, 92–93
  territory of, 20–21
  violence reported, 63, 66, 107, 180
Oesel (Saaremaa), 199, 248
order, ideas of, 114, 184
Org-Esch, 72
Orthodox Church, 32
Ostforschung, 253, 255–56
Ostland, see Nazis

Pan-Germans, 23, 61
  war aims of, 95, 164, 165
"Panje," 156
Pan-Slavism, 23, 24
Päts, Konstantin, 208
Papen, Franz von, 61
Patriotic Instruction program, 55, 125, 150
  n147, 213

passes
  movement and, 100–1
  pass commando units, 102–4
  principle of, 101
  vaccines and, 106
Penck, Albrecht, 255
Petition of the Intellectuals, 165
poems, soldiers', 157, 158, 161
Poland and Poles, 16, 205
  civil administration, 21, 54, 56, 64, 100
  conquest by Germans, 19
  economic influence, 67
  German plans for, 163, 196–98, 202
  kingdom declared, 195
  legionnaires, 228
  national identity, 32
  Nazi occupation of, 265
  Ober Ost and, 32, 62, 210
  Prussian Poles, 58–59, 187, 213
  schools and, 125
police (gendarmes), 56, 61, 78, 102, 213
  abuses alleged, 78, 107
  central office in the East, 63, 92
  inefficacy against bandits, 181
  origins of concept, 168
  railroad police, 104–5
Polish-Lithuanian Commonwealth, 31, 32,
    36, 125
"Polnische Wirtschaft," 25
Pommerania, 57
postal system, 61, 99
  natives and, 100
POWs, 32, 72–74, 79, 98
  German, 213, 241
Present Time, The, 118, 123, 183
press section, 115, 258
  censorship, 119, 123, 133, 190
  failure of, 123
  field bookstores, 136
  Land Ober Ost, The, 116
  press conferences, 116
  tours for journalists, 116–17
  travel accounts, 162
  wire service, 116
Pripet marshes, 26
Prittwitz und Gaffron, Maximilian von, 15
prostitution
  disease and, 105, 186
  officers' brothels, 188
  regulation of, 80, 133
Prussia, 16, 209
  ancient Baltic Prussians, 31, 35
  East Prussian Settlement Society, 61
  model of administration, 62–63
  officials, 57, 58

Prussian Lithuanians, 59, 123, 187, 192
Prussian Poles, 58–59, 187, 213
Russian occupation, 14–15

Radviliškis, 243
railways
  future plans for, 199
  military use by Germans, 16–17
  Railroad directorate, 63, 96–97
  rebuilding, 96–97
  state of, 90, 96
Ratzel, Friedrich, 166, 167, 169, 253–54,
  255
Raum, 94, 162
  Lebensraum, 254, 256–57, 259
  meaning of, 106–7, 252–53
  Ostraum, 107, 260
  postwar lessons on, 252–55, 256
  Nazis and, 256, 259, 263–65, 268–72
  spatial ordering (Raumordnung), 264, 268
rear areas (Etappe), 55, 61
refugees, 21
regulations and orders, 77
Reichskommissariat Ostland, see Nazis
Reichstag, 62, 189, 196, 201, 204, 206
  demands in Ober Ost, 64, 198, 211
  Peace Resolution, 197
relief organizations, native, 75, 183, 200–1
religious conflict, 67–68, 180–81
Remarque, Erich Maria, 2, 247, 261
Rennenkampf, Pavel, 14, 15, 16
requisitions, 65, 73
  horses, 67–68, 182
  receipts, 67
  resisted, 182
resistance, native, 182–83, 208
Reval, 205, 215, 217, 229
  see also Tallinn
Revolution of 1905, 31, 33, 37
Rhodes, Cecil, 168
Richert, Dominik, 187–88
Riefenstahl, Leni, 150 n151
Riehl, Wilhelm Heinrich, 45, 167
  Die deutsche Arbeit, 45
  Land und Leute, 46, 167
Riga, 17, 31, 181, 199, 212, 215, 219, 228,
  267
  administration of, 57
  Freikorps attack on, 231, 232, 242
  front stabilizes at, 20
"Riga Marching Song," 239
Rilke, Rainer Maria, 24, 41
river traffic, 98
roads, 17, 67, 90, 97
  construction work on, 72

Roman Catholicism, 31, 32, 59, 180
  clergy, 180, 200
Romania, 176, 206
Romanovs, 33
Romanticism, 28, 167
Rosenberg, Alfred, 258, 259, 267, 268
Rümker, Kurt von, 96, 127
Russia and Russians
  Brest-Litovsk Treaty, 206
  Duma, 32
  February Revolution, 144, 177, 195, 196
  First Army, 14
  frontier fortifications, 17, 19
  German views of, 22, 152
  Nazi views of, 257
  in Ober Ost, 32
  Petrograd Soviet, 195
  Russification, 36
  Second Army, 14
  Soviet, 229
  White forces, 229, 231, 232, 242
  see also Soviet Union; Bolsheviks;
    scorched earth policy

Salomon, Ernst von, 234, 235, 236, 239,
  240
Samsonov, Aleksandr, 14, 15
Saxony, 209
  mercenaries, 229
Schaulen (Šiauliai), 57, 73, 77, 180
  Freikorps in, 242
  Jews in, 120, 160
  orders, 104
  taken by Germans, 17
Scheidemann, Phillip, 214
Scheubner-Richter, Max Erwin von,
  258–59
Schickedanz, Arno, 259
Schiemann, Theodor, 24, 211
Schiller, Friedrich, 47, 142
  Wallensteins Lager, 142–43
Schlieffen Plan, 12, 14, 16
Schmidt, Rochus, 78
Scholtz, General von, 17
schools, see education
Schwerin, Friedrich von, 95
scorched earth policy, 17, 19, 20, 90, 99
Seeberg, Reinhold, 165
Seraphim, 178
Serbia, 20
settlement programs
  Baltic German plans, 33, 208
  East Prussian Settlement Society, 61
  Freikorps and, 230, 238
  "inner colonization," 61, 95

settlement programs *(cont.)*
  Nazi plans for, 261, 265, 268–72
  in Ober Ost, 71, 94, 198, 203, 208
  soldier-farmers, 96, 163
Shakespeare, William, 143
Šiauliai, *see* Schaulen
Siegfried Line, 163
Silesia, 16, 30, 57
Skoropadsky, Pavlo, 211
Smetona, Antanas, 200–1
smuggling, 67, 78, 182
Social Democrats, 24, 163, 189, 196, 204,
  214
soldiers' councils, 212, 215–19
  Central Council for the Eastern Front,
  217–18
soldiers' homes, 134–35, 142, 160
songs, 213, 239, 243, 262–63
Soviet Union
  Nazi invasion, 266
  Nazi views of, 257, 266–67
  occupation of Baltic States, 266
space, see *Raum*
Spengler, Oswald, 24
Stalin, Josef, 266
statistics, 66, 168
Steputat-Steputaitis, Wilhelm, 123, 192
Stone, Norman, 3
Storosta-Vydūnas, Wilhelm, 183
Struck, Hermann, 115, 116
Sturm und Drang movement, 24
Stuttgart, Auslandsmuseum, 162
submarine warfare, 211
Sudermann, Hermann, 183
Supreme Commander in the East, *see* Ober
  Ost; Hindenburg
Susemihl, 192
Suwalki, 16
Suwalki-Wilna, 55

Tacitus, 28, 36
Tallinn, 229
  see also Reval
Tannenberg, 1914 Battle of, 15, 20, 164,
  269
  Battle in 1410, 36
  monument, 251
  naming of, 15
Tatars, 33
taxes, 65
  dog tax, 65, 102
  future plans for, 199
telegraph and telephone, 99
  symbolism of, 160
terrain games, 171, 261

Teutonic Knights, 19, 31, 35, 190
  castles of, 35, 235, 248
  invoked, 39, 234–35, 251, 257
theatre, 136–43
  front cinema, 141
  Fronttheater, 141–43, 161
  interaction in, 138
  native theatre, 137–39
  Nazi, 263
Theweleit, Klaus, 239
Thirty Years' War, 39–41
  Freikorps invoke, 236
  Landsknechte, 40
  Wallenstein and, 40
Tilsit, 123, 184
toilets, 81
total war, 55, 171
translation
  catalog, 117
  in courts, 75–76
  of orders, 77
  post, 77, 117
  Seven Language Dictionary, 117–19
trenches, 21, 134
Trotsky, Leon, 204–5
Turkey, 259
Turnip Winter (1916–17), 72

Ukraine and Ukrainians, 152, 204–5, 211,
  218
  Nazi occupation of, 266, 267, 271
Ulmanis, Kārlis, 228, 231–32
"*Undeutschen*," 39, 70
Urach, Wilhelm von, 209–10, 215

Vācietis, Jukums, 228
Verkehrspolitik, *see* movement policy
Versailles Treaty, 230, 232, 237, 259
Vytautas, Grand Duke, 36
Vilms, Jüri, 206
Vilna, *see* Wilna
Vilnius, 14
  see also Wilna

Wagner, Richard, 24, 142
Waldersee, Graf von, 198
Wallenstein, Albrecht von, 40, 41, 142–43,
  261
  Freikorps model, 230, 236
Wandervogel, 167, 171, 236, 248
Warsaw, 15, 16, 17
Wartenburg, Count Yorck von, 61
"war land," 26
War Press Office, 119
war socialism, 216

Weber, Paul, 130
Wenden (Cēsis), 231
Wertheimer, Fritz, 163
"Westerners," 16
White Russians, see Belarus
Wilhelm II of Hohenzollern, Kaiser of
    Germany, 35, 117, 196, 208, 209, 214
Wilna (Vilnius), 14, 43, 205, 214, 228
    administrative area, 61–62
    art history in, 130
    cleaning of, 154, 160
    German capture of, 19–20, 35
    German guidebook to, 43–44
    German impressions of, 43
    hunger deaths, 75
    Jewish center, 32, 43, 44
    legends of, 43–44
    refugees in, 30
    schools, 124, 209
    Wilnaer Zeitung, 115–16
    see also Vilnius
Wilno, see Wilna
Wilson, Woodrow, 196, 214
Winnig, August, 230

Winter, Jay, 4
Wohl, Robert, 4
women, 42, 43, 73, 159
    German women, 134, 188, 217
    treatment of, 63, 106
work rooms, 128, 206, 218
    exhibits, 128
Württemburg, 209

Yiddish, 20, 32, 40, 58, 119–20
    in newspapers, 116
    translation, 117, 118
    theatre, 138–39
Yudenich, N. N., 242

Zechlin, Erich, 56, 115
Zeppelins, 19
Zhilinksi, Yakov, 14, 15
Zimmerle, Ludwig, 215
Zweig, Arnold, 41, 58, 115, 191–92, 218,
    247–48
    The Case of Sergeant Grischa, 28, 35, 41,
        58, 59, 64, 76–77, 99, 160, 191, 248,
        261

Studies in the Social and Cultural History of Modern Warfare

Titles in the series:

1 *Sites of Memory, Sites of Mourning: The Great War in European Cultural History*
Jay Winter
ISBN 0 521 49682 9 (paperback)

2 *Capital Cities at War: Paris, London, Berlin, 1914–1919*
Edited by Jay Winter and Jean-Louis Robert
ISBN 0 521 57171 5 (hardback) 0 521 66814 X (paperback)

3 *State, Society and Mobilization in Europe During the First World War*
Edited by John Horne
ISBN 0 521 56112 4

4 *A Time of Silence: Civil War and the Culture of Repression in Franco's Spain, 1936–1945*
Michael Richards
ISBN 0 521 59401 4

5 *War and Remembrance in the Twentieth Century*
Edited by Jay Winter and Emmanuel Sivan
ISBN 0 521 64035 0

6 *European Culture in the Great War: The Arts, Entertainment and Propaganda, 1914–1918*
Edited by Aviel Roshwald and Richard Stites
ISBN 0 521 57015 8

7 *The Labour of Loss: Mourning, Memory and Wartime Bereavement in Australia*
Joy Damousi
ISBN 0 521 66004 1 (hardback) 0 521 66974 X (paperback)

8 *The Legacy of Nazi Occupation: Patriotic Memory and National Recovery in Western Europe, 1945–1965*
Pieter Lagrou
ISBN 0 521 65180 8

9 *War Land on the Eastern Front: Culture, National Identity, and German Occupation in World War I*
Vejas Gabriel Liulevicius
ISBN 0 521 66157 9